Contents

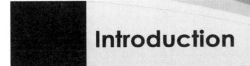

Introduction

Qualifications covered

This book has been written specifically to cover the unit 'Management Accounting Techniques' which is mandatory for the following qualifications:

AAT Level 3 Diploma in Accounting

AAT Diploma in Accounting – SCQF Level 7

The book contains a clear text with worked examples and case studies, chapter summaries and key terms to help with revision. Each chapter concludes with a wide range of activities, many in the style of AAT computer based assessments.

Spreadsheet skills for management accounting

This book includes case studies and questions applying spreadsheets skills to management accounting. It should be used in conjunction with the Osborne Books Spreadsheets for Management Accounting Tutorial text. If you do not know how to use a function, for example, look at how to do it in the spreadsheets book before completing the question in this book. Spreadsheet skills in the questions in this book are highlighted in **bold.**

Osborne Study and Revision Materials

Additional materials, tailored to the needs of students studying this unit and revising for the assessment, include:

- **Workbooks:** paperback books with practice activities and exams
- **Wise Guides:** pocket-sized spiral bound revision cards
- **Student Zone:** access to Osborne Books online resources
- **Osborne Books App:** Osborne Books ebooks for mobiles and tablets

Visit www.osbornebooks.co.uk for details of study and revision resources and access to online material.

1 An introduction to management accounting

this chapter covers...

- This first chapter examines the purpose of management accounting (which is often referred to as cost accounting) and its role in providing information to the managers of a business. In particular we see how the role of management accounting provides information to assist with:

    - decision-making

    - planning for the future

    - control of expenditure

    These themes will be developed in later chapters.

- We begin our introduction to management accounting with a recap on topics covered in Principles of Costing, part of the Level 2 Certificate in Accounting. We identify cost units and see how responsibility centres, cost centres, profit centres, revenue centres and investment centres are used to monitor the performance of sections of a business. We see how costs can be grouped together or classified in different ways:

    - by element

    - by nature

    - by function

    - by behaviour

    Each of these ways enables us to see the same business from a different viewpoint, which will help managers to run the business better.

- After studying this chapter you should have a clear idea of the role of management accounting and appreciate some of the ideas that it uses.

PURPOSE OF MANAGEMENT ACCOUNTING

Management accounting enables the managers of a business to know the cost of the firm's output, whether a product or a service, and the revenues from sales. Once this information is available, managers can use it to assist with:

- decision-making
- planning for the future
- control of expenditure

Management accounting (which is often referred to as cost accounting) is widely used by all types of businesses and organisations – whether they provide a service or make a product. Businesses and organisations need to keep their costs under review and in order to do this, they need accurate cost information. Thus a management accounting system will provide answers to questions such as:

What does it cost us to provide a student with a day's accountancy course?

What does it cost us to carry out a hip replacement operation?

What does it cost us to make a pair of trainers?

What does it cost us to serve a cheeseburger and fries?

What is the cost of a passenger-mile on a bus journey?

What does it cost us to provide a week's holiday in the Canaries?

The management accounting system helps managers with production planning and decision-making, such as:

- "how many items do we need to make and sell in order to break-even?"
- "if we increase production will we need to carry a bank overdraft?"

MANAGEMENT ACCOUNTING AND FINANCIAL ACCOUNTING

These two types of accounting, although they produce different reports and statements, obtain their data from the same set of transactions carried out by the business or organisation over a given period. This is illustrated in the diagram on the next page.

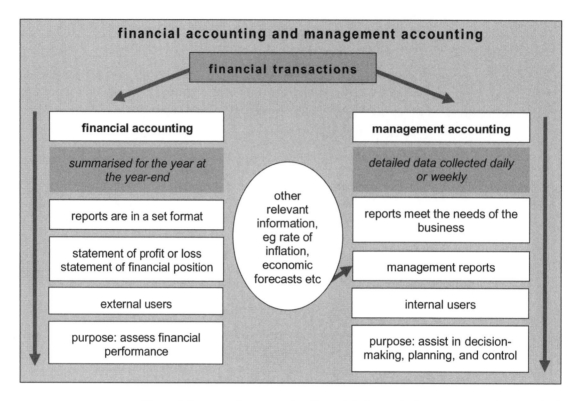

Financial accounting uses the financial data relating to transactions carried out over a period of time. The information is usually processed using accounting software and extracted in the form of financial statements – the statement of profit or loss and the statement of financial position. These statements are often required to be produced by law, eg the Companies Act, and are available to external users such as shareholders, suppliers, banks, HM Revenue & Customs, Companies House.

Management accounting uses the same data to produce reports containing financial information on the recent past and projections for the future. The reports are available to internal users, such as managers, directors, and owners (but not to shareholders generally), and may also be made available to third parties (such as banks). There is no legal requirement to produce this information and the content of the report and the principles used can be suited to the activities of the business or organisation and the requirements of its managers. The information is prepared as frequently as it is required, and speed is often vital as the information may go out-of-date very quickly. It is important that the information is prepared accurately and in line with the **ethical principle of integrity**, which requires accounting staff to be straightforward and honest in all professional and business relationships.

COST UNITS AND COMPOSITE COST UNITS

Cost units are units of output to which costs can be charged.

A cost unit can be:

- a unit of production from a factory such as a car, a television, an item of furniture
- a unit of service, such as a passenger on a bus, an attendant at a swimming pool

Composite cost units are units of output which comprise two variables.

Examples of composite cost units include:

- the cost of a bus passenger, per mile
- the cost of a hospital patient, per day

Note that composite cost units are common in service sector businesses.

RESPONSIBILITY CENTRES

Within a business different managers will have responsibilities at different levels, for example:

- a responsibility for controlling costs
- a responsibility to achieve a particular level of profit
- a responsibility to achieve a particular return on money invested
- a responsibility to achieve a level of sales revenue

Responsibility centres are segments of a business for which a manager is accountable.

Examples of responsibility centres are:

- cost centres
- profit centres
- revenue centres
- investment centres

COST CENTRES

As well as charging costs to cost units they also need to be charged to a specific part of a business – a **cost centre**.

Cost centres are segments of a business to which costs can be charged.

A cost centre in a manufacturing business, for example, is a department of a factory, a particular stage in the production process, or even a whole factory. In a college, examples of cost centres are the teaching departments, or particular sections of departments such as the college's administrative office.

Cost centres enable segmented costs – which relate to a particular centre – to be identified, and this assists with control of the business.

PROFIT CENTRES

For some sections of businesses the cost centre approach of analysing costs is taken to a further level by also analysing sales revenue to centres. As revenue less costs equals profit, such centres are called **profit centres**.

Profit centres are segments of a business to which costs can be charged, revenue can be identified, and profit can be calculated.

From the definition we can see that profit centres have both costs and revenue. For example, a garden centre has conservatory plants as a profit centre as shown in the following diagram:

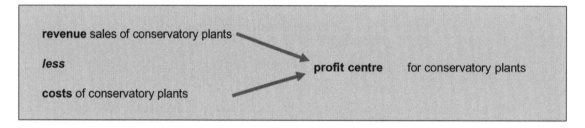

Note that many cost centres provide support services within a business or organisation and, so, cannot become profit centres because they do not have any significant revenue, for example, the administration department of a business.

The management of a profit centre has control over the centre's costs – both variable and fixed – and its revenues. By deducting costs from revenue the centre's management can quantify the profit made and can make comparisons with previous periods (eg last month, last quarter, last year, etc), with profit targets set for the current period (eg 'our profit is 10 per cent above target'), and also with other profit centres (eg 'our profit last month was higher than the other profit centres').

REVENUE CENTRES

In a **revenue centre**, the responsibility of the manager is only for the sales revenue generated.

Revenue centres are segments of a business where sales revenue from the product sold or service provided is measured.

Examples of revenue centres include shop departments, restaurants, coffee shops – where the manager is responsible for generating sales revenue.

INVESTMENT CENTRES

For **investment centres** the profit of the centre is compared with how much money the business has put in to earn that profit.

Investment centres are segments of a business where profit is compared with the amount of money invested in the centre.

Profit is compared with money invested by means of a percentage as shown in the following diagram for a garden centre's conservatory plants investment centre.

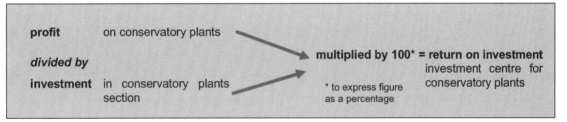

The management of an investment centre has control over the centre's costs – both variable and fixed – and its revenues, assets and liabilities. By calculating the return on investment, the centre's management will wish to make comparisons of the return for the current period with that of previous periods (eg 'have we done better than last year?') against targets set for the current period (eg 'are we on target for the current period?'), and also with the other investment centres of the business (eg 'how do we compare with the other investment centres?').

Case Study

PROVIDING INFORMATION FOR MANAGEMENT

situation

You are an Accounts Assistant at Severnvale Garden Centre.

The Managing Director, Charlie Rimmack, has asked you for accounting information that is needed for a meeting with the managers of two sections of the garden centre – the manager for conservatory plants and the manager for shrubs. Charlie wants the information in order to see which department is performing better; she requests details for each section of costs and revenue for last year, and the amount of money invested in each section at the end of the year. (She says that all figures can be rounded to the nearest £000.)

solution

You go to the accounts which have been set up to show segmented costs, revenue and money invested, and extract the following information for last year:

		Conservatory plants	Shrubs
		£000	£000
Costs:	materials	137	151
	labour	93	134
	expenses	45	70
Revenue		425	555
Money invested		450	400

In order to help the Managing Director you decide to present the management information for each cost centre in the following way:

Cost centre	Conservatory plants	Shrubs
	£000	£000
Materials	137	151
Labour	93	134
Expenses	45	70
Total	275	355

Here the cost centre for conservatory plants has the lower costs.

Profit Centre

	Conservatory plants	Shrubs
Revenue	425	555
less Costs (see above)	275	355
Profit	150	200

These figures show that shrubs is the better profit centre.

Revenue Centre

	Conservatory plants	Shrubs
Revenue	425	555

These figures show that shrubs is the better revenue centre.

Investment Centre

	Conservatory plants	Shrubs
$\dfrac{\text{Profit (see above)}}{\text{Investment}}$	$\dfrac{150}{450}$	$\dfrac{200}{400}$
Expressed as a percentage (multiplied by 100)	33%	50%

These figures show that shrubs is the better investment centre.

Conclusion

You complete a comparison table to summarise the results you have calculated:

Responsibility centre	Criteria	Conservatory plants	Shrubs
Cost centre	Low cost	£275,000 ✓	£355,000 **x**
Profit centre	High profit	£150,000 **x**	£200,000 ✓
Revenue centre	High sales	£425,000 **x**	£555,000 ✓
Investment centre	High %	33% **x**	50% ✓

Advice to Charlie Rimmack:

The shrubs department is performing better than the conservatory plants department for three of the four criteria. However, both sections are earning profits which contribute to the overheads of the business, so both should continue to trade.

Note that further use of management accounting techniques such as contribution and break-even (covered in later chapters) – can be used to provide additional information to managers.

CLASSIFICATION OF COSTS

Within any business, whether it manufactures a product or provides a service, there are certain costs involved at various stages to produce the units of output. The diagram on the next page shows the costs of a manufacturing business which are incurred by the three main sections or 'areas' of a manufacturing business.

These three separate sections are:

■ **factory** – where production takes place and the product is 'finished' and made ready for selling

■ **warehouse** – where finished goods are stored and from where they are despatched when they are sold

■ **office** – where the support functions take place – marketing, sales, administration, finance and so on

Note that while the diagram shows the costs of a manufacturing business, it can be adapted easily to fit non-manufacturing organisations, such as a shop, a hospital, a school or college, a church, a club. While the units of output of these organisations differ from those of a manufacturer, nevertheless they still incur costs at various stages of the 'production' process.

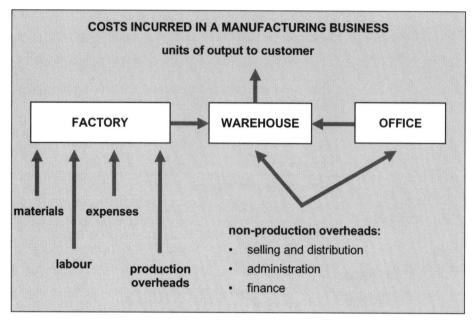

In order to prepare information for the managers of a business, costs must be classified, ie organised into sets in a way which the managers will find useful.

This can be done in four ways:

- by element
- by nature
- by function
- by behaviour

classification of costs by element

Businesses incur many different kinds of cost in the production of goods or 'output', including costs of the warehouse and the office. The most basic way of splitting up costs is according to expenditure type, under the headings:

- materials, eg the components to make a car
- labour, eg wages of employees
- expenses, eg rent and rates, telephone charges, insurance

Note: material, labour and expenses are often referred to as the three elements of cost.

Materials costs (physical items which you can see and touch) are the costs of raw materials, components and other goods used.

Labour costs are the costs of employees' wages and salaries.

Expenses are other costs, which cannot be included in 'materials' or 'labour'.

Splitting costs into these three elements applies to both manufacturing and service businesses. The classification provides important information to managers as they can see the breakdown of the total into different kinds of cost.

classification of costs by nature

Within each of the three elements of materials, labour and expenses, some costs can be identified directly with each unit of output. For example:

■ the cost of components used in making cars

■ the wages of workers on a production line in a factory

These are termed **direct costs**. In manufacturing, the total of all the direct costs is called the **prime cost** of the output.

A direct cost is a cost that can be identified directly with each unit of output.

Prime cost is the total of all direct costs.

Indirect costs (overheads) are all costs, other than those identified as 'direct costs', that cannot be identified directly with each unit of output.

There are many examples of overheads, including:

■ telephone and internet charges

■ insurance premiums

■ cost of wages of non-production staff, such as managers, office staff, accountants and so on

■ running costs of delivery vehicles

■ depreciation charge for non-current assets

Note particularly the last two examples. In management accounting, as in financial accounting, we distinguish between capital and revenue expenditure. In our analysis of costs we are referring to revenue expenditure, and therefore include the running costs and depreciation of non-current assets, rather than the capital cost of their purchase.

We now have six possible classifications for costs, each of the three elements of materials, labour and expenses being split by their nature into direct and indirect costs. These are illustrated for a manufacturing business in the table on the next page.

Classification of costs by element and by nature		
nature / element	**Direct Costs**	**Indirect Costs (Overheads)**
Materials	The cost of raw materials from which the finished product is made.	The cost of all other materials, eg grease for machines, cleaning materials.
Labour	Wages paid to those who work the machinery on the production line or who are involved in assembly or finishing of the product.	Wages and salaries paid to all other employees, eg managers and supervisors, maintenance staff, administration staff.
Expenses	Any expenses which can be identified with particular units of output, eg royalties payable to the designer of a product, fees linked directly to specific output and paid to people who are not employees.	All other expenses, eg rent, business rates, telephone, lighting and heating costs, depreciation of non-current assets, insurance, advertising, etc. These are costs which cannot be identified directly with units of output.
Total	**TOTAL DIRECT COSTS = PRIME COST**	**TOTAL INDIRECT COSTS = TOTAL OVERHEADS**

classification of costs by function

Another method of classifying costs is to look at the costs incurred in different sections of the organisation according to their 'function', or the kind of work being done.

In manufacturing, the main function is production of the goods. The business could not be run, however, without administrators, accountants, sales and delivery staff and so on – these are examples of non-production costs.

When costs are classified by function, the main headings generally used are:

production
administration
selling and distribution   non-production costs
finance

Other functions can be added to suit the needs of a particular business. For example, a 'Research and Development' heading could be used if a company spent large sums of money in researching and developing new products.

Non-manufacturing organisations – such as a hospital or a college – may use different 'function' headings, according to the kind of work each section of the organisation carries out.

Please note that, in classifying costs by their function, we are looking at the same set of costs for the business or organisation as before. We are simply presenting them in different groupings.

It is an important function of accounting that information should be presented in the form most suitable for the purpose for which it is required. For some management purposes, classification of costs by function provides better information.

classification of costs by behaviour

In management accounting, it is important to appreciate the behaviour of costs – in particular to understand that not all costs increase or decrease directly in line with increases or decreases in output. By behaviour, costs in the short term are:

■ fixed

■ semi-variable

■ variable

We shall be studying the relationship between fixed and variable costs and output in detail later in the book (Chapter 8). In particular, we will be looking at the technique of break-even analysis – the point at which costs are exactly equal to income.

fixed costs

Fixed costs remain constant over a range of output levels, despite other changes – for example, insurance, rent, business rates. In the form of a graph, they appear as follows (note that money amounts are shown on the vertical axis and units of output on the horizontal axis):

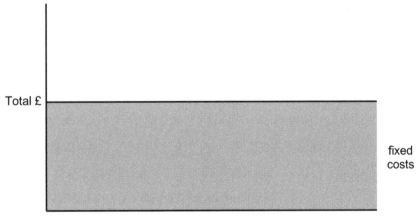

For fixed costs the **cost remains the same** at different levels of output.

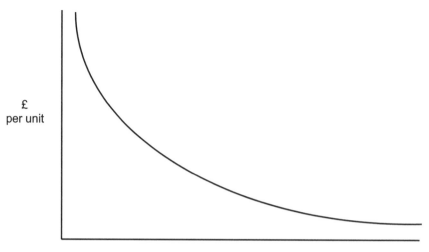

output: number of units

For fixed costs, the **cost per unit** falls as output increases. For example, with rent of £40,000 per year:

■ at output of 4,000 units, cost per unit equals £10 per unit

■ at output of 10,000 units, cost per unit equals £4 per unit

Whilst it is sensible to seek to achieve maximum output in order to reduce the cost per unit, fixed costs do not remain fixed at all levels of production. For example, a decision to double production is likely to increase the fixed costs – an increase in factory rent, for example, because an additional factory may need to be rented. Fixed costs are sometimes described as **stepped fixed costs**, because they increase by a large amount all at once; graphically, the cost behaviour is shown as a step:

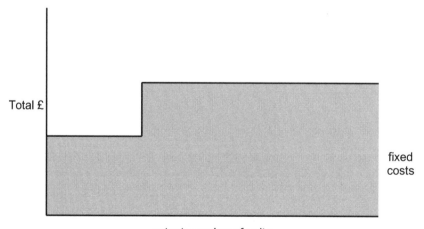

output: number of units

semi–variable costs

Semi-variable costs combine both a fixed and a variable cost. For example, an electricity bill comprises the fixed charges for the service, together with the variable amount for each unit of electricity. Such a **mixed cost** is expressed graphically as:

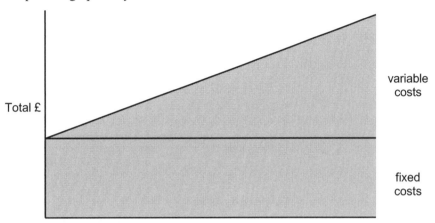

variable costs

Variable costs alter directly with changes in output levels, ie as activity increases, then the cost increases. Examples include direct materials, direct labour, and direct expenses such as royalties. Graphically, variable costs appear as follows:

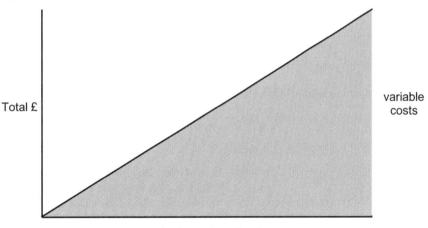

For example, a publishing company paying a royalty of £1 to an author for each book sold:

■ at sales of 1,000 books, equals variable cost of £1,000 royalties

■ at sales of 10,000 books, equals variable cost of £10,000 royalties

The cost per unit remains the same at different levels of output (unless there are economies of scale, eg bulk discount), as follows:

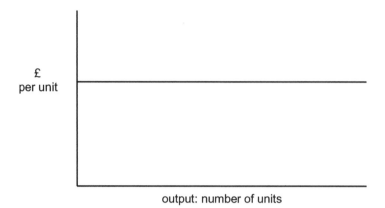

£
per unit

output: number of units

all costs are variable

Whilst we have made the distinction between fixed and variable costs, it is important to appreciate that these cost behaviours hold only in the short term – in the long term, all costs are variable. The example we saw earlier is of factory rent as a fixed cost but, if production increases, it may result in a larger, or another, factory being rented at an additional cost.

REASONS FOR CLASSIFYING COSTS

The question might be asked, "Why classify costs in four ways?" The answer is that we can see the same business from four different viewpoints – this will help managers to run the business better:

■ **by element**

looking for the high cost elements in order to make savings, eg labour might be identified as being too high

■ **by nature**

looking at the direct and indirect costs to see where savings could be made – eg the business might be able to reduce the cost of direct labour

■ **by function**

looking at the different departments to see which are the high-spending departments – perhaps savings can be made

■ **by behaviour**

identifying the costs as being fixed, semi-variable, or variable – the business might be able to make savings by altering the balance between fixed and variable costs

Thus classifying costs helps management with:

- decision-making, when implementing changes

- planning, when preparing forecasts and budgets

- control, when checking results against what was planned

CALCULATING THE COST OF GOODS AND SERVICES

The principles of management accounting will help to calculate the cost of a product –whether goods or services. Only when the cost of producing each unit of output is known, can a business make decisions about the selling price.

The steps towards calculating the cost of goods and services are:

identify the unit of output

The cost units for a particular business or organisation must be identified. As we have seen earlier, these are the units of output to which costs can be charged. Only by recovering costs through the sales of output can a business make a profit.

Examples of units of output include:

- cars

- meals

- passenger-miles

- hair cuts

- books printed

calculate the number of units of output for a particular time period

Once the unit of output is identified, the business is then able to calculate how many units can be produced or provided in a given time period, such as a day, week, month, quarter or year. For example, a garage will work out how many hours of mechanics' time are available, or a car manufacturer will calculate how many cars it can produce in a year.

calculate the direct costs

Having established the number of units of output for a particular time period, the next task is to calculate the direct costs, or prime cost, for that time period. As we have seen earlier in this chapter, the direct costs comprise:

direct materials	identifiable with the product
direct labour	the wages paid to those who make the product
direct expenses	identifiable with the product
Total direct costs **or** **Prime costs**	

calculate the indirect costs

The indirect costs, or overheads, of the production or service must be calculated for the particular time period. Indirect costs comprise:

indirect materials	materials used that are not identified directly with production
indirect labour	wages and salaries paid to those who are not directly involved in production
indirect expenses	expenses of the business not identified directly with production
Total indirect costs **or** **Overheads**	

Once the indirect costs have been calculated, we must then ensure that their total cost is charged to the cost units for a particular time period. Only by including indirect costs in the total cost of the output can a business recover their cost from the sales made.

calculate the total cost of a unit of output

Once the direct and indirect costs for a time period are known, the total cost of a unit of output can be calculated, as follows:

$$\frac{direct\ costs + indirect\ costs\ (overheads)}{number\ of\ units\ of\ output} = total\ cost\ of\ a\ unit\ of\ output$$

The total cost is also known as the absorption cost – because it absorbs (includes) both the direct costs and the indirect costs. Once total cost is known, the business can use the information to help it make pricing and other decisions. Note that, for inventory valuation purposes, only those indirect costs which relate to production are to be included in total cost (see page 57).

calculating the cost – a summary

The process of calculating the cost of output is illustrated in the diagram shown below.

costs for a service business

While the units of 'output' of businesses or organisations that produce a service are not manufactured products, they still incur the costs of:

- materials
- labour
- expenses

Some of the costs of a service business can be linked directly to the 'output' or the cost units of the organisation, but others are classified as overheads.

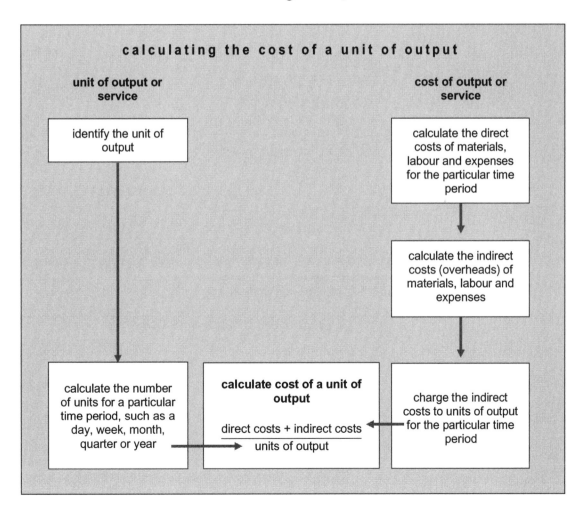

TOTAL COST STATEMENT

The total cost statement brings together all the costs involved in producing the output of a business. It can be prepared on the basis of:

- a single cost unit, eg the cost of making one car in a car factory

- a batch, eg the cost of making 1,000 'special edition' cars

- the whole factory, eg the cost of all the car factory's output for a given time period

The total cost statement is prepared using the following layout:

	TOTAL COST STATEMENT	£
	Direct materials	X
add	Direct labour	X
add	Direct expenses	X
equals	PRIME COST	X
add	Production overheads	X
equals	PRODUCTION COST*	X
add	Selling and distribution costs ┐	X
add	Administration costs ────┼─ non-production overheads**	X
add	Finance costs ┘	X
equals	TOTAL COST	X

* product cost

** period cost

By taking total cost away from revenue we can create a statement of profit or loss. This shows the profitability of the business after all costs have been taken into account. The statement of profit or loss is:

	STATEMENT OF PROFIT OR LOSS	£
	Revenue	X
less	Total cost	X
equals	PROFIT	X

From the total cost statement note the difference between **product cost** and **period cost**:

Product cost

The costs that become part of the manufactured product, that is, direct materials, direct labour, direct expenses (if any), and production overheads. Product costs are included in the closing inventory of the product at the year end and are carried forward to the next financial year.

Period cost

The costs that are not part of the manufactured product and cannot be assigned to products or closing inventory. Period costs – which are incurred in a period of time, eg monthly – are expensed to the statement of profit or loss in the accounting period in which they are incurred.

SPREADSHEET SKILLS FOR MANAGEMENT ACCOUNTING

the use of spreadsheets in management accounting

Spreadsheets are an invaluable tool when it comes to producing management accounting information. Every organisation will require different types of management information and will want this to be presented in different ways. This management information will help the managers to understand the business, enabling them to make decisions, plan and control the business effectively. Using spreadsheets to do this will be beneficial for both accounts staff, as it makes the process of producing management information more efficient and flexible, and business managers, who may then understand the information more easily due to a clear format or graphs that make it more clear.

applying spreadsheet skills to management accounting information

You may have learned some simple spreadsheet skills in Principles of Costing, part of the Level 2 Certificate in Accounting. In this book, we will apply spreadsheets to the management accounting you have learned in each chapter.

Each spreadsheet skill you need to learn is included in the Osborne Books Spreadsheets for Management Accounting Tutorial text. If you already know how to format the content of a cell to the currency format, for example, you may not need to refer to it. However, if you are required to use the 'goal seek' function, for example, and have not used this function before, you should look at how to do this in the Osborne Books Spreadsheets for Management Accounting Tutorial text, prior to tackling the management accounting questions in this book.

Each chapter includes a Spreadsheet Skills Case Study and also spreadsheet-related questions in the Chapter Activities. The spreadsheet skills required to answer each question are indicated in **bold**. Some of the questions will require you to download a spreadsheet containing information which you will need to work with. Spreadsheet files are available to download on the Management Accounting Techniques Tutorial product page on the Osborne Books website www.osbornebooks.co.uk.

Remember, spreadsheets are a tool to help you provide management information. As you learn the management accounting techniques, you will know what to expect the figures in a spreadsheet you produce to be – you can even check them using your calculator to begin with, until you feel more confident.

Work through the Spreadsheet Skills Case Study below, producing a simple statement of profit or loss, including the total cost statement covered earlier in the chapter. You should be able to apply some spreadsheet skills you already know from the Level 2 Certificate in Accounting, then refer to the Osborne Books Spreadsheets for Management Accounting Tutorial text for those you do not.

<table>
<tr><td>Case
Study</td></tr>
</table>

SPREADSHEET SKILLS TO PROVIDE MANAGEMENT ACCOUNTING INFORMATION

situation

Go Drink! produce insulated water bottles.

You are working in the management accounting department and have been asked to finish and format a partly completed spreadsheet of the statement of profit or loss, including the total cost statement, for the managing director.

Download the spreadsheet file 'MATST Ch 1 Spreadsheet Case Study Go Drink! data' from the Osborne Books website.

Save the spreadsheet file in an appropriate location and rename it 'MATST Ch 1 Spreadsheet Case Study Go Drink! answer'.

Open the renamed file.

You are required to:

1 **Merge and centre** the Statement of Profit or Loss heading across columns A to D. **Change the font to bold, size 14**.

2 Make 'Year ended 31 March 20-2' and '£' **bold**.

3 Use formulas to **calculate*** the Prime cost, the Production cost and the Total cost for the year ended 31 March 20-2.

4 **Insert a row** above the profit row (currently row 15).

5 Colour the cell **(fill)** containing the Prime cost amount yellow, the Production cost amount blue and the Total cost amount green.

6 Use a **formula** to **calculate*** the profit for the year ended 31 March 20-2 and highlight it, using a top and double bottom **border**.

7 **Format numbers** to show no decimal places and a thousand separator, with negative figures in brackets (0,000).

8 Enter 'Profit %' in A17, then **calculate** the profit margin (profit as a % of revenue) in D17, **format** it as a **percentage to two decimal places**, then make row 16 and row 17 **bold**.

***Calculate** allows you to use an appropriate **formula** or method. This could be **SUM** =SUM(D8:D9) or simply addition (=D8+D9) for example.

solution

So, when tackling the spreadsheet question, work through each row methodically. You could even tick them off in this book as you go.

The partly completed spreadsheet 'MATST Ch 1 Spreadsheet Case Study Go Drink! data' currently looks like this:

	A	B	C	D	E
1	Statement of Profit or Loss				
2	Year ended 31 March 20-2			£	
3					
4	Revenue			1,250,600	
5	Direct materials			-445,200	
6	Direct labour			-75,900	
7	Direct expenses			-3,600	
8	Prime cost				
9	Production overheads			-126,785	
10	Production cost				
11	Selling and distribution costs			-253,100	
12	Administration costs			-94,200	
13	Finance costs			-12,800	
14	Total cost				
15	Profit				
16					

Attempt points 1 to 3, then compare your answer to the spreadsheet on the next page:

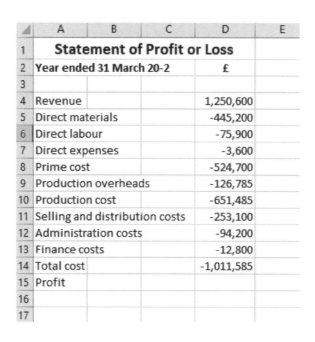

The formulas for Prime cost, Production overheads and Total cost that could be used here are:

Cell	Possible formula	
Prime Cost, D8	=D5+D6+D7	=SUM(D5:D7)*
Production cost, D10	=D8+D9	= SUM(D8:D9)*
Total cost, D14	=D10+D11+D12+D13	= SUM(D10:D13)*

* Using the **SUM** method is recommended but it will give you a warning triangle in the top left-hand corner of D8 (shown on the screen print on the next page).

Do not worry – this is simply a **formula warning** to ask you if you have included the right cells in your formula. Click on the cell to check the formula, then choose the option to ignore the error.

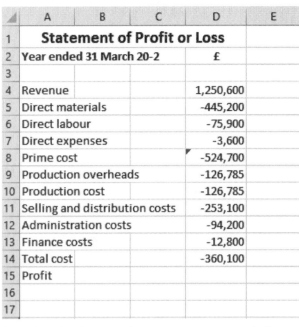

	A	B	C	D	E
1	**Statement of Profit or Loss**				
2	Year ended 31 March 20-2			£	
3					
4	Revenue			1,250,600	
5	Direct materials			-445,200	
6	Direct labour			-75,900	
7	Direct expenses			-3,600	
8	Prime cost			-524,700	
9	Production overheads			-126,785	
10	Production cost			-126,785	
11	Selling and distribution costs			-253,100	
12	Administration costs			-94,200	
13	Finance costs			-12,800	
14	Total cost			-360,100	
15	Profit				
16					
17					

Try points 4 to 6 now and compare your answer to the spreadsheet shown below.

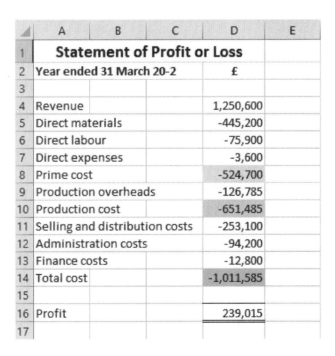

	A	B	C	D	E
1	**Statement of Profit or Loss**				
2	Year ended 31 March 20-2			£	
3					
4	Revenue			1,250,600	
5	Direct materials			-445,200	
6	Direct labour			-75,900	
7	Direct expenses			-3,600	
8	Prime cost			-524,700	
9	Production overheads			-126,785	
10	Production cost			-651,485	
11	Selling and distribution costs			-253,100	
12	Administration costs			-94,200	
13	Finance costs			-12,800	
14	Total cost			-1,011,585	
15					
16	Profit			239,015	
17					

You can see row 15 has been added, the relevant cost cells have been highlighted and the profit figure calculated in D16, is highlighted by the total borders.

Finally, complete the question by doing points 7 and 8, then compare your answer to the spreadsheet image below.

◢	A	B	C	D	E
1	**Statement of Profit or Loss**				
2	Year ended 31 March 20-2			£	
3					
4	Revenue			1,250,600	
5	Direct materials			(445,200)	
6	Direct labour			(75,900)	
7	Direct expenses			(3,600)	
8	Prime cost			(524,700)	
9	Production overheads			(126,785)	
10	Production cost			(651,485)	
11	Selling and distribution costs			(253,100)	
12	Administration costs			(94,200)	
13	Finance costs			(12,800)	
14	Total cost			(1,011,585)	
15					
16	**Profit**			**239,015**	
17	**Profit %**			**19.11%**	

If you wish to look at the spreadsheet answer, which will show you the spreadsheet in full colour, download 'MATST Ch 1 Spreadsheet Case Study Go Drink! answer', from the Management Accounting Techniques Tutorial product page on the Osborne Books website www.osbornebooks.co.uk.

Chapter Summary

- Management accounting (also referred to as cost accounting) is essential to provide information for managers of businesses in order to assist with decision-making, planning and control.

- Responsibility centres are segments of a business and include cost centres, profit centres, investment centres and revenue centres.

- Costs may be charged directly to cost units or to specific parts of a business called cost centres.

- Profit centres analyse costs and revenue to show profit (revenue less costs).

- Revenue centres measure sales revenue from the product sold or service provided.

- Investment centres compare profit with the amount of money invested in the centre.

- Costs may be classified by element, by nature, by function, or by behaviour, depending on the purpose for which the information is required.

- Classifying costs by element and by nature gives a six-way split:

DIRECT MATERIALS	INDIRECT MATERIALS
DIRECT LABOUR	INDIRECT LABOUR
DIRECT EXPENSES	INDIRECT EXPENSES
TOTAL DIRECT COSTS or PRIME COST	TOTAL INDIRECT COSTS or OVERHEADS

- Overheads may be classified by dividing them amongst the functions or sections of the business:

  - factory (or production)

  - selling and distribution

  - administration

  - finance

  - other section headings as appropriate to the organisation

- By behaviour, costs are fixed, or semi-variable, or variable, in relation to output.

- Total cost of a unit of output = $\dfrac{\text{direct costs + indirect costs (overheads)}}{\text{number of units of output}}$

- A total cost statement lists the total of the direct costs and the overheads.

- A statement of profit or loss shows revenue minus total cost equals profit.

integrity	ethical principle requiring accounting staff to be straightforward and honest in all professional and business relationships
cost unit	unit of output to which costs can be charged
composite cost unit	unit of output which comprises two variables
responsibility centre	segment of a business for which a manager is accountable
cost centre	segment of a business to which costs can be charged
profit centre	segment of a business to which costs can be charged, revenue can be identified, and profit can be calculated
revenue centre	segment of a business where sales revenue from the product sold or service provided is measured
investment centre	segment of a business where profit is compared with the amount of money invested in the centre
materials costs	the costs of raw materials, components and other goods used
labour costs	the costs of employees' wages and salaries
expenses	other costs, which cannot be included in 'materials' or 'labour'
direct cost	a cost that can be identified directly with each unit of output
indirect cost (overhead)	a cost that cannot be identified directly with each unit of output
prime cost (direct cost)	the total of all direct costs
fixed costs	costs which remain fixed over a range of output levels
stepped fixed costs	costs that are fixed but, under certain circumstances, increase by a large amount all at once
semi-variable	costs which combine a fixed and variable element
variable costs	costs which vary directly with output
total cost statement	list of the total of the direct costs and the overheads
product cost	costs that become part of the manufactured product
period cost	costs that cannot be assigned to the manufactured product and are incurred in a period of time, eg monthly

Activities

1.1   Which **one** of these is an example of an accounting technician applying the ethical principle of integrity?

(a)	Preparation of management accounting information that is inaccurate	
(b)	Making estimates of management accounting information in order to get the job done quickly	
(c)	Preparation of management accounting information without reference to source data	
(d)	Preparation of management accounting information in a straightforward and honest way	

1.2   The owner of a business with two departments – Cee and Dee – wishes to know which is performing better. The management accountant has produced the following results (shown below) and the owner now seeks your advice.

Complete the comparison table below and advise the owner – in a sentence – which department is performing better.

Responsibility centre	Criteria	Department Cee	Department Dee
Cost centre	Low cost	£10,000	£12,000
Profit centre	High profit	£5,000	£4,000
Revenue centre	High sales	£55,000	£35,000
Investment centre	High %	20%	15%
Advice to the owner:			

1.3 You work for Outdoors and Active!, a company making outdoor equipment. It has three divisions: tents, outdoor clothing and sleeping bags. The accounting system tracks the costs, revenue and money invested in each of these divisions separately.

The Finance Director would like you to produce a report for the company, showing each division's performance in the following order for:

- Revenue

- Costs, individual and total

- Profit earned and profit as a percentage of revenue

- Investment made and the return on investment expressed as a percentage.

He is considering moving away from reporting simply on a profit centre basis, so would like to see how each division performs as a revenue centre, cost centre, profit centre and investment centre.

The information for each division for the year ended 31 March 20-3 is set out below:

Division:	Tents	Outdoor Clothing	Sleeping Bags
Costs:	£000	£000	£000
Materials	1,600	2,060	1,900
Labour	1,970	1,430	650
Overheads	540	320	420
Revenue	4,920	5,630	3,680
Money invested	3,750	3,690	1,290

Open a new spreadsheet and name it 'Outdoors and Active! Divisional Performance 31 March 20-3'.

Set up suitable headings in cells A1 and A2, to indicate the company and the reporting period and **format** in bold.

Name the worksheet 'Divisional Performance'.

Produce a report showing the relevant information, in the order indicated by the Finance Director, using the information in the table.

Use **borders** to define each responsibility centre.

Format figures to show no decimal places with a thousand separator.

Include the additional percentages as required by the Finance Director, using **formulas** to calculate them and **format** these as **percentage** to one decimal place.

Use **cell fill** with one chosen colour to highlight the highest revenue, cost, profit as percentage of revenue and return on investment percentage.

Save the worksheet and check your answers at the back of the book or using the spreadsheet 'MATST Chapter 1 Outdoors and Active! Divisional Performance 31 March 20-3' on the Osborne website, www.osbornebooks.co.uk.

1.4 You work as an Accounts Assistant at City News and Books, a company which owns a group of shops selling newspapers and magazines, books and stationery. The accounting software shows costs, revenue and money invested for each of these three sections of the business: newspapers and magazines, books, stationery.

The Finance Director has requested details for all costs and revenue for last year, and the amount of money invested in each section of the business at the end of the year. (She says that all figures can be to the nearest £000.)

The Accounts Supervisor asks you to deal with this request and you go to the accounts and extract the following information for last year:

	Newspapers and magazines	Books	Stationery
	£000	£000	£000
Costs: materials	155	246	122
labour	65	93	58
expenses	27	35	25
Revenue	352	544	230
Money invested	420	850	250

The Accounts Supervisor asks you to present the information for the Finance Director in the form of a report which shows the costs, profit, return on investment (to the nearest percentage point), and revenue for each section of the business. Use the grid as part of your answer.

	Newspapers and magazines	Books	Stationery
Cost Centre	£000	£000	£000
• materials			
• labour			
• expenses			
• total			
Profit Centre			
Revenue			
less Costs (see above)			
Profit			
Revenue Centre			
Investment Centre			
Profit (see above)			
Investment			
Expressed as a percentage			

1.5 Classify each of the following costs by behaviour (ie fixed, or semi-variable, or variable):

- raw materials
- factory rent
- electricity
- direct labour, eg production workers paid on the basis of work done
- indirect labour, eg supervisors' salaries
- commission paid to sales staff

Taking the costs in turn, explain to a friend, who is about to set up a furniture manufacturing business, why you have classified each as fixed, or semi-variable, or variable. Answer the comment, 'What difference does it make anyway, they are all costs that have to be paid.'

1.6 Classify the following costs (tick the appropriate column):

		Fixed	Semi-variable	Variable
(a)	Rates of business premises			
(b)	Royalty paid to designer for each unit of output			
(c)	Car hire with fixed rental and charge per mile			
(d)	Employees paid on piecework basis			
(e)	Straight-line depreciation			
(f)	Direct materials			
(g)	Telephone bill with fixed rental and a charge for each call made			
(h)	Office salaries			

1.7   You are the Assistant Accountant for Tom's Nurseries, a business growing plants and selling them to local garden centres.

The Finance Director has been asked to produce some information analysing the quarterly costs of the business, as part of a possible cost restructuring programme. She wants you to complete categorising the costs into variable, semi-variable and fixed costs.

Download the spreadsheet file 'MATST Chapter 1 Activities data' from the Osborne Books website.

Save the spreadsheet file in an appropriate location and rename it to 'MATST Chapter 1 Activities answers', so you can refer back to it.

Open the renamed file.

You are required to:

1   **Merge and centre** the 'Tom's Nurseries' heading across columns C to D. **Change the font to size 13**.

2   **Merge and centre** the 'Quarter ended 30 June 20-5' heading across columns C to D. **Change the font to bold, size 12**.

3   **Spell check** the information on the Activity 1 spreadsheet.

4   Using the list of cost categories in F2:F4, apply **data validation** to cells D6 to D17, so only the categories of variable cost, semi-variable cost and fixed cost can be used.

Set the input message as 'Costs can only be categorised using the listed cost categories!'.

Choose a suitable warning message if an incorrect category was typed into the cell.

5   Enter the correct category for the remaining costs in the cost category column.

6   **Format** the **numbers** to **accounting format** £0,000 to no decimal places.

7   **Sort** the cost table into variable, semi-variable and fixed costs.

8   Ensure all the text is visible.

9   Delete column B. Delete row 5.

10   Use **SUBTOTAL** to **SUM** each type of cost, including a grand total in B21.

11   Highlight the Grand Total amount with a **total border**.

12   **Hide** the detailed cost information, so only the amount and subtotal by cost category are showing.

13   **Hide column** A.

Save the worksheet and check your answers at the back of the book or using the spreadsheet 'MATST Chapter 1 Activities answer' on the Osborne Books website, www.osbornebooks.co.uk.

1.8 Severn Manufacturing Limited makes chairs for school and college use. The chairs have plastic seats, and tubular steel legs. **You are to** classify the company's costs into:

- direct materials

- indirect materials

- direct labour

- indirect labour

- direct expenses

- indirect expenses

The cost items to be classified are:

Cost item	Classification (write your answer)
Tubular steel	
Factory supervisor's salary	
Wages of employee operating the moulding machine which produces the chair seats	
Works canteen assistant's wages	
Business rates of factory	
Electricity to operate machines	
Factory heating and lighting	
Plastic for making chair seats	
Hire of special machinery for one particular order	
Grease for the moulding machine	
Depreciation of factory machinery	
Depreciation of office equipment	

1.9 Betterwell NHS Trust is a large hospital with many departments. Costs of the general operating theatre have been identified and you are to classify them into:

- direct materials

- indirect materials

- direct labour

- indirect labour

- direct expenses

- indirect expenses

The cost items to be classified are:

Cost item	Classification (write your answer)
Dressings	
Disposable scalpels	
Surgeon's salary	
Floor cleaning materials	
Laundry	
Depreciation of staff drinks machine	
Theatre heat and light	
Porter's wages	
Anaesthetic gas	
Depreciation of theatre equipment	
Maintenance of theatre equipment	
CDs for music in theatre	
Anaesthetist's salary	

1.10 Wyvern Water Limited bottles natural spring water at its plant at Walcoll at the base of the Wyvern Hills. The natural spring is on land owned by a local farmer to whom a royalty is paid for each bottle of water produced.

You are an Accounts Assistant at Wyvern Water Limited and are asked to analyse the following cost items into the appropriate columns and to agree the totals:

Cost item	Total cost	Prime cost	Production overheads	Admin costs	Selling and distribution costs
	£	£	£	£	£
Wages of employees working on the bottling line	6,025				
Wages of employees in the stores department	2,750				
Bottles	4,050				
Safety goggles for bottling line employees	240				
Advertisement for new employees	125				
Depreciation of bottling machinery	500				
Depreciation of sales staff's cars	1,000				
Royalty paid to local farmer	750				
Trade exhibition fees	1,500				
Computer stationery	210				
Sales staff salaries	4,095				
TOTALS	21,245				

1.11 Which **one** of the following is normally classed as a fixed cost for a manufacturing business?

(a)	Raw materials to make the product	
(b)	Salaries of maintenance staff	
(c)	Production workers paid on the basis of work done	
(d)	Royalties paid to the designer of the product	

1.12   Which **one** of the following is normally classed as a variable cost for a 'high street' printing shop?

(a)	Supervisor's salary	
(b)	Rent of shop	
(c)	Electricity used	
(d)	Cost of paper	

1.13   Which **one** of these is a product cost?

(a)	Production overheads	
(b)	Selling and distribution costs	
(c)	Finance costs	
(d)	Administration costs	

1.14   Which **one** of these is a period cost?

(a)	Direct labour	
(b)	Direct materials	
(c)	Administration costs	
(d)	Production overheads	

1.15   Which **one** of the following statements is correct?

(a)	A period cost is included in inventory valuation	
(b)	Only direct costs are included in inventory valuation	
(c)	A product cost is included in inventory valuation	
(d)	Both product and period costs are included in inventory valuation	

1.16 Identify whether each of the following statements describe the purpose of management accounting or financial accounting within a limited company.

Statement	Management accounting	Financial accounting
Providing financial statements for shareholders		
Producing financial reports on future activities		
Providing financial information to assist with decision-making		
Controlling the expenditure of the business		
Liaising with HMRC for VAT and tax purposes		
Producing financial reports as and when they are needed		

2 Materials costs

this chapter covers...

In Chapter 1 we saw how costs can be classified in a variety of different ways including by element as materials, labour and expenses. In this chapter we focus on materials – or inventory – costs.

Businesses hold materials inventory in the form of raw materials and components, work-in-progress, finished goods, products bought for resale, and service items. Often the value of such materials is high, representing a considerable investment of money. In this chapter we explain:

- *purchasing and control of materials*

- *reordering procedures*

- *records that are kept for materials*

- *valuation of inventory*

- *use of inventory records*

- *bookkeeping entries for materials costs*

TYPES OF MATERIALS INVENTORY

Materials inventory is the cost of:

- raw materials and components bought for use by a manufacturing business, including work-in-progress and finished goods

- products bought for resale by a shop or a wholesaler

- service or consumable items, such as stationery, bought for use within a business

In management accounting we need to distinguish between direct materials and indirect materials. Thus a manufacturer classifies the cost of materials from which the finished product is made as direct materials; other materials used – grease for machines, cleaning materials, etc – are classified as indirect materials, and form part of the overheads of the business.

The buying of materials is normally undertaken by a firm's Purchasing or Procurement Department, although in smaller businesses the responsibility will be carried out by an individual or the owner. The job of the buyer(s) is to ensure that the purchases made by the business are bought in compliance with the inventory control policies of the business and at the lowest possible cost, consistent with quality and quantity and to meet sustainability measures.

At any time, most businesses will hold materials ready to use or for resale. The diagram shown on the next page examines the materials held by three types of business: a manufacturing business which makes products, a trading business such as a shop, which buys and sells goods, and a service business or organisation, which holds consumable materials.

PLANNING OF PURCHASES AND CONTROL OF MATERIALS

Planning for the purchase of materials and the control of materials inventory is critical to the efficiency of a business. However, holding materials is expensive:

- they have to be financed, possibly by using borrowed money (on which interest is payable)

- there are storage costs, including rent and rates, security, insurance

Within a business there are conflicting demands on its policy for materials. On the one hand, the finance department will want to minimise materials inventory levels to keep costs as low as possible; on the other hand, production and marketing departments will be anxious to keep materials inventory high so that output can be maintained and new orders satisfied speedily before customers decide to buy elsewhere.

MATERIALS HELD BY BUSINESSES		
Manufacturing Business	**Trading Business**	**Service Business**
Raw materials and components	**Goods for resale**	**Consumable materials**
Inventory of raw materials used in the production process at a level so that the business does not run short but does not have money tied up unnecessarily. A vehicle manufacturer will hold components ready to use, for example.	Items the retailer or wholesaler has bought in (eg from the manufacturer) and has available for sale to the customer. For example: ▪ *retailers* a supermarket will have cans of orange drink ready for sale ▪ *wholesalers* a timber merchant will have quantities of wood for sale to customers	Materials that are either for use in the organisation or for sale to the customer as part of the service provided. For example: ▪ *for use in the organisation* in a college there will be paper ready for use in the photocopiers ▪ *items for sale* an optician will sell reading glasses as part of the service provided
Work-in-progress		
Part-finished goods on the production line. In a car factory these would be cars partly assembled, for example.		
Finished goods		
Goods that have been completed and are ready for sale to customers. A vehicle manufacturer would have completed cars ready for sale, for example.		

There are a number of methods of planning purchases and of inventory control. The methods adopted will depend on the size and sophistication of the business. It is important that a business knows how much inventory it has at any time – either by making a physical count, or by keeping computer records (which need physical verification at regular intervals) – and it must know when it will have to reorder more inventory. The business then needs to know the quantity that needs to be reordered. The main methods are:

perpetual inventory

This system records receipt and issue of inventory as the items pass in and out of the business, and reorders are made accordingly. Inventory records are often kept digitally by computer, activated by the reading of bar codes. Many supermarkets work on this basis.

just in time (JIT)

A method favoured by manufacturing businesses where supplies of components are delivered to the production line just as they are needed. For JIT to operate effectively, quality suppliers are needed who can be contracted to deliver goods in accordance with manufacturing schedules. In this way inventory levels are kept very low.

formulas

Businesses need to calculate when to order inventory, and how much to order; formulas can be used to help with this. These are explained in the sections which follow.

MATERIALS PURCHASES: FIXED QUANTITY METHOD

Using the fixed quantity method of reordering, materials are ordered in set amounts, eg 750 reams of copy paper (a ream is 500 sheets). For such a system to operate, the business should know:

■ the **maximum inventory level** that can be held – this can be calculated, but may well be determined by the amount of storage space available in the warehouse, shop or office stationery 'cupboard'

■ the **buffer inventory**, ie the minimum level that inventory should not fall below before the new order from the supplier is delivered

■ the **lead time**, ie how long it takes for new inventory to be delivered after being ordered

■ the **reorder level**, ie the point at which a new order is to be placed – this is often the most critical factor to determine

■ the appropriate **reorder quantity,** including the maximum reorder quantity and the minimum reorder quantity

Many businesses use a computer inventory control system to keep a running record of the amount of each material held, the lead time for reordering, and the buffer inventory. The fixed quantity method of reordering is illustrated as follows:

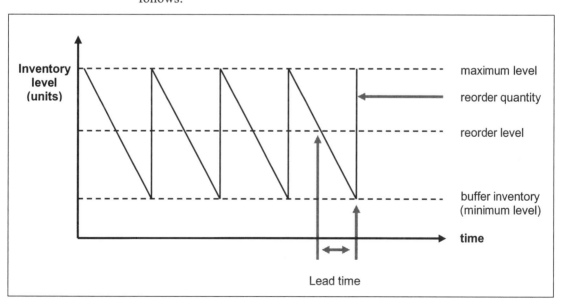

buffer inventory

= reorder level – (average usage* x average lead time)

* per day/week/month

This is the minimum inventory level to be held in order to meet unexpected emergencies and is set by the purchasing/procurement or the stores department – lead time will be known by the department.

reorder level =

= (average usage x average lead time) + buffer inventory

The reorder level is calculated so that replacement materials are delivered just as the inventory falls to the level of the buffer inventory.

Tutorial note: when completing calculations for buffer inventory or reorder level, AAT Assessments will give the values for either buffer inventory or reorder level.

maximum inventory level

= buffer inventory + maximum reorder quantity

The maximum inventory level is the highest level that the business wishes to hold. This maximum may be because of limited storage space, the cost of funding the inventory, or business practice. The disadvantage of holding too much inventory is that of obsolescence – inventory either going out of date or being superseded by an updated product.

maximum reorder quantity

= maximum inventory level – buffer inventory

Maximum reorder quantity will, when received, restore inventory to the maximum level.

Tutorial note: when completing calculations for maximum inventory level or maximum reorder quantity, AAT Assessments will give the values for either maximum inventory level or maximum reorder quantity.

minimum reorder quantity

= average usage x average lead time

Minimum reorder quantity will, when received, restore inventory to the reorder level (which means a further order will have to be placed).

worked example

A4, white copy paper

average daily usage	30 reams (a ream is 500 sheets)
average lead time	5 days
buffer inventory	100 reams
maximum inventory level	900 reams (due to limited storage space)

Calculations

Reorder level

    = (30 reams usage x 5 days' lead time)

    + 100 reams buffer inventory

    = (30 x 5) + 100

    = 250 reams (reorder level)

Maximum reorder quantity

    = 900 reams maximum inventory level – 100 reams buffer inventory

    = 800 reams maximum reorder quantity

Minimum reorder quantity

    = 30 reams usage x 5 days' lead time

    = 150 reams minimum reorder quantity

Note: by the time the minimum order is delivered – in five days' time – inventory will have fallen to 100 reams; the order will restore the inventory to 250 reams (which is the reorder level), so another order will have to be placed immediately.

It is important not to treat inventory calculations in isolation – there does need to be consideration of wider issues which may affect the business or organisation. Such issues include:

- needs of the business – for example, if an inventory item is being used less frequently than before, the calculations will need to be revised to suit current and future needs

- obsolescence of inventory – for example, if spare parts are kept for a particular make and model of vehicle, inventory levels will need to be run down when the vehicles are being replaced by those of a different make and model

- seasonal variations affecting usage and inventory levels – for example, a business using oil for heating may be offered a cheaper price when usage is low in the summer which may make it worthwhile to buy; by contrast, when usage is high in the winter, the supplier's price and lead times may increase

MATERIALS PURCHASES: ECONOMIC ORDER QUANTITY (EOQ)

It is clear that the reorder quantity is critical to the efficiency of inventory holding:

- if reorder amounts are **too large**, too much inventory will be held, which will be an expense to the business

- if reorder amounts are **too small**, the expense of constantly reordering will outweigh any cost savings of lower inventory levels, and there will be the danger that the item might 'run out'

The most economic reorder quantity – **the economic order quantity (EOQ)** – can be calculated by a mathematical formula which involves a number of different costs and other figures:

- **ordering cost** – the administration cost of placing each order, eg stationery, postage, wages, telephone, bank charges

- **inventory holding cost** – the cost of keeping the inventory on the shelves expressed as the cost of holding one unit of inventory per year; examples of inventory holding costs include rent and rates, insurance, wages, deterioration, obsolescence, security

- **annual usage** – the number of inventory units used per year

The formula is:

$$\text{Economic Order Quantity (EOQ)} = \sqrt{\frac{2 \times \text{annual usage} \times \text{ordering cost}}{\text{inventory holding cost}}}$$

On a calculator with a square root function, this formula can be worked out easily. Calculate the figures in the formula first, and then press the square root button ($\sqrt{}$).

For example, for a particular inventory item, the ordering cost of each order is £45, the inventory holding cost is £2 per unit per year, and annual usage is 2,000 units. The EOQ formula is applied as follows:

$$\text{Economic Order Quantity (EOQ)} = \sqrt{\frac{2 \times 2,000 \times £45}{£2}}$$

$$= \sqrt{\frac{180,000}{2}}$$

$$= \sqrt{90,000}$$

$$= \underline{300 \text{ units}}$$

As a result of using EOQ, a balance is struck between the cost of placing an order and the cost of holding inventory; EOQ represents the most efficient level of order to place because it minimises the total cost of ordering and storage.

Once the EOQ has been calculated, it is used as the quantity of inventory to be ordered each time an order is placed. This principle is illustrated in the Case Study on page 54.

INVENTORY RECORDS

Most businesses will have records of their inventories. Such records may be kept either by using computer inventory software, or manually on individual inventory records. Under both methods – computer and manual – a separate record is maintained for each type of inventory. The system is used whether the materials are held for resale by a retailer, or for use in production by a manufacturer. When supplies of the material are received they are entered in the inventory record, and when items are sold (or issued to production) they are shown as issues on the inventory record.

A typical inventory record is shown below. Note that:

■ a separate inventory record is used for each type of inventory

■ the 'quantity' column can be expressed in units, kg, litres, metres, etc – whatever is suitable for the inventory item

■ the 'cost per unit' and 'total cost' columns are always the cost price of the inventory

INVENTORY RECORD

Date	Receipts			Issues			Balance		
	Quantity (units)	Cost per unit	Total Cost	Quantity (units)	Cost per unit	Total Cost	Quantity (units)	Cost per unit	Total Cost
		£	£		£	£		£	£

The layout of the inventory record may vary from one business to another.

The way in which inventory records are used is shown in the Case Study on page 50.

VALUATION OF INVENTORY

The amount of materials inventory held by a business or organisation invariably has considerable value and ties up a lot of money. At the end of the financial year, it is essential to value the inventory for use in the calculation of profit in the financial statements. A process of counting inventory (usually known as stock-taking) is used to make a physical check of the inventory held, which is then compared with the inventory records. The inventory held is then valued as follows:

number of items held x cost per item = inventory value at cost

The auditors of a business may make random checks to ensure that the inventory value is correct.

The general rule is that inventory can be valued at *either*:

■ what it cost the business to buy (including additional costs to bring the product or service to its present location or condition, such as delivery charges), *or*

■ the net realisable value – which is the actual or estimated selling price (less any extra costs, such as selling and distribution) – ie what you would get for it

Inventory valuation is normally at the **lower of cost and net realisable value**. This valuation is taken from International Accounting Standard (IAS) No 2, entitled *Inventories*. This method of valuation is illustrated as follows:

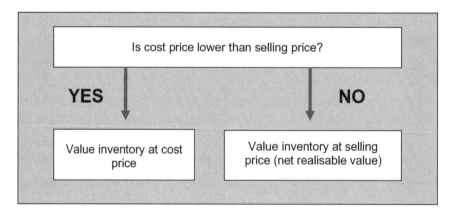

The difficulty with inventory valuation is in finding out the cost price of inventory – this is not easy when quantities of a particular item are continually being bought in – often at different prices – and then sold. Some organisations have inventory in a number of different forms, eg manufacturing businesses have raw materials, work-in-progress and finished goods.

METHODS OF INVENTORY VALUATION

issuing of materials and goods

The costing process requires that a value is given to raw materials (for a manufacturer) and goods (for a shop) when they are 'issued'. This means the point at which they are handed over to the production line or placed on the shop shelves. Traditionally the materials and goods were issued from 'stores' – a storage area – where they had been kept by the business since delivery from the supplier. The phrase 'issued from stores' is still used, although nowadays materials and goods are often delivered just before they are needed – this saves on storage and finance costs.

The cost of the materials or goods at the time of issue is normally the purchase cost – ie the price the business paid the supplier. But purchase costs do vary – so which cost do you take and what valuation do you give the materials or goods?

The two most commonly used methods for deciding which 'cost' to use for raw materials used in the production process or sold from shop shelves are either FIFO (first in, first out) or AVCO (weighted average cost). Both of these methods are permitted by IAS 2 for financial accounting purposes. The methods work as follows:

FIFO (First In, First Out)

In this method, the first (oldest) cost prices are used first when goods are issued from stores. This means that the remaining inventory is valued at the most recent cost prices.

AVCO (Weighted Average Cost)

In this method, a weighted average cost is calculated for the inventory held at a given time, using the formula:

$$\text{weighted average cost} = \frac{\text{total cost of inventory held}}{\text{number of items held}}$$

The weighted average cost is then used to attach a value to issues from stores. A new weighted average must be calculated each time that further purchases are made.

which method to use?

The use of a particular method of inventory valuation does not necessarily correspond with the method of physical distribution adopted in a firm's stores. For example, in a car factory one car battery of type X is the same as another, and no-one will be concerned if the issue is one from the last batch received, even if the FIFO system has been adopted. However, perishable goods are always physically handled on the basis of first in, first out, even if the accounting inventory records use another method.

Having chosen a suitable inventory valuation method, a business will continue to use that method unless there are good reasons for making the change.

Case Study

H RASHID COMPUTER SUPPLIES: INVENTORY RECORDS

situation

H Rashid runs a computer supplies company. One of the items he sells is the 'Zap' memory stick.

To show how the inventory records would appear under FIFO and AVCO, and the closing inventory valuation at 31 May 20-4, the following data is used for each method:

January	Opening inventory of 40 units at a cost of £3.00 each
February	Bought 20 units at a cost of £3.60 each
March	Sold 36 units for £6 each
April	Bought 20 units at a cost of £3.75 each
May	Sold 25 units for £6 each

Note: show the cost per unit to two decimal places.

What will be the profit for the period using each inventory valuation method?

Tutorial notes:

- This Case Study shows the inventory records using the two methods: FIFO and AVCO.

- The inventory records in this Case Study include, under the 'balance' heading, a column for 'cost per unit'. This column is not always given (see Case Study on page 54) but is included here to show the workings clearly.

- In the solution which follows there are often several calculations in the issues and balance columns – these are given to show clearly the calculations. However, in some layouts, you will only be able to record one entry in each inventory record cell: what you will record is the total of each cell, eg for February, below, you will record 60 in the quantity cell and 192.00 in the total cost cell.

- Where appropriate, make sure you know how many decimal places you should work to.

solution

Note: With FIFO, units issued at the same time may be valued at different costs. This is because the quantities received, with their costs, are listed separately and used in a specific order. There may be insufficient units at one cost, eg see the May issue below.

FIFO

For FIFO, in the 'Balance' columns, a new list of inventory quantities and costs is started after each receipt or issue. When inventory is issued, costs are used from the **top** of the list downwards.

INVENTORY RECORD: FIFO

Date	Receipts			Issues			Balance		
	Quantity (units)	Cost per unit	Total Cost	Quantity (units)	Cost per unit	Total Cost	Quantity (units)	Cost per unit	Total Cost
		£	£		£	£		£	£
20-4 Jan	Balance						40	3.00	120.00
Feb	20	3.60	72.00				40	3.00	120.00
							20	3.60	72.00
							—		——
							60		192.00
							—		——
March				36	3.00	108.00	4	3.00	12.00
							20	3.60	72.00
							—		——
							24		84.00
							—		——
April	20	3.75	75.00				4	3.00	12.00
							20	3.60	72.00
							20	3.75	75.00
							—		——
							44		159.00
							—		——
May				4	3.00	12.00			
				20	3.60	72.00			
				1	3.75	3.75			
				—		——			
				25		87.75	19	3.75	71.25
				—		——			

AVCO

For AVCO, each quantity issued is valued at the weighted average cost per unit, and so is the balance of inventory. The complete list of different costs does not have to be rewritten each time. Note that there are often rounding issues with AVCO.

INVENTORY RECORD: AVCO

Date	Receipts			Issues			Balance		
	Quantity (units)	Cost per unit	Total Cost	Quantity (units)	Cost per unit	Total Cost	Quantity (units)	Cost per unit	Total Cost
		£	£		£	£		£	£
20-4 Jan	Balance						40	3.00	120.00
Feb	20	3.60	72.00				40	3.00	120.00
							20	3.60	72.00
							60	3.20	192.00
March				36	3.20	115.20	24	3.20	76.80
April	20	3.75	75.00				24	3.20	76.80
							20	3.75	75.00
							44	3.45	151.80
May				25	3.45	86.25	19	3.45	65.55

Note: Weighted average cost is calculated by dividing the quantity of inventory held into the value of the inventory. For example, at the end of February, the weighted average cost is £192 ÷ 60 units = £3.20, and at the end of April it is £151.80 ÷ 44 = £3.45.

Each time a new receipt of inventory is recorded, a new weighted average cost is calculated. When inventory is issued, the cost is at the last calculated weighted average cost.

The closing inventory valuations at the end of May 20-4 show total cost prices of:

> FIFO   £71.25
>
> AVCO   £65.55

There is quite a difference, and this has come about because different inventory valuation methods have been used.

effect on profit

In the example above, the selling price was £6 per unit. The effect on gross profit of using the inventory valuations is shown below.

		FIFO	AVCO
		£	£
Revenue: 61 units at £6		366.00	366.00
Opening inventory:	40 units at £3	120.00	120.00
Purchases:	20 units at £3.60 and	147.00	147.00
	20 units at £3.75		
		267.00	267.00
Less Closing inventory	19 units	71.25	65.55
Cost of sales		195.75	201.45
Gross profit = Revenue – Cost of sales		170.25	164.55

Notice that the cost of sales figure in each case is also obtainable by adding up the values in the 'Issues' column. You can also check in each case that, both in Units and in Values:

opening inventory + receipts – issues = closing inventory

Here it is 40 units + 40 units – 61 units = 19 units.

This Case Study shows that in times of rising prices, FIFO produces a higher reported profit than AVCO. However, over the life of a business, total profit is the same in total, whichever method is chosen: the profit is allocated to different years depending on which method is used.

Accounting staff must resist being pressured into using a different inventory valuation in order to manipulate profits. The application of **ethical considerations** in accounting must ensure that information is prepared with **objectivity** – that is without manipulation or bias.

COMPARISON OF FIFO AND AVCO

The table on the next page compares the two inventory valuation techniques and consolidates what you have learned so far.

It is important to note that a business must adopt a consistent inventory valuation policy, ie it should choose one method of finding the cost price, and not change it without good reason.

Comparison of the FIFO and AVCO methods of inventory valuation		
	FIFO	**AVCO**
Method	The costs used for goods sold or issued follow the order in which the goods were received.	Does not relate issues to any particular batch of goods received, but uses a weighted average cost.
Calculation	It is easy to calculate costs because they relate to specific receipts of materials or goods.	More complex because of the need to calculate weighted average costs after each receipt of goods.
Inventory valuation	Inventory valuations are based on the most recent costs of materials or goods received.	Weighted average costs are used to value closing inventory.
Profits and taxation	In times of rising prices this method will result in higher reported profits than the other methods, resulting in more tax being payable. This method is acceptable for tax purposes and is permitted under IAS 2, *Inventories*.	The weighted average method will smooth out some of the peaks and troughs of profit and loss. This method is acceptable for tax purposes and is permitted under IAS 2, *Inventories*.
Administration	Use of this method will mean keeping track of each receipt until the goods are issued or sold.	There is no need to track each receipt as a weighted average cost is used. This also means it is easier to computerise the inventory records.
Cost of sales	If cost prices have changed, this method will use older, out of date prices for cost of sales or goods issued.	This method will give an average price for the cost of sales.

Case Study

USING ECONOMIC ORDER QUANTITY AND INVENTORY RECORDS

Tutorial note: In this Case Study note that the inventory record does not give a 'cost per unit' under the 'balance' heading.

situation

You are an Accounts Assistant at Stoke Park Limited and have been asked to help with the inventory records.

The management accountant has given you the following information for metal grade FE4.

- Annual demand – 28,125 kilograms
- Annual holding cost per kilogram – £0.50
- Fixed ordering cost – £20

(a) **You are to** calculate the Economic Order Quantity (EOQ) for FE4.

The inventory record shown below for metal grade FE4 for the month of September has only been fully completed for the first three weeks of the month.

(b) **You are to** complete the entries in the inventory record for the two receipts on 25 and 29 September that were ordered using the EOQ method.

(c) **You are to** complete all entries in the inventory record for the two issues in the month and for the closing balance at the end of September using the FIFO method of issuing inventory.

Note: show the cost per kilogram (kg) to two decimal places.

Inventory record for metal grade FE4

Date	Receipts			Issues			Balance	
	Quantity (kg)	Cost per kg	Total Cost	Quantity (kg)	Cost per unit	Total Cost	Quantity (kg)	Total Cost
Balance as at 23 September		£	£		£	£	740	£ 814
25 September		1.20						
27 September				850				
29 September		1.25						
30 September				1,630				

solution

(a)

$$\text{Economic Order Quantity (EOQ)} = \sqrt{\frac{2 \times 28{,}125 \text{ kg} \times £20}{£0.50}}$$

$$= \sqrt{\frac{1{,}125{,}000}{0.50}}$$

$$= \sqrt{2{,}250{,}000}$$

$$= \underline{1{,}500 \text{ kg}}$$

(b) and **(c)**

Inventory record for metal grade FE4

Date	Receipts			Issues			Balance	
	Quantity (kg)	Cost per kg	Total Cost	Quantity (kg)	Cost per unit	Total Cost	Quantity (kg)	Total Cost
		£	£		£	£		£
Balance as at 23 September							740	814
25 September	1,500	1.20	1,800				740	814
							1,500	1,800
							2,240	2,614
27 September				740	1.10	814		
				110	1.20	132		
				850		946	1,390	1,668
29 September	1,500	1.25	1,875				1,390	1,668
							1,500	1,875
							2,890	3,543
30 September				1,390	1.20	1,668		
				240	1.25	300		
				1,630		1,968	1,260	1,575

Tutorial notes:

- This Case Study uses the FIFO method of issuing inventory. You need to be able to identify and explain the principles behind the FIFO and AVCO methods.

- With the FIFO method you will note that issues may be valued at different costs – as here on 27 and 30 September. This is because the quantities received, with their costs, are listed separately and used in a specific order.

CATEGORIES OF INVENTORY

The principle of inventory valuation, as set out in International Accounting Standard No 2, *Inventories*, is that inventories should be valued at **'the lower of cost and net realisable value'**.

Note should be taken of:

■ separate items of inventory, or

■ groups of similar items

This means that the inventory valuation 'rule' must be applied to each separate item of inventory, or each group or category of similar inventory. The total cost cannot be compared with the total net realisable value.

INVENTORY VALUATION FOR MANUFACTURING BUSINESSES

The principle of 'the lower of cost and net realisable value' applies to a manufacturer for the three types of inventory that may be held at the year-end:

■ raw materials

■ part-finished goods or work-in-progress

■ finished goods

For raw materials, the comparison is made between cost (which can be found using the techniques of FIFO or AVCO) and net realisable value.

For part-finished and finished goods, IAS 2 requires that the cost valuation includes expenditure not only on direct materials but also on direct labour, direct expenses and production overheads. Thus for part-finished and finished goods, 'cost' means 'production cost', ie the total of:

■ direct materials

■ direct labour

■ direct expenses

■ production overheads (to bring the product to its present location or condition)

Such 'cost' is then compared with net realisable value – less any further costs necessary to complete the item or get it in a condition to be sold – and the lower figure is taken as the inventory valuation. (Remember that different items or groups of inventory are compared separately.)

ABC MANUFACTURING:
INVENTORIES VALUATION

situation

ABC Manufacturing started in business on 1 July 20-3 producing security devices for doors and windows. During the first year 2,000 units were sold and, at the end of the year, on 30 June 20-4, there were 200 units which were finished and 20 units which were exactly half-finished as regards direct materials, direct labour and production overheads.

Costs for the first year were:

	£
Direct materials used	18,785
Direct labour	13,260
Production overheads	8,840
Non-production overheads	4,420
Total cost for year	45,305

At 30 June 20-4 it was estimated that the net realisable value of each completed security device was £35. At the same date, the company holds raw materials as follows:

	Cost	Net realisable value
	£	£
Material A	1,400	1,480
Material B	400	360
Material C	260	280

Calculate the inventories valuation at 30 June 20-4 for:
- raw materials
- work-in-progress
- finished goods

solution

RAW MATERIALS

Using the IAS 2 rule of the 'lower of cost and net realisable value', and applying it to each group or category of inventory, the total value is:

	£	
Material A	1,400	(cost)
Material B	360	(net realisable value)
Material C	260	(cost)
	2,020	

WORK-IN-PROGRESS

To calculate the value of both work-in-progress and finished goods we need to know the production cost, ie direct materials, direct labour and production overheads. This is:

	£
Direct materials used	18,785
Direct labour	13,260
Production overheads	8,840
Production cost for year	**40,885**

All these costs are included because they have been incurred in bringing the product to its present location or condition. Non-production overheads are not included because they are not directly related to production.

Thus, a production cost of £40,885 has produced:

Units sold	2,000
Closing inventory of completed units	200
Closing inventory of work-in-progress –	
20 units exactly half-finished equals	
10 completed units	10
Production for year	**2,210**

The **cost per unit** is:

$$\frac{£40,885}{2,210} = \textbf{£18.50 per unit}$$

The 20 half-finished units have a cost of (20 ÷ 2) x £18.50 = **£185**.

They have a net realisable value of (20 ÷ 2) x £35 = **£350**.

The value of work-in-progress will, therefore, be shown in the financial statements as **£185**, which is the lower of cost and net realisable value.

FINISHED GOODS

The completed units held at the end of the year have a production cost of 200 x £18.50 = £3,700, compared with a net realisable value of 200 x £35 = £7,000. Applying the rule of lower of cost and net realisable value, finished goods inventory will be valued at the cost price, **£3,700**.

BOOKKEEPING FOR MATERIALS COSTS

In this section we look at the cost bookkeeping entries to record inventory transactions – the purchase of materials either on credit from suppliers or on cash terms, and the issue or return of inventory to or from production. These entries form part of the bookkeeping system for costing.

When making cost bookkeeping entries, remember to use the principles of double-entry bookkeeping:

- a debit entry records a gain in value for an asset or an expense

- a credit entry records a gain in value for a liability or an income item

With direct materials, the general ledger entries are:

- **purchase of materials on credit from a supplier**

    - debit inventory (asset gained)

    - credit trade payables control (liability incurred)

- **purchase of materials on cash terms** (ie immediate payment from bank)
    - debit inventory (asset gained)
    - credit bank (decrease in bank balance)

- **issue of materials to production**
    - debit production (asset of materials gained)
    - credit inventory (value of materials to production)

- **return of materials from production to inventory**
    - debit inventory (asset gained)
    - credit production (value from production)

Four accounts are involved in these transactions:
    - inventory account
    - production account
    - trade payables control account
    - bank account

The cost bookkeeping entries for direct materials are shown diagrammatically at the top of the next page.

With indirect materials (such as grease used to lubricate factory machinery) the general ledger entries for the issue of materials are:

- debit production overheads

- credit inventory

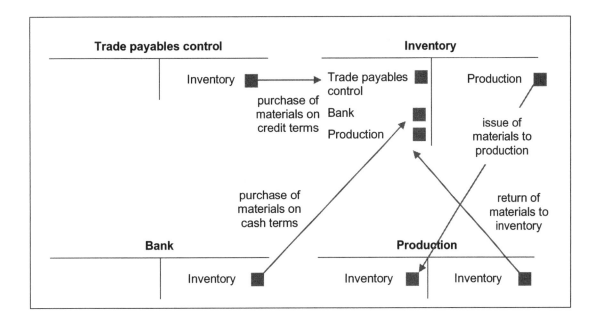

BLUE JEANS LIMITED:
BOOKKEEPING FOR MATERIALS COSTS

situation

Blue Jeans Limited manufactures and sells denim jeans and jackets. The company uses the first in, first out (FIFO) method for valuing issues of materials to production and for valuing inventory.

The company has been very busy in recent weeks and, as a consequence, some of the accounting records are not up-to-date. The inventory record shown at the top of the next page has not been completed.

All issues of blue denim are for the manufacture of blue jeans. The following cost accounting codes are used to record material costs:

Code number	Description
2000	inventory – blue denim
2200	production – blue jeans
4000	trade payables control

As an Accounts Assistant at Blue Jeans Limited, you are asked to complete the inventory record (showing the cost per metre to two decimal places) and to fill in the table opposite to record the journal entries for the two purchases and two issues of blue denim in the cost accounting records.

INVENTORY RECORD

Product: Blue denim

Date	Receipts			Issues			Balance	
	Quantity (metres)	Cost per metre	Total Cost	Quantity (metres)	Cost per metre	Total Cost	Quantity (metres)	Total Cost
20-4 Balance at 1 Oct		£	£		£	£	20,000	£ 10,000
11 Oct	10,000	0.60	6,000				30,000	16,000
14 Oct				25,000				
19 Oct	20,000	0.70	14,000					
25 Oct				20,000				

20-4	Code number	Debit £	Credit £
11 October	2000		
11 October	4000		
14 October	2000		
14 October	2200		
19 October	2000		
19 October	4000		
25 October	2000		
25 October	2200		

solution

The inventory record, using FIFO, is completed as shown below.

Note that the calculations for the issues are from more than one receipt cost.

14 October				£
20,000	metres at £0.50 per metre		=	10,000
5,000	metres at £0.60 per metre		=	3,000
25,000	metres		=	13,000

25 October				£
*5,000	metres at £0.60 per metre		=	3,000
**15,000	metres at £0.70 per metre		=	10,500
20,000	metres		=	13,500

* remainder of receipt on 11 October
** part of receipt on 19 October

INVENTORY RECORD

Product: **Blue denim**

Date	Receipts			Issues			Balance	
	Quantity (metres)	Cost per metre	Total Cost	Quantity (metres)	Cost per metre	Total Cost	Quantity (metres)	Total Cost
20-4 Balance at 1 Oct		£	£		£	£	20,000	£ 10,000
11 Oct	10,000	0.60	6,000				20,000 10,000	10,000 6,000
							30,000	16,000
14 Oct				20,000 5,000	0.50 0.60	10,000 3,000		
				25,000		13,000	5,000	3,000
19 Oct	20,000	0.70	14,000				5,000 20,000	3,000 14,000
							25,000	17,000
25 Oct				5,000 15,000	0.60 0.70	3,000 10,500		
				20,000		13,500	5,000	3,500

The cost bookkeeping entries are:

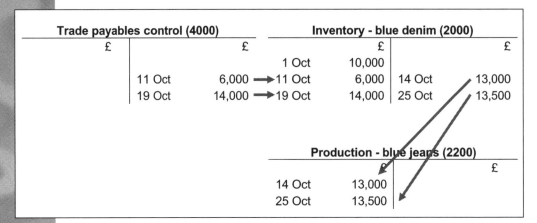

Trade payables control (4000)		Inventory - blue denim (2000)	
£	£	£	£
		1 Oct 10,000	
11 Oct 6,000	→11 Oct	6,000	14 Oct 13,000
19 Oct 14,000	→19 Oct	14,000	25 Oct 13,500

Production - blue jeans (2200)	
£	£
14 Oct 13,000	
25 Oct 13,500	

The cost bookkeeping transactions are recorded as journal entries in the following way:

20-4	Code number	Debit £	Credit £
11 October	2000	6,000	
11 October	4000		6,000
14 October	2000		13,000
14 October	2200	13,000	
19 October	2000	14,000	
19 October	4000		14,000
25 October	2000		13,500
25 October	2200	13,500	

SPREADSHEET SKILLS FOR MANAGEMENT ACCOUNTING

materials inventory

Many businesses that hold inventory for resale or as raw materials, consumables or work-in-progress may use spreadsheets to monitor and control it. A larger business may use an inventory system to manage inventory on a day-to-day basis and use spreadsheets to review inventory periodically. Smaller businesses often track inventory levels using spreadsheets to decide when to place an order to replenish inventory levels, or to value it at the end of the year for the financial statements.

When spreadsheets are used, it is important to protect the spreadsheet, in the same way a business keeps the physical inventory secure. If inventory is stolen and the inventory record amended, then the theft may not be identified for some time.

Spreadsheets can also be useful to automate certain procedures. For example, valuing inventory at the year end requires a company to undertake a detailed comparison of cost compared to net realisable value. This can be considerably quicker, and more accurate, when the information is loaded into a spreadsheet and a suitable formula is used.

Inventory can be a considerable investment by a business, so monitoring the level of inventory held is critical to meet customer and production needs, as well as monitor the amount of cash tied up in it. Setting order levels, using the fixed quantity method for example, will assist in managing this effectively.

Finally, analysing how much of particular products are held in inventory can be very useful, particularly when products have a short shelf life. Management may require an accountant to use charts to assist them with this.

Let's look at a Case Study (on the next page) to see how spreadsheets might be used in practice.

SPREADSHEET SKILLS TO PROVIDE MANAGEMENT ACCOUNTING INFORMATION

situation

Bumper Beds Ltd sells various styles and sizes of bed. The year end inventory valuation is in progress and some analysis of inventory is required. The year end is 31 March 20-6.

Matt Bush, the accountant, has asked you to assist in the year end valuation process. The inventory count has been performed at the two finished goods warehouses.

Download the spreadsheet file 'MATST Ch 2 Spreadsheet Skills Case Study Bumper Beds Ltd data' from the Osborne Books website.

Save the spreadsheet file in an appropriate location and rename it 'MATST Ch 2 Spreadsheet Skills Case Study Bumper Beds Ltd answer'.

Open the renamed file.

Part a)

Complete the following in the 'Summary' worksheet:

1 In column D, use a **formula** to **link** the appropriate items in Finished goods warehouse 1 and Finished goods warehouse 2 to find the total number of items held.

2 In column G, use an **IF statement** to select the correct inventory value, under IAS 2 rules, for the valuation of the closing inventory.

3 In column G, use **conditional formatting** to highlight inventory valued at net realisable value in red and cost in green.

4 In column H, use a **formula** to **calculate** the total inventory value on 31 March 20-6.

5 **Format** the numbers in column H to **currency** to two decimal places. Ensure all information in column H can be clearly seen.

6 In row 2, **wrap text** so headings are clearly visible.

The production manager has asked you to produce some further analysis of the closing inventory valuation.

Part b)

Complete the following in the 'Summary' worksheet:

1 Use **SUBTOTAL** to **calculate** the total inventory value for each range.

2 **Hide** the detail and **columns** B-G. Ensure the titles and ranges can be seen.

3 Copy the 'Summary' worksheet onto a **new worksheet**, rename it 'Inventory 31 March 20-6' and insert a **3D pie chart** onto it, excluding Grand Total.

4 Amend the title to 'Total year end inventory (value)' and add **data labels** to two decimal places. **Change the colour** of any segments where the data labels are not clearly visible.

5 **In the chart, explode the segment** for the range with the largest inventory value. Resize the chart, so all the data can be clearly seen.

solution

The 'Summary' worksheet looks like this initially.

	A	B	C	D	E	F	G	H	I	J
2	Range	Colour and cushion	Description	Total number	Cost	Net Realisable \	IAS 2 value of	Total inventory value		
3	Dreamy	Midnight	Single		£246.50	£199.00				
4	Dreamy	Midnight	Double		£455.50	£399.00				
5	Dreamy	Midnight	King size		£575.60	£549.00				
6	Dreamy	Midnight	Queen size		£465.50	£429.00				
7	Dreamy	Midnight	Super king size		£685.50	£599.00				
8	Cosy	Oatmeal	Single		£266.50	£299.00				
9	Cosy	Oatmeal	Double		£475.50	£499.00				
10	Cosy	Oatmeal	King size		£595.60	£629.00				
11	Cosy	Oatmeal	Queen size		£485.50	£539.00				
12	Cosy	Oatmeal	Super king size		£695.50	£749.00				
13	Dreamy City	Grey	Single		£226.50	£279.00				
14	Dreamy City	Grey	Double		£405.50	£469.00				
15	Dreamy City	Grey	King size		£545.60	£599.00				
16	Dreamy City	Grey	Queen size		£445.50	£499.00				
17	Dreamy City	Grey	Super king size		£665.50	£739.00				
18	Sleepy	Midnight	Single		£209.00	£199.00				
19	Sleepy	Midnight	Double		£405.50	£289.00				
20	Sleepy	Midnight	King size		£525.60	£489.00				
21	Sleepy	Midnight	Queen size		£425.50	£399.00				
22	Sleepy	Midnight	Super king size		£605.50	£589.00				
23	Cosy City	Grey	Single		£266.50	£299.00				
24	Cosy City	Grey	Double		£475.50	£499.00				
25	Cosy City	Grey	King size		£595.60	£629.00				
26	Cosy City	Grey	Queen size		£485.50	£539.00				
27	Cosy City	Grey	Super king size		£695.50	£749.00				
28	Sleepy City	Grey	Single		£209.00	£259.00				
29	Sleepy City	Grey	Double		£405.50	£459.00				
30	Sleepy City	Grey	King size		£525.60	£575.00				
31	Sleepy City	Grey	Queen size		£425.50	£499.00				
32	Sleepy City	Grey	Super king size		£605.50	£669.00				
33	Nest	Midnight	Single		£224.00	£199.00				
34	Nest	Midnight	Double		£420.50	£389.00				
35	Nest	Midnight	King size		£540.60	£529.00				
36	Nest	Midnight	Queen size		£440.50	£420.00				
37	Nest	Midnight	Super king size		£620.50	£579.00				
38	Cosset	Oatmeal	Single		£275.00	£339.00				
39	Cosset	Oatmeal	Double		£465.00	£529.00				

Summary | Finished goods warehouse 1 | Finished goods warehouse 2 | ⊕

For point 1, **link**ing the amount of inventory in each of the finished goods warehouse worksheets to the 'Summary' worksheet is straightforward. For example, in cell D3, the formula is:

='Finished goods warehouse 1'!D3+'Finished goods warehouse 2'!D3

If you are asked to do this, all the sheets will have the same range of inventory, so do not worry about having to make any adjustments.

Valuing inventory at the lower of cost or net realisable value, uses a simple **IF statement**. For cell G3, the formula is:

=IF(F3<E3,F3,E3). An alternative formula could also be =IF(E3<F3,E3,F3).

So whichever value is lower will be used for the IAS 2 value of the item. Remember, any spreadsheet is simply used to apply your accounting knowledge.

For a business, it is important to highlight where inventory is reduced in value, if the net realisable value is lower than the cost. **Conditional formatting** is a good tool to highlight this. When using it, sometimes it is easier to use two rules, rather than try to write one complicated one! The rules to use in this question are shown on the next page:

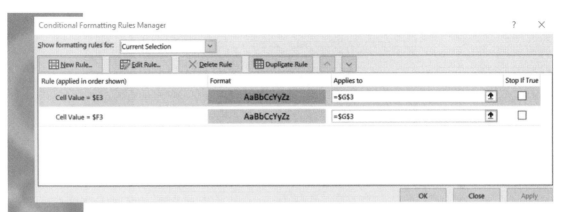

Remember the row in the cell value must not include **absolute referencing** (so no $ sign in front of the number) so the conditional formatting can be copied and pasted to the other cells.

The IAS 2 value of item is then used to find the total inventory cost - the total number multiplied by the IAS 2 value of each item.

After completing part a) points 5 & 6, compare your answer to this extract of the 'Summary' worksheet below:

	A	B	C	D	E	F	G	H	I
1	Year ended 31 March 20-6								
2	Range	Colour and cushions	Description	Total number	Cost	Net Realisable Value	IAS 2 value of item	Total inventory value	
3	Dreamy	Midnight	Single	32	£246.50	£199.00	£199.00	£6,368.00	
4	Dreamy	Midnight	Double	29	£455.50	£399.00	£399.00	£11,571.00	
5	Dreamy	Midnight	King size	10	£575.60	£549.00	£549.00	£5,490.00	
6	Dreamy	Midnight	Queen size	17	£465.50	£429.00	£429.00	£7,293.00	
7	Dreamy	Midnight	Super king size	10	£685.50	£599.00	£599.00	£5,990.00	
8	Cosy	Oatmeal	Single	13	£266.50	£299.00	£266.50	£3,464.50	
9	Cosy	Oatmeal	Double	25	£475.50	£499.00	£475.50	£11,887.50	
10	Cosy	Oatmeal	King size	12	£595.60	£629.00	£595.60	£7,147.20	
11	Cosy	Oatmeal	Queen size	12	£485.50	£539.00	£485.50	£5,826.00	
12	Cosy	Oatmeal	Super king size	25	£695.50	£749.00	£695.50	£17,387.50	
13	Dreamy City	Grey	Single	55	£226.50	£279.00	£226.50	£12,457.50	
14	Dreamy City	Grey	Double	59	£405.50	£469.00	£405.50	£23,924.50	
15	Dreamy City	Grey	King size	36	£545.60	£599.00	£545.60	£19,641.60	
16	Dreamy City	Grey	Queen size	29	£445.50	£499.00	£445.50	£12,919.50	
17	Dreamy City	Grey	Super king size	21	£665.50	£739.00	£665.50	£13,975.50	
18	Sleepy	Midnight	Single	13	£209.00	£199.00	£199.00	£2,587.00	
19	Sleepy	Midnight	Double	20	£405.50	£289.00	£289.00	£5,780.00	
20	Sleepy	Midnight	King size	19	£525.60	£489.00	£489.00	£9,291.00	
21	Sleepy	Midnight	Queen size	15	£425.50	£399.00	£399.00	£5,985.00	
22	Sleepy	Midnight	Super king size	31	£605.50	£589.00	£589.00	£18,259.00	
23	Cosy City	Grey	Single	23	£266.50	£299.00	£266.50	£6,129.50	
24	Cosy City	Grey	Double	6	£475.50	£499.00	£475.50	£2,853.00	
25	Cosy City	Grey	King size	17	£595.60	£629.00	£595.60	£10,125.20	
26	Cosy City	Grey	Queen size	6	£485.50	£539.00	£485.50	£2,913.00	
27	Cosy City	Grey	Super king size	14	£695.50	£749.00	£695.50	£9,737.00	
28	Sleepy City	Grey	Single	2	£209.00	£259.00	£209.00	£418.00	
29	Sleepy City	Grey	Double	5	£405.50	£459.00	£405.50	£2,027.50	
30	Sleepy City	Grey	King size	4	£525.60	£575.00	£525.60	£2,102.40	
31	Sleepy City	Grey	Queen size	9	£425.50	£499.00	£425.50	£3,829.50	
32	Sleepy City	Grey	Super king size	6	£605.50	£669.00	£605.50	£3,633.00	
33	Nest	Midnight	Single	13	£224.00	£199.00	£199.00	£2,587.00	
34	Nest	Midnight	Double	38	£420.50	£389.00	£389.00	£14,782.00	
35	Nest	Midnight	King size	24	£540.60	£529.00	£529.00	£12,696.00	
36	Nest	Midnight	Queen size	6	£440.50	£420.00	£420.00	£2,520.00	
37	Nest	Midnight	Super king size	13	£620.50	£579.00	£579.00	£7,527.00	
38	Cosset	Oatmeal	Single	26	£275.00	£339.00	£275.00	£7,150.00	
39	Cosset	Oatmeal	Double	15	£465.00	£529.00	£465.00	£6,975.00	
40	Cosset	Oatmeal	King size	21	£630.00	£699.00	£630.00	£13,230.00	
41	Cosset	Oatmeal	Queen size	10	£575.00	£659.00	£575.00	£5,750.00	
42	Cosset	Oatmeal	Super king size	9	£695.00	£799.00	£695.00	£6,255.00	
43	Nest City	Grey	Single	16	£219.00	£259.00	£219.00	£3,504.00	
44	Nest City	Grey	Double	30	£415.50	£489.00	£415.50	£12,465.00	
45	Nest City	Grey	King size	12	£535.60	£569.00	£535.60	£6,427.20	
46	Nest City	Grey	Queen size	12	£435.50	£529.00	£435.50	£5,226.00	
47	Nest City	Grey	Super king size	14	£615.50	£699.00	£615.50	£8,617.00	
48									

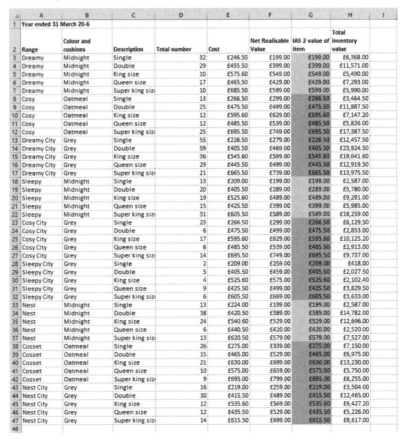

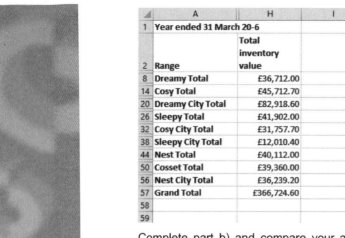

	A	H	I
1	Year ended 31 March 20-6		
2	Range	Total inventory value	
8	Dreamy Total	£36,712.00	
14	Cosy Total	£45,712.70	
20	Dreamy City Total	£82,918.60	
26	Sleepy Total	£41,902.00	
32	Cosy City Total	£31,757.70	
38	Sleepy City Total	£12,010.40	
44	Nest Total	£40,112.00	
50	Cosset Total	£39,360.00	
56	Nest City Total	£36,239.20	
57	Grand Total	£366,724.60	
58			
59			

Complete part b) and compare your answer to the 'Inventory 31 March 20-6' worksheet below.

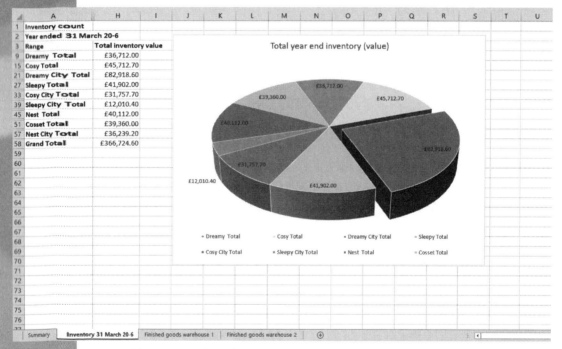

You can review the complete answer on the Osborne books website, by downloading the file 'MATST Ch 2 Spreadsheet Case Study Bumper Beds Ltd answer'. You should easily be able to read the chart and all the data labels. You will have had to **change the colour** for several **data series**.

If you found any elements of the chart difficult, go to the Osborne Books Spreadsheets for Management Accounting Tutorial and review the required skills.

To complete part b) you must use **SUBTOTAL** to **SUM** the inventory for e
range. This is a useful **formula**, which can also be used to average or find
minimum and maximum in a range. You may need to practice it a couple of tir
to be able to apply it correctly – use the Spreadsheets Skills for Managen
Accounting Tutorial to help you.

After applying **SUBTOTAL** for point 1, an extract of the 'Summary' worksheet lo
like this:

	A	B	C	D	E	F	G	Total
1	Year ended 31 March 20-6							
2	Range	Colour and cushions	Description	Total number	Cost	Net Realisable Value	IAS 2 value of item	Total inve value
3	Dreamy	Midnight	Single	32	£246.50	£199.00	£199.00	£6,
4	Dreamy	Midnight	Double	29	£455.50	£399.00	£399.00	£11,
5	Dreamy	Midnight	King size	10	£575.60	£549.00	£549.00	£5,
6	Dreamy	Midnight	Queen size	17	£465.50	£429.00	£429.00	£7,
7	Dreamy	Midnight	Super king size	10	£685.50	£599.00	£599.00	£5,
8	**Dreamy Total**							£36,
9	Cosy	Oatmeal	Single	13	£266.50	£299.00	£266.50	£3,
10	Cosy	Oatmeal	Double	25	£475.50	£499.00	£475.50	£11,
11	Cosy	Oatmeal	King size	12	£595.60	£629.00	£595.60	£7,
12	Cosy	Oatmeal	Queen size	12	£485.50	£539.00	£485.50	£5,
13	Cosy	Oatmeal	Super king size	25	£695.50	£749.00	£695.50	£17,
14	**Cosy Total**							£45,
15	Dreamy City	Grey	Single	55	£226.50	£279.00	£226.50	£12,
16	Dreamy City	Grey	Double	59	£405.50	£469.00	£405.50	£23,
17	Dreamy City	Grey	King size	36	£545.60	£599.00	£545.60	£19,
18	Dreamy City	Grey	Queen size	29	£445.50	£499.00	£445.50	£12,
19	Dreamy City	Grey	Super king size	21	£665.50	£739.00	£665.50	£13,
20	**Dreamy City Total**							£82,
21	Sleepy	Midnight	Single	13	£209.00	£199.00	£199.00	£2,
22	Sleepy	Midnight	Double	20	£405.50	£289.00	£289.00	£5,
23	Sleepy	Midnight	King size	19	£525.60	£489.00	£489.00	£9,
24	Sleepy	Midnight	Queen size	15	£425.50	£399.00	£399.00	£5,
25	Sleepy	Midnight	Super king size	31	£605.50	£589.00	£589.00	£18,
26	**Sleepy Total**							£41,
27	Cosy City	Grey	Single	23	£266.50	£299.00	£266.50	£6,
28	Cosy City	Grey	Double	6	£475.50	£499.00	£475.50	£2,
29	Cosy City	Grey	King size	17	£595.60	£629.00	£595.60	£10,
30	Cosy City	Grey	Queen size	6	£485.50	£539.00	£485.50	£2,
31	Cosy City	Grey	Super king size	14	£695.50	£749.00	£695.50	£9,
32	**Cosy City Total**							£31,
33	Sleepy City	Grey	Single	2	£209.00	£259.00	£209.00	£
34	Sleepy City	Grey	Double	5	£405.50	£459.00	£405.50	£2,
35	Sleepy City	Grey	King size	4	£525.60	£575.00	£525.60	£2,
36	Sleepy City	Grey	Queen size	9	£425.50	£499.00	£425.50	£3,
37	Sleepy City	Grey	Super king size	6	£605.50	£669.00	£605.50	£3,
38	**Sleepy City Total**							£12,(

And once you **hide the detail** of the **SUBTOTAL** formula, after you **hide colun**
B to G, the Summary worksheet looks like this:

Chapter Summary

- ■ Businesses and other organisations hold materials inventory in the form of raw materials and components bought for production, products bought for resale, and service items bought for use within the business.

- ■ Two important inventory costs are the ordering cost and the inventory holding cost.

- ■ Materials purchases can be made using:
  - – the fixed quantity method
  - – Economic Order Quantity (EOQ)

- ■ The quantity of inventory is recorded on an inventory record, which also indicates:
  - – the level at which inventory should be ordered
  - – the quantity of inventory that should be reordered

- ■ Inventory valuation is normally made **at the lower of cost and net realisable value** (IAS 2).

- ■ Inventory valuation methods:
  - – FIFO (first in, first out)
  - – AVCO (weighted average cost)

- ■ For a manufacturer, cost comprises the direct manufacturing costs of materials, labour and expenses, together with the production overheads which bring the product to its present location or condition.

- ■ Cost bookkeeping entries are made to record inventory transactions such as:
  - – purchase of materials on credit from suppliers or on cash terms
  - – issue of materials to production
  - – return of materials from production to inventory

Key Terms

materials	the cost of: – raw materials and components used in production – products bought for resale – service items bought for use within the business
fixed quantity method	the reordering of materials in set amounts
reorder level	(average usage x average lead time) + buffer inventory
maximum inventory level	buffer inventory + maximum reorder quantity

maximum reorder quantity	maximum inventory level – buffer inventory
minimum reorder quantity	average usage x average lead time
Economic Order Quantity (EOQ)	a method of minimising ordering costs and inventory holding costs; calculated by the formula:

$$\sqrt{\frac{2 \text{ x annual usage x ordering cost}}{\text{inventory holding cost}}}$$

inventory record	record held for each inventory item which shows receipts of supplies and sales (or issues to production)
inventory value	number of items held x inventory valuation per item
cost	the amount it cost to buy the inventory (including additional costs to bring the product to its present location or condition)
net realisable value	selling price (less any extra costs, such as selling and distribution)
FIFO	'First in, first out' method of attaching a value to each issue of materials or goods from stores, using the oldest cost prices first
AVCO	'Average cost' method of attaching a value to each issue of materials or goods from stores, using a weighted average of the cost prices of all items in inventory at the date of issue
inventory record	method of recording inventory data in order to ascertain the cost at which materials are issued, and to ascertain a valuation of closing inventory
cost bookkeeping	double-entry system to record costing transactions; uses the principles of double-entry bookkeeping

Activities

2.1 Calculate, for inventory items D and E, the reorder level and the maximum reorder quantity from the following information:

- average daily usage of D = 3 units, of E = 4 units

- buffer inventory of D = 30 units, of E = 40 units

- there is space available in the store for 350 units of each item of inventory

- average lead time is 7 days

2.2 Beautiful Bamboo Ltd is a small business making furniture using bamboo. There are few raw materials required – bamboo, glue and wax – but recently there have been occasions where the workshop has run out of an item, making production inefficient.

The owner, Sali, would like to know when to order bamboo, glue and wax, as well as how much to order, so he does not run out of materials. He has kept a spreadsheet of amounts used each week in the factory for recent orders for each material. He has also collected the following information:

Material	Maximum inventory possible in workshop	Inventory buffer	Average lead time, days
Bamboo	5,000 kg	1,000 kg	6
Glue	150 litres	50 litres	4
Wax	80 litres	40 litres	4

Download the spreadsheet file 'MATST Chapter 2 Activities data' from the Osborne Books website.

Save the spreadsheet file in an appropriate location and rename it to 'MATST Chapter 2 Activities answers', so you can refer back to it.

Using the worksheet '2.2 Usage', complete the following:

1   Using the **DAYS** function, determine the number of days from the first to the last order, and enter this in cell A18. Enter the word 'Days' in B18.

2   **Calculate** the total amount ordered for each material in row 18 and enter 'Total' in F18. **Format the borders** of the total cells containing numbers to show a single line at the top and a double line at the bottom.

3   **Calculate** the average daily usage in row 21, using **ROUND** to the nearest whole number.

4   Enter the average lead time in row 22 and inventory buffer in row 23 for each material and use a formula to **calculate** the reorder level for each material in row 24.

5   **Enter** the maximum inventory possible in the warehouse from the information above for all the materials (cells C20:E20). **Calculate** the maximum order quantity in row 25, including the information above, in a suitable formula.

6   **Calculate** the minimum order quantity in row 26, using a suitable formula.

7   **Highlight in green** the reorder level quantities.

8   **Highlight in orange** the maximum order quantities.

9   **Highlight in yellow** the minimum order quantities.

10 **Format numbers as** 0,000.

11 **Protect cells** C3:E26 on the worksheet using the password 123.

Save the worksheet and check your answers at the back of the book or using the spreadsheet 'MATST Chapter 2 Activities answers', available to download on the Osborne Books website, www.osbornebooks.co.uk.

2.3   The following information is available for material XX5:

   •   annual demand – 72,000 kilograms

   •   annual holding cost per kilogram – £2

   •   fixed ordering cost – £20

   You are to calculate the Economic Order Quantity (EOQ) for material XX5.

2.4   The following is an extract of the inventory movements for January to May 20-1 taken from your computer system:

Inventory record Product X			
20-1	Purchase price	Purchases	Sales
January	£3.00	20 units	
February	£3.60	10 units	
March			8 units
April	£4.00	10 units	
May			16 units

You are to:

Prepare an inventory record for Product X using:

(a)   FIFO

(b)   AVCO

Notes:

   •   a blank inventory record, which may be photocopied, is provided in the Appendix
   •   where appropriate, work to the nearest penny, ie to two decimal places

2.5 XY Limited is formed on 1 January 20-4 and, at the end of its first half-year of trading, the inventory records, taken from the computer system, are as follows:

20-4	TYPE X		TYPE Y	
	Receipts (units)	Issues (units)	Receipts (units)	Issues (units)
January	100 at £4.00		200 at £10.00	
February		80	100 at £9.50	
March	140 at £4.20			240
April	100 at £3.80		100 at £10.50	
May		140	140 at £10.00	
June	80 at £4.50			100

You are to prepare inventory records for products X and Y using **(a)** FIFO, **(b)** AVCO

Notes:

* a blank inventory record, which may be photocopied, is provided in the Appendix
* where appropriate, work to the nearest penny, ie to two decimal places

2.6 Breeden Bakery Limited makes 'homestyle' cakes which are sold to supermarket chains.

The company uses the first in, first out (FIFO) method of issuing inventory.

As an Accounts Assistant at Breeden Bakery you have been given the following tasks.

Task 1

Complete the following inventory record for wholewheat flour for May 20-4 (showing the cost per kilogram to two decimal places):

INVENTORY RECORD

Product: Wholewheat flour

Date	Receipts			Issues			Balance	
	Quantity (kgs)	Cost per kg	Total Cost	Quantity (kgs)	Cost per kg	Total Cost	Quantity (kgs)	Total Cost
20-4 Balance at 1 May		£	£		£	£	10,000	£ 2,500
6 May	20,000	0.30	6,000				30,000	8,500
10 May				20,000				
17 May	10,000	0.35	3,500					
20 May				15,000				

Task 2

All issues of wholewheat flour are for the manufacture of fruit cakes. The following cost accounting codes are used to record materials costs:

Code number	Description
3000	inventory account – wholewheat flour
3300	production account – fruit cakes
5000	trade payables control account

Complete the table below to record the journal entries for the two purchases and two issues of wholewheat flour in the cost accounting records.

20-4	Code number	Debit £	Credit £
6 May			
6 May			
10 May			
10 May			
17 May			
17 May			
20 May			
20 May			

2.7   The following data is available for plastic grade P5:

- Annual demand – 57,600 kilograms
- Annual holding cost per kilogram – £2
- Fixed ordering cost – £25

(a)   You are to calculate the Economic Order Quantity (EOQ) for P5.

Economic Order Quantity (EOQ) = [   ] kg

The inventory record shown below for plastic grade P5 for the month of June has only been fully completed for the first three weeks of the month.

(b)   Complete the entries in the inventory record for the two receipts on 23 and 26 June that were ordered using the EOQ method.

(c)   Complete ALL entries in the inventory record for the two issues in the month and for the closing balance at the end of June using the AVCO method of issuing inventory.

Show the costs per kilogram (kg) in £ to three decimal places, and the total costs in whole £.

INVENTORY RECORD

Product: **Plastic grade P5**

Date	Receipts			Issues			Balance	
	Quantity (kg)	Cost per kg	Total Cost	Quantity (kg)	Cost per kg	Total Cost	Quantity (kg)	Total Cost
		£	£		£	£		£
Balance as at 22 June							4,400	10,560
23 June		2.634						
25 June				1,000				
26 June		2.745						
29 June				1,500				

2.8 Crossways Limited uses the following accounts to record inventory transactions in its cost bookkeeping system:

– inventory account

– trade payables control account

– bank account

– production account

For each of the four transactions in the following table show the account which will be debited and the account which will be credited.

Transaction		Account debited	Account credited
1	Receipt of materials into inventory, paying on credit		
2	Issue of materials from inventory to production		
3	Receipt of materials into inventory, paying immediately by bank transfer		
4	Return of materials from production to inventory		

2.9 Which **one** of these is an example of unethical behaviour by an accounting technician?

(a)	Valuing inventory in an objective way	
(b)	Valuing inventory in accordance with IAS 2, *Inventories*	
(c)	Valuing inventory without being influenced by the business owner	
(d)	Valuing inventory in order to maximise profit	

2.10 Bumper Beds Ltd sells various styles and sizes of bed. The year end is 31 March 20-6.

Matt Bush, the accountant, has asked you to assist in some analysis of the year end inventory, using some of the information you previously produced in the Spreadsheet Skills for Management Accounting Case Study earlier in the chapter. The inventory summary has been copied onto the Activities data worksheet.

Download the spreadsheet file 'MATST Chapter 2 Activities data' if you have not already done so.

Save the spreadsheet file in an appropriate location and rename it 'MATST Chapter 2 Activities answers'.

Using the worksheet '2.10 Inventory Analysis' complete the following:

1   **Copy and paste values and formats** from the '2.10 Inventory Analysis' worksheet onto a new worksheet named 'NRV Cost Analysis'. Ensure all information can be seen clearly.

2   On 'NRV Cost Analysis' **delete columns** E and F.

3   On 'NRV Cost Analysis' **sort** the information on valuation method, to filter the items between cost and NRV.

4   On 'NRV Cost Analysis', use **SUBTOTAL** to find the minimum inventory value of items held at cost and items held at net realisable value.

5   On 'NRV Cost Analysis', use **SUBTOTAL** to find the maximum inventory value of items held at cost and items held at net realisable value.

Matt Bush is considering removing the queen size bed from the range. He would like you to produce a **bar chart** showing the amount of inventory held by bed size, excluding the Midnight style beds.

Using the information on the '2.10 Inventory Analysis' worksheet:

6   Create a **pivot table and chart** in a new worksheet, named 'Inventory by size chart' showing the number of beds held by size, excluding the Midnight colour and cushions beds.

7   Amend the column chart to be a **2D bar chart**.

8   Change the **colour (cell) fill** for the queen size bed to orange.

9   **Amend the title** to 'Inventory held by size'.

10   **Amend the scale on the axis** for the number of beds to show intervals of 25.

11   **Add data labels** to the chart.

12   **Move the legend** to the right of the chart.

13   **Resize the chart** so it is clear to read.

Save the worksheet and check your answers at the back of the book or using the spreadsheet 'MATST Chapter 2 Activities answers', available to download on the Osborne website, www.osbornebooks.co.uk.

3 Labour costs

this chapter covers...

In Chapter 1 we saw how costs can be classified in a variety of different ways including by element as materials, labour and expenses. In this chapter we focus on labour costs and explain:

■ factors that affect labour costs

■ methods by which the direct labour employees of a business can be paid

■ how payroll information is gathered

■ overtime, idle time and equivalent units

■ use of a time sheet to calculate gross wages

■ bookkeeping entries for labour costs

ACCOUNTING FOR LABOUR COSTS

Labour cost is one of the elements of costs – all businesses incur labour costs, which are the costs of wages and salaries of all their employees.

factors that affect labour costs

There are many factors that need to be considered by a business when deciding how much to pay employees. The starting point will always be the amount that is paid by other businesses in the area for similar grades of employees but, at the same time, the wider economic implications of supply and demand will affect wage rates.

The factors to consider include:

- wage rates paid by other local businesses

- comparisons with national average wage rates

- the national minimum and living wage rates set by government

- any government incentives to take on additional employees, such as young people or the long-term unemployed

- local employment conditions – high unemployment in the area will drive down wage rates; conversely low unemployment, and especially a shortage of skilled labour, will increase wage rates

- housing and transport costs in the locality

- the impact of interest rate changes on business confidence

- for a new business, it might be prudent to choose to locate in an area of high unemployment – in addition to lower wage rates, there may be government incentives in the form of reduced rents and business rates, training and other grants

Before taking on labour, a business must decide how to calculate gross pay for its employees. Labour payment methods are looked at in detail on the next page. Wages are usually calculated according to time worked or work done, or a combination of both. Most businesses use a computer accounting program for wages calculations.

LABOUR PAYMENT METHODS

Direct labour cost is the wages paid to those who work on a production line, are involved in assembly, or are involved in the output of a service business.

The three main payment methods for direct labour are:

time rate   Time rate, or basic pay, is where the employee is paid on the basis of time spent at work. Overtime is often paid for hours worked beyond a standard number of hours, or for work carried out on days which are not part of the working week, eg Saturdays or Sundays. Overtime is often paid at rates such as 'time-and-a-quarter', 'time-and-a-half', or 'double-time'. 'Time-and-a-half', for example, means that 1.5 times the basic hourly rate is paid.

      Time rate is often referred to as a 'day rate'.

piecework rate   The employee is paid an agreed sum for each task carried out or for each unit of output completed. Units of output can be based on an agreed output per hour, which is referred to as 'standard hour produced'.

      In many cases, employees have a guaranteed minimum wage.

bonus system   The employee is paid a time rate and then receives a bonus if output is better than expected when comparing the time allowed with the time taken. The bonus is calculated as an agreed percentage of the time saved multiplied by the time rate.

      Bonus systems base employees' earnings on a combination of time taken and work done.

Most other employees, eg factory supervisors, sales staff, office staff, are usually paid on a weekly or monthly basis. Such wages and salaries – classed as indirect labour costs – may be increased by bonus payments; for example, a production bonus for factory supervisors, commissions for sales staff, a profit-sharing scheme for all employees.

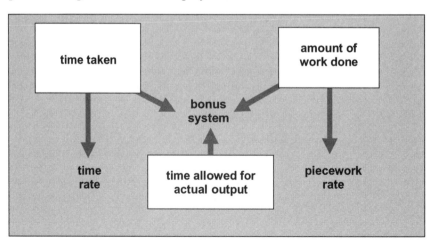

There are many variations on the three methods outlined above and, indeed, changing patterns of employment create different payment methods from those that would have been the norm just a few years ago. For example, the contracting out of many business support services – such as cleaning, security, computers – means that the costing of such services by the provider may incorporate time rates and bonus systems whereas previously the employees would have been paid on a weekly or monthly basis.

In order to calculate gross wages, information about hours worked and/or work done must be recorded. The methods – which are usually computerised and linked to payroll software – include:

- **time sheets**, where employees record the hours they have worked
- **clock cards**, where employees 'clock in' at the start of work, and 'clock out' at the end
- **piecework tickets**, completed by employees who work on a batch of output
- **job cards**, where each employee records the amount of time spent on each job
- **route cards** – which are used to follow a product through the production process – on which employees record the amount of time they spend working on the product
- **computer cards** – 'swipe' cards which link direct into the computerised payroll are used by employees to record their attendance

qualities of a good labour payment method

- reward should be related to effort and fair to all staff
- the method should be easy to manage and administer, and cheap and efficient to run
- it should be easy for employees to understand how pay is calculated
- payment should be made at regular intervals and soon after the event, eg employees on piecework should be paid in the week after the production has been achieved
- the principles of the scheme should remain constant, but there should be flexibility to deal with changes in production techniques

summary

The three main labour payment methods, together with some alternative systems, are summarised in the table on the next page.

As an Accounts Assistant, always remember that payroll information is confidential and any queries should be referred to the appropriate person –for example, the Payroll Manager, or the Accounts Supervisor.

Labour payment methods – a summary			
	Time rate	**Piecework rate**	**Bonus system**
Situation	This method is used where it is difficult to measure the quantity of output and where quality is more important than volume of output.	This method is used where the work is repetitive and quantity of output is more important than quality.	This method is used to motivate employees, where the work is not so repetitive as in piecework but is measurable.
Gross Pay Calculation	*Hours worked x rate per hour = basic pay.* Easy to calculate and understand. Overtime often paid for extra hours worked	*Number of items produced x rate per item.* Easy to calculate and understand.	*Basic pay + often proportion of the time saved.* Time saved is the difference between time allowed and time taken to do a task. More complex to calculate and understand.
Motivation	Pay is not linked to output and therefore there is no incentive to work hard. Slower workers may get paid overtime at higher rates.	Pay is related directly to output. There is a direct incentive to work as the amount of output determines the amount paid.	There is some incentive to work in order to earn a bonus as well as basic pay.
Quality of Output	There is no pressure on time and so quality should be maintained.	The fact that pay is related to output means it is important that quality standards of output are met.	The link between pay and output means that the quality of output needs to be checked.
Control	Important that the volume and quality of output is maintained.	Important that the volume and quality of output is maintained.	Important that the volume and quality of output is maintained.
Administration	No need to set time allowances for output.	A need to set time allowances for work done and to keep these up to date.	A need to set time allowances for work done and to keep these up to date.
Payment to Employees	A regular amount is earned by the employee plus any overtime payments.	The amount earned by the employee varies with the output the employee produces.	There is regular income but pay can be increased by additional effort.
Alternative Systems	**High day rate –** employees are paid a higher than average rate per hour but agree to produce a given amount of output at a given quality.	**Attendance allowance** – to ensure employees turn up. **Guaranteed day rate** – to give employees a minimum payment. **Differential piecework** – to pay efficient workers more for output beyond a given level of output, ie an extra amount per unit.	**Group bonus schemes** – used where employees work as a group. This can include all workers, eg cleaners. This may create problems as the most efficient workers may be held back by the less efficient workers.

WESTMID MANUFACTURING: LABOUR PAYMENT

situation

Westmid Manufacturing Company has three factories in the West Midlands making parts for the car industry. Each factory was bought from the previous owners and, as a result, each has a different method for paying its direct labour workforce. The details of the labour payment methods in each factory, together with data on two employees from each factory, are as follows:

WALSALL FACTORY

In this factory, which is involved in heavy engineering, employees are paid on the basis of a time rate. Employees are required to 'clock in' and 'clock out' each day.

Jayne Brown is a machine operator and her clock card for last week shows that she worked 39 hours; her basic pay is £12 per hour.

Stefan Wozniak is a skilled lathe operator and his clock card shows that he worked 42 hours; his basic pay is £14 per hour, with overtime for hours worked beyond 37 hours at 'time-and-a-half'.

DUDLEY FACTORY

This factory operates a number of light engineering production lines making car components such as windscreen wiper blades, headlamp surrounds, interior mirrors etc. The production line employees are all paid on a piecework basis; however, each employee receives a guaranteed time rate which is paid if the piecework earnings are less than the time rate. This may happen if, for example, there are machine breakdowns and the production line has to be halted.

Tracey Johnson works on the line making headlamp surrounds. For each one that passes through her part of the process, she is paid 50p; her guaranteed time rate is 35 hours each week at £11 per hour. Last week's production records show that she processed 910 units.

Pete Bronyah is on the line which makes interior mirrors. For his part of the process he receives £1.30 for each one, with a guaranteed time rate of 35 hours at £11 per hour. Last week there was a machine failure and he was only able to process 250 units.

WOLVERHAMPTON FACTORY

In this factory a number of engineering production lines are operated. The direct labour force is paid on a time rate basis, but a bonus is paid if work can be completed faster than the time allowed. The bonus is for the savings achieved to be shared equally between employer and employee. Wages are, therefore, paid on the following basis: time rate + 50% of time saved x time rate. If no bonus is due, then the time rate applies.

Martin Lee worked 38 hours last week; his time rate is £12 per hour. He is allowed a time of 30 minutes to carry out his work on each unit of production; last week he completed 71 units.

Sara King has a time rate of £11 per hour; last week she worked 40 hours. She is allowed a time of 15 minutes to carry out her work on each unit of production; last week she completed 184 units.

What were the gross earnings of each employee?

solution

WALSALL FACTORY

Jayne Brown	39 hours x £12.00 per hour	=	£468.00
Stefan Wozniak	37 hours x £14.00 per hour = £518		
	5 hours x £21.00 per hour = £105	=	£623.00

DUDLEY FACTORY

Tracey Johnson	Piecework rate, 910 units x 50p per unit	=	£455.00
	Guaranteed time rate, 35 hours x £11.00 per hour	=	£385.00
	Therefore piecework rate of £455.00 is paid.		
Pete Bronyah	Piecework rate, 250 units x £1.30 per unit	=	£325.00
	Guaranteed time rate, 35 hours x £11.00 per hour	=	£385.00
	Therefore guaranteed time rate of £385.00 is paid.		

WOLVERHAMPTON FACTORY

Martin Lee	Time rate, 38 hours x £12.00 per hour	=	£456.00
	Bonus, time allowed 71 units x 30 minutes each = 35 hours 30 minutes		
	Therefore no time saved, so no bonus payable.		
	Time rate of £456 paid.		
Sara King	Time rate, 40 hours x £11.00 per hour	=	£440.00
	Bonus, time allowed 184 x 15 minutes each	=	46 hours
	Therefore time saved is 6 hours		
	Bonus is 50% of (6 hours x £11.00)	=	£33.00
	Therefore wages are £440.00 + £33.00	=	£473.00

The Case Study illustrates some of the direct labour payment methods in use, however it should be appreciated that there are many variations on these.

OVERTIME, IDLE TIME AND EQUIVALENT UNITS

In Chapter 1 we divided labour costs between:

■ **direct costs**, labour costs of production-line employees

■ **indirect costs**, labour costs of other employees, such as supervisors, office staff, etc

Whilst this distinction appears clear enough, there are times when a proportion of the labour costs of production-line employees is classed as an indirect cost (rather than a direct cost) and is included amongst the overheads of the business. This is done if part of the cost of wages of the direct workers cannot be linked to specific work.

overtime payments and overtime premium

When production-line employees work overtime they are usually paid at a rate above the time rate. For example, overtime might be paid at 'time-and-a-half'; thus an employee with a time rate of £12 an hour will receive **overtime payments** of £18 an hour. The additional £6 per hour is called **overtime premium**. For normal cost accounting purposes, any overtime worked is charged at £12 an hour to direct labour, and £6 an hour to indirect labour.

Example:

A group of employees on a production line has a working week consisting of 35 hours each. Anything over that time is paid at time-and-a-half. One employee has worked 40 hours during the week at a normal rate of £12.

■ direct wages cost is 40 hours at £12 = £480

■ overtime premium is 5 hours at £6 (half of £12) = £30, which is charged to indirect labour

■ total wages cost £510 (35 hours at £12, plus 5 hours at £18)

The overtime premium is spread across all output and is not charged solely to the output being worked on during the overtime period. As another issue, management will wish to know why there was the need to work overtime, and will seek to control such an increase in labour costs.

However, where a customer requests overtime to be worked to get a rush job completed, then the full overtime rate (£18 an hour in the above example) is charged as direct labour, and passed on as a cost to the customer.

Other additional payments made to employees – such as a bonus – will be treated in a similar way to overtime premium and will normally be treated as an indirect labour cost.

idle time

Idle time occurs when production is stopped through no fault of the production-line employees – for example, a machine breakdown, or a shortage of materials. Employees paid under a piecework or a bonus system will receive time rate for the period of the stoppage. Such wages costs are normally charged to overheads as indirect labour.

Similarly, time spent by direct workers on non-productive work – eg attendance on a training course – would also usually be treated as an overhead.

equivalent units

When production employees are paid on the basis of output, a calculation of equivalent units may need to be made. This happens when part of the production at the end of the accounting period is work-in-progress for the labour content.

Example:

10,000 units have been completed during the month and, at the month-end, 2,000 units are work-in-progress and are 50 per cent complete for the labour content. The equivalent units completed for the month will be:

10,000 units + (2,000 units x 50%) = 11,000 equivalent units

USING A TIME SHEET

In order to calculate gross wages, as noted earlier (page 85), a business or organisation must obtain information about hours worked and/or work done.

A time sheet – often kept electronically – is used for each employee to record:

- hours worked each day, split between production and indirect work
- amount of basic pay each day (using the hourly rate paid to the employee)
- amount of overtime premium each day (using the hourly rate)
- total pay each day
- total hours worked for the week
- total basic pay, overtime premium and pay for the week

A time sheet, which includes overtime premium is shown in the Case Study which follows:

CALCULATING THE PAY

situation

You are an Accounts Assistant at Onslow Limited and have been asked to help with calculating labour costs.

The cost accountant has given you the electronic time sheet for one of Onslow Limited's employees, P Cusack, who is paid as follows:

- For a basic seven-hour shift every day from Monday to Friday – basic pay at £12.00 per hour for both production and indirect work

- For any overtime in excess of the basic seven hours on any day from Monday to Friday – the extra hours are paid at time-and-a-half (basic pay plus an overtime premium equal to half of basic pay)

- For any hours worked on a Saturday or Sunday – double-time (basic pay plus an overtime premium equal to basic pay)

You are to complete the time sheet columns headed basic pay, overtime premium and total pay (enter a zero figure, '0', in the columns where nothing is to be paid).

Note: overtime premium is just the premium paid for the extra hours worked.

The employee's weekly time sheet for the week ending 14 June 20-2 is shown below.

Employee:	P Cusack			Production Centre: Metal cutting			
Employee number:	260			Basic pay per hour: £12.00			
	Hours spent on production	Hours worked on indirect work	Notes	Basic pay £	Overtime premium £	Total pay £
Monday	7	0				
Tuesday	5	2	2 hours first aid course			
Wednesday	7	0				
Thursday	6	1	1 hour cleaning			
Friday	8	0				
Saturday	3	0				
Sunday	0	0				
Total	36	3				

solution

P Cusack's time sheet is completed as follows:

Employee: P Cusack			Production Centre: Metal cutting			
Employee number: 260			Basic pay per hour: £12.00			
	Hours spent on production	Hours worked on indirect work	Notes	Basic pay £	Overtime premium £	Total pay £
Monday	7	0		84	0	84
Tuesday	5	2	2 hours first aid course	84	0	84
Wednesday	7	0		84	0	84
Thursday	6	1	1 hour cleaning	84	0	84
Friday	8	0		96	6	102
Saturday	3	0		36	36	72
Sunday	0	0		0	0	0
Total	36	3		468	42	510

BOOKKEEPING FOR LABOUR COSTS

In this section we look at the cost bookkeeping entries to record labour costs – the transfer of labour costs to production and to overheads. These entries form part of the bookkeeping system for costing.

A **wages control account** – which can also include salaries – links to the payroll accounting system. It is used to charge labour costs to the various cost, profit, or investment centres of a business or organisation. In this way:

■ direct labour costs are charged to production

■ indirect labour (eg factory supervisor) costs are charged to production overheads

■ administration labour (eg office staff) costs are charged to non-production overheads

Note:

– production overheads are also referred to as operating overheads

– non-production overheads are also referred to as non-operating overheads

With labour costs the general ledger entries are:

■ **transfer of direct labour costs to production**

– debit production

– credit wages control

■ **transfer of indirect labour costs to production overheads**

– debit production overheads

– credit wages control

■ **transfer of administration labour costs to non-production overheads**

– debit non-production overheads, eg administration

– credit wages control

The cost bookkeeping entries for labour costs are shown diagrammatically below:

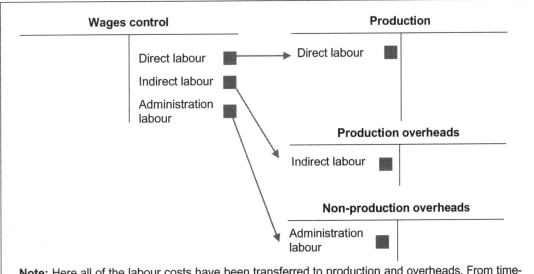

Note: Here all of the labour costs have been transferred to production and overheads. From time-to-time, however, some part of labour costs may relate to capital expenditure – for example, own workforce used to build an extension to the premises; here the bookkeeping entries for the relevant labour costs are:

– debit premises account (or relevant capital expenditure account)

– credit wages control account

BLUE JEANS LIMITED:
BOOKKEEPING FOR LABOUR COSTS

situation

Blue Jeans Limited manufactures and sells denim jeans and jackets. The payroll for the week ended 21 May 20-4 has been completed with the following amounts to pay:

• net wages to be paid to employees	£5,000
• Income Tax and National Insurance Contributions (NIC) to HMRC	£1,000
• pension contributions to be paid to the pension fund	£500
Total	£6,500

The payroll for the week has been analysed as:

• direct labour costs	£3,500
• indirect labour costs	£2,000
• administration labour costs	£1,000
Total	£6,500

All of the direct labour costs are for the manufacture of blue jeans. The following cost accounting codes are in use to record labour costs:

Code number	Description
2200	production – blue jeans
2400	production overheads
2600	non-production overheads – administration
4200	wages control

As an Accounts Assistant at Blue Jeans Limited, you are asked to prepare the wages control account and to fill in the table below to record the journal entries which show how the total cost of the payroll is split between the various cost centres of the business.

20-4	Code number	Debit £	Credit £
21 May	2200		
21 May	4200		
21 May	2400		
21 May	4200		
21 May	2600		
21 May	4200		

solution

Wages control account is prepared as follows:

Dr		Wages Control Account (4200)		Cr
	£			£
Cash/bank (net wages)	5,000	Production (direct labour)		3,500
HM Revenue & Customs (income tax and NIC)	1,000	Production overheads (indirect labour)		2,000
Pension contributions	500	Non-production overheads (administration)		1,000
	6,500			6,500

The cost bookkeeping entries are:

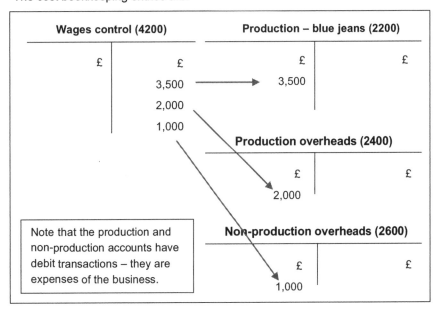

Note that the production and non-production accounts have debit transactions – they are expenses of the business.

The cost bookkeeping transactions are recorded as journal entries in the following way:

20-4	Code number	Debit £	Credit £
21 May	2200	3,500	
21 May	4200		3,500
21 May	2400	2,000	
21 May	4200		2,000
21 May	2600	1,000	
21 May	4200		1,000

In this way, the total cost of the payroll is split between the various cost centres of the business.

SPREADSHEET SKILLS FOR MANAGEMENT ACCOUNTING

calculating labour costs

Labour costs are often significant in a business. It is important to record and monitor these costs accurately and, as it is easy for the Payroll Clerk to make a mistake adding up the hours worked for an employee or to calculate a bonus incorrectly, spreadsheets are often used to ensure arithmetic accuracy of payroll information. Setting up timesheet templates and having summaries that are used each week or month can make producing the payroll more efficient for smaller businesses.

payroll systems and spreadsheets

Payroll software can be used to ensure compliance with tax rules and real-time information reporting for HMRC, so spreadsheets may be used to collect payroll data initially and provide a comparison to the reports produced by the payroll system.

Simple payroll software may not be capable of reporting information by department to allow a business to post direct and indirect costs accurately to the general ledger. The payroll information may need to be downloaded from the system into a spreadsheet, then manipulated to produce a journal for posting to the general ledger. Even if an integrated payroll software produces detailed reports, posting automatically into the general ledger, information may be downloaded from it into spreadsheets and used to monitor labour costs, providing information to managers, perhaps in graphical form.

So let's look at how a business uses a spreadsheet to collect hours worked by staff. This information is used to calculate the basic pay for the employees and the gross pay amount. A simple graph indicates the labour cost for each employee.

SPREADSHEET SKILLS TO PROVIDE MANAGEMENT ACCOUNTING INFORMATION

situation

Karen's Kitchen, a small catering business, uses a spreadsheet to record the hours worked by staff for June 20-9. Karen Parsons, the owner, has asked you to do some analysis on the data for her.

Download the spreadsheet file 'MATST Ch 3 Spreadsheet Case Study Karen's Kitchen data' from the Osborne Books website.

Save the spreadsheet file in an appropriate location and rename it 'MATST Ch 3 Spreadsheet Case Study Karen's Kitchen answer'.

Open the renamed file.

You are required to:

1 In the worksheet called 'June hours' use a **lookup** function on the 'Person name' data to fill in column E with the wage rate for the person, using information from the 'Wage rate' worksheet.

2 Retitle column E 'Wage rate'.

3 Check for and **remove duplicates** in the wages. Enter the number found in cell H1.

4 Use column F to **calculate** the Wage rate multiplied by Hours to give the 'Gross wages'.

5 **Format** the 'Wage rate' and 'Gross wages' to **currency £** to two decimal places.

6 **Rename worksheet** Sheet3 'Gross Pay'.

7 Use **SUMIF**, and the information from the 'June hours' worksheet, to **calculate** the Gross Pay for June for each employee. Insert 'Total' in A11 and **calculate** the total gross pay in B11.

8 Insert a **2D pie chart** showing the Gross Pay by person. Resize it so the key is clearly visible.

9 Insert a **title** above the graph 'Gross Pay per Employee for June'.

10 Use **data labels** on the outside edge to show the gross pay for each employee.

solution

The top part of the worksheet 'June hours', used to record the hours, currently looks like this:

	A	B	C	D	E	F	G	H
1	Date	Job	Person name	Hours	Wages	Gross wages		
2	1/6/20X9	Woodward party	Anish Bhatt	6				
3	1/6/20X9	Woodward party	Ben Williams	6				
4	1/6/20X9	Woodward party	Cam Long	3				
5	1/6/20X9	Woodward party	Karen Parsons	8				
6	1/6/20X9	Woodward party	Mariyah Sadiq	4				
7	1/6/20X9	Woodward party	Mo Gee	6				
8	1/6/20X9	Woodward party	Phil Morris	8				
9	1/6/20X9	Woodward party	Tonya Wysocki	4				
10	14/6/20X9	Patel Party	Anish Bhatt	6				
11	14/6/20X9	Patel Party	Ben Williams	4				
12	14/6/20X9	Patel Party	Cam Long	4				
13	14/6/20X9	Patel Party	Karen Parsons	9				
14	14/6/20X9	Patel Party	Mariyah Sadiq	5				
15	14/6/20X9	Patel Party	Mo Gee	4				
16	14/6/20X9	Patel Party	Phil Morris	8				
17	14/6/20X9	Patel Party	Tonya Wysocki	6				
18	15/6/20X9	Salenko wedding	Anish Bhatt	4				
19	15/6/20X9	Salenko wedding	Anish Bhatt	4				
20	15/6/20X9	Salenko wedding	Ben Williams	5				
21	15/6/20X9	Salenko wedding	Cam Long	5				

June hours | Wage rate | Sheet3 | ⊕

Lookup functions can be either **VLOOKUP** or **HLOOKUP.** The Wage rate worksheet shows the pay rate for each person, in a vertical list:

	A	B	C	D
1		Rate per hour		
2	Karen Parsons	£17.00		
3	Phil Morris	£15.50		
4	Cam Long	£14.50		
5	Mariyah Sadiq	£14.50		
6	Mo Gee	£14.50		
7	Ben Williams	£14.50		
8	Anish Bhatt	£14.50		
9	Tonya Wysocki	£14.50		
10	Hannah Wilson	£14.50		
11				
12				

June hours | **Wage rate** | Sheet3

The formula we need is **VLOOKUP**, as the Rate per hour is in a vertical column. You may need to refer to the Osborne Books Spreadsheets for Management Accounting Tutorial to help you, if you are unfamiliar with this formula.

The formula needs to be copied down to the last entry in E48. If you are learning new functions, it is a good idea to check the result, to make sure it is what you expect. So, compare Phil Morris's wage rate in E48 to that in the 'Wage rate' worksheet and you should find the wage rate is 15.5. If this is not the case, go back and review your formula.

Once you have completed points 1 and 2, compare your answer to the spreadsheet extract below.

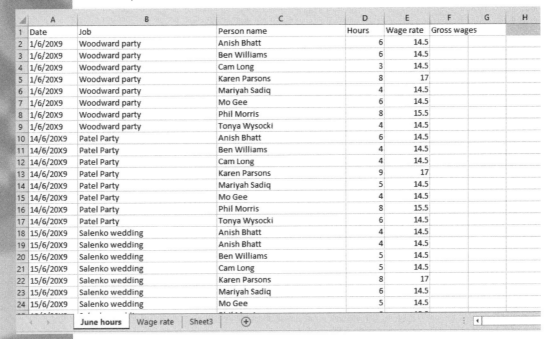

	A	B	C	D	E	F	G	H
1	Date	Job	Person name	Hours	Wage rate	Gross wages		
2	1/6/20X9	Woodward party	Anish Bhatt	6	14.5			
3	1/6/20X9	Woodward party	Ben Williams	6	14.5			
4	1/6/20X9	Woodward party	Cam Long	3	14.5			
5	1/6/20X9	Woodward party	Karen Parsons	8	17			
6	1/6/20X9	Woodward party	Mariyah Sadiq	4	14.5			
7	1/6/20X9	Woodward party	Mo Gee	6	14.5			
8	1/6/20X9	Woodward party	Phil Morris	8	15.5			
9	1/6/20X9	Woodward party	Tonya Wysocki	4	14.5			
10	14/6/20X9	Patel Party	Anish Bhatt	6	14.5			
11	14/6/20X9	Patel Party	Ben Williams	4	14.5			
12	14/6/20X9	Patel Party	Cam Long	4	14.5			
13	14/6/20X9	Patel Party	Karen Parsons	9	17			
14	14/6/20X9	Patel Party	Mariyah Sadiq	5	14.5			
15	14/6/20X9	Patel Party	Mo Gee	4	14.5			
16	14/6/20X9	Patel Party	Phil Morris	8	15.5			
17	14/6/20X9	Patel Party	Tonya Wysocki	6	14.5			
18	15/6/20X9	Salenko wedding	Anish Bhatt	4	14.5			
19	15/6/20X9	Salenko wedding	Anish Bhatt	4	14.5			
20	15/6/20X9	Salenko wedding	Ben Williams	5	14.5			
21	15/6/20X9	Salenko wedding	Cam Long	5	14.5			
22	15/6/20X9	Salenko wedding	Karen Parsons	8	17			
23	15/6/20X9	Salenko wedding	Mariyah Sadiq	6	14.5			
24	15/6/20X9	Salenko wedding	Mo Gee	5	14.5			

June hours | Wage rate | Sheet3 | ⊕

The **VLOOKUP** formula used in E2, for example, is:

=VLOOKUP(C2,'Wage rate'!A$2:B$10,2,FALSE)

Did you use **absolute referencing** when you copied the formula down initially? If not, some cells will have contained '#N/A'. This is a very common mistake and one that will disappear with practice.

Now complete points 3 to 5 and compare your answer to the spreadsheet extract on the next page.

	A	B	C	D	E	F	G	H
1	Date	Job	Person name	Hours	Wage rate	Gross wages		2
2	1/6/20X9	Woodward party	Anish Bhatt	6	£14.50	£87.00		
3	1/6/20X9	Woodward party	Ben Williams	6	£14.50	£87.00		
4	1/6/20X9	Woodward party	Cam Long	3	£14.50	£43.50		
5	1/6/20X9	Woodward party	Karen Parsons	8	£17.00	£136.00		
6	1/6/20X9	Woodward party	Mariyah Sadiq	4	£14.50	£58.00		
7	1/6/20X9	Woodward party	Mo Gee	6	£14.50	£87.00		
8	1/6/20X9	Woodward party	Phil Morris	8	£15.50	£124.00		
9	1/6/20X9	Woodward party	Tonya Wysocki	4	£14.50	£58.00		
10	14/6/20X9	Patel Party	Anish Bhatt	6	£14.50	£87.00		
11	14/6/20X9	Patel Party	Ben Williams	4	£14.50	£58.00		
12	14/6/20X9	Patel Party	Cam Long	4	£14.50	£58.00		
13	14/6/20X9	Patel Party	Karen Parsons	9	£17.00	£153.00		
14	14/6/20X9	Patel Party	Mariyah Sadiq	5	£14.50	£72.50		
15	14/6/20X9	Patel Party	Mo Gee	4	£14.50	£58.00		
16	14/6/20X9	Patel Party	Phil Morris	8	£15.50	£124.00		
17	14/6/20X9	Patel Party	Tonya Wysocki	6	£14.50	£87.00		
18	15/6/20X9	Salenko wedding	Anish Bhatt	4	£14.50	£58.00		
19	15/6/20X9	Salenko wedding	Ben Williams	5	£14.50	£72.50		
20	15/6/20X9	Salenko wedding	Cam Long	5	£14.50	£72.50		
21	15/6/20X9	Salenko wedding	Karen Parsons	8	£17.00	£136.00		
22	15/6/20X9	Salenko wedding	Mariyah Sadiq	6	£14.50	£87.00		
23	15/6/20X9	Salenko wedding	Mo Gee	5	£14.50	£72.50		
24	15/6/20X9	Salenko wedding	Phil Morris	8	£15.50	£124.00		

June hours | Wage rate | Sheet3 | ⊕

Karen Parsons wants to know the gross pay per employee and **SUMIF** is a good formula to use to find this. Again, it is important to use **absolute references** in the formula, so when you copy it down from top to bottom, the formula continues to look at the correct information on the June hours worksheet.

Once you have completed points 6 and 7, the spreadsheet should look like this:

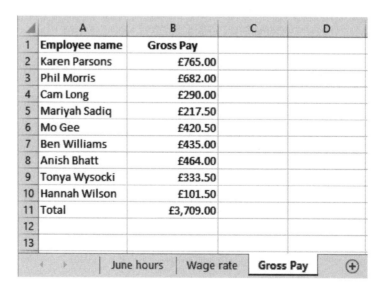

	A	B	C	D
1	**Employee name**	**Gross Pay**		
2	Karen Parsons	£765.00		
3	Phil Morris	£682.00		
4	Cam Long	£290.00		
5	Mariyah Sadiq	£217.50		
6	Mo Gee	£420.50		
7	Ben Williams	£435.00		
8	Anish Bhatt	£464.00		
9	Tonya Wysocki	£333.50		
10	Hannah Wilson	£101.50		
11	Total	£3,709.00		
12				
13				

June hours | Wage rate | **Gross Pay** | ⊕

The **SUMIF** formula adds up only those rows in the 'June hours' worksheet that relate to a particular person.

For example, to find the gross pay for Mo Gee, the formula in B6 is:

=SUMIF('June hours'!C$2:C$46,'Gross Pay'!A6,'June hours'!F$2:F$46).

You can check part of the answer, if you are unsure, using a calculator. Add up the wages for Mo Gee for each job in 'June hours' and it should agree to the answer in B6, £420.50.

If you wish, you could confirm the total gross pay is correct here: use **SUM** to add up the Gross wages column in the 'June hours' worksheet and confirm it agrees to the total gross pay in B11 on the 'Gross Pay' worksheet, £3,709.

The last part of the question is to produce a graph showing the gross pay per employee for June. If you have not produced graphs before, refer to the Osborne Books Spreadsheets for Management Accounting Tutorial before attempting this.

Now complete points 8 to 10 and compare your answer to the spreadsheet below.

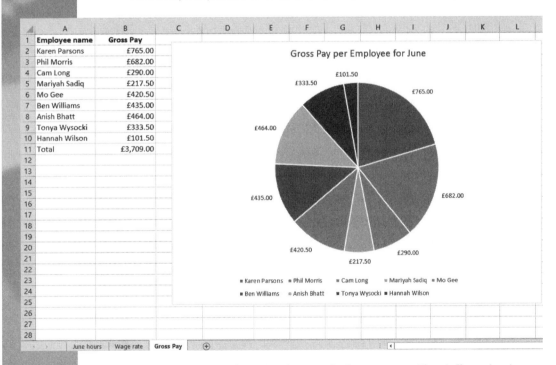

By presenting the information in a graph, the wages cost by staff member is easy for Karen to understand.

Chapter Summary

- Labour costs – the costs of wages and salaries – are incurred in every kind of business.

- Levels of wage rates paid to employees are influenced by a number of factors including the rates paid by similar local businesses, national living wage rate and national averages.

- The main labour payment methods are based either on time or amounts of work done or on a combination of both.

- Certain wages costs of direct workers may be classed as indirect labour costs: these include overtime premium and payment for idle or non-productive time.

- Cost bookkeeping entries are made to charge labour costs to the various cost centres of a business or organisation.

Key Terms

time rate	labour payment method based on the time worked by an employee, giving the formula: hours worked x rate per hour
piecework rate	labour payment method based on the work done by an employee, giving the formula: number of items produced x rate per unit
bonus system	labour payment method in which an employee is paid a time rate and then receives a bonus if output is better than expected when comparing the time allowed with the time taken – the bonus is often calculated as an agreed percentage of the time saved multiplied by the time rate
time sheet	method by which employees record the hours they have worked
overtime payment	an overtime pay rate paid at more than time rate, for example, 'time-and-a-half'
overtime premium	the additional pay above normal rates which is paid to employees working overtime, for example, the premium part of 'time-and-a-half' is the extra 'half' of the hourly rate; this is often charged as indirect labour rather than direct labour

idle time	time during which work is stopped, due to reasons such as machine breakdown or shortage of materials; employees usually receive time rate for idle time, and the cost is normally classified as an indirect cost
equivalent units	completed units plus work-in-progress at the percentage complete for labour
wages control account	used to charge labour costs to the various cost, profit or investment centres:

– direct labour to production

– indirect labour to production overheads

– administration labour to non-production overheads

Activities

3.1 A manufacturing business pays its production workers on a time rate basis. A bonus is paid where production is completed faster than the time allowed for a standard hour's production; the bonus is paid at half of the time rate for production time saved. How much will each of the following employees earn for the week?

Employee	Time rate	Hours worked	Time allowed (output per hour)	Actual production
N Ball	£11.00 per hour	35	30 units	1,020 units
T Smith	£10.00 per hour	37	40 units	1,560 units
L Lewis	£10.00 per hour	38	20 units	820 units
M Wilson	£12.00 per hour	36	25 units	950 units

3.2   A company pays its production-line employees on a piecework basis, but with a guaranteed time rate. How much will each of the following employees earn during the week?

Employee	Time rate	Hours worked	Production	Piecework rate
L Fry	£10.00 per hour	40	1,200 units	30p per unit
R Williams	£12.00 per hour	37	500 units	90p per unit
P Grant	£11.00 per hour	36	725 units	60p per unit

3.3   Deerpark Ltd are a company making branded luxury T-shirts, shirts and sweatshirts, using a workforce paid on piecework. The pay per item was amended this week, so now each worker earns £11.00 for a shirt, £8.00 for a sweatshirt and £6.00 for a T-shirt. All the staff are part-time homeworkers, so the amount of clothing they make varies from day to day. The information of who makes the products each day is collected on a spreadsheet.

You must use the employees' daily activity information to determine the gross pay for each employee for last week.

Download the spreadsheet file 'MATST Chapter 3 Activities data' from the Osborne Books website.

Save the spreadsheet file in an appropriate location and rename it to 'MATST Chapter 3 Activities answers', so you can refer back to it.

Open the renamed file and work on the worksheet '3.3 Piecework payroll'.

You are required to:

1   In the Gross pay summary table, cells J4:P6, using the **COUNTIF** function, determine how many

- Sweatshirts
- T-shirts
- Shirts

each person has made, referring to the items produced in cells I4:I6 and using the data in cells A3:G42.

2   **Calculate**, using appropriate **formulas**, the total per item in cells Q4:Q6.

3   Use an **IF statement** in Q6, including the **COUNTA** function, to check all items have been included in the gross pay calculation, showing 'OK' if correct and "Check" if not. Highlight Q6 in green.

4   **Calculate**, using appropriate formulas, the gross pay per employee and the total gross pay in cells J8:Q8, using the information in cells J4:P6 and the rate per item in cells J14:J16.

5   Produce a **2D bar chart** of the gross pay by employee underneath the gross pay table. Give the chart an appropriate **title** and add **data labels (data callout format)** to show the amount earned by each employee and their name.

6   In the bar chart, **fill** the bar for the employee earning the highest gross pay in blue and the lowest gross pay in red.

Save your worksheet as 'MATST Chapter 3 Activities answers' and compare your spreadsheet to the answers in the back of the book or the spreadsheet on the Osborne Books website.

3.4 Print 'n' Go is a print shop that specialises in printing headed notepaper for businesses. It employs two printers, Anna Kurtin and Pete Singh. Both are paid a basic rate per hour for a 35-hour week with two overtime rates: time-and-a-third for weekdays (rate 1), and time-and-a-half for weekends (rate 2). In addition, a production bonus is paid of 50p per 1,000 copies printed.

Details for last week are as follows:

	Anna Kurtin	Pete Singh
Basic rate per hour	£10.50	£12.00
Total hours worked	39	42
Overtime hours: rate 1	4	3
rate 2	–	4
Number of copies printed	45,000	57,000

You are to

- calculate the gross wages earned by each employee for last week (to include any bonus)

- calculate the piecework rate per 1,000 copies printed that would be equal to the gross wages earned by Anna Kurtin for the week, assuming the same output level of 45,000 copies, rounded to the nearest penny.

3.5 Wyvern Fabrication Company has two departments – moulding and finishing. Data relating to labour for a four-week period is given on the labour cost sheet below.

The company uses a bonus scheme whereby employees receive 50 per cent of the time saved in each department, paid at the actual labour rate per hour. This is not included in the actual wages cost, which shows actual time taken multiplied by the actual wage rate.

LABOUR COST SHEET for the four weeks ended 26 February 20-7		
	MOULDING	FINISHING
Actual wages cost (£)	£41,160	£45,450
Time allowed	4,000 hours	5,000 hours
Time taken	4,100 hours	4,500 hours
Time saved		
Bonus (£)		
Total labour cost (£)		

You are to calculate the total labour cost for each department.

3.6 The direct workers of Haven Limited are paid a basic wage of £10.20 per hour. For time worked above 40 hours per week, they receive overtime pay at time-and-a-half. For two particular weeks, we have the following information for a team of 10 direct workers:

Week 1: Total hours worked = 450 hours, including 50 hours of overtime.

Week 2: Total hours worked = 400 hours, including 20 hours of non-production work, clearing up and re-organising a section of the factory during a machine breakdown.

For each of the two given weeks you are to:

(a) Calculate the gross earnings in total for the team of 10 employees.

(b) State how much of the gross earnings would normally be treated as an indirect labour cost.

3.7 You are an Accounts Assistant at Durning Limited and have been asked to help with calculating labour costs.

The electronic timesheet of T Mantle, one of Durning Limited's employees, is shown on the next page.

- For a basic six-hour shift every day from Monday to Friday – basic pay for both production and indirect work.

- For any overtime in excess of the basic six hours on any day from Monday to Friday – the extra hours are paid at time-and-a-half (basic pay plus an overtime premium equal to half of basic pay).

- For three contracted hours each Saturday morning – basic pay.

- For any hours worked in excess of three hours on a Saturday or any hours worked on a Sunday – double-time (basic pay plus an overtime premium equal to basic pay).

You are to complete the time sheet columns headed basic pay, overtime premium and total pay (enter a zero figure, '0', in the columns where nothing is to be paid).

Note: overtime premium is just the premium paid for the extra hours worked.

Employee's weekly time sheet for week ending 15 April 20-6

Employee:		T Mantle	Production Centre:		Finishing	
Employee number:		170	Basic pay per hour:		£14.00	
	Hours spent on production	Hours worked on indirect work	Notes	Basic pay £	Overtime premium £	Total pay £
Monday	6	0				
Tuesday	5	2	2 hours maintenance			
Wednesday	7	0				
Thursday	6	3	3 hours training			
Friday	8	0				
Saturday	5	0				
Sunday	0	0				
Total	37	5				

3.8 Breeden Bakery Limited makes 'homestyle' cakes which are sold to supermarket chains. The payroll for the week ended 26 March 20-4 has been completed with the following amounts taken from the computer payroll software:

•	net wages to be paid to employees	£7,500
•	Income Tax and National Insurance Contributions (NIC) to HMRC	£1,450
•	pension contributions to be paid to the pension fund	£750
	Total	£9,700
•	direct labour costs	£6,500
•	indirect labour costs	£2,700
•	administration labour costs	£500
	Total	£9,700

As an Accounts Assistant at Breedon Bakery you have been given the following tasks:

Task 1

Prepare wages control account for the week ended 26 March 20-4

Dr	Wages Control Account		Cr
	£		£

Task 2

All of the direct labour costs are for the manufacture of fruit cakes. The following cost accounting codes are in use to record labour costs:

Code number	Description
3300	production – fruit cakes
3500	production overheads
3700	non-production overheads – administration
5200	wages control

Complete the table below to record the journal entries on 26 March which show how the total cost of the payroll is split between the various cost centres of the business.

20-4	Code number	Debit £	Credit £
26 March			
26 March			
26 March			
26 March			
26 March			
26 March			

3.9   You have recently joined Cosy Jumpers, a business making handmade aran jumpers, as their Accounts Clerk.

You are completing the gross pay calculation for December for the staff and the payroll journal, using the monthly payroll spreadsheet. You must calculate the December pay information for gross basic pay, overtime payment, bonus and total pay for all employees, and complete the payroll journal. At the start of December a supervisor, Rosie Twigg, was employed and the payroll journal must be updated for her.

The previous Accounts Clerk was not confident on spreadsheets and set up the payroll journal, which contains errors. Cosy Jumpers treats overtime premium and bonuses as production overheads, along with supervisor's pay.

Download the spreadsheet file 'MATST Chapter 3 Activities data' from the Osborne Books website.

Save the spreadsheet file in an appropriate location and rename it to 'MATST Chapter 3 Activities answers', so you can refer back to it.

Open the renamed file and work on the worksheet '3.9 Staff payroll Dec'.

You are required to:

1   Enter 'Basic pay rate 2' into A4 and 18 into B4. **Format** B3 and B4 to **currency £** to two decimal places.

2   All employees except Rosie Twigg, who is the supervisor, are paid at Basic pay rate 1. Rosie Twigg is paid at Basic pay rate 2. **Using appropriate formulas, calculate** the basic pay for all the employees, using **absolute referencing** for the correct basic pay rate (cells B3 and B4) and the hours worked (column B), completing column D in the December pay table.

3   Using an **IF statement** and **absolute referencing**, in an appropriate **formula, calculate** the overtime premium for each employee if more than the basic hours are worked, using the hours worked (column B), the basic hours in the month (cell B2), the basic rate (cell B3) and the overtime rate (cell B5).

4   A £5 bonus is payable to a production worker for each jumper they produce in excess of the expected jumpers per hour. Using an **IF statement**, complete the bonus column in the December pay table.

5   A £2 bonus is payable to Rosie Twigg, the production supervisor for all jumpers produced in excess of the expected jumpers per hour. Using an **IF statement**, complete the bonus payable to Rosie Twigg for December in cell F18.

6   Add a **comment** to F8 stating the bonus calculation for Rosie Twigg is £2 per excess jumper and for production workers it is £5 per excess jumper.

7   Use **trace precedents** to find one error in the formulas in row 19.

8   In cell G20, enter a **formula** to confirm the wages information adds correctly both down and across.

9   Using a **formula, calculate** the overtime premium only in cell F28, and post it to the correct account code.

10   **Insert a row** in the payroll journal between rows 28 and 29, then post the supervisor's basic pay to the relevant cost code, in B30, entering the description 'Production - overheads (basic pay - supervisor)' in C29 and the amount in the relevant column, debit or credit.

11 Ensure the payroll journal and the December pay table balance to each other.

12 **Adjust the orientation** of the page to landscape.

13 **Set the print area** to A22 to H35. **Insert a custom footer** showing today's date, the worksheet name and the file name.

Save your worksheet as 'MATST Chapter 3 Activities answers' and compare your spreadsheet to the answers in the back of the book or the spreadsheet on the Osborne Books website.

3.10 Icod Limited manufactures golf clubs. The following data relates to the production of its 'Mulligan' brand of clubs for October 20-4:

Total direct labour hours worked	16,000 hours
Normal time hours	14,400 hours
Overtime hours	1,600 hours
Normal time rate per hour	£10 per hour
Overtime premium per hour	£5 per hour

In the company's cost bookkeeping system all direct labour overtime payments are included in direct costs.

The following cost accounting codes are in use to record labour costs:

Code number	Description
1500	production – 'Mulligan' clubs
5000	wages control

You are to:

• Calculate the total cost of direct labour for October.

• Show the cost bookkeeping entries, together with account codes, in order to transfer the direct labour costs to production.

3.11   Wyvern Manufacturing Limited pays some of its production employees on a piecework system, based on an agreed output per hour – called the standard hours produced.

The following information relates to one of these employees last week:

Day	Actual hours worked	Standard hours produced
Monday	8	7
Tuesday	7	7
Wednesday	9	10
Thursday	10	11
Friday	10	8

The employee is paid £15 per standard hour produced.

You are to complete the sentences below by entering the correct figures:

(a)   The employee's total pay for the week was £ [   ] .

Now assume that the company offers a guaranteed minimum daily payment of £120.

(b)   The employee's total pay for the week would now be £ [   ] .

Now assume that, instead of a guaranteed minimum daily payment, the company offers a guaranteed minimum weekly payment of £650.

(c)   The employee's total pay for the week would now be £ [   ] .

Now assume that, instead of a guaranteed minimum weekly payment, the company pays for actual hours worked at the standard hour rate, together with a flat-rate bonus of £75 for the week.

(d)   The employee's total pay for the week would now be £ [   ] .

3.12 Excalibur Limited, a manufacturing business, has a Production Department where the employees work in teams. Their basic rate is £10.00 per hour and there are two rates of overtime as follows:

Overtime rate 1: basic pay + 25%

Overtime rate 2: basic pay + 50%

Excalibur sets a target for production of every component each month. A team bonus equal to 5% of basic hourly rate is payable for every equivalent unit of production in the month in excess of the target.

The target for March was 10,000 units.

In March the production was 12,000 equivalent units.

All overtime and bonuses are included as part of the direct labour cost.

(a) Complete the gaps in the table below to calculate the total labour cost.

Labour cost	Hours	£
Basic pay	416	
Overtime rate 1	30	
Overtime rate 2	15	
Total cost before team bonus		
Bonus payment		
Total cost including team bonus		

(b) Calculate the total labour cost per equivalent unit of the finished production for March. Give your answer in £s to **two** decimal places.

The direct labour cost per equivalent unit for March is £ [   ]

(c) Excalibur has forecast the following information for the Production Department for April:

The basic hourly rate will be increased to £10.60 per hour. The target for production is still 10,000 units and the bonus, equal to 5% of basic hourly rate, is still payable for equivalent units of production in excess of this.

9,800 units will be completed in April and the closing work-in-progress is expected to be 1,500 units which will be 80% complete with regard to labour. No opening work-in-progress was expected at the start of April.

Complete the following sentence by filling in the blanks.

The equivalent units of production with regard to labour for April will be [   ] units.

The bonus payable will be £ [   ] .

4 Overheads and expenses

this chapter covers...

In this chapter we turn our attention to the way in which the overheads and expenses of a business are incorporated into the cost of the output. In particular we look at:

- *nature of overheads as period costs*

- *need to recover the cost of overheads through units of output*

- *process of allocating and apportioning the cost of overheads into the units of output*

- *different bases of apportionment of overheads*

- *apportionment of service department costs, using the direct and step-down methods*

- *commonly-used overhead absorption (recovery) rates and their relative merits in given circumstances*

- *bookkeeping entries for overheads*

OVERHEADS

In Chapter 1 'An Introduction to Management Accounting' we saw that costs could be classified as follows:

	Direct materials		Indirect materials
+	Direct labour	+	Indirect labour
+	Direct expenses	+	Indirect expenses
=	Total direct costs	=	Total indirect costs
	or Prime cost		or Overheads

Direct costs are product costs which can be identified directly with each unit of output, whilst indirect costs (overheads) are period costs which cannot be identified directly with each unit of output.

The indirect costs – indirect materials, indirect labour, and indirect expenses – form the overheads of a business. Overheads do not relate to particular units of output but must, instead, be shared amongst all the cost units (units of output to which costs can be charged) to which they relate. For example, the cost of the factory rent must be included in the cost of the output.

The important point to remember is that all the overheads of a business, together with the direct costs, must be covered by revenue from the output – the sales of products or services.

In practice, businesses usually plan – or budget – their overheads in advance, often on an annual basis. By doing this they can work out how to 'recover' the overheads through their output – using an overhead absorption rate.

In larger businesses and organisations, overheads are usually classified by function under headings such as:

- factory or production, eg factory rent and business rates, indirect factory labour, indirect factory materials, heating and lighting of factory

- selling and distribution, eg salaries of sales staff, vehicle costs, delivery costs

- administration, eg office rent and rates, office salaries, heating and lighting of office, indirect office materials

- finance, eg bank interest

Each of these functions or sections of the business is likely to be what is known as a cost centre, a term which was defined in Chapter 1 as follows:

Cost centres are segments of a business or organisation to which costs can be charged.

As well as cost centres, businesses may also have profit centres, investment centres and revenue centres – all four types of centres are collectively called responsibility centres.

In order to deal with the overheads we need to know the responsibility centres of the organisation. This will depend on the size of the business and the way in which the work is organised.

COLLECTING OVERHEADS IN RESPONSIBILITY CENTRES

Depending on the type of cost, overheads are either **allocated** to responsibility centres – cost centres, profit centres, investment centres, revenue centres – or they are **apportioned** to centres.

allocation of overheads

Some overheads belong entirely to one particular centre, for example:

- the wages of a supervisor who works in only one centre

- the rent of a separate building in which there is only one centre

- the cost of indirect materials that have been issued to one particular centre

Overheads like these can therefore be allocated to the centre to which they belong.

Allocation of overheads is the charging to a particular responsibility centre of overheads that are incurred entirely by that centre.

apportionment of overheads

Overheads that cannot be allocated to a particular centre have to be shared or **apportioned** between those responsibility centres that have shared the benefits of the relevant cost.

Apportionment of overheads is the sharing of overheads over a number of responsibility centres to which they relate. Each centre is charged with a proportion of the overhead cost.

For example, a department which is a cost centre within a factory will be charged a proportion of the factory rent and rates. Another example is where a supervisor works within two departments, both of which are separate cost centres: the indirect labour cost of employing the supervisor is shared between the two cost centres.

With apportionment, a suitable **basis** – or method – must be found to apportion overheads between centres; the basis selected should be related to the type of cost. Different methods might be used for each overhead, for example:

Overhead	Basis of apportionment
rent, rates	floor space (or volume of space) of centres
heating, lighting	floor space (or volume of space) of centres
buildings insurance	floor space (or volume of space) of centres
buildings depreciation	floor space (or volume of space) of centres
machinery insurance	cost or carrying amount of machinery and equipment
machinery depreciation	cost or carrying amount of machinery; or machine usage (hours)
canteen	number of employees in each centre
supervisory costs	number of employees in each centre, or labour hours worked by supervisors in each centre

It must be stressed that apportionment is used only for those overheads that cannot be allocated to a particular centre. For example, if a college's Business Studies Department occupies a building in another part of town from the main college building, the business rates for the building can clearly be allocated to the Business Studies cost centre. By contrast, the business rates for the main college building must be apportioned amongst the cost centres on the main campus.

review of allocation and apportionment

It is important that the allocation and apportionment of overheads are reviewed at regular intervals to ensure that the methods being used are still valid. For example:

■ **allocation**

The role of a supervisor may have changed – whereas previously the supervisor worked in one department only, he or she might now be working in two departments.

■ **apportionment**

Building work may have expanded the floor space of a department, so that the apportionment basis needs to be reworked.

Any proposed changes to allocation and apportionment must be discussed with senior staff and their agreement obtained before any changes to methods are implemented. Accounting staff will often have to consult with managers and supervisors who work in operational departments, to discuss how overheads are charged to their departments, and to resolve any queries.

apportionment and ratios

It is important to understand the method of apportionment of overheads using ratios. For example, overheads relating to buildings are often shared in the ratio of the floor space used by the cost centres.

Now read through the Worked Example and the Case Study which follow.

worked example: apportionment using ratios

A business has four cost centres: two production departments, A and B, and two non-production cost centres, stores and maintenance. The total rent per year for the business premises is £24,000. This is to be apportioned on the basis of floor space, given as:

	Production dept A	Production dept B	Stores	Maintenance
Floor space (square metres)	400	550	350	200

Step 1

Calculate the total floor space: 400 + 550 + 350 + 200 = 1,500 square metres

Step 2

Divide the total rent by the total floor space: £24,000 ÷ 1,500 = £16

This gives a rate of £16 per square metre.

Step 3

Multiply the floor space in each cost centre by the rate per square metre. This gives the share of rent for each cost centre. For example, in Production Department A, the share of rent is 400 x £16 = £6,400. The results are shown in the table:

	Production dept A	Production dept B	Stores	Maintenance
Floor space (square metres)	400	550	350	200
Rent apportioned	£6,400	£8,800	£5,600	£3,200

Step 4

Check that the apportioned amounts agree with the total rent:

£6,400 + £8,800 + £5,600 + £3,200 = £24,000

Case Study

PILOT ENGINEERING LIMITED:
OVERHEAD ALLOCATION AND APPORTIONMENT

situation

Pilot Engineering Limited, which makes car engine components, uses some of the latest laser equipment in one department, while another section of the business continues to use traditional machinery. Details of the factory are as follows:

Department X is a 'hi-tech' machine shop equipped with laser-controlled machinery with a carrying amount of £80,000. This department has 400 square metres of floor space. There are three machine operators: the supervisor spends one-third of their time in this department.

Department Y is a 'low-tech' part of the factory equipped with machinery with a carrying amount of £20,000. The floor space is 600 square metres. There are two workers who spend all their time in this department: the supervisor spends two-thirds of their time in this department.

The budgeted overheads for the next financial year to be allocated or apportioned are:

1	Factory rates	£12,000
2	Wages of the supervisor	£33,000
3	Factory heating and lighting	£2,500
4	Depreciation of machinery	£20,000
5	Buildings insurance	£2,000
6	Insurance of machinery	£1,500
7	Specialist materials for the laser equipment	£2,500

How should each of these be allocated or apportioned to each department?

solution

The recommendations are:

1   Factory rates – apportioned on the basis of floor space.

2   Supervisor's wages – apportioned on the basis of time spent, ie one-third to Department X, and two-thirds to Department Y. If the time spent was not known, an alternative basis could be established, based on the number of employees.

3   Factory heating and lighting – apportioned on the basis of floor space.

4   Depreciation of machinery – apportioned on the basis of the carrying amount of machinery.

5   Buildings insurance – apportioned on the basis of floor space.

6   Insurance of machinery – apportioned on the basis of the carrying amount of machinery.

7   Specialist materials for the laser equipment – allocated to Department X because this cost belongs entirely to Department X.

It is important to note that there are no fixed rules for the apportionment of overheads – the only proviso is that a fair proportion of the overhead is charged to each department which has shared the benefits of the relevant cost. Methods of apportionment will need to be reviewed at regular intervals to ensure that they are still valid; changes can only be implemented with the agreement of senior staff.

The apportionment of budgeted overheads for Pilot Engineering Limited is as follows (sample workings are shown below the table):

Budgeted overheads	Basis of Apportionment	Total £	Dept X £	Dept Y £
Factory rates	Floor space	12,000	4,800	7,200
Wages of supervisor	Time spent	33,000	11,000	22,000
Heating and lighting	Floor space	2,500	1,000	1,500
Dep'n of machinery	Carrying amount	20,000	16,000	4,000
Buildings insurance	Floor space	2,000	800	1,200
Machinery insurance	Carrying amount	1,500	1,200	300
Specialist materials	Allocation	2,500	2,500	–
		73,500	37,300	36,200

workings:

For example, the floor space of the two departments is:

Dept X	400	square metres
Dept Y	600	square metres
Total	1,000	square metres

Factory rates are apportioned as follows:

$$\frac{£12,000}{1,000} = £12 \text{ per square metre}$$

Dept X rates	£12 x 400 =	£4,800
Dept Y rates	£12 x 600 =	£7,200
Total (check)		£12,000

SERVICE DEPARTMENTS

Many businesses have departments which provide services within the business; for example, maintenance, transport, stores or stationery. Each service department is a cost centre, to which a proportion of overheads is charged. As service departments do not themselves have any cost units to which their overheads may be charged, the costs of each service department must be **re-apportioned** to the production departments (which do have cost units) to which overheads can be charged. A suitable basis of re-apportionment must be used, for example:

- the overheads of a maintenance department might be re-apportioned to production departments on the basis of value of machinery or equipment, or on the basis of time spent in each production department

- the overheads of a stores or stationery department could be re-apportioned on the basis of value of goods issued to production departments

- the overheads of a subsidised canteen could be re-apportioned on the basis of the number of employees

RE-APPORTIONMENT OF SERVICE DEPARTMENT OVERHEADS

The overheads of service cost centres are charged to production cost centres using:

- either **direct apportionment** where service departments provide services to production departments only

- or the **step-down method** where service departments provide services to production departments *and* to other service departments

To illustrate re-apportionment, we will apply these techniques to a business with two production departments, A and B, and two service departments, stores and maintenance. After allocation and apportionment of production overheads, the totals are:

	Total £	Production dept A £	Production dept B £	Stores £	Maintenance £
Overheads	20,400	10,000	5,000	2,400	3,000

direct apportionment

Initially, we will assume that the service departments do not provide services to one another. Their costs are directly apportioned to production departments using a suitable basis. In the example on the previous page:

■ stores overheads are re-apportioned on the basis of the number of stores requisitions – department A has made 150 requisitions; department B has made 50

■ maintenance overheads are re-apportioned on the value of machinery – department A has machinery with a carrying amount (net book value) of £20,000, department B's machinery has a value of £10,000

Using direct apportionment, the overheads of the service departments are re-apportioned as shown in the table below. The method of calculation using ratios is the same as we used for apportionment.

Notice that the total is taken out of the service cost centre column when it is shared between the production cost centres.

	Total £	Production dept A £	Production dept B £	Stores £	Maintenance £
Overheads	20,400	10,000	5,000	2,400	3,000
Stores	–	1,800	600	(2,400)	–
Maintenance	–	2,000	1,000	–	(3,000)
	20,400	13,800	6,600	–	–

Thus all the overheads have now been charged to the production departments where they can be 'absorbed' into the cost units which form the output of each department. We will see how the absorption is carried out later in this chapter.

step-down method

This is used where, as well as to production departments, one service department provides services to another. We will now assume this is the case and, using the example, the stores department deals with requisitions from the maintenance department, but no maintenance work is carried out in the stores department. Under the step-down method we re-apportion **firstly** the overheads of the stores department (because it does not receive any services from the maintenance department), and **secondly** the overheads of the maintenance department:

■ stores requisitions

- department A 150

- department B 50

- maintenance 50

■ value of machinery

- department A £20,000

- department B £10,000

The re-apportionment of the production overheads of the service departments, using the step-down method, is as follows:

	Total £	Production dept A £	Production dept B £	Stores £	Maintenance £
Overheads	20,400	10,000	5,000	2,400	3,000
Stores	–	1,440	480	(2,400)	480
				–	*3,480
Maintenance	–	2,320	1,160	–	(3,480)
	20,400	13,760	6,640	–	–

* Note that a new total is calculated for the maintenance department before it is re-apportioned. £480 from stores is added to the original £3,000 overheads in the maintenance department.

All the overheads have now been charged to the production departments.

ALLOCATION AND APPORTIONMENT – A SUMMARY

The diagram on the next page summarises the allocation and apportionment of overheads that we have seen in this chapter. It shows:

■ allocation of overheads directly to cost centres

■ apportionment of overheads on an equitable basis to cost centres

■ re-apportionment of service department costs to production cost centres

The Case Study which follows on page 125 is a comprehensive example of allocation and apportionment.

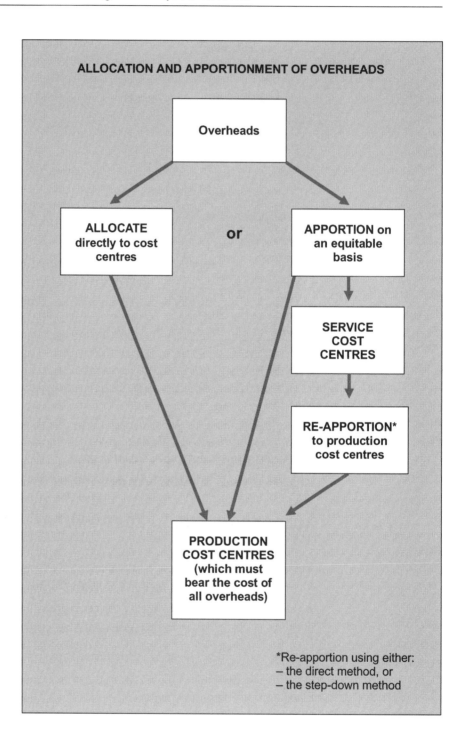

Case
Study

KORECKI LIMITED: ALLOCATION AND APPORTIONMENT OF OVERHEADS

situation

You work as an Accounts Assistant for Korecki Limited, a manufacturing business. The company has two production centres: cutting and assembly – and three support cost centres: maintenance, stores and administration.

Korecki Limited's budgeted overheads for the next financial year are:

	£	£
Depreciation charge for machinery		3,900
Power for production machinery		4,680
Rent and rates of premises		21,450
Light and heat for premises		8,250
Indirect labour costs:		
Maintenance	45,400	
Stores	27,250	
Administration	62,100	
Totals	134,750	38,280

The following information is also available:

See table on the next page.

Overheads are allocated or apportioned on the most appropriate basis. The total overheads of the support cost centres are then re-apportioned to the two production centres, using the direct method.

- 75% of the maintenance cost centre's time is spent maintaining production machinery in the cutting production centre and the remainder in the assembly production centre.

- The stores cost centre makes 60% of its issues to the cutting production centre, and 40% to the assembly production centre.

- Administration supports the two production centres equally.

- There is no reciprocal servicing between the three support cost centres.

Department	Carrying amount of machinery	Production machinery power usage (KwH)	Floor space (square metres)	Number of employees
Production centres:				
Cutting	175,000	25,500	600	6
Assembly	85,000	13,500	400	8
Support cost centres:				
Maintenance			300	3
Stores			200	2
Administration			150	4
Total	260,000	39,000	1,650	23

You are to use the information to allocate and apportion the budgeted overheads for the next financial year.

s o l u t i o n

Before completing an apportionment table you identify that:

- indirect labour is to be allocated to the support cost centres

- all other overheads are to be apportioned to the production centres and support cost centres, using a suitable basis

The basis of apportionment you decide to use is:

- depreciation charge for machinery – carrying amount of machinery

- power for production machinery – power usage

- rent and rates of premises – floor space

- light and heat for premises – floor space

As noted earlier, the indirect labour of the support centres will be allocated.

The apportionment table, including the re-apportionment of the service cost centres, is completed (see next page).

Budgeted overheads	Basis of apportionment	Cutting £	Assembly £	Maintenance £	Stores £	Admin £	Totals £
Depreciation charge for machinery	Carrying amount of machinery	2,625	1,275				3,900
Power for production machinery	Power usage	3,060	1,620				4,680
Rent and rates of premises	Floor space	7,800	5,200	3,900	2,600	1,950	21,450
Light and heat for premises	Floor space	3,000	2,000	1,500	1,000	750	8,250
Indirect labour	Allocated			45,400	27,250	62,100	134,750
Totals		16,485	10,095	50,800	30,850	64,800	173,030
Re-apportion Maintenance		38,100	12,700	(50,800)			
Re-apportion Stores		18,510	12,340		(30,850)		
Re-apportion Administration		32,400	32,400			(64,800)	
Total overheads to production centres		105,495	67,535				173,030

OVERHEAD ABSORPTION (RECOVERY)

Once overheads have been allocated or apportioned to production cost centres, the final step is to ensure that the overheads are charged to cost units. In the language of management accounting this is known as 'absorption' or 'recovery', ie the cost of overheads is charged to the cost units which pass through that particular production department.

For example, if you take a car to be repaired at a garage, the bill may be presented as follows:

	£
Parts	70.00
Labour: 3 hours at £40 per hour	120.00
Total	190.00

Within this bill are the three main elements of cost: materials (parts), labour and overheads. The last two are combined as labour – the garage mechanic is not paid £40 per hour; instead the labour rate might be £15 per hour, with the rest, ie £25 per hour, being a contribution towards the overheads and profit of the garage. Other examples are accountants and solicitors, who charge a 'rate per hour', part of which is used to contribute to the cost of overheads and profit.

To be profitable, a business must ensure that its selling prices more than cover all its costs:

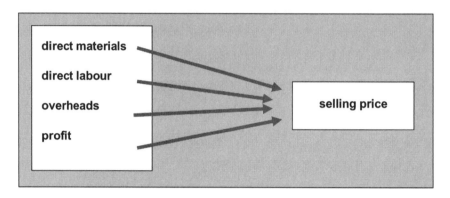

calculating overhead absorption (recovery) rates

In order to recover the overheads of a department, there are two steps to be followed:

1 calculation of the overhead absorption rate (OAR)

2 application of this rate to actual work done

The overhead absorption rate is calculated using estimated or budgeted figures as follows, for a given time period:

$$OAR = \frac{\textit{total budgeted cost centre overheads}}{\textit{total planned work in the cost centre}}$$

The amount of work must be measured in a suitable way – for a manufacturing business this is usually:

■ direct labour hours, or

■ machine hours

Other businesses and organisations – especially those which provide a service – will use other ways, eg an accountancy firm may use an hourly rate, or a bus company may use miles travelled.

direct labour hour method

With this method, production overhead is absorbed on the basis of the number of direct labour hours worked. It is most commonly used where production is labour intensive.

1 Calculation of the overhead absorption rate, using budgeted figures:

$$\frac{\textit{total cost centre overheads}}{\textit{total direct labour hours (in cost centre)}} = \textit{cost per direct labour hour}$$

2 Application of the rate:

direct labour hours worked x overhead absorption rate

= overhead absorbed

worked example

Department A   total budgeted cost centre overheads for year   £40,000

expected direct labour hours for year   5,000

actual direct labour hours in March   450

1   Overhead absorption rate:

$$\frac{£40,000}{5,000 \text{ hours}} = £8 \text{ per direct labour hour}$$

2   Application of the rate:

450 hours x £8 = £3,600 of overhead absorbed in March

machine hour method

Here the production overhead is absorbed on the basis of machine hours. It is most commonly used where production is machine intensive.

1 Calculation of the overhead absorption rate, using budgeted figures:

$$\frac{\textit{total cost centre overheads}}{\textit{total machine hours (in cost centre)}} = \textit{cost per machine hour}$$

2 Application of the rate:

machine hours worked x overhead absorption rate

= overhead absorbed

worked example

Department B   total budgeted cost centre overheads for year £216,000

expected machine hours for year   36,000

actual machine hours in March   3,500

1   Overhead absorption rate:

$$\frac{£216,000}{36,000 \text{ hours}} = £6 \text{ per machine hour}$$

2   Application of the rate:

3,500 hours x £6 = £21,000 of overhead absorbed in March

service sector – hourly rate (or sales price / unit method)

This method is often used by businesses such as accountants, solicitors, dentists, garages, where the overhead is absorbed on the basis of chargeable time or sales price or units sold.

1   Calculation of the overhead absorption rate, using budgeted figures:

$$\frac{\textit{total cost centre* overheads}}{\textit{total chargeable hours** (in cost centre)}} = \textit{cost per hour of chargeable time}$$

* for a firm of accountants, an example of a cost centre would be a department (eg tax department), or the whole of a small office

** can be adapted to use sales price/units sold

2   Application of the rate:

chargeable hours (or sales price/units sold) x overhead absorption rate

= overhead absorbed

worked example

Tax department of accounting firm

total budgeted cost centre overheads for year £120,000

expected chargeable hours for year   6,000

actual chargeable hours in May   450

1 Overhead absorption rate:

$$\frac{\pounds120,000}{6,000 \text{ hours}} = \pounds20 \text{ per chargeable hour}$$

2 Application of the rate:

450 chargeable hours x £20 = £9,000 of overhead absorbed in May

service sector – miles travelled

Here the overhead is absorbed on the basis of miles travelled.

1 Calculation of the overhead absorption rate, using budgeted figures:

$$\frac{total\ cost\ centre^*\ overheads}{total\ miles\ travelled\ (in\ cost\ centre)} = cost\ per\ mile\ travelled$$

* for a bus company, an example of a cost centre would be a route number, a bus or a garage

2 Application of the rate:

miles travelled x overhead absorption rate = overhead absorbed

worked example

Buses on route 73	total budgeted cost centre overheads for year	£100,000
	expected miles travelled for year	200,000
	actual miles travelled in March	18,000

1 Overhead absorption rate:

$$\frac{\pounds100,000}{200,000 \text{ miles}} = \pounds0.50 \text{ per mile travelled}$$

2 Application of the rate:

18,000 miles travelled x £0.50 = £9,000 of overhead absorbed in March

which method to use?

Only one overhead absorption rate will be used in a particular department, and the method selected must relate to the reason why the costs are incurred. For example, a cost centre which is machine based, where most of the overheads incurred relate to machinery, will use a machine hour basis.

The direct labour hour method is a very popular method (eg the garage mentioned earlier) because overheads are absorbed on a time basis. Thus the cost unit that requires twice the direct labour of another cost unit will be charged twice the overhead.

A machine hour rate is particularly appropriate where expensive machinery is used in the department.

It is important to select the best method of overhead absorption for the particular business, otherwise wrong decisions will be made on the basis of the costing information. The particular absorption method selected for a department will need to be reviewed at regular intervals to ensure that it is still valid. For example, the direct labour hour method is unlikely to continue to be appropriate where a machine has been brought in to automate processes that were previously carried out by hand. Any proposed changes must be discussed with senior managers and their agreement obtained before any changes to methods are implemented. The changes will need to be discussed with managers and supervisors in operational departments to explain how overheads will be charged to their departments in the future, and any queries will need to be resolved.

using a pre-determined rate

Most businesses and organisations calculate a pre-determined overhead absorption rate for each department. This is then applied to all production passing through that department.

The OAR is calculated in advance using estimates – this avoids having to calculate the rate regularly, which may result in changes over quite short time periods. Instead the rate is smoothed out over fluctuations in cost and activity over a longer accounting period.

Appropriate consultation will need to be made with staff from the operating departments before a pre-determined rate is established for a particular department.

OVER- OR UNDER-ABSORPTION OF OVERHEADS

Most businesses will find that the amount of overheads absorbed into the cost of their actual work during the year is not the same as the amount that has been spent. If the amount absorbed is greater, the difference is called 'over-absorption' or 'over-recovery' of overheads. If the amount absorbed is less than the amount spent, the difference is called 'under-absorption' or 'under-recovery'.

Over-absorption or under-absorption (recovery) is the difference between the total amount of overheads absorbed (recovered) in a given period and the total amount spent on overheads.

over-absorption of overheads

The following example shows a calculation for over-absorption – with the overhead absorption rate based on direct labour hours.

worked example

Department C

overhead absorption rate (based on direct labour hours)	£6.00 per labour hour
actual labour hours in year	6,300 hours
actual overheads for year	£36,000

- actual overheads for the department are £36,000

- actual overhead absorbed: 6,300 hours x £6.00 per hour = £37,800

- over-absorption of overhead: £37,800 – £36,000 = £1,800

At the end of the financial year the statement of profit or loss is credited with the amount of over-absorbed overhead, which cancels out the extra overhead expense charged.

On first impressions, over-absorption of overheads seems to be a 'bonus' for a business – profits will be higher; however, it should be remembered that the overhead rate may have been set too high. As a consequence, sales might have been lost because the selling price has been too high. The overhead absorption rate (OAR) will need to be reviewed with the manager and supervisors of the operational department if over-absorption continues on a regular basis – they may be able to explain the reason for the difference.

under-absorption of overheads

With under-absorption, the actual overhead absorbed is less than the actual overheads for the department. For example, if in Department C (above) actual labour hours in the year were 5,500, the calculations would be:

- actual overheads for the department are £36,000

- actual overhead absorbed: 5,500 hours x £6.00 per hour = £33,000

- under-absorption of overhead: £36,000 – £33,000 = £3,000

At the end of the financial year the statement of profit or loss is debited with the amount of under-absorbed overhead, which brings the overhead expense up to the correct level.

Under absorption of overheads is a cost to a business, so reducing profitability. It may be that the selling price of output has been set too low, or output is less than expected, or actual overhead is more than expected. The OAR will need to be revised if under-absorption continues on a regular basis.

BOOKKEEPING ENTRIES FOR OVERHEADS

In this section we look at the cost bookkeeping entries to record the transfer of the cost of overheads to production, together with the entries for over- or under-absorption of overheads (which are transferred to the statement of profit or loss). These entries form part of the bookkeeping system for costing.

A production overheads account is used to:

■ transfer production overheads to production

■ credit the amount of over-absorbed overheads to the statement of profit or loss

■ debit the amount of under-absorbed overheads to the statement of profit or loss

The cost bookkeeping entries are:

■ **transfer production overheads (amount absorbed) to production**
   - debit production
   - credit production overheads

■ **credit over-absorbed overheads to the statement of profit or loss**
   - debit production overheads
   - credit statement of profit or loss

Here, the amount of over-absorbed overheads reduces the total cost of production, and so increases profits.

■ **charge under-absorbed overheads to the statement of profit or loss**
   - debit statement of profit or loss
   - credit production overheads

Here the amount of under-absorbed overheads adds to the total cost of production, and so reduces profits.

These cost bookkeeping entries are shown diagrammatically on the opposite page.

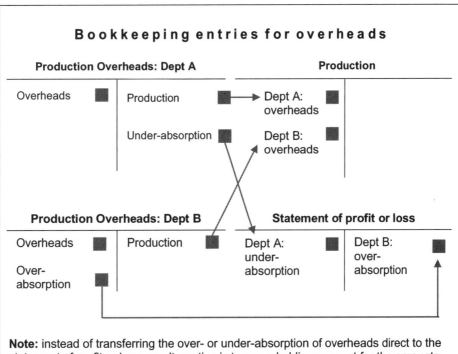

Bookkeeping entries for overheads

Note: instead of transferring the over- or under-absorption of overheads direct to the statement of profit or loss, an alternative is to use a holding account for the amounts. At the end of the financial year, the balance of this account is then transferred to the statement of profit or loss – as either a debit or a credit entry, depending on the balance.

BOXIT LIMITED:
BOOKKEEPING FOR OVERHEADS

situation

Boxit Limited manufactures and sells cardboard boxes which are used for packaging and storage. The boxes pass through two departments – cutting and assembly. Details of overheads for the departments for the four weeks ended 24 March 20-8 are as follows:

Cutting Department

- overhead absorption rate is £10.00 per machine hour

- machine hours used were 1,000

- actual cost of production overhead was £11,000

Assembly Department

- overhead absorption rate is £4.00 per direct labour hour
- direct labour hours worked were 2,000
- actual cost of production overhead was £7,500

The following cost accounting codes are in use to record overheads:

Code number	Description
2200	production
2500	production overheads: cutting department
2600	production overheads: assembly department
5500	statement of profit or loss

As an Accounts Assistant at Boxit Limited, you are asked to prepare the two production overheads accounts and to fill in the table below to record the journal entries for the overheads and for the over- and under-absorption of overheads.

20-8	Code number	Debit £	Credit £
24 March	2200		
24 March	2500		
24 March	2200		
24 March	2600		
24 March	5500		
24 March	2500		
24 March	2600		
24 March	5500		

solution

The production overheads accounts are prepared as follows:

Dr	**Production Overheads Account: Cutting Department (2500)**		Cr
	£		£
Bank (overheads incurred)	11,000	Production	10,000
		Statement of profit or loss	
		(under-absorption)	1,000
	———		———
	11,000		11,000
	———		———

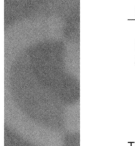

Dr	**Production Overheads Account: Assembly Department (2600)**		Cr
	£		£
Bank (overheads incurred)	7,500	Production	8,000
Statement of profit or loss			
(over-absorption)	500		
	——		——
	8,000		8,000
	——		——

The cost bookkeeping entries are:

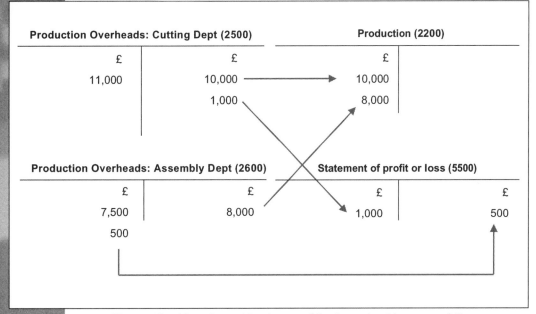

The cost bookkeeping entries to record the journal entries are as follows:

20-8	Code number	Debit £	Credit £
24 March	2200	10,000	
24 March	2500		10,000
24 March	2200	8,000	
24 March	2600		8,000
24 March	5500	1,000	
24 March	2500		1,000
24 March	2600	500	
24 March	5500		500

In this way, the cost of the pre-determined overhead rates is charged to production, while the amount of over- or under-absorption of overheads is transferred to the statement of profit or loss.

SPREADSHEET SKILLS FOR MANAGEMENT ACCOUNTING

using spreadsheets to allocate and apportion overheads

Over the course of the chapter, you have allocated and apportioned overheads, using both the direct and step-down methods, to determine an overhead recovery rate. The apportionment process is very repetitive, and it can take a long time to do the calculations on a calculator. It is also easy to make mistakes and time consuming to find and fix them, so spreadsheets are the perfect tool for 'automating' this process.

So, let's start off with a partly completed spreadsheet for Beautiful Tableware Ltd.

Case Study

SPREADSHEET SKILLS TO PROVIDE MANAGEMENT ACCOUNTING INFORMATION

situation

Beautiful Tableware Ltd has been operating for many years and produces stoneware dishes for cooking and serving food in.

Your manager, Claire, has set up a template for the overhead absorption rates for next year. She has asked you to complete the calculations and has given you the raw data and costs in a spreadsheet.

Download the spreadsheet file 'MATST Ch 4 Spreadsheet Case Study Beautiful Tableware data' from the Osborne Books website.

Save the spreadsheet file in an appropriate location and rename it 'MATST Ch 4 Spreadsheet Case Study Beautiful Tableware answer'.

Open the renamed file.

You are required to:

1 In the worksheet called 'Apportionment calculation' use a **lookup** function and **absolute cell referencing** to find the values for the basis of apportionment on the table from F6 to K10. The basis of apportionment is on the worksheet 'Basis of apportionment'.

2 Apportion the total costs in the Apportionment £' table. Use an appropriate calculation **formula** and **link** the data from the 'Apportionment basis' table using **absolute cell referencing**.

3 In row containing figures, **SUM** the allocated costs across into cells K15 to K25.

4 Use an **IF statement** in L15 to compare total cost in E15 to the calculated cost in K15, showing 'OK' if correct and 'Error' if not. **Copy** this down to L19.

5 Apportion the stores and maintenance costs, using the direct method, using the following information:

	% of department time		
	Moulding	**Glazing**	**Finishing**
Stores	60	30	10
Maintenance	75	15	10

6 **Format** the cost information in E15 to K25 to GBP £0,000.00.

7 The overheads are to be apportioned on machine hours for moulding and glazing and labour hours for finishing.

	Moulding	**Glazing**	**Finishing**
Machine hours	25,380	3,865	200
Labour hours	1,300	750	1,232

Calculate the overhead absorption rate for the correct department in F27, G27 and H27, using **ROUNDUP** to the nearest pence, formatting to **currency**.

8 **Amend the column width** to ensure the descriptions and data can be viewed.

9 Make the title of the 'Apportionment £' table **bold.**

10 **Hide column** E.

solution

The 'Apportionment calculation' worksheet currently looks like the one shown on the next page:

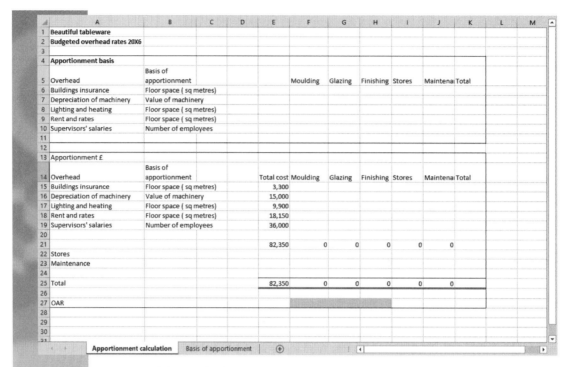

And the 'Basis of apportionment' worksheet looks like this:

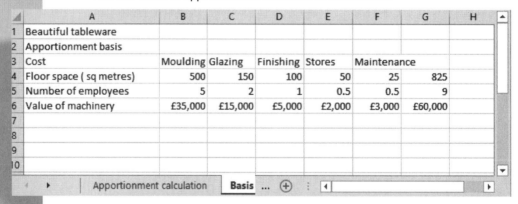

As you are given the basis of apportionment already – buildings insurance, for example, is apportioned on the basis of floor space (sq metres) – you can use a **VLOOKUP** formula to apportion this cost, referring to the table in the 'basis of apportionment' worksheet. However, this situation is slightly more complex than previously covered, as you must amend the formula for each department, so the correct basis of apportionment is used.

The formula in F6 for the Moulding department is:

=VLOOKUP($B6,'Basis of apportionment'!$A$4:$G$6,2,FALSE) and can be copied down to F10. However, when the formula is copied across, this happens:

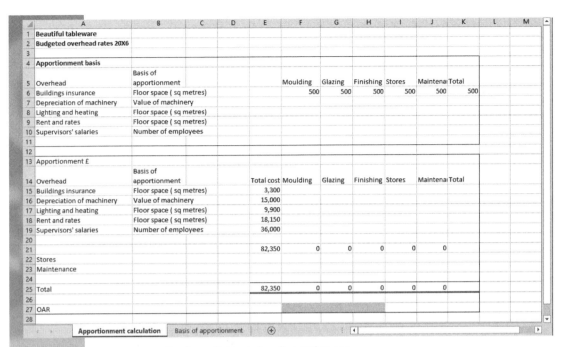

	A	B	C	D	E	F	G	H	I	J	K	L	M
1	Beautiful tableware												
2	Budgeted overhead rates 20X6												
3													
4	Apportionment basis												
5	Overhead	Basis of apportionment				Moulding	Glazing	Finishing	Stores	Maintenai	Total		
6	Buildings insurance	Floor space (sq metres)				500	500	500	500	500	500		
7	Depreciation of machinery	Value of machinery											
8	Lighting and heating	Floor space (sq metres)											
9	Rent and rates	Floor space (sq metres)											
10	Supervisors' salaries	Number of employees											
11													
12													
13	Apportionment £												
14	Overhead	Basis of apportionment			Total cost	Moulding	Glazing	Finishing	Stores	Maintenai	Total		
15	Buildings insurance	Floor space (sq metres)			3,300								
16	Depreciation of machinery	Value of machinery			15,000								
17	Lighting and heating	Floor space (sq metres)			9,900								
18	Rent and rates	Floor space (sq metres)			18,150								
19	Supervisors' salaries	Number of employees			36,000								
20													
21						82,350	0	0	0	0	0		
22	Stores												
23	Maintenance												
24													
25	Total					82,350	0	0	0	0	0		
26													
27	OAR												
28													

Apportionment calculation | Basis of apportionment | ⊕

... as the formula in each cell remains as:

=VLOOKUP($B6,'Basis of apportionment'!$A$4:G$6,**2**,FALSE)

In the VLOOKUP, the column number stayed as 2, the Moulding column, so you must change the formulas to look at the correct column in the table on the 'Basis of apportionment' worksheet. For example, for the Finishing department, column 4, the formula would be:

=VLOOKUP($B6,'Basis of apportionment'!$A$4:$G$6,**4**,FALSE.)

Each time it is copied across, it must be amended to refer to the correct department's column. However, it can be copied down, as long as you use absolute referencing for the table reference - $A$4:$G$6.

Once this is complete, the 'Apportionment basis' table looks like this:

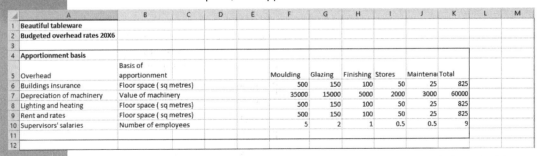

	A	B	C	D	E	F	G	H	I	J	K	L	M
1	Beautiful tableware												
2	Budgeted overhead rates 20X6												
3													
4	Apportionment basis												
5	Overhead	Basis of apportionment				Moulding	Glazing	Finishing	Stores	Maintenai	Total		
6	Buildings insurance	Floor space (sq metres)				500	150	100	50	25	825		
7	Depreciation of machinery	Value of machinery				35000	15000	5000	2000	3000	60000		
8	Lighting and heating	Floor space (sq metres)				500	150	100	50	25	825		
9	Rent and rates	Floor space (sq metres)				500	150	100	50	25	825		
10	Supervisors' salaries	Number of employees				5	2	1	0.5	0.5	9		
11													
12													

So you can now complete the Apportionment table below. It is important to use absolute referencing to refer to the Total cost in column E and the Total in the Apportionment basis table, so the formula can be copied correctly.

Remember you can confirm what the answer should be using your calculator if you are unsure, as you know how to apportion costs.

You can then complete point 4 - the **IF statement**. Use the formula wizard to help you and refer to the Osborne Books Spreadsheets for Management Accounting Tutorial if you are unfamiliar with this formula.

Once you have completed points 1 to 4, compare your Apportionment calculation worksheet with the one below.

	A	B	C	D	E	F	G	H	I	J	K	L	M
1	Beautiful tableware												
2	Budgeted overhead rates 20X6												
3													
4	Apportionment basis												
5	Overhead	Basis of apportionment				Moulding	Glazing	Finishing	Stores	Maintena	Total		
6	Buildings insurance	Floor space (sq metres)				500	150	100	50	25	825		
7	Depreciation of machinery	Value of machinery				35000	15000	5000	2000	3000	60000		
8	Lighting and heating	Floor space (sq metres)				500	150	100	50	25	825		
9	Rent and rates	Floor space (sq metres)				500	150	100	50	25	825		
10	Supervisors' salaries	Number of employees				5	2	1	0.5	0.5	9		
11													
12													
13	Apportionment £												
14	Overhead	Basis of apportionment			Total cost	Moulding	Glazing	Finishing	Stores	Maintena	Total		
15	Buildings insurance	Floor space (sq metres)			3,300	2000.00	600.00	400.00	200.00	100.00	3300.00	OK	
16	Depreciation of machinery	Value of machinery			15,000	8750.00	3750.00	1250.00	500.00	750.00	15000.00	OK	
17	Lighting and heating	Floor space (sq metres)			9,900	6000.00	1800.00	1200.00	600.00	300.00	9900.00	OK	
18	Rent and rates	Floor space (sq metres)			18,150	11000.00	3300.00	2200.00	1100.00	550.00	18150.00	OK	
19	Supervisors' salaries	Number of employees			36,000	20000.00	8000.00	4000.00	2000.00	2000.00	36000.00	OK	
20													
21						82,350	47,750	17,450	9,050	4,400	3,700	82350.00	
22	Stores												
23	Maintenance												
24													
25	Total					82,350	47,750	17,450	9,050	4,400	3,700	82350.00	
26													
27	OAR												
28													
29													

Point 5 requires a straightforward apportionment of the Stores and Maintenance departments, using the direct method and the information you are given.

The total departments' costs for the overhead recovery rates, once this is completed, are Moulding: £53,165, Glazing: £19,325 and Finishing: £9,860.

For point 6, the **ROUNDUP** function is required as, when we recover overheads, we want to recover all of them. If we simply rounded the overhead absorption rate for the Moulding department, this rounds down to £2.09 per machine hour. Multiplying this by the machine hours of 25,380, recovers £53,044.20 – £120.80 less than £53,165 budgeted for the Moulding department. In a larger organisation, this under-recovery could add up, so it should be avoided. Using the **ROUNDUP** function results in an overhead recovery rate of £2.10 per machine hour, recovering £53,298 – £133 more than budgeted.

After you have completed points 8 to 10, compare your answer to the extract of the 'Apportionment calculation' worksheet below.

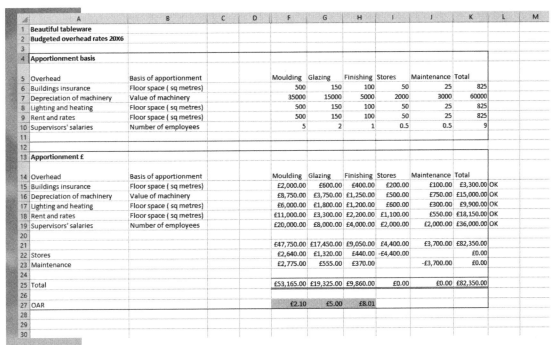

	A	B	F	G	H	I	J	K	L
1	Beautiful tableware								
2	Budgeted overhead rates 20X6								
3									
4	Apportionment basis								
5	Overhead	Basis of apportionment	Moulding	Glazing	Finishing	Stores	Maintenance	Total	
6	Buildings insurance	Floor space (sq metres)	500	150	100	50	25	825	
7	Depreciation of machinery	Value of machinery	35000	15000	5000	2000	3000	60000	
8	Lighting and heating	Floor space (sq metres)	500	150	100	50	25	825	
9	Rent and rates	Floor space (sq metres)	500	150	100	50	25	825	
10	Supervisors' salaries	Number of employees	5	2	1	0.5	0.5	9	
11									
12									
13	Apportionment £								
14	Overhead	Basis of apportionment	Moulding	Glazing	Finishing	Stores	Maintenance	Total	
15	Buildings insurance	Floor space (sq metres)	£2,000.00	£600.00	£400.00	£200.00	£100.00	£3,300.00	OK
16	Depreciation of machinery	Value of machinery	£8,750.00	£3,750.00	£1,250.00	£500.00	£750.00	£15,000.00	OK
17	Lighting and heating	Floor space (sq metres)	£6,000.00	£1,800.00	£1,200.00	£600.00	£300.00	£9,900.00	OK
18	Rent and rates	Floor space (sq metres)	£11,000.00	£3,300.00	£2,200.00	£1,100.00	£550.00	£18,150.00	OK
19	Supervisors' salaries	Number of employees	£20,000.00	£8,000.00	£4,000.00	£2,000.00	£2,000.00	£36,000.00	OK
20									
21			£47,750.00	£17,450.00	£9,050.00	£4,400.00	£3,700.00	£82,350.00	
22	Stores		£2,640.00	£1,320.00	£440.00	-£4,400.00		£0.00	
23	Maintenance		£2,775.00	£555.00	£370.00		-£3,700.00	£0.00	
24									
25	Total		£53,165.00	£19,325.00	£9,860.00	£0.00	£0.00	£82,350.00	
26									
27	OAR		£2.10	£5.00	£8.01				
28									
29									
30									

To allow you to compare the formulas in detail, you can download the answer file, 'MATST Chapter 4 Spreadsheet Skills Case Study Beautiful Tableware answer', from the Osborne Books website.

designing spreadsheets to support absorption and allocation of overheads

As part of your exam, you may be required to design spreadsheets to support absorption and allocation of overheads.

When designing a spreadsheet, you should make it as straightforward as possible. You may wish to use every spreadsheet skill you know, without considering who may use the document.

You may not always be the person using the spreadsheet, so keeping each formula simple and using formatting to highlight cells that need to be updated and cells that do not, can also help maintain the integrity of the spreadsheet. You may want to protect the data, and restrict choices of apportionment basis, and using **data validation** and **protecting cells** will achieve this.

Chapter Summary

- Overheads are the indirect costs – indirect materials, indirect labour and indirect expenses.

- Overheads are:
  - allocated to a specific responsibility centre, if they belong entirely to that centre
  - apportioned between centres, if they are shared

- Apportionment is done on a suitable basis, using ratios of floor space, numbers of employees and so on.

- Methods of allocation and apportionment should be reviewed regularly.

- The total overheads allocated and apportioned to the service cost centres are then re-apportioned to profit centres or production cost centres using either direct apportionment or the step-down method.

- After re-apportionment of the service cost centre overheads, the total overheads in each profit centre or production cost centre can be calculated.

- All the above steps can be carried out using expected or budgeted overhead amounts.

- Overhead absorption rates are calculated using the total expected or budgeted overheads in each cost centre.

- An overhead absorption rate is calculated as follows:

$$\text{overhead absorption rate} = \frac{\text{total budgeted cost centre overheads}}{\text{total planned work in cost centre}}$$

  where the planned amount of work may be measured, often in terms of direct labour hours or machine hours for a manufacturing company, although service sector organisations will use other methods, eg miles travelled for a bus company.

- Overhead absorption rates are applied to the actual work carried out. A direct labour hour absorption rate is applied as follows, for example:

  Direct labour hours worked x overhead absorption rate

  = overhead absorbed

- At the end of a given period, the amount of overhead absorbed may differ from the amount actually spent on the overheads. The difference is:
  - either, an over absorption (when the amount absorbed is more than the amount spent)
  - or, an under-absorption (when the amount absorbed is less than the amount spent)

- Cost bookkeeping entries are made to record:
  - overheads debited to production
  - over-absorption of overheads credited to the statement of profit or loss
  - under-absorption of overheads debited to the statement of profit or loss

Key
Terms

overheads	indirect costs, made up of: indirect materials + indirect labour + indirect expenses
cost centres	segments of a business to which costs can be charged
allocation of overheads	the charging to a particular responsibility centre of overheads that are incurred entirely by that centre
apportionment of overheads	the sharing of overheads over a number of responsibility centres to which they relate – each centre is charged with a proportion of the overhead cost
service department	a non-production cost centre that provides services to other cost centres in the business
re-apportionment of service department overheads	the sharing of the total overheads from a service department, a proportion being charged to each cost centre it serves; after all re-apportionment has been carried out, the overheads will be charged to profit centres or production cost centres
direct apportionment	method of re-apportionment used where service departments provide services to production departments only
step-down	method of re-apportionment used where service departments provide services to production departments and to other service departments
absorption (recovery)	the charging of overheads to cost units (units of output)
overhead absorption rate	the rate used to charge overheads to cost units – calculated in advance, as: budgeted total overhead ÷ planned amount of work
basis of absorption	the measurement of work used to calculate the overhead absorption rate, for example: – direct labour hours – machine hours – hourly rate – miles travelled

over- or under-absorption (recovery) — the difference between the total amount of overheads absorbed (recovered) in a given period and the total amount spent on overheads

over-absorption of overheads — overheads absorbed are more than the amount spent on overheads

under-absorption of overheads — overheads absorbed are less than the amount spent on overheads

Activities

4.1 Wyvern Fabrication Company has two production departments – moulding and finishing.

The company charges overheads on the basis of machine hours and the following overhead analysis information is available to you (note that service department overheads have already been apportioned to production departments):

OVERHEAD ANALYSIS SHEET		
	MOULDING	FINISHING
Budgeted total overheads (£)	9,338	3,298
Budgeted machine hours	1,450	680
Budgeted overhead absorption rate (£)		

Details of a particular job of work are as follows:

JOB OVERHEAD ANALYSIS SHEET		
	MOULDING	FINISHING
Job machine hours	412	154
Budgeted overhead absorption rate (£)		
Overhead absorbed by job (£)		

You are to:

(a) Calculate the overhead absorption rate (to two decimal places) for each of the two departments and complete the overhead analysis sheet.

(b) Calculate the production overhead absorbed by the job (to two decimal places) and complete the job overhead analysis sheet.

(c) Suggest another overhead absorption rate that the company might use and comment on the circumstances that would make it appropriate.

4.2 ABC Limited is a manufacturing business with three production centres: Departments A, B and C. The following are the budgeted factory overheads for the forthcoming year:

Rent and rates   £7,210

Depreciation of machinery   £10,800

Supervisor's salary   £33,000

Insurance of machinery   £750

Departmental information is:

	Dept A	Dept B	Dept C
Floor space (square metres)	300	150	250
Carrying amount of machinery	£25,000	£15,000	£10,000
Number of production-line employees	8	4	3

You are to:

(a) Using the following table, apportion the overheads to the production centres, stating the basis of apportionment.

Budgeted overheads	Basis of apportionment	Total £	Dept A £	Dept B £	Dept C £
Totals					

(b) Calculate the overhead absorption rate (to two decimal places) of each department, based on direct labour hours. Note that the factory works a 37 hour week for 48 weeks in a year.

4.3   Wye Engineering Limited offers specialist engineering services to the car industry. It has two production departments – machining and finishing – and a service department which maintains the machinery of both departments. The budgeting software shows that expected production overheads for the forthcoming year are:

	£
Rent and rates	5,520
Buildings insurance	1,320
Insurance of machinery	1,650
Lighting and heating	3,720
Depreciation of machinery	11,000
Supervisor's salary	30,000
Maintenance department salary	23,590
Factory cleaning	4,800

The following information is available:

	Machining	Finishing	Maintenance
Floor space (square metres)	300	200	100
Number of employees	6	3	1
Carrying amount of machinery	£40,000	£15,000	–

The factory works a 35 hour week for 47 weeks each year.

You are to:

Using the following table:

(a) • Prepare an analysis of production overheads showing the basis of allocation and apportionment to the three departments of the business (round to whole £s).

  • Re-apportion the service department overheads to production departments on the basis of value of machinery.

Budgeted overheads	Basis of apportionment	Total £	Machining £	Finishing £	Maintenance £

(b) Calculate an overhead absorption rate (to two decimal places) based on direct labour hours for each of the two production departments.

4.4 Mercia Tutorial College has two teaching departments – business studies and general studies – and two service departments – administration and technical support. The overheads of each department are as follows:

		£
•	Business studies	40,000
•	General studies	20,000
•	Administration	9,600
•	Technical support	12,000

The basis for re-apportioning the overheads of the service departments is:

- technical support, on the value of equipment in each department – business studies, £50,000; general studies, £25,000; administration, £25,000

- administration, on the number of students in the teaching departments – business studies, 500; general studies, 250

You are to use the table below and the step-down method to re-apportion the two service department overheads to the two teaching departments.

Budgeted overheads	Total	Business studies	General studies	Administration	Technical support
	£	£	£	£	£

4.5   Rossiter and Rossiter is a firm of chartered accountants, with two partners. The budgeting software shows that overhead costs for next year are estimated to be:

	£
Office rent	10,000
Office salaries	45,000
Rates	4,800
Heating and lighting	2,400
Stationery	2,000
Postage and telephone	5,100
Car expenses	5,600

The two partners plan to work for 47 weeks next year. They will each be in the office for 40 hours per week, but will be working on behalf of their clients for 35 hours per week.

(a)   What is the overhead absorption rate per partner hour (to two decimal places)?

(b)   If each partner wishes to earn a salary of £50,000 per year, what is the combined hourly rate per partner they should charge to clients, which includes overheads and their salaries (to two decimal places)?

(c)   If both partners actually work on their clients' behalf for 37 hours per week, what will be the total over-absorption of overheads for the year (to two decimal places)?

4.6   A friend of yours is about to start in business making garden seats. She plans to make two different qualities – 'Standard' and 'De Luxe'. Costs per unit for direct materials and labour are expected to be:

	Standard	De Luxe
	£	£
Direct materials	12.50	20.00
Direct labour:		
3 hours at £10.00 per hour	30.00	–
3.5 hours at £12.00 per hour	–	42.00
	42.50	62.00
Machine hours	1	2.5

Production overheads are expected to be £1,000 per month.

Production is expected to be 80 'Standard' seats and 40 'De Luxe' seats per month.

(a)   Suggest and calculate two different methods by which overheads can be absorbed.

(b)   Calculate the production cost (to two decimal places) of each of the two qualities of garden seats using the two different methods of overhead absorption.

(c)   Compare the results of your calculations and suggest to your friend the most appropriate method of overhead absorption for this business.

4.7 Durning Limited manufactures and sells household furniture. The company's operations are organised by departments, as follows:

- Warehouse
- Manufacturing
- Maintenance
- Administration

Information from the computer system shows that the budgeted fixed overheads of the company for November 20-1 were as follows:

	£
Depreciation of non-current assets	9,150
Rent	11,000
Other property overheads	6,200
Administration overheads	5,450
Staff costs:	
– warehouse	3,600
– manufacturing	9,180
– maintenance	8,650
– administration	5,940
Total budgeted fixed overheads	59,170

The following information is also relevant:

Department	% of floor space occupied	Carrying amount of non-current assets
		£000
Warehouse	15%	120
Manufacturing	60%	400
Maintenance	10%	20
Administration	15%	60
	100%	600

Overheads are allocated and apportioned between departments using the most appropriate basis.

Task 1

Please see next page.

Task 2

Manufacturing fixed overheads are absorbed on the basis of budgeted machine hours. The budgeted number of machine hours for November 20-1 was 10,000 hours.

You are to calculate the budgeted fixed overhead absorption rate (to two decimal places) for the manufacturing department for November 20-1.

Task 1

Complete the following table showing the allocation and apportionment of budgeted fixed overheads between the four departments.

Budgeted fixed overheads for November 20-1	Basis	Total £	Warehouse £	Manufacturing £	Maintenance £	Admin £
Depreciation		9,150				
Rent		11,000				
Other property overheads		6,200				
Administration overheads		5,450				
Staff costs		27,370				
		59,170				

4.8 You work as an Accounts Assistant at the Trevaunance Hotel which is part of a group of hotels. Each month it is one of your tasks to record and report cost information to head office.

The Trevaunance Hotel has fifty bedrooms and its operations are organised into five departments, as follows:

- Accommodation
- Restaurant
- Bar
- Kitchen
- Administration

Information from the computer system shows that the budgeted fixed overheads for the Trevaunance Hotel for August 20-3 were as follows:

	£
Bedroom repairs	3,200
Electricity	1,700
Rent of premises	9,000
Kitchen repairs	1,025
Staff costs:	
– accommodation	4,550
– restaurant	6,740
– bar	3,045
– kitchen	2,310
– administration	6,950
Other property overheads	4,000
Total budgeted fixed overheads	42,520

The following information is also relevant:

Department	% of floor space occupied	Metered electricity costs
		£
Accommodation	65%	550
Restaurant	15%	250
Bar	10%	150
Kitchen	5%	700
Administration	5%	50
	100%	1,700

Overheads are allocated and apportioned to the five departments using the most appropriate basis. The total administration overheads are then re-apportioned to the other four departments using the following percentages:

- Accommodation   60%
- Restaurant   20%
- Bar   10%
- Kitchen   10%

Task 1

Complete the following table showing the allocation and apportionment of budgeted fixed overheads between the five departments.

Budgeted fixed overheads for August 20-3	Basis	Total £	Accommodation £	Restaurant £	Bar £	Kitchen £	Administration £
Bedroom repairs		3,200					
Electricity		1,700					
Rent		9,000					
Kitchen repairs		1,025					
Staff costs		23,595					
Other property overheads		4,000					
		42,520					
Administration							( )
		42,520					

Task 2

Kitchen fixed overheads are absorbed on the basis of budgeted labour hours. The budgeted number of labour hours for the kitchen during August 20-3 was 1,000 hours.

You are to calculate the budgeted fixed overhead absorption rate per labour hour (to two decimal places) for the kitchen for August 20-3.

4.9 Bill's Bicycles Ltd produces bicycles.

You are calculating the overhead recovery rate for the production departments for the year ending 30 November 20-6. You have been given a partly completed spreadsheet by your manager to assist you in this task that includes the budgeted fixed overheads and relevant departmental information for the company.

You must decide which basis of apportionment is appropriate for each cost, then allocate or apportion it.

You must then re-apportion the two non-production departments – warehouse and administration – using the direct method.

- 60% of the warehouse's time is spent on issues to assembly, with the remaining 40% being spent on issues to frame making.
- The administration department supports the frame making and assembly equally.

Finally, calculate the overhead recovery rate, formatting the spreadsheet so the information is as clear as possible. The overheads for frame making are to be apportioned on machine hours and assembly on labour hours.

	Frame making	Assembly
Machine hours	250,000	12,300
Labour hours	53,400	59,400

Download the spreadsheet file 'MATST Chapter 4 Activities data' from the Osborne Books website.

Save the spreadsheet file in an appropriate location and rename it to 'MATST Chapter 4 Activities answers', so you can refer back to it.

Open the renamed file.

On the worksheet '4.9 Apportionment', you are required to:

1. Create a drop down list in cells B6 to B10 and B15 to B20 using **data validation**, referring to the list in L6 to L9. Enter the input message 'Complete the basis of apportionment using those given in the list.', as well as a suitable warning. Select the most appropriate basis of apportionment from the drop down list for each expense.

2. Using a suitable **HLOOKUP** formula along with the information on the worksheet '4.9 Basis of apport't', complete the 'Apportionment basis' table, F6 to J10. **Format** these cells as percentages or currency, £0,000, as appropriate.

3. Allocate and apportion the total costs in the 'Budgeted fixed overheads for year to 30 November 20-6' table, using appropriate **formulas** and the data from the 'Apportionment basis' table and the '4.9 Basis of apport't' worksheet.

4. Use **autosum** in cells J15 to J20 to total each row.

5. Put an **IF statement** in K15 to compare total cost in E15 to the calculated cost in J15, showing 'OK' if correct and 'Error' if not. Copy this down to K20.

6. Complete the re-apportionment of warehouse and administration, using information given in the question and suitable **formulas**.

7. Enter the correct machine or labour hours for each department in B29 and B30 and **calculate** the overhead recovery rate, using the **ROUNDUP** formula to two decimal places for Frame making in C29 and Assembly in E30.

8   **Hide column** E. Ensure all remaining information can be seen.

9   **Format** the Overhead Recovery Rate table to show the **cells in green** and **bold** the titles.

Save your worksheet as 'MATST Chapter 4 Activities answers' and compare your spreadsheet to the answers in the back of the book or the spreadsheet on the Osborne Books website.

4.10   You work as an Accounts Assistant for Sekula Limited, a manufacturing business. The company has two production centres: moulding and finishing – and three support cost centres: maintenance, stores and administration.

The company's budgeting software shows overheads for the next financial year are:

Budgeted overheads	£
Depreciation charge for machinery	1,950
Power for production machinery	2,604
Rent and rates of premises	4,275
Light and heat for premises	2,925
Indirect labour costs:	
Maintenance	32,200
Stores	27,150
Administration	28,450
Total	99,554

The following information is also available:

Department	Carrying amount of machinery	Production machinery power usage (KwH)	Floor space (square metres)	Number of employees
Production centres:				
Moulding	80,000	16,000	300	4
Finishing	50,000	8,000	160	5
Support cost centres:				
Maintenance			120	2
Stores			140	1
Administration			180	2
Total	130,000	24,000	900	14

Overheads are allocated or apportioned on the most appropriate basis. The total overheads of the support cost centres are then re-apportioned to the two production centres, using the direct method.

- 75% of the maintenance cost centre's time is spent maintaining production machinery in the moulding production centre and the remainder in the finishing production centre.

- The stores cost centre makes 60% of its issues to the moulding production centre, and 40% to the finishing profit centre.

- Administration supports the two production centres equally.

- There is no reciprocal servicing between the three support cost centres.

You are to complete the apportionment table below using the data above.

Budgeted overheads	Basis of apportionment	Moulding £	Finishing £	Maintenance £	Stores £	Admin £	Totals £
Depreciation charge for machinery							
Power for production machinery							
Rent and rates of premises							
Light and heat for premises							
Indirect labour							
Totals							
Re-apportion Maintenance							
Re-apportion Stores							
Re-apportion Administration							
Total overheads to production centres							

4.11 Wentworth Limited's budgeted overheads and activity levels for the next quarter are:

	Cutting	Assembly
Budgeted overheads (£)	165,600	318,750
Budgeted direct labour hours	18,400	12,750
Budgeted machine hours	8,280	4,250

(a) What would be the budgeted overhead absorption rate for each department if this were set based on their both being heavily automated?

(a)	cutting £9 per hour; assembly £25 per hour	
(b)	cutting £9 per hour; assembly £75 per hour	
(c)	cutting £20 per hour; assembly £25 per hour	
(d)	cutting £20 per hour; assembly £75 per hour	

(b) What would be the budgeted overhead absorption rate for each department if this were set based on their both being labour intensive?

(a)	cutting £9 per hour; assembly £25 per hour	
(b)	cutting £9 per hour; assembly £75 per hour	
(c)	cutting £20 per hour; assembly £25 per hour	
(d)	cutting £20 per hour; assembly £75 per hour	

Additional data

At the end of the quarter actual overheads incurred were found to be:

	Cutting	Assembly
Actual overheads (£)	158,200	322,250

(c) Assuming that exactly the same amount of overheads was absorbed as budgeted, what were the budgeted under- or over-absorptions in the quarter?

(a)	cutting over-absorbed £7,400; assembly over-absorbed £3,500	
(b)	cutting over-absorbed £7,400; assembly under-absorbed £3,500	
(c)	cutting under-absorbed £7,400; assembly under-absorbed £3,500	
(d)	cutting under-absorbed £7,400; assembly over-absorbed £3,500	

4.12   AggieSurf Limited manufactures and sells surfboards. The boards pass through two departments – moulding and finishing. Data for production overheads for the departments for the four weeks ended 26 May 20-6 are as follows:

Moulding Department

- overhead absorption rate is £8.00 per machine hour

- machine hours worked were 600

- actual cost of production overhead was £5,000

Finishing Department

- overhead absorption rate is £5.00 per direct labour hour

- direct labour hours worked were 1,500

- actual cost of production overhead was £7,000

The following cost accounting codes are in use to record production overheads:

Code number	Description
3000	production
3400	production overheads: moulding department
3500	production overheads: finishing department
6000	statement of profit or loss

As an Accounts Assistant at AggieSurf Limited, you are asked to prepare the two production overheads accounts and to fill in the table (on the next page) as at 26 May 20-6 to record the journal entries for the overheads and the over- and under-absorption of overheads.

Dr	**Production Overheads Account: Moulding Department (3400)**	Cr
	£	£

Dr	**Production Overheads Account: Finishing Department (3500)**	Cr
	£	£

20-6	Code number	Debit £	Credit £
26 May	3000		
26 May	3400		
26 May	3000		
26 May	3500		
26 May	6000		
26 May	3400		
26 May	3500		
26 May	6000		

4.13 You work in the accounts department of Treasured Trainers Ltd, a company producing trainers. There are two production departments – Cutting and Stitching. Details for the production overheads for the five weeks ended 24 March 20-8 are as follows:

	Cutting	Stitching
Overhead recovery rate	£6.00 per machine hour	£4 per labour hour
Machine / labour hours worked	7,400 hrs	10,800 hrs
Actual production overheads	£39,500	£45,100

The following cost codes are in use to record production overheads:

Code number	Description
2800	Production
3200	Production overheads: cutting department
3400	Production overheads: stitching department
8000	Statement of profit or loss

Note: Actual production overheads are paid through the bank, and posted automatically to the accounts, so the journal is not required to include this.

(a) The financial controller would like you to design a spreadsheet to automatically calculate and produce a journal for the under- or over-recovery of overheads, inputting on date and actual machine or labour hours and actual overheads incurred for the period.

Open a new spreadsheet and name it 'Treasured Trainers Overhead Recovery Calculation and Journal'.

Name the worksheet 'Overhead Recovery Journal'.

The worksheet should include the table below, to include the overhead information and calculations.

	Cutting	Stitching
	£	£
Overhead recovery rate		
Machine/labour hours worked		
Overheads recovered		
Actual production overheads		
(Under)/ over-recovery		

This table should be linked to a journal. You may wish to refer to the journal layout in 4.12 when designing it.

Produce a worksheet that will:

1   Automatically **calculate** the overheads recovered for a period for the cutting and stitching departments. The actual machine or labour hours must be input cells.

Use the data for the five weeks to 24 March 20-8 to illustrate this works correctly.

2   Automatically **calculate** the under- or over-recovery of the overheads for this period. The actual overheads incurred must be input cells in the spreadsheet. Show under-recovery as red and over-recovery as green, using **conditional formatting.**

3   Underneath the overhead information, produce a template journal. This must:
  – post the overheads recovered for the cutting production department using the data for the five weeks to 24 March 20-8.
  – post the overheads recovered for the stitching production department using the data for the five weeks to 24 March 20-8.
  – post the under- or over-absorption of overheads for the cutting production department. Use an **IF statement** to post this correctly as either a debit or a credit, to the statement of profit or loss.
  – post the under- or over-absorption of overheads for the stitching production department. Use an **IF statement** to post this correctly as either a debit or a credit, to the statement of profit or loss.

Identify each set of journal entries in a different **cell colour.**

4   **Protect** the worksheet so only the input cells – period, date, machine and labour hours worked and actual overheads for the cutting and stitching department and journal date – can be amended. Leave the password blank.

(b)   The financial controller has also asked you to produce a **3D column chart**, including a **data table**, for the production manager, showing overheads recovered and actual production overheads for both production departments.

1   Using the data from (a), produce a **3D column graph** on a separate worksheet showing the overheads recovered and the actual overheads incurred for both the cutting and stitching production department.

2   Give the **3D chart** a suitable **title** and include a **data table**.

3   Name the worksheet 'Production Overheads 24Mar20-8'.

Save the file as 'Treasured Trainers Overhead Recovery Calculation and Journal' and compare your answer to the back of the book or the spreadsheet on the Osborne Books website.

4.14 Fancy Cakes Limited manufactures and sells iced cakes and chocolate cakes. The cakes pass through two departments – baking and finishing. Data for production overheads for the departments for the four weeks ended 11 March 20-6 is as follows:

Baking Department

- overhead absorption rate is £10.00 per machine hour

- machine hours worked were 1,200

- actual cost of production overhead was £11,500

Finishing Department

- overhead absorption rate is £6.00 per direct labour hour

- direct labour hours worked were 800

- actual cost of production overhead was £5,000

The following cost accounting codes are in use to record production overheads:

Code number	Description
2000	production
2600	production overheads: baking department
2800	production overheads: finishing department
5000	statement of profit or loss

As an Accounts Assistant at Fancy Cakes Limited, you are asked to prepare the two production overheads accounts and to fill in the table as at 11 March 20-6 to record the journal entries for the overheads and the over- and under-absorption of overheads.

Dr	**Production Overheads Account: Baking Department (2600)**	Cr
	£	£

Dr	**Production Overheads Account: Finishing Department (2800)**	Cr
	£	£

20-6	Code number	Debit £	Credit £
11 March	2000		
11 March	2600		
11 March	2000		
11 March	2800		
11 March	2600		
11 March	5000		
11 March	5000		
11 March	2800		

4.15   You are the Management Accounts Assistant at Paint and Wallpaper Ltd. The two departments of the business are for paint and for wallpaper. Information from the computer system shows:

- the quarterly overhead absorption rates for each department on the basis of budgeted direct labour hours to be

Department	£
Paint	10.60
Wallpaper	12.40

- the actual results for the quarter are

	Paint	Wallpaper
Actual overhead	£14,360	£9,690
Actual direct labour hours	1,320	840

(a) Calculate the overhead absorbed for each department. Enter your answers to the nearest whole £.

Department	£
Paint	
Wallpaper	

(b) Calculate the amount of under- or over-absorbed overheads for each department, and indicate whether it is under-absorbed or over-absorbed.

Department		£	over-absorbed ✔	under-absorbed ✔
Paint				
Wallpaper				

(c) Complete the following statements by selecting the correct options to complete the gaps.

Select your options from the following list: added, credited, debited, financial position, increase, profit or loss, reduce

Over-absorbed overheads are .... to production overheads and .... to the statement of ....

Under-absorbed overheads are .... to the total cost of production and .... profits.

5 Methods of costing

this chapter covers...

In this chapter we examine appropriate methods of costing for different types of businesses. We look at:

- *principles of unit costing*

- *methods of costing used for specific orders: job costing and batch costing*

- *methods of costing used when the work is continuous: unit costing and service costing*

- *method of costing that would be used in various types of businesses and organisations*

- *calculation of job or batch costs and selling prices from given data*

- *calculation of average costs per cost unit in unit and service costing*

- *work-in-progress – equivalent unit calculations*

- *normal and abnormal wastage, including scrap sales*

- *bookkeeping entries for production where there is wastage*

UNIT COSTING

Unit costing is the cost incurred to produce one cost object.

A **cost object** is a unit of product, service or activity for which costs can be ascertained. Examples of cost objects in unit costing are:

- for a manufacturing business, per item manufactured
- for a hotel, per meal served
- for a chemical business, per kilogram (kg) or litre of output
- for a transport company, per passenger mile
- for a hospital, per day per patient

Note that, in the service sector, the units of output are often composite cost units (see page 5) which comprise two variables, eg passenger mile.

The principles of unit costing are the same whatever method of costing is used by the business. The unit cost of production or output is always calculated as:

$$\frac{cost\ of\ production\ or\ output}{number\ of\ cost\ units} = unit\ cost$$

There are four unit costs that can be calculated:

- prime cost
- marginal cost
- absorption cost
- total cost

Each of these includes different costs of production, as follows:

Direct costs

- direct materials
- direct labour
- variable production overheads

Direct materials and direct labour together give the **prime cost** of production.

Prime cost plus variable production overheads gives the **marginal cost** of production.

Indirect costs

- fixed production overheads

Marginal cost plus fixed production overheads gives the **absorption cost** of production.

Fixed non-production overheads

- such as administration, selling and distribution

Absorption cost plus fixed non-production overheads gives the **total cost** of production.

Study the worked example below, where the unit cost is calculated.

---

worked example – unit costing

A toy manufacturer makes a popular type of doll. During the four-week period which has just ended 10,000 dolls were produced, with the following costs:

Product: doll	
Direct costs	**£**
Direct materials	16,500
Direct labour	17,500
Prime cost	**34,000**
Variable production overheads	5,000
Marginal cost of production	**39,000**
Indirect costs	
Fixed production overheads	15,000
Absorption cost of production	**54,000**
Fixed non-production overheads	15,000
Total cost of production	**69,000**

The unit costs are calculated as follows:

- prime cost of one unit $\dfrac{£34,000}{10,000 \text{ dolls}} = £3.40$

- *marginal cost of one unit $\dfrac{£39,000}{10,000 \text{ dolls}} = £3.90$

- *absorption cost of one unit $\dfrac{£54,000}{10,000 \text{ dolls}} = £5.40$

- total cost of one unit $\dfrac{£69,000}{10,000 \text{ dolls}} = £6.90$

*We look at marginal and absorption costing in more detail in Chapter 6.

In this chapter we look at a number of different costing methods and see that most calculate a unit cost of production.

We look firstly at costing methods for specific orders, and secondly at costing for continuous work (page 174).

COSTING METHODS FOR SPECIFIC ORDERS

Specific order costing is where customers order what they want, before it is made. Thus, the customer places the specific order, and agrees to buy the product before the work is done.

Many service businesses also carry out work to customers' requirements, for example, accountants and solicitors. Each piece of work is different and is kept separate from the others.

Costing methods which are used by businesses to collect costs and to calculate the total cost of their output include:

- job costing
- batch costing

These are used in conjunction with absorption costing to recover the cost of overheads. Remember that businesses must recover their overheads in the total price charged to their customers – this applies both to manufacturing businesses and to service industries, such as hairdressers, banks, shops and transport companies.

Case Study

RACERS LIMITED: MANUFACTURING RACING BIKES

situation

Otto Kranz, a former cycling champion, is setting up a company to manufacture racing bikes. The business is to be called Racers Limited.

Otto is aware that he has two very distinct markets into which to sell his bikes:

- Some of his bikes will be produced to the specific requirements of individual customers for international level competition racing – this is the area which really interests Otto. He can charge a premium price for these custom-built designs.

- He also plans to sell quality racing bikes to the mass-market which will be made in batches of 20 to standard designs. These will be sold in specialist shops and are cheaper, both to manufacture and in terms of selling price.

But Otto is confused about how he is going to cost out these two different methods of production – the 'one-off' and the standard design. He says:

'I can record the costs of the direct materials and labour hours used to make the 'one-off' bike and the batches of 20. But what about the overheads? Will I need more than one costing system here?'

solution

Racers Limited is likely to use two different methods of costing, depending on the kind of work being done:

- job costing – for the one-off designs
- batch costing – for the mass-market bikes

SPECIFIC ORDERS: JOB COSTING

Job costing is used where each job can be separately identified from other jobs and costs are charged to the job.

The job becomes the cost unit to which costs are charged.

Examples of job costing include engineering firms that produce 'one-offs' to the customer's specifications, printing businesses, vehicle repairs, jobbing builders, wedding and party services.

The diagram below shows the main steps involved in job costing.

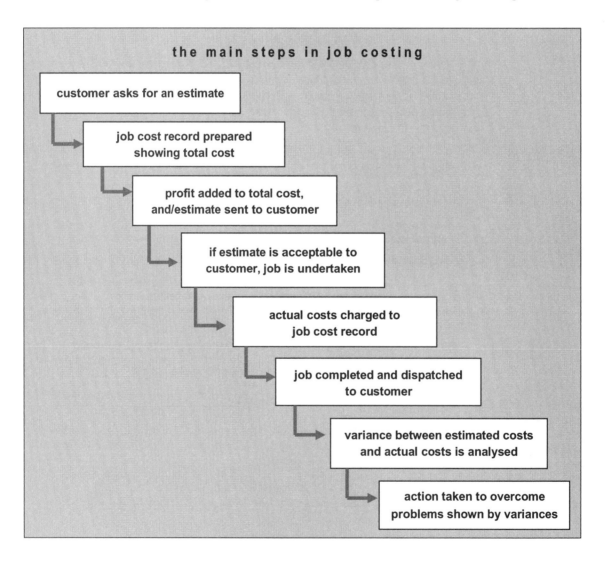

the main steps in job costing

- customer asks for an estimate
- job cost record prepared showing total cost
- profit added to total cost, and/estimate sent to customer
- if estimate is acceptable to customer, job is undertaken
- actual costs charged to job cost record
- job completed and dispatched to customer
- variance between estimated costs and actual costs is analysed
- action taken to overcome problems shown by variances

The important points to note from the diagram are:

■ each job is given a number in order to identify it

■ a separate job cost record is prepared for each job, listing the estimates of direct materials, direct labour, direct expenses and overheads (most businesses nowadays use a computer spreadsheet program to help with their costing and, in practice, the job cost sheet is held as a computer file)

■ the actual costs incurred are compared with the estimated costs, and the differences (called 'variances') between the two are analysed; action can then be taken to correct the variances, which will help when preparing future estimates. Additional costs can sometimes be passed on to the customer but, in other situations, the business might have to bear the loss

Case Study

FASHIONAID: JOB COSTING

situation

The youth group at a local church has decided to organise an evening fashion show, to be called 'FashionAid'. The objective of the show is to raise money for a children's charity. One of the organisers has asked for your help in arranging the construction of staging for the evening's events. You approach Pearshore Builders for an estimate of the cost of constructing the staging for the event.

solution

Pearshore Builders allocate a reference number to the job. They prepare a job cost record from their computer database as follows:

JOB NO. 6789 'FashionAid': construction of staging	
	£
Direct Materials	
Pine timber: 50mm x 76mm	82.00
Boards: 18 mm	55.00
Paint: white gloss	25.00
Direct Labour	
Construction: 4 hours at £20 per hour	80.00
Painting: 2 hours at £18 per hour	36.00
Overheads (based on direct labour hours)	
6 hours at £22.00 per hour	132.00
TOTAL COST	410.00
Profit mark-up (30% of total cost)	123.00
SELLING PRICE	533.00

These estimated costs will be obtained as follows:

- **direct materials**, from the inventory records for materials already held, and from the firm's Purchasing or Procurement Department for items that need to be bought in especially for this job

- **direct labour**, from the payroll records of the different grades of labour to be employed on this job

- **overheads**, from the pre-determined overhead absorption rate based, for this job, on direct labour hours

Assuming that the price is acceptable to the customer, the job will go ahead and Pearshore Builders will record the actual costs of the job. These can then be compared with the estimated costs, and any differences or 'variances' between the two can be investigated. For example, it might be that actual labour costs are higher than was estimated – this could mean that the employees took longer to do the job than was expected, or that pay rates had increased, or that more skilled staff – earning higher rates of pay – were used to do the job. This type of analysis, called 'variance analysis', is covered in Chapter 7.

SPECIFIC ORDERS: BATCH COSTING

Batch costing is used where the output consists of a number of identical items which are produced together as a batch.

Examples of batch costing include a bakery producing a batch of standard white loaves, and then a batch of croissants; or a clothing factory producing a batch of jackets, and then a batch of trousers, or a batch of blue scarves, and then a batch of red scarves. Each batch is the cost unit to which the costs are charged. Once the batch has been produced, the total cost per unit is calculated as follows:

$$\frac{total\ batch\ cost}{number\ of\ units\ of\ output} = total\ cost\ per\ unit$$

In essence, batch costing is very similar to job costing, but in a batch a number of identical units are produced. The batch is costed as a job during manufacture and the costs are collected together. Upon completion of the batch, the cost per unit can be calculated.

Batch numbers are frequently used to identify the output of a particular time – examples include paint colours and wallpaper production. The reason for identifying batches in this way is that there might be slight production variations – for example, in the quantities of raw materials used.

Case Study

AMBER LIMITED:
BATCH COSTING FOR CHILDREN'S CLOTHES

situation

Amber Limited is a company that designs and manufactures children's clothes. The company's products are noted for their design flair, and the use of fabrics that appeal to children and also wear well. The clothes sell through specialist shops and department stores.

This week, Amber Limited is making a batch of 1,000 sequin dresses for a department store. The costs of the batch are expected to be:

• direct materials, £3,500
• direct labour: cutting, 100 hours at £11 per hour
                 sewing, 200 hours at £10 per hour
                 finishing, 100 hours at £12 per hour
• the overhead absorption rate is £6 per direct labour hour
• a profit mark-up of 40% is added to the total cost

The Accounts Supervisor asks you, an Accounts Assistant, to calculate the total cost of producing the batch of sequin dresses, and to add the profit mark-up. She also asks you to calculate the company's cost per dress and the selling price per dress.

solution

Batch cost: 1,000 sequin dresses		
	£	£
Direct materials		3,500
Direct labour:		
cutting, 100 hours at £11 per hour	1,100	
sewing, 200 hours at £10 per hour	2,000	
finishing, 100 hours at £12 per hour	1,200	
		4,300
Variable overheads: 400 direct labour hours at £6 per hour		2,400
TOTAL COST		10,200
Profit mark-up (40% x £10,200)		4,080
SELLING PRICE		14,280

• $\text{total cost per unit} = \dfrac{\text{total batch cost}}{\text{number of units of output}} = \dfrac{£10,200}{1,000} = £10.20$

- selling price = $\dfrac{\text{total batch cost + profit}}{\text{number of units of output}} = \dfrac{£14,280}{1,000} = £14.28$

As with most types of costing, the estimated costs above need to be compared with the actual costs of making the batch. Any significant differences or 'variances' will need to be investigated.

SUMMARY – SPECIFIC ORDER COSTING

The diagram below summarises the costing methods for specific orders. Note that each of these separate pieces of work is a **cost object**, ie an item for which costs can be ascertained.

SPECIFIC ORDERS (separate pieces of work)

job costing	**batch costing**
for example:	for example:
• making one racing bike	• brewing a batch of beer
• preparing one client's accounts	• producing a batch of wallpaper
• putting a central heating system into one house	• baking a batch of loaves

---

COSTING METHODS FOR CONTINUOUS WORK

In both manufacturing and service industries, work may be done continuously rather than in separate jobs. This requires specific costing methods appropriate to those types of business. For example:

- a bus company runs a continuous service of buses, available for customers to use, and customers pay for their use of the service – the output will be costed using the **service costing** method

- in the manufacture of chocolate bars, production is a continuous process and the chocolate bars are available for customers to buy at all times – the output will be costed using the **unit costing** method

These two methods are summarised as follows:

CONTINUOUS WORK

service costing	**unit costing**
for example:	for example:
• running a nursing home	• making bikes
• providing a bus service	• manufacturing cars
• providing banking services	• manufacturing paint or chemicals

---

CONTINUOUS WORK: SERVICE COSTING

Service businesses are where work is done continuously rather than in separate jobs. Examples of service businesses are:

- a nursing home
- a bus service
- banking services
- room hire

Such businesses use **service costing** to establish the unit cost of the service provided. For example, the cost per passenger mile of a bus or train service, or the cost per student hour at a school or college. Service costing can be used for both external services, as above, and for internal services within the business, such as the unit service cost of issuing an item from a stores department to the production department.

Features of service costing are:

- the use of composite cost units (see page 5), such as patient/day, passenger/mile, room hire/day
- a low level of direct materials, in relation to total costs
- intangible output, in the form of performance, rather than tangible finished goods

The calculation of the cost per service unit is:

$$\frac{total\ costs\ of\ providing\ the\ service\ for\ the\ period}{number\ of\ service\ units\ for\ the\ period} = cost\ per\ service\ unit$$

Once the cost per service unit is known, for external services, a mark-up can be applied in order to calculate the amount to be charged to the customer.

worked example – service costing

A nursing home has capacity for fifteen residents at any one time. The home achieves an occupancy rate of 80%, ie an average of twelve beds are occupied at any one time. Costs for last year were:

	£
food and other supplies	54,580
nursing and medical staff	232,680
other support services	45,300
overheads	58,820
	391,380

The cost per day of each resident is calculated as follows:

- The occupancy in days is (15 residents x 365 days) x 80% = 4,380 days

- Cost per day per resident is: $\dfrac{\text{total cost}}{\text{number of days}} = \dfrac{£391,380}{4,380} = £89.36$ per resident

- This is the service unit cost for this organisation

CONTINUOUS WORK: UNIT COSTING

Unit costing is used by businesses that continuously produce a single product. Here the cost objects are identical and have the same costs. Units are measured in terms of output, including liquids (eg per litre), areas (eg per square metre), weights (eg per kilogram), etc.

The cost per unit is calculated as

$$\frac{total\ costs\ of\ production\ for\ the\ period}{number\ of\ units\ for\ the\ period} = cost\ per\ unit$$

Total costs comprise material, labour and overheads. Once the cost per unit is known, a mark-up can be applied in order to calculate the amount to be charged to the customer.

Two considerations for unit costing are:

- how to calculate the number of units and value of work-in-progress at a given time
- how to account for wastage, both normal and abnormal wastage

These are explained and calculated in the sections which follow.

WORK-IN-PROGRESS – EQUIVALENT UNITS

Cost calculations are more straightforward when all the items on the production line are completed at the end of the accounting period. In a more complex environment there will be items that have been started but not completed. This is known as **part-finished goods** or **work-in-progress** – see also Chapter 2 (page 59) – which can be calculated using either FIFO or AVCO.

For example, the production line at a car factory will always have cars which vary from being only just started, to those nearing the end of the line which are almost complete.

In calculating the cost per unit, it is necessary to take into account the degree of completeness of the work-in-progress. This is done by making equivalent unit calculations:

number of units in progress x percentage of completeness = equivalent units

Thus, 100 units which are exactly 40% complete are equal to 40 completed units.

The formula for calculating the cost per unit now becomes:

$$\frac{total\ cost\ of\ production}{number\ of\ units\ of\ output\ +\ equivalent\ units\text{-}in\text{-}progress} = cost\ per\ unit$$

worked example – work-in-progress

Racers Limited manufactures racing bikes. The company has just started production of a new model, the 'Triple X'. The figures for the first month's production are:

total cost of production	£8,500
units completed	40 bikes
units-in-progress	20 bikes

The units-in-progress are exactly half-finished. The equivalent units-in-progress, and the cost per bike, for the month are as follows:

completed units		= 40 bikes
equivalent units	20 x 50%	= 10 bikes
cost per unit	$\dfrac{£8,500}{40 + 10}$	= £170 per bike

Although, in the example above, it was assumed that the work-in-progress was exactly half-finished, this may well not be the case for all the elements of cost. For example, while direct materials might be 100% complete, direct labour and variable production overheads might be 50% complete.

Allowance has to be made for these differences in the calculation of the valuation of work-in-progress, and the layout used in the example below is one way in which the calculations can be made.

worked example – work-in-progress

The Toy Manufacturing Company makes a plastic toy called a 'Humber-Wumber'. The figures for the first month's production are:

direct materials	£6,600
direct labour	£3,500
production overheads	£4,000
units completed	900
units-in-progress	200

The units-in-progress are complete as regards materials, but are 50% complete for direct labour and production overheads.

Cost element	Costs	Completed units	Work-in-progress			Total equivalent units	Cost per unit	WIP value
			Units	% complete	Equivalent units			
	A	B	C	D	E	F	G	H
					C x D	B + E	A ÷ F	E x G
	£			%			£	£
Direct materials	6,600	900	200	100	200	1,100	6.00	1,200
Direct labour	3,500	900	200	50	100	1,000	3.50	350
Production overheads	4,000	900	200	50	100	1,000	4.00	400
Total	14,100						13.50	1,950

Note: columns are lettered to show how calculations are made.

Using an average cost basis (AVCO), the cost per unit of the first month's production and the month-end valuation figure for work-in-progress (WIP) is as follows:

900 completed units at £13.50 each	=	£12,150
work-in-progress valuation	=	£1,950
		———
costs for month	=	£14,100

ACCOUNTING FOR WASTAGE

An important aspect of most costing methods is that you don't always get out what you put in, ie there is often **wastage**. This is illustrated by the example of ordering a steak in a restaurant; the menu will say '250g fillet steak' (explaining that this is the uncooked weight); what comes on the plate will weigh rather less because, when the steak is grilled, fat and liquids are cooked away. Thus, by cooking a steak, the output is less than the input.

The aspect of costing where you don't get out what you put in is described as a **normal wastage**. This is unavoidable wastage arising during the production process. For example, the normal wastage on a 250g steak might be 50g. Normal wastage, which occurs as a result of factors such as evaporation, shrinkage, breakage, sampling and testing, are included as part of the cost of the output.

Once a standard of normal wastage has been established, this then forms the expectation for future production. Any variation from this normal wastage is treated separately in the bookkeeping as **abnormal wastage**.

If any of the normal wastage can be sold as **scrap sales**, the amount of money received is treated as a reduction in the total costs of production. Examples include: wood chippings and shavings sold off from a fence manufacturer, scrap metal from an engineering company.

The **production account** gathers together the costs of production (that is the inputs of material, labour and overheads) and records the amounts of normal and abnormal wastage.

Here the production account is credited with the expected quantity of normal wastage. No money amounts are recorded but a note of the wastage is recorded against production. In this way, the cost of normal wastage is included as part of the costs of the output.

For example, 11,000 kg of materials are input into production, with normal wastage of 1,000 kg, giving 10,000 kg as finished goods:

Dr				Production			Cr
	quantity kg	unit cost £	total cost £		quantity kg	unit cost £	total cost £
Inputs*	11,000	1.00	11,000	Normal wastage	1,000	-	-
				Finished goods	10,000	1.10	11,000
	11,000		11,000		11,000		11,000

* inputs = material, labour and overheads

Here it can be seen that the cost of inputs is £1 per kg but, after normal wastage, the cost of finished goods is £1.10 per kg (£11,000 ÷ 10,000 kg). Thus normal wastage has been absorbed into the cost of output.

The cost bookkeeping entries are shown diagrammatically as follows:

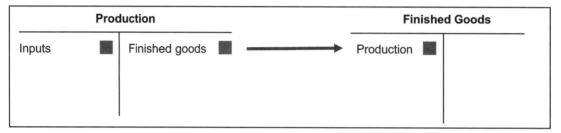

abnormal wastage

Abnormal wastage is where output is lower than after normal wastage. For example:

	kg
inputs	11,000
less normal wastage	1,000
expected output	10,000
actual output	9,400
abnormal wastage	600

The value of abnormal wastage is credited to the production account at the same cost per unit for output after allowing for normal wastage. Referring to the normal wastage from the production account, above, this will be £1.10 per kg. The production account with both normal and abnormal wastage is as follows:

Dr				Production			Cr
	quantity kg	unit cost £	total cost £		quantity kg	unit cost £	total cost £
Inputs	11,000	1.00	11,000	Normal wastage	1,000	-	-
				Finished goods	9,400	1.10	10,340
				Abnormal wastage	600	1.10	660
	11,000		11,000		11,000		11,000

Both the transfer to finished goods and the abnormal wastage are valued at the cost per unit of the expected output of £1.10 per kg, which gives:

finished goods   9,400 kg x £1.10 = £10,340

abnormal wastage   600 kg x £1.10 = £660

The amount of abnormal wastage is debited to a separate expense account:

Dr	Abnormal Wastage		Cr
	£		£
Production	660		

In this way, the cost of abnormal wastage is not charged to production – and management of the business will need to identify the reasons for the wastage. At the end of the financial year, the balance of abnormal wastage account is debited to the statement of profit or loss:

- debit statement of profit or loss
- credit abnormal wastage account

By doing this, abnormal wastage is treated as a period cost instead of being included with production cost and carried forward in the valuation of closing inventory.

The cost bookkeeping entries are shown diagrammatically below:

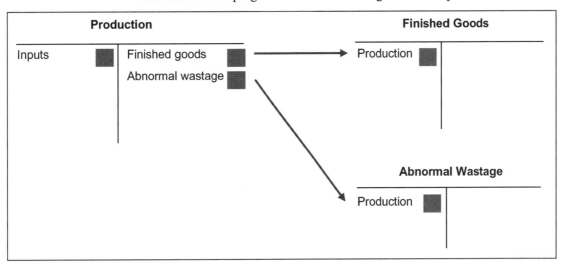

scrap sales

Wastage can often be sold as scrap, eg scrap metal from an engineering company. Where there are revenues from scrap sales for both normal wastage and abnormal wastage, we must be careful to distinguish between the two amounts:

■ revenue from normal wastage is credited to the production account, where it reduces the cost of production (including the cost of abnormal wastage – see example below)

■ revenue from abnormal wastage is credited to abnormal wastage account, so reducing the cost of abnormal wastage

In the example, which follows on with the same costs used before, all wastage – both normal and abnormal – is sold at a price of 50p per kg (which is received into the bank account). Remember that expected output is 10,000 kg, but actual output is 9,400 kg.

Dr				**Production**				Cr
	quantity kg	unit cost £	total cost £		quantity kg	unit cost £	total cost £
Inputs	11,000	1.00	11,000	Normal wastage	1,000	0.50	500
				Finished goods	9,400	1.05	9,870
				Abnormal wastage	600	1.05	630
	11,000		11,000		11,000		11,000

Both the transfer to finished goods and the abnormal wastage are valued at the cost per unit of the expected output, ie 10,000 kg.

$$\frac{\text{input cost} - \text{scrap value of normal wastage}}{\text{expected output}} = \frac{£11,000 - £500}{10,000 \text{ kg}} = £1.05 \text{ per kg}$$

This gives:

Finished goods 9,400 kg x £1.05   = £9,870

Abnormal wastage 600 kg x £1.05   = £630

The value of abnormal wastage is debited to abnormal wastage account; the revenue received from scrap sales is credited to the account:

Dr		**Abnormal Wastage**		Cr
	£			£
Production	630	Bank (600 kg x 50p)		300

At the end of the financial year, the balance of this account (£630 – £300 = £330) is debited to the statement of profit or loss.

The value of normal wastage is debited to normal wastage account and revenue received from scrap sales is credited – this leaves a nil balance on the account as follows:

Dr		Normal Wastage	Cr
	£		£
Production	500	Bank (from scrap sales)	500

The cost bookkeeping entries are shown diagrammatically as follows:

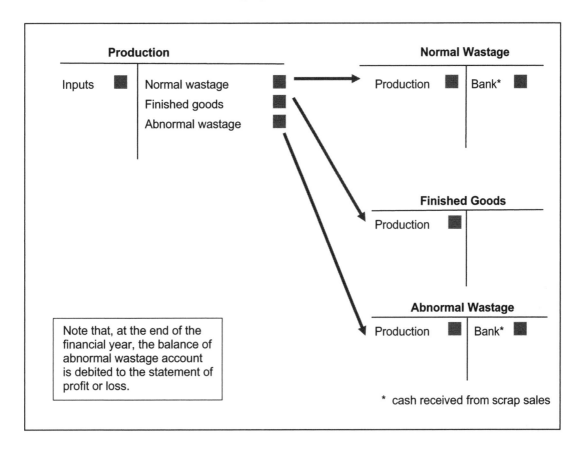

SPREADSHEET SKILLS FOR MANAGEMENT ACCOUNTING

using spreadsheets to cost production

In this chapter, you have studied how different types of costing are suitable for different products. The products used as illustrations have been quite simple, with a few direct and indirect costs. In real life, a job, such as fitting a kitchen, may have many different direct and indirect costs, which need to be included in the cost calculations when quoting for a job. Similarly, the costs of providing an hour of care to an elderly person at home is not simply the wages of the carer but must allow for all related costs.

Spreadsheets can be a useful aid to help a salesperson include all relevant costs in a quote or to ensure production are including all the costs of making a batch of items, including items such as waste. As additional costs are determined, which must be included in the cost of a job, batch, product or service, the relevant costing spreadsheets will be added to and amended. It is important to be aware of this when building a spreadsheet, so formulas and graphs update automatically, where possible.

Let's work through the Case Study for Cakes and Bakes by Karim Ltd together, seeing how spreadsheets can be used for costing products.

Case Study

SPREADSHEET SKILLS TO PROVIDE MANAGEMENT ACCOUNTING INFORMATION

situation

Cakes and Bakes by Karim Ltd is a small owner-managed business operating from a shop in Bradford. It is run by Karim, who makes fresh cakes, buns and bread daily, using batch production. You are its bookkeeper and Karim has asked you to help him look at the costs and pricing of one of its products, a large chocolate fudge cake supplied to local restaurants and sold as birthday cakes.

Download the spreadsheet file 'MATST Ch 5 Spreadsheet Case Study Cakes & Bakes by Karim Ltd data' from the Osborne Books website.

Save the spreadsheet file in an appropriate location and rename it 'MATST Ch 5 Spreadsheet Case Study Cakes & Bakes by Karim Ltd answer'.

Open the renamed file.

In the worksheet called 'Batch costs', you are required to:

1   Use the **COUNT** function in D3, to determine the number of batches. **Fill** cell G3 in orange.

2   **Merge and centre** the title 'Actual cost per batch' over columns F to R.

3   Change the **format** in F8:S15 to **currency** to two decimal places.

4   Use **formulas** to **calculate** the direct labour cost per batch (in row 17) and the overhead absorbed (in row 18), based on labour hours, using the information in D4 and D5 respectively.

5   In column S, use the **AVERAGE** function, to determine the average cost per batch of each material (S8:S15), the direct labour hours (S16), the direct labour (S17) and the overheads absorbed (S18).

6   Use **wrap text**, so the title 'Average cost per batch' in column S can be clearly read.

7   Use **formulas** to complete the average cost per batch of direct materials, direct labour, overheads and total cost, in C22 to C25. **Calculate** the prime cost per cake (C27) and the total cost per cake (C28), using the batch size in C2.

8   Use a **formula** to **calculate** the amount of markup of 45% in C29 and **ROUND** to two decimal places. **Calculate** the selling price in C30.

9   Use a top and double bottom **border** to highlight the 'Total cost' and a double underline **border** to highlight the 'Selling price'. **Fill** cells A21:C31 in light green.

solution

The 'Batch costs' worksheet currently looks like this:

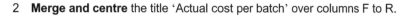

	A	B	C	D	E	F	G	H	I	J	K	L	M	N	O	P	Q	R	S	T
1	Information for batches of chocolate fudge cakes																			
2	Batch size			30																
3	Number of batches																			
4	Cost per labour hour			£15.00																
5	Overhead rate per labour hour			£8.00																
6						Actual cost per batch														
7	Direct costs		Per cake	Per batch		01-Mar	06-Mar	14-Mar	18-Mar	21-Mar	23-Mar	31-Mar	04-Apr	08-Apr	14-Apr	17-Apr	22-Apr	26-Apr	Average co	
8	Self raising flour		0.35	10.5		6.30	6.49	6.62	6.48	6.30	5.99	6.43	6.49	6.30	6.10	6.29	6.49	6.30		
9	Eggs		6	180		45.00	42.00	45.00	46.00	41.00	45.00	42.00	40.00	43.00	41.00	40.00	42.00	43.00		
10	Sugar		0.35	10.5		19.95	21.00	20.50	19.80	20.50	22.00	19.65	21.20	20.80	19.90	20.40	20.60	19.80		
11	Butter		0.3	9		61.04	63.17	64.59	63.10	61.04	57.90	62.41	63.17	61.01	58.84	60.98	63.17	61.04		
12	Vanilla extract		1	30		9.00	9.10	9.20	9.00	8.90	9.00	9.10	9.30	9.30	9.00	9.10	9.00	8.90		
13	Cocoa powder		0.15	4.5		65.16	63.00	62.00	65.00	63.00	61.00	62.00	60.00	61.00	63.00	60.00	62.00	63.00		
14	Double cream		0.2	6		95.56	92.76	91.89	90.65	86.56	81.23	88.69	89.76	86.52	83.26	86.46	89.76	86.56		
15	Chocolate, kg		0.2	6		12.00	12.50	11.50	12.00	11.50	11.00	12.00	11.50	12.50	12.20	12.00	12.60	13.00		
16	Direct labour, hrs			4		5.00	5.20	5.00	5.40	5.00	5.20	5.10	5.00	5.00	5.10	5.00	5.00	5.20		
17	Direct labour cost per batch																			
18	Overhead absorbed (labour hours)																			
19																				
20																				
21	Average cost per batch		£																	
22	Direct materials																			
23	Direct labour																			
24	Overheads																			
25	Total cost																			
26	Cost per cake		£																	
27	Prime cost																			
28	Total cost																			
29	Markup: 45%																			
30	Selling price																			

The **COUNT** function is useful when you need to know how many numbers are in a set of data. **COUNTA** will count cells with data in, ie not blank, and not just numbers.

The formula in D3 is straightforward to complete:

=COUNT(F7:R7)

so the average cost per batch is based on 13 batches of chocolate fudge cake. The remaining skills used in points 1 to 3 are those we have used before, so compare your answer to the worksheet below, once these are completed.

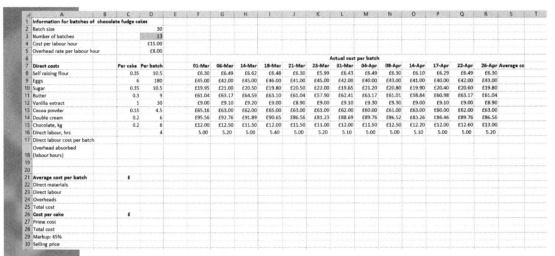

The direct labour cost per batch is the cost per labour hour of £15 in D4 multiplied by the hours for each batch in row 16, using absolute referencing. So, for example, in J17 the formula for the direct labour cost for the batch made on 21 March is:

=J16*$D$4

The calculation of the overheads absorbed per batch is similar to the labour costs per batch, so in J18, the formula is:

=$D$5*J16

The **AVERAGE** function is required in point 5 and is available using the Insert Function on the Formulas ribbon. If you do not know how to use the **AVERAGE** function, refer to the Osborne Books Spreadsheets for Management Accounting Tutorial to find out.

The formula used in S17, for example, is:

=AVERAGE(F17:R17)

Once points 1 to 6 are completed, the worksheet looks like this:

A	B	C	D	E	F	G	H	I	J	K	L	M	N	O	P	Q	R	S
1 Information for batches of chocolate fudge cakes																		
2 Batch size			30															
3 Number of batches			13															
4 Cost per labour hour			£15.00															
5 Overhead rate per labour hour			£8.00															
6											Actual cost per batch							
7 Direct costs		Per cake	Per batch		01-Mar	06-Mar	14-Mar	18-Mar	21-Mar	23-Mar	31-Mar	04-Apr	08-Apr	14-Apr	17-Apr	22-Apr	26-Apr	Average cost per batch
8 Self raising flour		0.35	10.5		£6.30	£6.49	£6.62	£6.48	£6.30	£5.99	£6.43	£6.49	£6.30	£6.10	£6.29	£6.49	£6.30	£6.35
9 Eggs		6	180		£45.00	£42.00	£45.00	£46.00	£41.00	£45.00	£42.00	£40.00	£43.00	£41.00	£40.00	£42.00	£43.00	£42.69
10 Sugar		0.35	10.5		£19.95	£21.00	£20.50	£19.80	£20.50	£22.00	£19.65	£21.20	£20.80	£19.90	£20.40	£20.60	£19.80	£20.47
11 Butter		0.3	9		£61.04	£63.17	£64.59	£63.10	£61.04	£57.90	£62.41	£63.17	£61.01	£58.84	£60.98	£63.17	£61.04	£61.65
12 Vanilla extract		1	30		£9.00	£9.10	£9.20	£9.00	£8.90	£9.00	£9.10	£9.30	£9.30	£9.00	£9.10	£9.00	£8.90	£9.07
13 Cocoa powder		0.15	4.5		£65.16	£63.00	£62.00	£65.00	£63.00	£61.00	£62.00	£60.00	£61.00	£63.00	£60.00	£62.00	£63.00	£62.32
14 Double cream		0.2	6		£95.56	£92.76	£91.89	£90.65	£86.56	£81.23	£88.69	£89.76	£86.52	£83.26	£86.46	£89.76	£86.56	£88.44
15 Chocolate, kg		0.2	6		£12.00	£12.50	£11.50	£12.00	£11.50	£11.00	£12.00	£11.50	£12.50	£12.20	£12.00	£12.60	£13.00	£12.02
16 Direct labour, hrs			4		5.00	5.20	5.00	5.40	5.00	5.20	5.10	5.00	5.00	5.10	5.00	5.00	5.20	5.09
17 Direct labour cost per batch					£75.00	£78.00	£75.00	£81.00	£75.00	£78.00	£76.50	£75.00	£75.00	£76.50	£75.00	£75.00	£78.00	£76.38
18 Overhead absorbed (labour hours)					£40.00	£41.60	£40.00	£43.20	£40.00	£41.60	£40.80	£40.00	£40.00	£40.80	£40.00	£40.00	£41.60	£40.74
19																		
20																		
21 Average cost per batch		£																
22 Direct materials																		
23 Direct labour																		
24 Overheads																		
25 Total cost																		
26 Cost per cake		£																
27 Prime cost																		
28 Total cost																		
29 Markup: 45%																		
30 Selling price																		

The average cost per batch information, summarised in C22 to C25, and the prime and total cost per cake all use straightforward formula. These are shown below:

	A	B	C	D
21	**Average cost per batch**		**£**	
22	Direct materials		=SUM(S8:S15)	
23	Direct labour		=S17	
24	Overheads		=S18	
25	Total cost		=SUM(C22:C24)	
26	**Cost per cake**		**£**	
27	Prime cost		=(C23+C22)/D2	
28	Total cost		=C25/D2	
29	Markup: 45%		=ROUND(+C28*0.45,2)	
30	Selling price		=C28+C29	
31				
32				
33				
34				

Markup and margin are both used when calculating the selling price of a product, so you must be careful to read which one is required. The markup on cost of 45% is the total cost per cake multiplied by 45%.

Finally, adding the total cost and the markup for each cake gives the selling price. After completing point 9, compare your answer to the worksheet below.

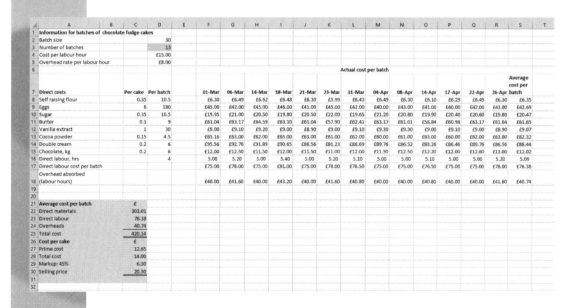

You can download the answer file, 'MATST Ch 5 Spreadsheet Skills Case Study Cakes & Bakes by Karim Ltd answer', from the Osborne Books website to compare your answer in detail.

Chapter Summary

- The method chosen for cost accounting within a business depends on the kind of work being done.

- In manufacturing and in service industries, work may consist of separately identifiable jobs or it may be continuous.

- Separately identifiable jobs are usually done to a customer's specific order.

- The costing method to be used for specific orders is:
  - job costing for a single unit of work
  - batch costing for a batch of identical units

- The costing method to be used for continuous work is:
  - service costing for service businesses
  - unit costing for manufacturing processes

- To obtain a cost per cost unit for continuous work, the total costs for a time period are collected together, then divided by the number of cost units produced or provided in the time period, ie:

$$\frac{total\ costs\ for\ the\ period}{number\ of\ units\ for\ the\ period} = cost\ per\ unit$$

- If there is work-in-progress at the end of the period, the number of equivalent complete units is calculated, for example 500 units that are 50% complete are equivalent to 500 x 50% = 250 completed units.

- Cost bookkeeping uses a production account to calculate the cost per unit of output. Possible outcomes to be recorded in the accounts are:
  - normal wastage, with or without scrap sales
  - abnormal wastage, with or without scrap sales

  At the end of a financial year, the balance of abnormal wastage account is debited to the statement of profit or loss.

Key Terms		
	costing method	techniques used to collect costs and to calculate the total cost of output
	job/batch costing	a form of specific order costing which applies costs to jobs/batches
	job cost record	record (often on a computer database) which shows the estimated and actual direct and indirect costs for a particular job
	variance	the difference between an estimated cost and an actual cost
	unit costing	method of costing for continuous manufacturing processes
	service costing	method of costing for service industries
	work-in-progress (WIP)	part-finished goods at a particular time
	equivalent units	number of units in progress x percentage of completeness
	production account	bookkeeping account which calculates the cost per unit of output
	normal wastage	unavoidable wastage arising from the production process
	abnormal wastage	where the wastage in a process is greater than the normal wastage
	scrap sales	money received from sale of normal and abnormal wastage

Activities

5.1 State, with reasons, the method of costing you think would be appropriate for:

- an accountant
- a bus company
- a baker
- a sports centre
- a hotel
- a wedding

5.2 A clothing manufacturer has been asked to give a quotation for the supply of a batch of uniforms for a band. Materials for the uniforms will be:

- 100 metres of cloth at £7.50 per metre
- 75 metres of braiding at £4.00 per metre

It is estimated that the job will take the machinists a total of 28 hours.

They are paid at the rate of £12.50 per hour.

The overhead absorption rate is £10.00 per direct labour hour.

You are to:

(a) Calculate the total cost of the job.

(b) Calculate the selling price if the company is to make a profit of 20% on the total cost price.

5.3   Rowcester Engineering Limited is asked to quote for the supply of a replacement cylinder head for a large stationary engine installed in a local factory.

The item will need to be cast in the foundry and then passed to the finishing shop for machining to specification.

Materials needed will be a 100 kg ingot of high-strength steel, which costs £10 per kg.

Direct labour will be 10 hours in the foundry, and 15 hours in the finishing shop. It will need 12 hours of machine hours in the finishing shop.

Foundry workers are paid £15 per hour, while machine operators in the finishing shop are paid £12 per hour.

Overheads are charged on the basis of 80% of direct labour cost in the foundry, and on the basis of £20 per machine hour in the finishing shop.

Profit is to be 25% of cost price.

You are to complete the following job cost record to show the estimated total cost of the job, and the selling price.

JOB COST RECORD Replacement Cylinder Head	£
Direct Materials	
Direct Labour	
Foundry:	
Finishing:	
Overheads	
Foundry:	
Finishing:	
TOTAL COST	
Profit	
SELLING PRICE	

5.4   MC Resurfacing Ltd surfaces and upgrades surfaces of carparks.

You are calculating a quotation for job MC980. You have been given a partly completed spreadsheet by your manager to assist you in this task that includes some of the relevant cost information for the job.

The job will be completed in period 27, three months from now. The tarmac PM821, required for the job had been subject to price increases, so you must forecast the expected cost in period 27 for this material. You must then complete the job cost calculations.

You have been given the direct labour rates for each team.

Site preparation team £15 per hour

Tarmac laying team £18.10 per hour

The sales manager would like you to produce a graph, showing her the relevant costs and margin of this job.

Download the spreadsheet file 'MATST Chapter 5 Activities data' from the Osborne Books website.

Save the spreadsheet file in an appropriate location and rename it to 'MATST Chapter 5 Activities answers', so you can refer back to it.

Open the renamed file.

On the worksheet '5.4 Forecast PM821', you are required to:

1   Use **FORECAST** to determine the price per tonne of PM821 for period 27. **Fill** the specific quote information cells (B28:C28) in green.

On the worksheet '5.4 Job cost', you are required to:

2   **Link** the forecast price per tonne calculated on worksheet '5.4 Forecast PM821' to the relevant price cell and use **ROUND** to **calculate** it to two decimal places. **Centre align** the titles for rows 4 and 5.

3   **Enter** the labour rates for the direct labour elements of the job.

4   Using appropriate **formulas, calculate** the cost for each element of the job and the total cost in column E.

5   Use **formulas** to find the margin of 20% in E16 and the selling price in E17.

6   Use an **IF statement** in E18 to confirm the margin (E16) is the correct % of the selling price (E17), stating 'OK' if it is correct and 'Check' if it is not.

7   **Add a comment** to E9, 'Confirmed with Site Prep Manager'.

8   **Copy** the worksheet '5.4 Job cost' and paste it into the worksheet named 'MC980 graph'.

On the worksheet '5.4 Job MC980 graph', you are required to:

9   **Hide** rows 8,11,14 and 15 and columns B to D.

10   **Insert a 3D pie chart** showing the costs and margin. Label the chart 'Quotation for Job MC980 - Total selling price £22,045'.

11   Add **data labels** showing the amount and %.

12   **Change the colour** for the segments 'Site preparation O/H' to light blue and 'Margin 20%' to light green.

13   Move the **legend** to the right-hand side of the graph.

14   **Resize the graph** so it can be easily read.

15   **Amend the header** to show 'Quotation for Job MC980'.

Save the worksheet and check your answers at the back of the book or using the spreadsheet 'MATST Chapter 5 Activities answers' on the Osborne Books website, www.osbornebooks.co.uk.

5.5 City Transit plc is a small train operating company which runs passenger rail services on a commuter line in a large city. The line links the docks area, which has been redeveloped with flats and houses, with the city centre, and then runs on through the suburbs. An intensive service is operated from early morning to late at night carrying people to and from work, school children, shoppers and leisure travellers.

The tracks that City Transit uses are leased from the track owner, Railnet plc.

The modern fleet of six electric trains is owned and maintained by City Transit.

The following information is available from the computer system in respect of last year's operations:

	Cost	Estimated life
Electric trains	£1,300,000 each	20 years

Depreciation is on a straight-line basis, assuming a residual value of £100,000 for each train.

Leasing charges for track	£1,000,000 pa
Maintenance charges for trains	£910,000 pa
Power for trains	£210,000 pa
Wages of drivers and conductors	£480,000 pa
Administration	£520,000 pa

There were one million passenger journeys last year with an average distance travelled of four miles.

You are to calculate the total cost per passenger mile (to two decimal places) of operating the railway for last year.

5.6 A manufacturer of plastic toys has the following information from its computer system concerning the first month of production:

Direct materials	£11,500
Direct labour	£9,000
Production overheads	£18,000
Toys completed	20,000
Toys in progress	5,000

The work-in-progress is complete as regards materials, but is 50% complete as regards direct labour and production overheads.

You are to complete the following layout to show the cost per toy (to two decimal places) of the first month's production and the month-end valuation for work-in-progress.

Cost element	Costs	Completed units	Work-in-progress			Total equivalent units	Cost per unit	WIP valuation
			Units	% complete	Equivalent units			
	A	B	C	D	E	F	G	H
	£				C x D	B + E	A ÷ F £	E x G £
Direct materials								
Direct labour								
Production overheads								
Total								

5.7 Agro Chemicals Limited produces a chemical.

For the four weeks ended 27 February 20-8, the company input 22,000 litres of direct materials, had an output of 20,000 litres and a normal wastage of 2,000 litres. The input costs were: materials £5,500, labour £3,300, overheads £2,200. Normal wastage was sold to a specialist reprocessing company for 20p per litre.

There was no opening or closing inventory at the beginning and end of production; all output was complete.

(a) As an Accounts Assistant, you are to complete the following production account for the four weeks ended 27 February 20-8.

Dr	Quantity	Unit cost	Total cost	Production Account	Quantity	Unit cost	Total cost	Cr
	(litres)	£	£		(litres)	£	£	
Materials				Normal wastage				
Labour				Finished goods				
Overheads								

(b) Identify the entry to be made in normal wastage account:

	Debit £	Credit £
Normal wastage account		

5.8 GrowFast Limited produces a granular lawn fertiliser.

For the four weeks ended 21 May 20-7, the company input 42,000 kg of direct materials and had an output of 39,500 kg – the difference of 2,500 kg was made up of normal wastage of 2,000 kg and abnormal wastage of 500 kg.

The input costs were: materials £10,500, labour £4,200, overheads £2,100. All wastage was sold to a specialist reprocessing company for 20p per kg.

There was no opening or closing inventory at the beginning and end of production; all output was complete.

As an Accounts Assistant, you are to complete the following production account, the abnormal wastage account, and the normal wastage account for the four weeks ended 21 May 20-7.

Dr				Production Account			Cr
	Quantity (kg)	Unit cost £	Total cost £		Quantity (kg)	Unit cost £	Total cost £
Materials				Normal wastage			
Labour				Finished goods			
Overheads				Abnormal wastage			

Dr	Normal Wastage Account	Cr
£		£

Dr	Abnormal Wastage Account	Cr
£		£

5.9   Excalibur Limited, a manufacturing business, uses both batch and unit costing as appropriate in its Production Department. It is currently costing a new product, EX321 which will start production in batches of 24,000 units.

From the computer database it is estimated that the following costs will be incurred in producing one batch of 24,000 units of EX321:

Product EX321 cost estimates	£ per batch
Direct materials	8,400
Direct labour	6,240
Variable overheads	4,560
Fixed manufacturing overheads	3,600
Fixed administration, selling and distribution costs	2,880
Total costs	25,680

You are to:

(a)   Calculate the prime cost of one unit of EX321.

£ _____

(b)   Calculate the full absorption cost of one unit of EX321.

£ _____

(c)   Calculate the marginal cost of one unit of EX321.

£ _____

(d)   Calculate the marginal production cost of one batch of EX321.

£ _____

(e)   Calculate the full absorption cost of one batch of EX321.

£ _____

5.10 PeachTree Ltd manufactures fashion clothes. In current production is a batch of 1,500 'Bude' jackets. The cost of the batch has been estimated as follows:

- Direct material

  - Cloth, design number P20, 2,500 metres at £5.50 per metre

  - Lining, type Y45, 2,000 metres at £2.50 per metre

- Direct labour

  - Cutting, 1,200 hours at £14 per hour

  - Sewing, 2,000 hours at £12 per hour

  - Finishing, 750 hours at £15 per hour

- Variable production overhead is £6 per direct labour hour

- Fixed production overhead is £15,000 per batch

(a) Complete the cost card for the batch of Bude jackets.

Cost card for 1,500 'Bude' jackets	£
Direct material:	
Cloth	
Lining	
Total direct material	
Direct labour:	
Cutting	
Sewing	
Finishing	
Total direct labour	
Variable production overhead	
Fixed production overhead	
Total estimated absorption cost	

(b)   Show the journal entry to transfer the cost of direct labour for finishing to production of the batch.

Select your journal entries from the following list: Bank, Production, Payables ledger control, Receivables ledger control, Wages control.

Debit		
Credit		

(c)   Calculate the estimated prime cost per batch.

£ [   ]

Calculate the estimated marginal cost per batch.

£ [   ]

(d)   PeachTree Ltd will sell each of the 'Bude' jackets for £110.

Calculate the total revenue PeachTree will receive for the batch.

£ [   ]

Calculate the estimated profit for each jacket.

£ [   ]

5.11   You work as an Assistant Accountant for Nixon Garden Furniture Ltd, a company making garden furniture. You have been asked to cost an order for 600 deckchairs from a hotel chain and determine the possible margin %. Your colleague, who left recently, had started this quotation using a spreadsheet and you must now finish it.

You have been given the following information for the batch:

Direct materials:

Weather-proof canvas: 1,200 metres costing £8.50 per metre

Wood: 3,600 metres of dowelling at £4 per metre

Direct labour:

Cover makers are outsourced and paid £6 per cover.

Frame makers are paid £15 per hour, with 25% premium for overtime. Overtime is classed as a direct cost. It will take 800 hrs to make the deckchairs, including 200 hrs of overtime.

Assembly staff are paid £15 per hour, plus £0.80 per deckchair completed. It usually takes 20 minutes to assemble each deckchair.

Overheads

Variable production is £3 per direct labour hour.

Fixed production overheads are £5,000.

The price is £135 per deckchair.

Download the spreadsheet file 'MATST Chapter 5 Activities data' from the Osborne Books website if you have not already done so.

Save the spreadsheet file in an appropriate location and rename it to 'MATST Chapter 5 Activities answers', so you can refer back to it.

Open the renamed file.

On the worksheet '5.11 Quotation 600 DC', you are required to:

1   **Amend the format** for rows 1 & 2 to font size 14 bold.

2   Using **formulas**, complete the direct materials costs (B4 to B5). **Fill the cells** of the direct materials section of the cost card (Columns A & B, rows 3 to 6) in light orange.

3   Use **trace precedents** to find the problem with the total direct labour formula (B11) and correct it.

4   Using **formulas, calculate** the direct labour costs (B8 to B10). **Fill the cells** of the direct labour section of the cost card (Columns A & B, rows 7 to 11) in blue.

5   Using **formulas, calculate** the variable production overhead cost (B12), then complete the fixed production overhead cost (B13). **Fill the cells** of the overheads section of the cost card (Columns A & B, rows 12 to 13) in green.

6   Using a **formula, calculate** the total estimated absorption cost per batch (B14). Put a thick **border** around the cost card (A2:B14).

7   **Format** the cells B4 to B14 to 0,000.

8   Using a **formula, calculate** the marginal cost per batch.

9   Using a **formula, calculate** the estimated revenue per batch. Format cell B18 to **currency** to 0 decimal places.

10   Using a **formula, calculate** the expected profit. Using **conditional formatting**, highlight the expected profit in B20 in green, with black text, if the expected profit exceeds £25,000.

Save the file as 'MATST Chapter 5 Activities answers' and compare this to the answer on the Osborne Books website.

6 Marginal, absorption and activity based costing

this chapter covers...

This chapter studies the costing methods of marginal and absorption costing and compares the profit made by a business under each method. Also included is activity based costing, which has developed from absorption costing.

This chapter explains:

- *the different treatment of product costs and period costs in marginal costing and absorption costing*

- *how marginal costing works, including the calculation of contribution, and its role in short-term decision-making*

- *how absorption costing works, including the valuation of closing inventory*

- *a comparison of profits when marginal costing and absorption costing are used*

- *how activity based costing charges overheads to production on the basis of activities*

MARGINAL AND ABSORPTION COSTING SYSTEMS

These two costing systems are often used in management accounting, but for different purposes:

- marginal costing – helps with short-term decision-making

- absorption costing – is used to calculate inventory valuations and profit or loss in financial statements

The use of each system is dependent on the information needs of the business or organisation:

- 'can we afford to sell 1,000 units of our product each month to Megastores Limited at a discount of 20 per cent?' (use marginal costing)

- 'what profit have we made this year?' (use absorption costing)

These costing systems use the same product and period costs, but they are treated differently according to their behaviour. Remember that:

- product costs are those costs that become part of the manufactured product

- period costs are those costs that cannot be assigned directly to the manufactured product, eg rent of a factory, and are charged in full to the statement of profit or loss

MARGINAL COSTING

Marginal cost is the cost of producing one extra unit of output.

To help with short-term decision-making, costs are classified by their behaviour as either variable costs or fixed costs (with semi-variable costs being split between their fixed and variable parts). Such a classification of costs is used in marginal costing to work out how much it costs to produce each extra unit of output.

Marginal cost is often – but not always – the total of the variable costs of producing a unit of output. For most purposes, marginal costing is not concerned with **fixed period costs** (such as the rent of a factory); instead it is concerned with **variable product costs** – direct materials, direct labour, direct expenses, and variable production overheads – which increase as output increases. For most decision-making, the marginal cost of a unit of output is, therefore, the variable cost of producing one more unit.

Knowing the marginal cost of a unit of output enables the managers of a business to focus on the contribution provided by each unit. The contribution is the sales revenue after marginal/variable product costs have been paid. The contribution formula is:

selling price less variable cost = contribution

Contribution can be calculated on a per unit basis, or for a batch of output (eg 1,000 units), or for a whole business.

It follows that the difference between the sales revenue and the variable costs of the units sold in a period is the total contribution that the sales of all the units in the period make towards the fixed period costs of the business. Once these are covered, the remainder of the contribution is profit.

Thus a business can work out the profit from its operations, using a marginal costing statement, using the total contribution and fixed costs figures:

total contribution less fixed production costs = operating profit

A marginal costing statement can be prepared in the following format:

		£
	Sales revenue	X
less	Variable production costs	X
equals	Contribution	X
less	Fixed production overheads	X
equals	OPERATING PROFIT	X

Note from the marginal costing statement how the contribution goes towards the fixed production overheads and, when they have been covered, goes to covering non-production overheads before calculating profit.

The relationship between marginal costing, contribution and profit is shown in the Case Study which follows.

Case Study

WYVERN BIKE COMPANY: MARGINAL COSTING

situation

The Wyvern Bike Company makes 100 bikes each week and its costs are as follows:

Direct materials	£4,000
Direct labour	£5,000
Production overheads	£5,000

Investigations into the behaviour of costs has revealed the following information:

- direct materials are variable costs

- direct labour is a variable cost

- of the production overheads, £2,000 is a fixed cost, and the remainder is a variable cost

The selling price of each bike is £200.

As an Accounts Assistant at the Wyvern Bike Company, you are asked to:

- calculate the marginal cost of producing each bike

- show the expected contribution per bike

- prepare a marginal costing statement to show clearly the total contribution and the total operating profit each week

solution

Marginal cost per bike

		£
Variable costs per unit:		
	Direct materials (£4,000 ÷ 100)	40
	Direct labour (£5,000 ÷ 100)	50
	Production overheads (£3,000* ÷ 100)	30
	Marginal cost per bike	120

* £5,000 – £2,000 fixed costs

Contribution per bike

	Selling price per bike	200
less	Variable cost per bike	120
equals	Contribution per bike	80

Marginal costing statement

		£	£
	Sales £200 x 100 bikes		20,000
less	Variable costs:		
	Direct materials	4,000	
	Direct labour	5,000	
	Production overheads	3,000	
			12,000
equals	Total contribution		8,000
less	Fixed production overheads		2,000
equals	Operating profit for the week		6,000

ABSORPTION COSTING

Absorption costing absorbs (recovers) the costs of the business amongst the cost units.

Absorption costing answers the question, 'What does it cost to make one unit of output?'

The absorption cost of a unit of output is made up of the following costs:

		£
	Direct materials	X
add	Direct labour	X
add	Direct expenses	X
add	Production overheads (fixed and variable)	X
equals	ABSORPTION COST	X

Note that the production overheads comprise the factory costs of indirect materials, indirect labour, and indirect expenses.

Case Study

WYVERN BIKE COMPANY: ABSORPTION COSTING

situation

The Wyvern Bike Company makes 100 bikes each week and its costs are as follows:

Direct materials	£4,000
Direct labour	£5,000
Production overheads	£5,000

The selling price of each bike is £200.

As an Accounts Assistant at the Wyvern Bike Company, you are asked to:

• calculate the absorption cost of producing each bike

• calculate the total operating profit each week

solution

Absorption cost per bike

Total costs per week:	£
Direct materials	4,000
Direct labour	5,000
Production overheads	5,000
Total cost	14,000

The absorption cost of producing one bike is:

$$\frac{\text{Total cost}}{\text{Units of output}} = \frac{£14,000}{100 \text{ bikes}} = £140 \text{ per bike}$$

Profit each week		£
	Selling price (100 bikes x £200)	20,000
less	Total cost	14,000
equals	Operating profit for the week	6,000

Conclusion

Operating profit for the week of £6,000 is the same as with the marginal costing method, so we could say 'Does it matter whether we use marginal or absorption costing?' The answer to this is that it does:

– marginal costing, with its focus on variable costs and contribution, is useful for short-term decision-making

– absorption costing is a simple method of calculating the cost of output and is used in financial statements for inventory valuation

As the Case Study shows, each cost unit bears an equal proportion of the costs of the production overheads of the business. Because of its simplicity, absorption costing is a widely used system which tells us how much it costs to make one unit of output. It works well where the cost units are identical, eg 100 identical bikes, but is less appropriate where some of the cost units differ in quality, eg 100 bikes, of which 75 are standard models and 25 are handbuilt to the customers' specifications. It also ignores the effect of changes in the level of output on the cost structure. For example, supposing the bike manufacturer reduces output to 50 bikes a week:

▪ will direct materials remain at £40 per bike? (buying materials in smaller quantities might mean higher prices)

▪ will direct labour still be £50 per bike? (with lower production, the workforce may not be able to specialise in certain jobs, and may be less efficient)

▪ will the production overheads remain at £5,000? (perhaps smaller premises can be used and the factory rent reduced)

A further costing method – which has developed from absorption costing – is activity based costing (page 211).

MARGINAL AND ABSORPTION COSTING COMPARED

Marginal costing tells the managers of a business or organisation the cost of producing one extra unit of output. Nevertheless, we must always remember that one of the objectives of the costing system is to ensure that all the costs of a business or organisation are recovered by being charged to production. This is achieved by means of overhead absorption (see Chapter 4). Below is a comparison between marginal and absorption costing:

■ **marginal costing**

Marginal costing recognises that period costs vary with time rather than activity, and identifies the variable production cost of one extra unit. For example, the rent of a factory relates to a certain time period, eg one month, and remains unchanged whether 100 units of output are made or whether 500 units are made (always assuming that the capacity of the factory is at least 500 units); by contrast, the production of one extra unit will incur an increase in variable costs, ie direct materials, direct labour, direct expenses (if any), and variable overheads – this increase is the **marginal cost**.

■ **absorption costing**

This technique absorbs all product costs into each unit of output through the use of an overhead absorption rate (see Chapter 4). Therefore the more units that are produced, the cheaper will be the cost per unit – because the overheads are spread over a greater number of units.

The diagram below demonstrates how the terms in marginal costing relate to the same production costs as those categorised under absorption costing terms. As noted above, when using marginal costing it is the behaviour of the cost – fixed or variable – that is important, not the origin of the cost.

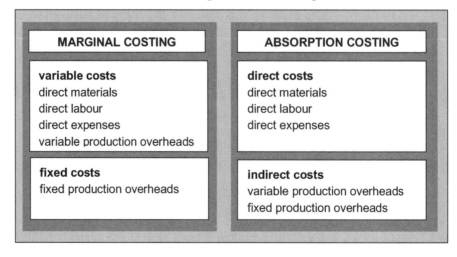

MARGINAL COSTING	ABSORPTION COSTING
variable costs direct materials direct labour direct expenses variable production overheads	**direct costs** direct materials direct labour direct expenses
fixed costs fixed production overheads	**indirect costs** variable production overheads fixed production overheads

The table on page 216 gives a comparison between marginal costing and absorption costing – together with activity based costing (see page 211) – including a note on the usefulness and the limitations of each.

marginal and absorption costing: profit comparisons

Because of the different ways in which marginal costing and absorption costing treat period costs, the two techniques produce different levels of profit when there is a closing inventory figure. This is because, under marginal costing, the closing inventory is valued at variable production cost; by contrast, absorption cost includes a share of fixed production costs in the closing inventory valuation. This is illustrated in the Case Study which follows, looking at the effect of using marginal costing and absorption costing on the statement of profit or loss of a manufacturing business.

The marginal cost approach is often used to help with short-term decision-making (see Chapter 8). However, for financial statements, absorption costing must be used for inventory valuation purposes in order to comply with IAS 2 (see page 48). Under IAS 2, *Inventories*, the closing inventory valuation is based on the product costs of direct materials, direct labour, direct expenses (if any), and production overheads. Note that non-production overheads are not included in either costing method, as they are period costs which are charged to the statement of profit or loss in the year to which they relate.

Although these two methods can be used to calculate different levels of profit, they must not be used to manipulate profits. Those working in accounting must apply ethical principles so that the users of profit statements can be assured that such statements have been prepared with objectivity, ie with no manipulation or bias.

Case Study

CHAIRS LIMITED:
MARGINAL AND ABSORPTION COSTING

situation

Chairs Limited commenced business on 1 January 20-7. It manufactures a special type of chair designed to alleviate back pain. Information on the first year's trading is as follows:

number of chairs manufactured	5,000
number of chairs sold	4,500
selling price	£110 per chair
direct materials	£30 per chair
direct labour	£40 per chair
fixed production overheads	£100,000
non-production overheads	£50,000

As an Accounts Assistant at Chairs Limited, the directors ask for your help in producing profit statements using the marginal costing and absorption costing methods. They say that they will use 'the one that shows the higher profit' to the company's Bank Manager.

solution

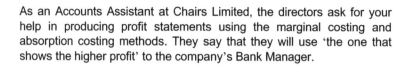

CHAIRS LIMITED

Statement of profit or loss for the year ended 31 December 20-7

	MARGINAL COSTING		ABSORPTION COSTING	
	£	£	£	£
Sales revenue 4,500 at £110 each		495,000		495,000
Variable costs 5,000 chairs				
Direct materials at £30 each	150,000		150,000	
Direct labour at £40 each	200,000		200,000	
Prime cost	350,000		350,000	
Less Closing inventory (marginal cost)				
500 chairs at £70 each	35,000			
		315,000		
Fixed production overheads	100,000		100,000	
				450,000
Less Closing inventory (absorption cost)				
500 chairs at £90 each			45,000	
Less Cost of sales		415,000		405,000
GROSS PROFIT		80,000		90,000
Less Non-production overheads		50,000		50,000
NET PROFIT		30,000		40,000

Tutorial notes:

- Closing inventory is always calculated on the basis of this year's costs:

  marginal costing, variable costs only, ie £30 + £40 = £70 per chair

  absorption costing, variable and fixed costs, ie £450,000 ÷ 5,000 chairs = £90 per chair

- The difference in the profit figures is caused only by the closing inventory figures: £35,000 under marginal costing and £45,000 under absorption costing – the same costs have been used, but fixed production overheads have been treated differently.

- Only fixed production overheads are dealt with differently using the techniques of marginal and absorption costing.

- Non-production overheads are charged in full to the statement of profit or loss in the year to which they relate.

With marginal costing, the full amount of the fixed production overheads has been charged in this year's statement of profit or loss; by contrast, with absorption costing, part of the fixed production overheads (here, £10,000) has been carried forward in the inventory valuation.

With regard to the directors' statement that they will use 'the one that shows the higher profit', the following points should be borne in mind:

- A higher profit does not mean more money in the bank.

- The two methods simply treat fixed production overheads differently and, in a year when there is no closing inventory, total profits to date are exactly the same – but they occur differently over the years. Over time, profits are identical under both methods.

- For financial statements, Chairs Limited must use the absorption cost inventory valuation of £45,000 in order to comply with IAS 2, *Inventories*.

- Ethical considerations must apply – those working in accounting must prepare profit statements without manipulation or bias.

ACTIVITY BASED COSTING

Activity based costing (ABC) charges overheads to production on the basis of activities.

ABC is a costing method which has developed from absorption costing but with a different approach to charging overheads to production. ABC identifies what causes overheads to be incurred, rather than charging total overheads for a particular period. Instead of using overhead recovery methods based around, for example, labour hours or machine hours, ABC uses cost drivers linked to the way in which a business is conducted.

Cost drivers are activities which cause costs to be incurred.

By identifying relevant cost drivers, as illustrated in the Case Study which follows, the cost per unit of a product can be calculated based on its use of activities.

Case Study

AYEBEE LIMITED: ACTIVITY BASED COSTING

situation

AyeBee Limited manufactures two products: Aye and Bee. Aye is a standard product which is produced in batches of 500 units; Bee is a product which is made for a number of customers who each require different specifications – it is produced in batches of 100 units. Each unit of production – whether Aye or Bee – requires one direct labour hour.

Production of each batch of Aye and Bee incurs the following overheads:

- the machinery to be set up at a cost of £400 per batch (to cover the engineer's time and test running of the machinery)

- quality inspection costs of £200 per batch (to cover inspection time and cost of rejects)

In a typical week the company produces 500 units of Aye and 500 units of Bee, so the set up costs and quality inspection costs are:

1 set-up cost of Aye (1 batch) at £400	=	£400
5 set-up costs of Bee (5 batches) at £400	=	£2,000
1 quality inspection of Aye at £200	=	£200
5 quality inspections of Bee at £200	=	£1,000
WEEKLY TOTAL		£3,600

How should AyeBee Limited charge overheads to production?

solution

As each unit of production requires one direct labour hour, ie product Aye 500 hours, product Bee 500 hours, the overhead costs of set-ups and quality inspections, using a direct labour basis, will be charged to production as follows:

Product Aye =	£1,800
Product Bee =	£1,800
TOTAL	£3,600

We can see that this is an incorrect basis on which to charge overheads to production because product Aye required just one set-up and one quality inspection, whereas product Bee required five set-ups and five quality inspections.

By using activity based costing, with set-up and quality inspection as the cost drivers, overheads can be charged to production as follows:

Product Aye:

1 set-up at £400	=	£400
1 quality inspection at £200	=	£200
TOTAL		£600

Product Bee:

5 set-ups at £400	=	£2,000
5 quality inspections at £200	=	£1,000
TOTAL		£3,000

In this way, by using activity based costing, there is a more accurate reflection of the cost of set-ups and quality inspections. The cost of 500 units of product Aye is reduced by £1,200 (ie £1,800 – £600), while the cost of 500 units of product Bee is increased by £1,200 (ie from £1,800 to £3,000). This increased accuracy of costing may have implications for the viability of product Bee, and for the selling price of both products.

other cost drivers

Cost drivers must have a close relationship with an activity, which can then be related to output. Examples of activities and their cost drivers include:

Activity	Cost driver
• set-ups	• number of set-ups
• quality control	• number of quality inspections
• processing orders to suppliers	• number of orders
• processing invoices received	• number of invoices
• processing orders to customers	• number of orders
• processing invoices to customers	• number of invoices
• marketing	• number of advertisements
• telephone sales	• number of telephone calls made

As has been seen in the example above, by using activity based costing, the emphasis is placed on which activities cause costs. It answers the question of why costs are incurred, instead of simply stating the amount of the cost for a given period. By using ABC, the responsibility for the cost is established and so steps can be taken to minimise the cost for the future.

THE USE OF COST POOLS

Cost pools are groups of overhead costs that are incurred by the same activity.

When using activity based costing it is advisable to group together those overhead costs which are attributed to the same activity in a cost pool. For example, the purchasing costs for goods to be used in production will include the wages of the firm's purchasing staff, the cost – or proportionate cost – of the purchasing office and the cost of computer and internet services relating to purchasing.

The use of a cost pool makes the attribution of costs through cost drivers much easier – there is no need to seek a separate cost driver for each overhead cost when similar activities can be grouped together.

using activity based costing

The steps to applying activity based costing are illustrated in the following diagram:

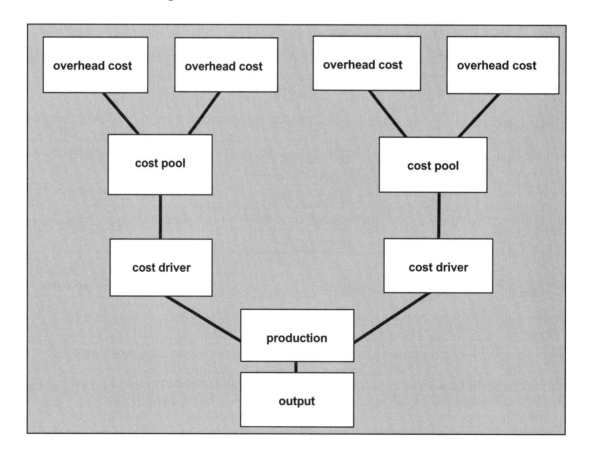

- The first step is to group together in a cost pool the overhead costs which are incurred by the same activity, for example, the purchasing costs for goods to be used in production.

- The second step is to identify the factor which influences the costs – the cost driver. Once identified, the rate for each cost can be calculated. For example, the cost driver could be the cost of placing an order for the purchase of goods to be used in production.

- The third step is to charge the rate for each cost to production based on the use of the activity. For example, if a product requires two purchase orders to be placed, it will be charged with the cost of two activities.

advantages of using activity based costing

The main advantages of using ABC:

- cost information is more accurate because cost drivers are used to identify the activity which causes costs to be incurred

- it is more objective because it is able to identify the overhead costs relating to different products, rather than the overheads of the whole business

- with its focus on overhead costs ABC gives the management of a business a good understanding of why costs are incurred and how they will be altered by changes in production

- it leads to the more accurate calculation of selling prices because overhead costs are attributed to the products which use the activities

- it may identify areas of waste and inefficiency

- management decision-making is improved, eg in pricing policy

- ABC is appropriate for capital-intensive industries where overheads are high and complex in nature

COMPARISON OF COSTING METHODS

The table on the next page gives a comparison between marginal costing, absorption costing, and activity based costing, including a note on the usefulness and the limitations of each.

Comparison of marginal, absorption and activity based costing		
	Marginal costing	**Absorption costing**	**Activity based costing**

Main use	• to help with short-term decision-making (see Chapter 8) in the forms of
	   – break-even analysis
	   – margin of safety
	   – target profit
	   – contribution – sales ratio
	   – 'special order' pricing
		• to calculate selling prices using cost plus profit
		
		• to calculate inventory valuation for financial statements
			• to identify what causes overheads to be incurred for a particular activity

How does it work?	• focuses on product costs • costs are classified as either fixed or variable • contribution to fixed costs is calculated as selling price less variable costs	• focuses on product and period costs • production overheads are charged to production through an overhead absorption rate, often on the basis of direct labour hours or machine hours	• focuses on product costs • cost drivers and cost pools are identified • production overheads are charged to production on the basis of activities
Main focus	• marginal cost • contribution	• production overheads charged to production • calculating selling prices and profit • calculating inventory values	• identifying cost drivers and cost pools as a way of charging production overheads to production
Usefulness	• concept of contribution is easy to understand • useful for short-term decision-making, but no consideration of overheads	• acceptable under IAS 2, *Inventories* • appropriate for traditional industries where production overheads are charged to production on the basis of direct labour hours or machine hours	• acceptable under IAS 2 *Inventories* • more accurate calculation of selling prices because production overheads are analysed to the products which use the activities • appropriate for capital-intensive industries where overheads are high and complex in nature
Limitations	• costs have to be identified as either fixed or variable • all overheads have to be recovered, otherwise a loss will be made • not acceptable under IAS 2, *Inventories* • calculation of selling prices may be less accurate than other costing methods	• not as useful in short-term decision-making as marginal costing • may provide less accurate basis for calculation of selling prices where overheads are high and complex in nature	• time-consuming to set up and record costs (because of the detail required) • the selection of cost drivers can be difficult • the cost drivers need to be kept up-to-date • period costs – such as rent and rates – still need to be recovered

SPREADSHEET SKILLS FOR MANAGEMENT ACCOUNTING

using spreadsheets for marginal, absorption and activity based costing

In this chapter, you have studied marginal, absorption and activity based costing methods. Marginal costing is often used to help make short-term management decisions. It is important to categorise costs into variable production or fixed production costs when using this method and spreadsheets can help with this.

Absorption costing is used for year-end financial statements, as the inventory valuation used must include an element of production overheads. You produced a manual absorption costing statement in the Chair Ltd Case Study. Using a spreadsheet to determine the cost of production, then using this to calculate closing inventory, can make the process more accurate and efficient.

Activity based costing uses cost drivers to determine how much overhead should be charged to each product. Once the information is gathered, undertaking this process is repetitive, so using a spreadsheet will save time.

The Case Study below is the production of a marginal cost statement using spreadsheets.

Case Study

SPREADSHEET SKILLS TO PRODUCE MANAGEMENT ACCOUNTING INFORMATION

situation

Nish runs a business making rucksacks from recycled materials. You work in the accounts department and have been asked to finish producing a marginal costing statement for the year ended 30 June 20-9.

The sales and production information for each product has been collected on a spreadsheet, along with pricing information and a draft marginal cost statement.

You have been given the following information for the year ended 30 June 20-9:

Overheads	£
Fixed production overheads	36,500
Administration	18,352
Marketing	13,695
Distribution	13,800

The labour rate per hour was £16.20 for the year for direct labour.

There was no opening inventory for any product.

Download the spreadsheet file 'MATST Ch 6 Recycled Rucksacks data' from the Osborne Books website.

Save the spreadsheet file in an appropriate location and rename it 'MATST Ch 6 Spreadsheet Case Study Recycled Rucksacks answer'.

Open the renamed file.

In the worksheet called 'Sales & production information', you are required to:

1   **Format** the titles in row 5 to **centre aligned, bold** and **italic**.

2   **Calculate**, using an appropriate formula, the total materials cost for each product (cells F6:F23).

3   **Insert** the labour cost per hour into cell D1. Use **absolute referencing**, along with an appropriate **formula**, to **calculate** the total labour cost (cells H6:H23).

4   Using appropriate **formulas, calculate** the total variable overhead cost (cells J6:J23) and the marginal cost of production (cells K6:K23).

5   Use an appropriate **formula**, incorporating **VLOOKUP**, to find the price for each product line on worksheet 'Pricing', to **calculate** the total sales revenue for each item sold in the year (cells M6:M23).

6   Using appropriate **formulas**, **calculate** the items in closing inventory (cells N6:N23) and the closing inventory value using the marginal cost of production (cells O6:O23).

7   **Format** all monetary amounts with the **accounting format**, excluding the '£', and all hours to **0,000.00**.

8   Using appropriate **formulas, calculate** the totals on row 25, indicated by the total lines (cells C25, F25, H25, J25:O25).

In the worksheet called 'Marginal cost statement 30Jun-9':

9   **Link** the appropriate totals from the worksheet 'Sales and production information', to complete sales revenue (cell D4), direct materials costs (cell C6), direct labour costs (cell C7), variable overhead costs (cell C8) and closing inventory (cell C10).

10 **Enter** the correct overhead figures from the overhead table above into column D of the marginal cost statement.

11 Use **formulas** to **calculate** the prime production cost in cell C9, the subtotal in cell C11 and the cost of sales in cell D13.

12 In cell E9, use an **IF statement** to confirm the calculated prime production cost agrees to cell K25 on the 'Sales & production information' worksheet, stating "ok" if it agrees and "Check" if it does not.

13 Use **formulas** to **calculate** the gross profit (cell D14) and net profit (cell D19).

14 In cell E14, use an appropriate **formula** to **calculate** the gross profit margin, **formatting** the cell to show it to the nearest whole **percentage**.

solution

The 'Sales & production information' worksheet intially looks like this:

Product Line	Colour	Number of items produced	Material used per item, metres	Material cost per metre £	Total materials cost	Labour per item, hrs	Total labour cost £	Variable overheads per item £	Total variable overhead cost £	Marginal cost of production £	Number of items sold	Total sales revenue £	Items in closing inventory	Closing inventory value £
Shabby Chic	Pink	650	1.30	3.25		1		3.6			621			
Shabby Chic	Blue	520	1.30	3.45		1		3.6			512			
Shabby Chic	Yellow	340	1.30	3.78		1		3.6			280			
Shabby Chic	Purple	251	1.30	3.85		1		3.6			242			
Shabby Chic	Multi coloured	463	1.30	3.32		1		3.6			425			
Army Surplus	Camouflage	950	1.00	2.45		0.75		4.5			900			
Army Surplus	Navy	634	1.00	2.6		0.75		4.5			601			
Army Surplus	Black	183	1.00	2.8		0.75		4.5			175			
Double Denim	Indigo	769	1.10	4.2		1.25		2.6			742			
Double Denim	Stone washed	943	1.10	4.1		1.25		2.6			853			
Double Denim	White	428	1.10	4.25		1.25		2.6			420			
Double Denim	Black	653	1.10	4.25		1.25		2.6			614			
Cool Canvas	White	825	1.00	3.5		1		3.1			768			
Cool Canvas	Blue	523	1.00	3.7		1		3.1			504			
Cool Canvas	Green	241	1.00	3.9		1		3.1			231			
Cool Canvas	Yellow	365	1.00	3.9		1		3.1			325			
Cool Canvas	Pink	842	1.00	3.6		1		3.1			836			
Cool Canvas	Red	149	1.00	3.9		1		3.1			130			
Total														

Recycled Rucksacks — Labour cost per hour. Production and sales information. Year ended 30 June 20-9

The first four points are straightforward, using simple formulas and absolute referencing to calculate the relevant costs. Once points 1 to 4 are complete, the 'Sales & production information' worksheet looks like this:

Recycled Rucksacks — Labour cost per hour £16.20. Production and sales information. Year ended 30 June 20-9

Product Line	Colour	Number of items produced	Material used per item, metres	Material cost per metre £	Total materials cost	Labour per item, hrs	Total labour cost £	Variable overheads per item £	Total variable overhead cost £	Marginal cost of production £	Number of items sold	Total sales revenue £	Items in closing inventory	Closing inventory value £
Shabby Chic	Pink	650	1.30	3.25	2746.25	1	10530	3.6	2340	15616.25	621			
Shabby Chic	Blue	520	1.30	3.45	2332.2	1	8424	3.6	1872	12628.2	512			
Shabby Chic	Yellow	340	1.30	3.78	1670.76	1	5508	3.6	1224	8402.76	280			
Shabby Chic	Purple	251	1.30	3.85	1256.255	1	4066.2	3.6	903.6	6226.055	242			
Shabby Chic	Multi coloured	463	1.30	3.32	1998.308	1	7500.6	3.6	1666.8	11165.708	425			
Army Surplus	Camouflage	950	1.00	2.45	2327.5	0.75	11542.5	4.5	4275	18145	900			
Army Surplus	Navy	634	1.00	2.6	1648.4	0.75	7703.1	4.5	2853	12204.5	601			
Army Surplus	Black	183	1.00	2.8	512.4	0.75	2223.45	4.5	823.5	3559.35	175			
Double Denim	Indigo	769	1.10	4.2	3552.78	1.25	15572.25	2.6	1999.4	21124.43	742			
Double Denim	Stone washed	943	1.10	4.1	4252.93	1.25	19095.75	2.6	2451.8	25800.48	853			
Double Denim	White	428	1.10	4.25	2000.9	1.25	8667	2.6	1112.8	11780.7	420			
Double Denim	Black	653	1.10	4.25	3052.775	1.25	13223.25	2.6	1697.8	17973.825	614			
Cool Canvas	White	825	1.00	3.5	2887.5	1	13365	3.1	2557.5	18810	768			
Cool Canvas	Blue	523	1.00	3.7	1935.1	1	8472.6	3.1	1621.3	12029	504			
Cool Canvas	Green	241	1.00	3.9	939.9	1	3904.2	3.1	747.1	5591.2	231			
Cool Canvas	Yellow	365	1.00	3.9	1423.5	1	5913	3.1	1131.5	8468	325			
Cool Canvas	Pink	842	1.00	3.6	3031.2	1	13640.4	3.1	2610.2	19281.8	836			
Cool Canvas	Red	149	1.00	3.9	581.1	1	2413.8	3.1	461.9	3456.8	130			
Total														

Compare your answer to this carefully.

Point 5 asks you to use **VLOOKUP** for the sales price for each product, so you can multiply it by the number of items sold to find the sales revenue for each product. So, for example, the formula for sales revenue for Double Denim Indigo is:

=VLOOKUP(A14,Pricing!$A$3:$B$6,2,FALSE)*L14

The closing inventory calculation is Number of items produced minus Number of items sold.

The marginal cost statement you are producing requires the closing inventory value in point 6 to include only the variable costs of those items left unsold. The formula for closing inventory for Shabby Chic Pink rucksacks is as follows:

=N6*(K6/C6)

Complete points 7 and 8, then compare your totals to those in the answer on the next page – these must be correct, as they will be used for the marginal cost statement now.

	A	B	C	D	E	F	G	H	I	J	K	L	M	N	O	P
1	Recycled Rucksacks		Labour cost per hour	£16.20												
2	Production and sales information															
3	Year ended 30 June 20-9															
4									Variable	Total				Items in	Closing	
			Number of items	Material used per item,	Material cost per metre £	Total materials	Labour per item,	Total labour	overheads per item	variable overhead	Marginal cost	Number of	Total sales	closing	inventory	
5	Product Line	Colour	produced	metres		cost	hrs	cost £	£	cost £	of production £	items sold	revenue £	inventory	value £	
6	Shabby Chic	Pink	650	1.30	3.25	2,746.25	1.00	10,530.00	3.60	2,340.00	15,616.25	621	27,945.00	29	696.73	
7	Shabby Chic	Blue	520	1.30	3.45	2,332.20	1.00	8,424.00	3.60	1,872.00	12,628.20	512	23,040.00	8	194.28	
8	Shabby Chic	Yellow	340	1.30	3.78	1,670.76	1.00	5,508.00	3.60	1,224.00	8,402.76	280	12,600.00	60	1,482.84	
9	Shabby Chic	Purple	251	1.30	3.85	1,256.26	1.00	4,066.20	3.60	903.60	6,226.06	242	10,890.00	9	223.25	
10	Shabby Chic	Multi coloured	463	1.30	3.32	1,998.31	1.00	7,500.60	3.60	1,666.80	11,165.71	425	19,125.00	38	916.41	
11	Army Surplus	Camouflage	950	1.00	2.45	2,327.50	0.75	11,542.50	4.50	4,275.00	18,145.00	900	31,500.00	50	955.00	
12	Army Surplus	Navy	634	1.00	2.60	1,648.40	0.75	7,703.10	4.50	2,853.00	12,204.50	601	21,035.00	33	635.25	
13	Army Surplus	Black	183	1.00	2.80	512.40	0.75	2,223.45	4.50	823.50	3,559.35	175	6,125.00	8	155.60	
14	Double Denim	Indigo	769	1.10	4.20	3,552.78	1.25	15,572.25	2.60	1,999.40	21,124.43	742	25,970.00	27	741.69	
15	Double Denim	Stone washed	943	1.10	4.10	4,252.93	1.25	19,095.75	2.60	2,451.80	25,800.48	853	29,855.00	90	2,462.40	
16	Double Denim	White	428	1.10	4.25	2,000.90	1.25	8,667.00	2.60	1,112.80	11,780.70	420	14,700.00	8	220.20	
17	Double Denim	Black	653	1.10	4.25	3,052.78	1.25	13,223.25	2.60	1,697.80	17,973.83	614	21,490.00	39	1,073.48	
18	Cool Canvas	White	825	1.00	3.50	2,887.50	1.00	13,365.00	3.10	2,557.50	18,810.00	768	34,560.00	57	1,299.60	
19	Cool Canvas	Blue	523	1.00	3.70	1,935.10	1.00	8,472.60	3.10	1,621.30	12,029.00	504	22,680.00	19	437.00	
20	Cool Canvas	Green	241	1.00	3.90	939.90	1.00	3,904.20	3.10	747.10	5,591.20	231	10,395.00	10	232.00	
21	Cool Canvas	Yellow	365	1.00	3.90	1,423.50	1.00	5,913.00	3.10	1,131.50	8,468.00	325	14,625.00	40	928.00	
22	Cool Canvas	Pink	842	1.00	3.60	3,031.20	1.00	13,640.40	3.10	2,610.20	19,281.80	836	37,620.00	6	137.40	
23	Cool Canvas	Red	149	1.00	3.90	581.10	1.00	2,413.80	3.10	461.90	3,456.80	130	5,850.00	19	440.80	
24																
25	Total		9,729			38,149.76		161,765.10		32,349.20	232,264.06	9,179	370,005.00	550	13,231.91	
26																
27																

You can now move on to produce the marginal costing statement. Linking worksheets is commonly used, so any changes to the sales and production information will automatically update the marginal cost statement.

Once points 9 and 10 are completed, the marginal cost statement looks like this:

	A	B	C	D	E	F
1	Recycled Rucksacks					
2	Marginal cost statement year ended 30 June 20-9					
3			£	£		
4	Sales revenue			370,005.00		
5	Variable costs					
6	Direct materials costs		38,149.76			
7	Direct labour costs		161,765.10			
8	Variable overhead costs		32,349.20			
9	Prime production cost					
10	Closing inventory		13,231.91			
11						
12	Fixed production overheads		36,500.00			
13	Cost of sales					
14	Gross profit					
15	Overheads:					
16	Administration			18,352.00		
17	Marketing			13,695.00		
18	Distribution			13,800.00		
19	Net profit					
20						

Points 11 to 14 include spreadsheets skills we have already covered, applied to the marginal cost statement.

The completed marginal cost statement is below.

	A	B	C	D	E	F	G
1	**Recycled Rucksacks**						
2	**Marginal cost statement year ended 30 June 20-9**						
3			£	£			
4	**Sales revenue**			370,005.00			
5	*Variable costs*						
6	Direct materials costs		38,149.76				
7	Direct labour costs		161,765.10				
8	Variable overhead costs		32,349.20				
9	*Prime production cost*		232,264.06		ok		
10	Closing inventory		13,231.91				
11			219,032.15				
12	Fixed production overheads		36,500.00				
13	**Cost of sales**			255,532.15			
14	**Gross profit**			114,472.86		31%	
15	*Overheads:*						
16	Administration			18,352.00			
17	Marketing			13,695.00			
18	Distribution			13,800.00			
19	**Net profit**			68,625.86			
20							

Your formulas should agree to those in the spreadsheet on the next page.

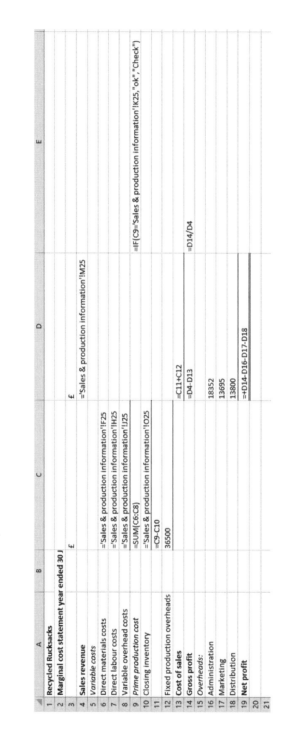

	A	B	C	D	E
1	**Recycled Rucksacks**				
2	**Marginal cost statement year ended 30 J**				
3		£	£	£	
4	**Sales revenue**			='Sales & production information'!M25	
5	*Variable costs*				
6	Direct materials costs		='Sales & production information'!F25		
7	Direct labour costs		='Sales & production information'!H25		
8	Variable overhead costs		='Sales & production information'!J25		
9	*Prime production cost*		=SUM(C6:C8)		
10	Closing inventory		='Sales & production information'!O25		
11			=C9-C10		
12	Fixed production overheads	36500			
13	**Cost of sales**			=C11+C12	
14	**Gross profit**			=D4-D13	=IF(C9='Sales & production information'!K25,"ok","Check")
15	*Overheads:*				
16	Administration		18352		
17	Marketing		13695		
18	Distribution		13800		
19	**Net profit**			=+D14-D16-D17-D18	=D14/D4
20					
21					

You can download the answer file, 'MATST Ch 6 Spreadsheet Case Study Recycled Rucksacks answer', from the Osborne Books website.

Chapter Summary

- Marginal and absorption costing treat product and period costs differently according to their behaviour.

- Marginal costing classifies costs by their behaviour – variable product costs or fixed period costs. Such a classification is used to cost units of output on the basis of their variable (or marginal) costs.

- Marginal costing helps with short-term decision-making.

- Absorption costing absorbs the period costs of the business amongst the cost units by means of overhead absorption rates. It is used to cost units of output to calculate inventory valuations and profit or loss in financial statements.

- Activity based costing (ABC) charges overheads to production on the basis of activities.

- ABC makes use of cost drivers and cost pools.

Key Terms

product cost	costs that become part of the manufactured product
period cost	costs that cannot be assigned to the manufactured product
marginal cost	the product cost of one extra unit of output
contribution	selling price – variable cost
absorption cost	the period production costs of the business are absorbed amongst the cost units through the use of an overhead absorption rate
objectivity	ethical principle of accounting that does not permit manipulation or bias
activity based costing	technique which charges overheads to production on the basis of activities
cost drivers	activities which cause costs to be incurred
cost pools	groups of overhead costs that are incurred by the same activity

Activities

6.1 Coffeeworks Limited manufactures coffee machines for domestic use. The management of the company is considering next year's production and has asked you to help with certain financial decisions.

The following information is available:

Selling price (per machine)	£80
Direct materials (per machine)	£25
Direct labour (per machine)	£20
Fixed production overheads	£270,000 per year
Non-production overheads	£200,000 per year

The company is planning to manufacture 15,000 coffee machines next year.

(a) Calculate the marginal cost per coffee machine.

(b) Calculate the absorption cost per coffee machine.

(c) Prepare a statement of profit or loss to show the profit or loss if 15,000 coffee machines are sold.

6.2 Cook-It Limited makes garden barbecues. The management of the company is considering the production for next year and has asked for help with certain financial decisions.

The following information is available:

Selling price (per barbecue)	£90
Direct materials (per barbecue)	£30
Direct labour (per barbecue)	£25
Fixed production overheads	£150,000 per year
Non-production overheads	£125,000 per year

The company is planning to manufacture 10,000 barbecues next year.

Required:

You are to calculate:

(a) The marginal cost per barbecue.

(b) The absorption cost per barbecue.

(c) The profit or loss if 10,000 barbecues are sold.

6.3 Maxxa Limited manufactures one product, the Maxx. For the month of January 20-7 the following information is available from the computer system:

Number of units manufactured	4,000
Number of units sold	3,000
Selling price	£8 per unit
Direct materials for month	£5,000
Direct labour for month	£9,000
Fixed production overheads for month	£6,000
Non-production overheads for month	£4,000

There was no finished goods inventory at the start of the month. Both direct materials and direct labour are variable costs.

Required:

You are to produce statements of profit or loss using marginal costing and absorption costing methods.

6.4 Bill's Bicycles Ltd started producing a new bicycle, the Freewheeler Electric Bicycle, on 1 December 20-5. The owners have asked you to produce statements of profit or loss using both marginal and absorption costing methods (similar to those produced in question 6.3).

Some information has been provided to you on a worksheet '6.4BB MC AC statements' and you must complete the statements.

You have been given the following information.

Frame making team £16.50 per hour, 3 hours per unit.

Assembly team £18.00 per hour, 5 hours per unit.

Fixed production overheads for the year are £862,400.

Download the spreadsheet file 'MATST Chapter 6 Activities data' from the Osborne Books website.

Save the spreadsheet file in an appropriate location and rename it to 'MATST Chapter 6 Activities answers', so you can refer back to it.

Open the renamed file.

On the worksheet '6.4BB MC AC Statements', you are required to:

1   **Insert** the labour hours and rate information for each department (cells B7 to B10) and the fixed production overheads (cell B11).

2   Using appropriate **formulas**, **calculate** the sales revenue (cells C15 and E15) and the variable costs for the marginal cost statement (cells B17 to B19) and the absorption cost statement (cells D17 to D19).

3   **Link** the fixed production overheads to the appropriate cell in the marginal cost statement (column B) and absorption cost statement (column D).

4 **Calculate** subtotals where appropriate and format these with a single **border** at the top of the cell. Using appropriate **formulas**, **calculate** the closing inventory value to be included in the appropriate place in the marginal cost statement (column B) and the absorption cost statement (column D).

5 Using appropriate **formulas**, **calculate** the cost of sales (cell C26), gross profit (cell C27), and net profit (cell C33) for the marginal cost statement.

6 Using appropriate **formulas**, **calculate** the cost of sales (cell E26), gross profit (cell E27), and net profit (cell E33) for the absorption cost statement.

7 **Format** the titles in rows 12 to 14 in bold.

8 **Merge** and **centre** the titles for each statement over cells B13 to C13 and cells D13 to E13.

9 Using an appropriate **formula**, **calculate** the additional profit under absorption costing (cell E34). Using an appropriate **formula**, **calculate** the production overhead absorbed per unit of production, (cell E36), using **ROUND** to two decimal places.

10 **Fill** cells B13 to C33 in pale yellow and cells D13 to E33 in green. **Fill** cells A34 to E36 in blue.

Save the file as 'MATST Chapter 6 Activities answers' and compare this to the answer on the Osborne Books website.

6.5 Activtoys Limited commenced business on 1 January 20-1. It manufactures the 'Activ', an outdoor climbing frame. Information from the computer system on the first year's trading is as follows:

Number of climbing frames manufactured	1,500
Number of climbing frames sold	1,300
Selling price	£125 per frame
Direct materials	£25 per frame
Direct labour	£30 per frame
Fixed production overheads	£82,500
Non-production overheads	£8,000

Required:

(a) The directors ask for your help in producing statements of profit or loss using the marginal costing and absorption costing methods. They say that they will use 'the one that gives the higher profit' to show to the company's Bank Manager.

(b) Prepare a note for the directors explaining the reason for the different profit figures and commenting on their statement.

6.6 Explain the following terms:

(a) activity based costing

(b) cost driver

(c) cost pool

6.7 The Financial Director of Elwin Limited is considering changing the method of calculating the selling price of the company's products from absorption cost plus a mark-up to activity based costing plus a mark-up.

Prepare a note for the directors of Elwin Limited which explains the benefits of activity based costing over absorption costing.

6.8 You work for Pizzaiola Ltd, a company making pizza ovens. Traditionally, the company has used absorption costing to cost its four products – Piccolo, Medio, Grande and Gigante. Prices are set on a cost plus 40% basis. Some products are not selling well and the new finance director believes they may be over priced, due to the amount of overhead being absorbed by them.

The new finance director has collected some information for next quarter's budget, so she can calculate the product cost using activity based costing. She thinks this will give a better indication of how much each product costs to make and may mean the pricing of some products can be changed.

She has asked you to complete the analysis, determining a suggested price for each product, comparing it to the current price and identifying which are under- or over-priced.

The current selling prices are:

Piccolo	£300
Medio	£340
Grande	£480
Giganto	£590

Download the spreadsheet file 'MATST Chapter 6 Activities data' from the Osborne Books website.

Save the spreadsheet file in an appropriate location and rename it to 'MATST Chapter 6 Activities answers', so you can refer back to it.

Open the renamed file.

On the worksheet '6.8 Overhead information', you are required to:

1 **Calculate**, using an appropriate **formula**, the absorption overhead rate (cell C27), using the total machine hours for production (cell G25), and using **ROUNDUP** to two decimal places. **Calculate**, using appropriate **formulas**, the overhead rate per product, using the overhead rate in cell C27 and the machine hours for each product (cells C24 to F24), in cells C29 to F29. **Format** the cells as **currency** to two decimal places.

2 Using the information in cells C17 to G19 and the budgeted production overheads in cells C5 to C7, **calculate**, using appropriate **formulas**, the amount of each type of overhead attributable to each product using activity based costing (cells G34 to F36). **Calculate** the total overhead costs (cells G34 to G37) and the total overhead per product (C37 to F37). **Format** the totals in row 37 as **double underline, single top line**.

3　　　**Calculate**, using appropriate **formulas**, the overhead per product for activity based costing in cells C39 to F39. **Format** the cells as **currency** to two decimal places.

On the worksheet '6.8 Product costing', you are required to:

4　　　**Link** the production overhead from worksheet '6.8 Overhead information' for each product for both absorption costing (cells C19 to F19) and activity based costing (cells H19 to K19).

5　　　Correct the production cost formula, using **trace precedents** in cells C20 to F20 and H20 to K20. **Format** the row **bold**.

6　　　Using appropriate **formulas, calculate** the markup of 40% in cells C21 to F21 and cells H21 to K21 and the suggested price in cells C22 to F22 and cells H22 to K22. **Format cells** A22 to K22 with orange fill.

7　　　**Insert** the current prices into cells H25 to K25. **Format cells** A25 to K25 with light blue fill.

8　　　Using appropriate **formulas, calculate** the difference (the under-charged or over-charged price) between the amended price and the current price in cells H27 to K27 for each product. Show items where the current price is below the suggested price as negative numbers and items where the current price is higher than the suggested price as positive numbers. Use **conditional formatting** to show negative numbers with red text on a red fill and positive numbers with green text on a green fill.

9　　　**Hide columns** C to G.

Save the file as 'MATST Chapter 6 Activities answers' and compare this to the answer on the Osborne Books website.

6.9　Which **one** of these is an example of ethical behaviour by an accounting technician employed in a limited company?

(a)　Agreeing with the finance director to include period costs in the closing inventory	
(b)　Agreeing with the finance director to use marginal costing for the closing inventory	
(c)　Agreeing with the finance director to use absorption costing for the closing inventory	
(d)　Agreeing with the finance director to use either marginal or absorption costing for the closing inventory depending on which gives the higher profit	

7 Aspects of budgeting

this chapter covers...

In this chapter we turn our attention to budgets and how they are used to help with the financial planning of a business. In particular we see:

- *the need for budgets as part of the decision-making, planning and control processes*

- *how budgeted costs and revenues are set*

- *fixed and flexible budgets*

- *the behaviour of fixed, semi-variable and variable costs*

- *the use of the high/low method to identify the amounts of fixed and variable costs*

- *the preparation of a flexible budget for total revenues and costs*

- *how budgets are a method of cost control through the use of variances*

- *how budgets are used in responsibility accounting to make managers and supervisors responsible for the costs and revenues of their section of the business, and as a way of motivating employees*

- *the monitoring process for budget reports, together with an example of a flexible budget and the calculation of resulting variances*

- *the causes of variances for costs and revenues*

- *rolling budgets*

WHAT IS A BUDGET?

A budget is a financial plan for a business that is prepared in advance.

Budgets are based on pre-determined costs and revenues set in advance of production. These will be set for materials, labour, overheads, selling prices and operating profit. Such pre-determined costs and revenues are often referred to as **standard costs** and **standard selling prices**.

All businesses need methods of controlling the costs of materials, labour, and overheads that go to make up the finished product. Imagine a car factory where the cost and amount of materials to make the car is not known; where the hours of work and rates of pay are not known, where the cost of overheads is not known. Under such circumstances, the costs could not be controlled, and it would be impossible to quote a selling price for the product. To overcome this problem many businesses establish budgeted costs and revenues for their output in advance of production. Thus a budgeted cost can be calculated for things as diverse as a product manufactured in a factory, a hospital operation, servicing a car, a meal in a restaurant, a passenger-mile on a bus.

Budgeted/standard costs and revenues are set for:

- **direct materials**

  The quantity and quality of each type of material to be used in producing the output, and the price of such materials, is pre-determined. Budgeted materials cost is the expected quantity and quality of materials multiplied by the expected material price.

- **direct labour**

  The labour hours required to manufacture a quantity of goods or provide a service, together with the cost of the labour, is pre-determined. Budgeted labour cost is the expected labour hours multiplied by the expected wage rates.

- **production overheads**

  The expected volume of output within a time period, multiplied by the overhead absorption rate, determines the budgeted overhead cost.

- **sales revenue**

  The expected volume of sales within a time period multiplied by the expected selling price determines the budgeted sales revenue.

- **operating profit**

  The expected operating profit within a time period (note that operating profit is sales revenue minus direct materials, direct labour and production and non-production overheads).

Budgets are usually set for each of the responsibility centres – cost, profit, revenue and investment centres – of the business. Once budgets have been set, they can be used as part of the decision-making, planning, and control processes:

- **decision-making**

  The budgeted cost can be used to make pricing decisions, and to consider the effect of using different qualities of materials and grades of labour on the cost of the output.

- **planning**

  Budgets can be prepared to plan the production of goods or services for the next accounting period, and to budget for materials, labour, overheads, sales revenue and operating profit.

- **control**

  Monitoring can be carried out on a regular basis to identify cost and revenue variances from the budget, together with a reconciliation of budgeted and actual costs, revenues and operating profit.

FIXED AND FLEXIBLE BUDGETS

fixed budgets

A fixed budget remains the same whatever the level of activity.

A **fixed budget** is set at the beginning of the time period for planning purposes and then adhered to and monitored, whatever the circumstances – ie the budgeted figures do not change. Fixed budgets are useful in situations where circumstances are stable – for example, a departmental budget for a school or a college, where a set amount of money is allowed for buying stationery each year.

flexible budgets

A flexible budget changes with the level of activity and takes into account different cost behaviour patterns.

In reality, situations do change. For example, the sales revenue can vary quite widely from the figure set in the budget: a new product can be more successful than expected – or it can be a complete disaster. In either case the budgeted figures for sales revenue (and production costs too) will be wide of the mark. The answer is to use a **flexible budget**, which is altered for control purposes to vary in line with the **level of activity** of a business – ie with output of products sold or services provided. By doing this the right costs and revenues are matched and variances can be calculated.

A business may therefore prepare a flexible budget to show different levels of activity. For example, if production is at 80 per cent of the expected amount, then the budget is 'flexed' to 80 per cent and appropriate variances calculated.

flexible budgets – sales revenue, variable and fixed costs

When calculating sales revenue and variable costs for a flexible budget, the revenue or cost per unit is unchanged – it is the total revenue/cost that is 'flexed' to the level of activity. For example, direct materials at £2 per unit: with a budget for 10,000 units, the budgeted cost is £20,000; if the actual performance is 12,000 units, the flexed budget cost is £24,000.

The other costs of making a product or providing a service – the overheads – fall into three categories:

■ fixed overheads, eg the rent of a factory
■ variable overheads, eg unit costs of telephone calls
■ semi-variable overheads, eg a utility bill with a fixed standing charge and a variable unit cost

The important point to note is that, when preparing a flexible budget, fixed overheads will not change due to changes in the level of output, but they may change due to price (eg the rent is increased). **For an increase in fixed overheads, it is the actual cost that is compared with the budget figure.**

FIXED AND VARIABLE COSTS IN BUDGETING AND DECISION-MAKING

In Chapter 1 we saw that:

■ fixed costs remain constant over a range of output levels
■ variable costs alter directly with changes in output levels
■ semi-variable costs combine a fixed and a variable element

Identifying costs as being fixed, semi-variable or variable helps with budgeting and decision-making – the business might be able to alter the balance between fixed and variable costs in order to increase profits. A product could be made:

■ either, by using a labour-intensive process, with a large number of employees supported by basic machinery
■ or, by using expensive machinery in an automated process with very few employees

In the first case, the cost structure will be high variable costs (direct labour) and low fixed costs (straight-line depreciation of machinery). In the second case, there will be low variable costs and high fixed costs. Management will need to examine the relationship between the costs – together with the likely sales figures, and the availability of finance with which to buy the machinery – before making a decision.

More specifically, a knowledge of the behaviour of costs can be used to help management to:

- identify the amount of fixed costs within a semi-variable cost

- prepare flexible budgets for revenue and costs

- identify the point at which costs are exactly equal to income – known as the break-even point (covered in Chapter 8)

IDENTIFYING THE AMOUNT OF FIXED AND VARIABLE COSTS

With semi-variable costs we have already seen (in Chapter 1) how these combine both a fixed and a variable cost. It is important to be able to identify the amount of each, as this will help with budgeting and decision-making. Where the total costs are known at two levels of output, the amounts of fixed and variable costs can be identified using the 'high/low' method as the difference in the costs at different output levels will be due solely to the variable costs.

example

- at output of 1,000 units, total costs are £7,000

- at output of 2,000 units, total costs are £9,000

What are the fixed costs? What are the variable costs?

Using the 'high/low' method to identify the fixed and variable costs:

- The low output and costs are deducted from the high output and costs, as follows:

	high output	2,000 units	£9,000
less	low output	1,000 units	£7,000
equals	differences	1,000 units	£2,000

- The amount of the variable cost per unit is now calculated as:

$$\frac{\text{difference in cost}}{\text{difference in units}} = \frac{£2,000}{1,000} = £2 \text{ variable cost per unit}$$

- Therefore, at 1,000 units of output the cost structure is:

	total cost	£7,000
less	variable costs (1,000 units x £2 per unit)	£2,000
equals	fixed costs	£5,000

■ Check this now at 2,000 units of output when the cost structure is:

	variable costs (2,000 units x £2 per unit)	£4,000
add	fixed costs (as above)	£5,000
equals	total costs	£9,000

The 'high/low' method can only be used when variable costs increase by the same money amount for each extra unit of output (ie there is a constant unit variable cost), and where there are no stepped fixed costs. Having established the fixed and variable elements, these can then be applied to any other level of output.

BUDGETS FOR REVENUE AND COSTS

Once fixed and variable costs are known for the three elements of costs – materials, labour and expenses – at a particular level of output, it is relatively simple to calculate how the costs will change at different levels of output. For example, if variable materials costs at an output of 1,000 units are £2,000 then, at an output of 1,100 units, they will be £2,200 (ie a 10 per cent increase in both output and cost). By contrast, the fixed expense of factory rent of, say, £5,000 will be unchanged if output increases by 10 per cent. (Note that such calculations assume a constant unit variable cost and that there are no stepped fixed costs.)

Such changes in costs and revenues can be incorporated, as part of the planning process, into a **flexible budget**. This calculates total revenues and costs and shows the cost per unit and profit per unit at flexed (either increased or decreased) activity levels, as shown in the Case Study which follows.

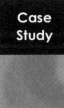

Case Study

FLEXIBLE BUDGET FOR REVENUE AND COSTS, INCLUDING SEMI-VARIABLE COSTS

situation

Note: In this Case Study batches of output are treated as the units of output.

Cannit Limited makes cans for customers in the food and drink industry. The company has prepared a budget for the next quarter for one of its cans, AB24. This can is produced in batches and the budget is based on producing and selling 800 batches.

One of the customers of Cannit Limited has indicated that it may be significantly increasing its order level for can AB24 for the next quarter and it appears that activity levels of 1,000 batches and 1,500 batches are feasible.

The semi-variable costs should be calculated using the high/low method. If 2,000 batches are sold the total semi-variable cost will be £6,500 and there is a constant unit variable cost up to this volume.

Complete the flexible budget below and calculate the budgeted profit per batch of AB24 at the activity levels of 1,000 and 1,500 batches.

Batches produced and sold	800	1,000	1,500
	£	£	£
Sales revenue	24,000		
Variable costs:			
• Direct materials	4,400		
• Direct labour	6,800		
• Overheads	4,800		
Semi-variable costs:	4,100		
• Variable element			
• Fixed element			
Total cost	20,100		
Total profit	3,900		
Profit per batch (to two decimal places)	4.88		

solution

- Sales revenue is £30.00 per batch (£24,000 ÷ 800 batches)
- Direct materials are £5.50 per batch (£4,400 ÷ 800)
- Direct labour is £8.50 per batch (£6,800 ÷ 800)
- Overheads are £6.00 per batch (£4,800 ÷ 800)

Each of these can be multiplied by 1,000 and 1,500 to give the revenue and costs at these activity levels as they all vary directly with output.

The semi-variable cost is split between the amounts for fixed and variable costs by using the high/low method:

	high output	2,000	batches	*£6,500
less	low output	800	batches	£4,100
equals	difference	1,200	batches	£2,400

*from text at the start of the Case Study

- The amount of the variable cost per batch is £2.00 (£2,400 ÷ 1,200 batches)
- The amount of the fixed cost is £2,500 (at 800 batches £4,100 – [800 x £2.00])

The **flexible budget** of revenue and costs completed for activity levels of 1,000 and 1,500 batches is as follows:

Batches produced and sold	800	1,000	1,500
	£	£	£
Sales revenue	24,000	30,000	45,000
Variable costs:			
• Direct materials	4,400	5,500	8,250
• Direct labour	6,800	8,500	12,750
• Overheads	4,800	6,000	9,000
Semi-variable costs:	4,100		
• Variable element		2,000	3,000
• Fixed element		2,500	2,500
Total cost	20,100	24,500	35,500
Total profit	3,900	5,500	9,500
Profit per batch (to two decimal places)	4.88	5.50	6.33

Service businesses

Whilst this Case Study has used the schedule of revenue and costs for a manufacturing business, the same format can be used for a service business. For example, a bus company could budget revenues and costs on the basis of miles travelled, and a care home could budget revenues and costs on the basis of the cost per day per resident.

BUDGETED CONTRIBUTION

Many budgets are set out in such a way as to show the **contribution** to fixed overheads. Contribution, which is **selling price less variable cost**, is an important factor in short-term decision-making and is discussed fully on page 272.

The Case Study which follows shows how a business has gathered its budgeted or standard information and uses this to calculate its costs and contribution per unit, and to calculate a budgeted profit or loss.

Case Study

MURRAY MANUFACTURING: BUDGETED CONTRIBUTION

situation

Murray Manufacturing Limited makes a single product, the MM6. It has prepared budgeted/standard data for the next financial year, as follows:

	MM6
Sales revenue (£)	137,500
Direct materials (£)	35,000
Direct labour (£)	23,750

The company expects to produce and sell 25,000 units of MM6. Budgeted fixed overheads are £42,950.

The company directors ask you to prepare data to show the budgeted contribution per unit of MM6 sold, and the company's budgeted profit or loss for the year.

solution

You present the budgeted data in the form of a table, as follows (with working notes shown):

	MM6	
Selling price per unit	£5.50	£137,500 ÷ 25,000 units
Less: variable costs per unit		
Direct materials	£1.40	£35,000 ÷ 25,000 units
Direct labour	£0.95	£23,750 ÷ 25,000 units
Contribution per unit	£3.15	£5.50 – (£1.40 + £0.95)
Sales volume (units)	25,000	
Total contribution	£78,750	£3.15 x 25,000 units
Less: fixed overheads	£42,950	
Budgeted profit	£35,800	£78,750 – £42,950

The table provides useful data for the directors who can see the budgeted information on a per unit basis. From this they can consider the effects of any changes they are able to make regarding sales volume, revenues and costs.

BUDGETS AND VARIANCES

A variance is the difference between the budgeted/standard cost or revenue and the actual cost or revenue.

A particular feature of budgets is their use as a method of cost and revenue control. This is done by comparing the budgeted cost or revenue with the actual cost or revenue of the output in order to establish the variance. The calculations below are shown differently for costs and revenues in order to always show a favourable variance as a positive figure and an adverse variance as a negative figure. This is particularly relevant when using a spreadsheet.

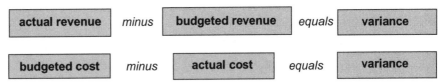

Variances can be either **favourable** (F) or **adverse** (A):

- **favourable variances**
  - a favourable cost variance is where actual costs are lower than budgeted costs
  - a favourable revenue variance is where actual revenues are higher than budgeted revenues
  - a favourable operating profit is where actual profit is higher than budgeted profit

- **adverse variances**
  - an adverse cost variance is where actual costs are higher than budgeted costs
  - an adverse revenue variance is where actual revenues are lower than budgeted revenues
  - an adverse operating profit is where actual profit is lower than budgeted profit

management by exception

The control systems of a business will set down procedures for acting on variances, but only for significant variances. This type of system is known as **management by exception**, ie acting on variances that are exceptional. Managers will normally work to **tolerance limits** – a tolerance limit is an acceptable percentage variance on the budgeted amount. If a cost or revenue exceeds the tolerance limit, the variance will be significant and investigative action will need to be taken.

who needs to know about variances?

Variances against budgeted cost or revenue need to be reported to the **appropriate** level of management within the business. This level will depend on the significance of the variance, for example:

- **the cost of the materials used is going up by 1 per cent**

The Managing Director is unlikely to be interested – it will be up to the purchasing department to see if there is a way around the increase.

- **a major failure in an automated process has cut output by 50 per cent**

This is a matter to bring to the attention of higher management and the directors of the company: production patterns, purchasing and staffing will have to be re-organised so that production can be increased.

motivating employees

As a means of motivating employees, budgets are an example of **responsibility accounting.** Managers and supervisors are made responsible for the costs and revenues of their section but, in order to be effective, managers must participate in the budget-setting process. As a method of motivation, budgets can be seen by employees as either a 'carrot' or a 'stick', ie as a form of encouragement to achieve the amounts set, or as a form of punishment if pre-determined costs are exceeded or sales revenues not achieved.

reporting and investigating variances

The variances for the cost elements and sales revenues are summarised on a **budget report**. Such reports reconcile the budgeted cost and the actual cost for each cost element (materials, labour, expenses, fixed and variable overheads) and the budgeted revenues, and show the variances. An example of a budget report is shown below.

	Budget	Actual	Variance	Favourable (F) or Adverse (A)
Units sold	145,000	145,000		
	£000	£000	£000	
Sales revenue	870	899	29	F
Less costs:				
Direct materials	200	170	30	F
Direct labour	260	260	0	0
Variable overheads	180	230	50	A
Fixed overheads	100	90	10	F
Operating profit	130	149	19	F

A budget report shows the variances for revenue and for each cost element by comparing the budget amount with the actual amount or as a percentage. Percentages are always calculated by dividing the variance by the budgeted figure. Variances are:

- sales revenue
- direct materials
- direct labour
- variable overheads
- fixed overheads

From the budget report on the previous page:

- revenue variance: sales revenue £899,000 – £870,000 = £29,000 or 3.3% (£29,000/£870,000) favourable (F), because actual revenue is better than the budget

- cost variance: direct materials £200,000 – £170,000 = £30,000 or 15% (£30,000/£200,000) favourable (F)

- cost variance: direct labour £260,000 – £260,000 = £0, ie no variance, so '0' (zero) is shown in the variance column

- cost variance: variable overheads £180,000 – £230,000 = £50,000 or 28% (£50,000/£180,000) adverse (A)

- cost variance: fixed overheads £100,000 – £90,000 = £10,000 or 10% (£10,000/£100,000) favourable (F)

The effect of variances on operating profit is that:

- favourable revenue variances increase profit
- adverse revenue variances reduce profit
- favourable cost variances increase profit
- adverse cost variances reduce profit

In the budget report the revenue and cost variances are reconciled to the operating profit variance, ie the net amount of the variances for costs and revenues is equal to the operating profit variance, £19,000 or 15% (£19,000/£130,000) favourable in the example on the previous page.

The order for investigating variances shown by the budget report, using either money amounts or percentages, is usually as follows:

- large variances – favourable and adverse
- other adverse variances
- any remaining favourable variances

Note that small variances may not be worth investigating – the cost of the investigation might outweigh the benefits.

The variances need to be investigated by the appropriate level of management:

■ less significant variances are dealt with by managers and supervisors

■ significant variances need to be referred to a higher level of management who will decide what further investigation is required

Note that constant adverse or favourable variances need to be investigated as the budgeted costs and revenues may have been set incorrectly.

reporting cycle

For budget reports to be used effectively it is essential that employees are trained to record information accurately about actual costs and revenues. The quality of the information must be:

■ accurate

■ timely

■ in the appropriate format, highlighting the major features

The reporting cycle of the budget report will depend on the time periods used. For example, if a business establishes budget reports on the basis of monthly – or four-weekly – periods, then variances are likely to be reported within the first two weeks of the next period – often in the form of a computer report from the finance department. Generally a senior manager will call a meeting at a fixed point in each period – with the staff responsible for the costs and revenues – in order to review variances from the previous period.

revision of budgets

At regular intervals – annually, or more often – the budgeted costs and revenues need to be revised to take note of:

■ cost increases caused by inflation – which will affect materials, labour and overheads (although not necessarily to the same extent) – and other external factors

■ changes to the specifications and quality of materials, eg an improvement in quality may lead to less wastage and easier, faster, production

■ changes to work practices, eg an increase in automation may lead to reduced labour costs, or the employment of different grades of employees

■ changes to selling prices, which may be limited by what competitors are charging for similar products

controllable and non-controllable costs and revenues

When investigating variances, it is important to appreciate that not all of the costs and revenues can be controlled directly by managers and supervisors in the short term.

Period costs, such as the cost of rent paid on the premises, is outside the control of the Purchasing or Procurement Manager – the rent being negotiated by the Administration Manager. Nevertheless, a proportion of rent will be included amongst the budgeted cost of overheads.

By contrast, the Purchasing Manager has control over product costs, such as the cost of materials (unless there is a world market price – eg for coffee or crude oil – over which he or she can have no influence).

Thus we can distinguish between:

- **controllable costs** – costs and revenues which can be influenced by the manager/supervisor
- **non-controllable costs** – costs which cannot be influenced by the manager/supervisor in the short term

Note that, in the longer-term, all costs and revenues are controllable. For example, a business may decide to move to premises where the rent is cheaper, or to close its operations at one location, or even – in the extreme – to cease trading altogether.

MONITORING OF BUDGET REPORTS

A business or organisation using budgets will monitor the outcomes by comparing the budgeted amounts set with the results that actually occurred. An outline of the monitoring process is shown in the diagram below.

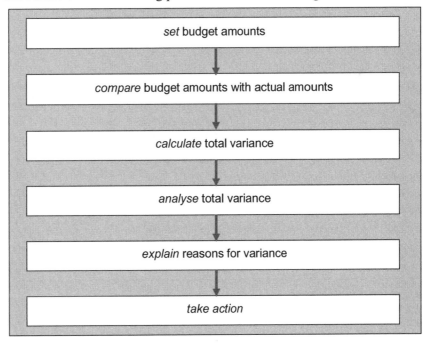

EXBURY LIMITED:
VARIANCES IN FLEXIBLE BUDGETS

situation

You work as an Accounts Assistant for Exbury Ltd, a manufacturing business.

Exbury Ltd budgeted to manufacture and sell 10,000 units of product 10EX for the year ended 31 December. However, due to an increase in demand it was able to manufacture and sell 12,000 units.

You are to complete the following table to show a flexed budget and the resulting variances against this budget for the year. Show the actual variance amount, for sales revenue and each cost, in the column headed 'Variance'.

Note:

• Adverse variances must be denoted with a minus sign or brackets

• Enter 0 where any figure is zero

	Original budget	Flexed budget	Actual	Variance
Units sold	10,000	12,000	12,000	
	£000	£000	£000	£000
Sales revenue	250		290	
Less costs:				
Direct materials	80		90	
Direct labour	110		140	
Fixed overheads	30		35	
Operating profit	30		25	

solution

You complete the table as follows:

	Original budget	Flexed budget	Actual	Variance
Units sold	10,000	12,000	12,000	
	£000	£000	£000	£000
Sales revenue	250	300	290	−10
Less costs:				
Direct materials	80	96	90	6
Direct labour	110	132	140	−8
Fixed overheads	30	30	35	−5
Operating profit	30	42	25	−17

Working notes

- The budget is flexed from 10,000 to 12,000 units. This is a 20 per cent increase (2,000/10,000 x 100).

- The budget figures for sales revenue, direct materials and direct labour are all increased by 20 per cent to give the amount for the flexed budget. For example, sales revenue £250,000 x 1.2 = £300,000. Note that variable overheads would be flexed in the same way.

- For fixed overheads, the actual figure of £35,000 is used. The increase from the budget figure of £30,000 shows an adverse variance of £5,000.

- The variance column is completed by comparing the flexed budget with the actual figures. The total variance, here £17,000 adverse, is reconciled with the change in operating profit from that shown by the flexed budget to the actual figure.

What information does the flexed budget tell us?

- Impact on profit

  As the actual profit of £25,000 is £17,000 less than the flexed budget profit of £42,000, the managers of the business will wish to identify which variance has had the greatest impact on decreasing operating profit. Here, sales revenue is the largest adverse variance and the cause of this will need to be investigated.

- Causes of variances

  There are a number of reasons for variances – as discussed in more detail in the next section. For example, the flexed budget and actual figures show a favourable variance of £6,000 for direct materials. This could be caused by factors such as a decrease in materials prices, less wastage of materials, or a change of specifications to use cheaper materials.

CAUSES OF VARIANCES

Budgeted/standard costs and revenues are set in order to give individual departmental managers, who are responsible for aspects of the business' output, suitable targets to aim for. When actual costs are compared with budgeted costs, an investigation can be carried out to find the causes of the variances and to see what can be done about them for the future.

The main causes of variances are listed on the next page.

Direct materials	Adverse	Favourable
increase in materials prices	✓	
decrease in materials prices		✓
cheaper materials used		✓
more expensive materials used	✓	
more materials wasted	✓	
fewer materials wasted		✓
theft of materials	✓	
change to cheaper specifications		✓
change to more expensive specifications	✓	
Direct labour		
increase in pay	✓	
reduction in pay		✓
more efficient use of labour		✓
less efficient use of labour	✓	
higher paid grade of labour used	✓	
lower paid grade of labour used		✓
Overheads		
increase in price	✓	
reduction in price		✓
stepped fixed cost	✓	
more expensive supplier	✓	
cheaper supplier		✓
Sales revenue		
increase in selling price		✓
decrease in selling price	✓	
increase in number sold		✓
decrease in number sold	✓	

Note the following examples of inter-relationship within variances, referred to as **sub-variances**:

■ an adverse direct material variance may be resolved by:

– reducing the amount of materials wasted (material usage variance), or

– buying the materials at a cheaper price (material price variance), or

– training staff so that materials are used more efficiently (material usage variance)

- an adverse direct labour variance may be resolved by:
  - training staff to work more efficiently (labour efficiency variance), or
  - using labour at a lower grade of pay (labour rate variance), or
  - reorganising the production process so that staff work more efficiently (labour efficiency variance)
- an adverse overhead variance may be resolved by:
  - buying from cheaper suppliers (eg telephones, electricity, gas), or
  - more efficient use of overheads (eg sub-letting part of the premises), or
  - making changes to the production process (eg by reviewing the balance between labour work and machine work)

ROLLING BUDGETS

A rolling (continuous) budget is continually kept up-to-date by adding a new budget period once the most recent budget period is completed.

For example, a business has prepared a month-by-month budget for next year from January to December. With a rolling budget, at the end of each month, the business will add another month – January for this year will 'drop out' of the budget, but January for the following year will be added. This rolling process – often referred to as the moving annual total (MAT) – continues so that the business always has a budget that extends into the future for the same period.

The advantages of rolling budgets include:

- there is always a budget that extends into the future
- the data for the new budget period is adjusted to take note of the current information from the period just completed
- management of the business will reassess the budget after each budget period
- the focus of management is on one budget period at a time instead of the whole year
- seasonal variations are eliminated because a full year is compared with a full year's budget which means that developing trends can be seen

The disadvantages of rolling budgets include:

- it can be costly and time-consuming to keep revisiting the planning process to add a new budget period
- the focus of the business may be more concerned with updating the rolling budget than controlling actual costs and revenues

- the overall budget totals will vary as one period drops out and a new one is added, leading to a lack of focus on key issues from those working with the budget

- adding a new budget period may become a routine activity without full consideration of changes within the business or the wider economy

A rolling budget is an ideal spreadsheet application, with figures for the entire budget period being updated every time a completed budget period is replaced by a new period.

SPREADSHEET SKILLS FOR MANAGEMENT ACCOUNTING

using spreadsheets for budget preparation, sensitivity analysis and reporting

In this chapter, you have studied how to prepare budgets that include fixed, semi-variable and variable costs. In real life, spreadsheets will be used to make the budgeting process as efficient as possible. A well-built spreadsheet will be flexible enough to allow managers to amend budgetary assumptions such as price per product, discounts and variable costs per unit. The budget may also be produced for several levels of activity, so a spreadsheet that automatically updates revenues and costs when these are amended is particularly useful.

When the budget is produced, managers may want to understand the impact of different assumptions on the budgeted profit for the business. This is known as 'sensitivity analysis' and could be performed by using the initial budget as a model, copying it onto a new worksheet, then amending certain assumptions to create alternative scenarios. Alternatively, a business could show several budgeted outputs side by side, to highlight how the budgeted profit responds to changes in activity levels.

Budgets will be shared with managers, so budgetary information should be clear and easy to read. When budget reports are produced by the accounts department, perhaps for a flexed budget, conditional formatting can highlight significant variances. This can help managers know exactly what to investigate, improving performance and profits for the business.

In summary, a good accountant will produce reports to help the employees in the business understand *what* has happened and spreadsheets are a great tool to use for this. Managers are then able to ask the *right* questions, finding out *why* it happened and then take appropriate action.

Let's look at performing some sensitivity analysis on a budget using spreadsheets in the following Case Study.

Case Study

SPREADSHEET SKILLS TO PROVIDE MANAGEMENT ACCOUNTING INFORMATION

situation

Miss Molly Pet Treats makes training treats for dogs. The company is due to launch a new line of treats, Woofily Good Treats. The management are considering spending money on additional marketing, so would like you to produce a budget for three alternative outputs.

At 550,000 bags, all variable costs change in line with the increase in production.

At 700,000 bags:

- Revenue will decrease by £0.20 for all units.

- Variable material costs will decrease by 5% per unit for all units.

- Variable labour costs will decrease by 2% for all units.

- Fixed marketing costs, included in selling and distribution overheads, will increase by £35,000.

The management would also like to know how many bags must be sold to make a profit of £150,000.

Download the spreadsheet file 'MATST Ch 7 Spreadsheet Case Study Miss Molly Pet Treats Ltd data' from the Osborne Books website.

Save the spreadsheet file in an appropriate location and rename it 'MATST Ch 7 Spreadsheet Case Study Miss Molly Pet Treats Ltd answer'.

Open the renamed file.

In the worksheet called 'Woofily Good Treats Budget', you are required to:

1 **Input** the price per bag into C26 and D26.

2 **Spell check** the worksheet.

3 **Format cells** B9:D24 to currency, £0,000.

4 **Calculate**, using appropriate formulas, the budgeted costs and revenues at outputs of 550,000 and 700,000, allowing for any expected changes in revenue or cost per unit.

5 **Total** the variable costs (B18:D18) and fixed costs (B23:D23). Amend the format to **italic** for these rows.

6 **Calculate** the contribution (B19:D19) and the forecast profit or loss (B24:D24).

7 **Format** the revenue, contribution and forecast profit or loss rows to bold.

8 Use **borders** to show contribution as a total – single underlined – and the forecast profit or loss as a total – double underlined.

9 **Cell fill** B8:D28 in the colours to match the bags sold in row 6.

10 **Calculate** the contribution per bag in B27:D27 and the forecast profit/(loss) per bag in B28:D28.

11 Use **TODAY** to insert today's date into D1.

12 **Copy and paste, including formats and formulas** the worksheet 'Woofily Good Treats Budget' into a new worksheet and name it 'Target Profit £150,000'.

13 In the worksheet named 'Target Profit £150,000', use **GOALSEEK** to find the number of bags sold to earn profits of £150,000 in cell D24.

solution

The 'Woofily Good Treats Budget' worksheet currently looks like this:

	A	B	C	D	E
1	**Miss Molly Pet Treats Ltd**	**Date produced**			
2	**Product : Woofily Good Treats**				
3	**Budget for year ending 30 June 20-3**				
4					
5					
6	**Bags sold**	**400,000**	**550,000**	**700,000**	
7					
8		£	£	£	
9	Revenue	1000000			
10	*Direct materials (all variable):*				
11	Rice	32000			
12	Vitmins	160000			
13	Cheese	160000			
14	Suasage	120000			
15	*Direct labour (all variable):*				
16	Baking	78000			
17	Packaging	86000			
18	Total variable costs				
19	Contribution				
20	*Fixed costs:*				
21	Production overheads	269000			
22	Selling and distrbution overheads	112000			
23	Total fixed costs				
24	Forecast profit/ (loss)				
25					
26	**Price per bag**	**£2.50**			
27	**Contribution per bag**				
28	**Forecast profit / (loss) per bag**				
29					

Woofily Good Treats Budget

Points 1 to 4 use spreadsheet skills you have already used in the activities in this book. Once you have completed points 1 to 4, the 'Woofily Good Treats Budget' worksheet will look like this:

	A	B	C	D	E
1	**Miss Molly Pet Treats Ltd**	**Date produced**			
2	**Product : Woofily Good Treats**				
3	**Budget for year ending 30 June 20-3**				
4					
5					
6	**Bags sold**	**400,000**	**550,000**	**700,000**	
7					
8		£	£	£	
9	Revenue	£1,000,000	£1,375,000	£1,610,000	
10	*Direct materials (all variable):*				
11	Rice	£32,000	£44,000	£53,200	
12	Vitamins	£160,000	£220,000	£266,000	
13	Cheese	£160,000	£220,000	£266,000	
14	Sausage	£120,000	£165,000	£199,500	
15	*Direct labour (all variable):*				
16	Baking	£78,000	£107,250	£133,770	
17	Packaging	£86,000	£118,250	£147,490	
18	Total variable costs				
19	Contribution				
20	*Fixed costs:*				
21	Production overheads	£269,000	£269,000	£269,000	
22	Selling and distribution overheads	£112,000	£112,000	£147,000	
23	Total fixed costs				
24	Forecast profit/ (loss)				
25					
26	**Price per bag**	**£2.50**	**£2.50**	**£2.30**	
27	**Contribution per bag**				
28	**Forecast profit / (loss) per bag**				
29					

Check your numbers carefully as the revenue and variable costs for direct materials and direct labour both change when 700,000 bags are sold. It is important you read the text in the top of the question carefully, to ensure you produce the budget as required. Any information given to you *will* be relevant!

The formulas are shown on the next page and indicate where costs and revenues have been amended.

	A	B	C	D	E
1	**Miss Molly Pet Treats Ltd**	**Date produced**			
2	**Product : Woofily Good Treats**				
3	**Budget for year ending 30 June 20-3**				
4					
5					
6	**Bags sold**	**400000**	**550000**	**700000**	
7					
8		£	£	£	
9	Revenue	1000000	=C6*C26	=D6*D26	
10	*Direct materials (all variable):*				
11	Rice	32000	=B11/$B$6*$C$6	=B11/B$6*D$6*0.95	
12	Vitamins	160000	=B12/$B$6*$C$6	=B12/B$6*D$6*0.95	
13	Cheese	160000	=B13/$B$6*$C$6	=B13/B$6*D$6*0.95	
14	Sausage	120000	=B14/$B$6*$C$6	=B14/B$6*D$6*0.95	
15	*Direct labour (all variable):*				
16	Baking	78000	=B16/$B$6*$C$6	=B16/B$6*D$6*0.98	
17	Packaging	86000	=B17/$B$6*$C$6	=B17/B$6*D$6*0.98	
18	Total variable costs				
19	Contribution				
20	*Fixed costs:*				
21	Production overheads	269000	=B21	=B21	
22	Selling and distribution overheads	112000	=B22	=B22+35000	
23	Total fixed costs				
24	Forecast profit/ (loss)				
25					
26	**Price per bag**	**=B9/B6**	2.5	2.3	
27	**Contribution per bag**				
28	**Forecast profit / (loss) per bag**				
29					

Totalling the variable and fixed costs is straightforward using the **SUM** function. The contribution is revenue minus variable costs, so the formula for the contribution for 400,000 units, for example, is:

=B9-B18.

Similarly, the formula for the forecast profit/(loss), contribution less fixed costs, for 400,000 units is:

=B19-B23.

Points 5 to 9 use formatting to make it easy for managers to pick out key numbers or focus on one particular output. Have a look at the worksheet below, once you have completed points 5 to 10, and compare it to the one above when points 1 to 4 were completed. Do you think the key information is highlighted more clearly? When producing spreadsheets at work, think about your formatting for a moment - how easy is it for others in the company to understand the information, not just the accounts department?

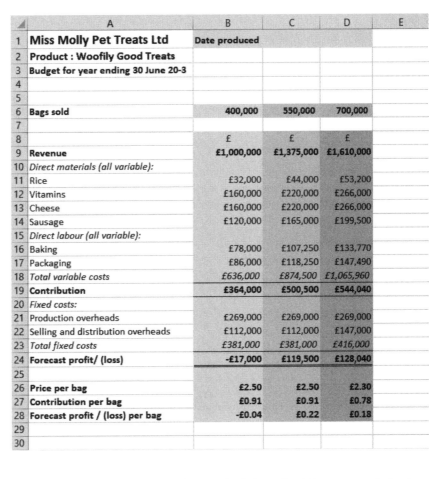

	A	B	C	D	E
1	**Miss Molly Pet Treats Ltd**	**Date produced**			
2	**Product : Woofily Good Treats**				
3	**Budget for year ending 30 June 20-3**				
4					
5					
6	**Bags sold**	400,000	550,000	700,000	
7					
8		£	£	£	
9	**Revenue**	**£1,000,000**	**£1,375,000**	**£1,610,000**	
10	*Direct materials (all variable):*				
11	Rice	£32,000	£44,000	£53,200	
12	Vitamins	£160,000	£220,000	£266,000	
13	Cheese	£160,000	£220,000	£266,000	
14	Sausage	£120,000	£165,000	£199,500	
15	*Direct labour (all variable):*				
16	Baking	£78,000	£107,250	£133,770	
17	Packaging	£86,000	£118,250	£147,490	
18	*Total variable costs*	*£636,000*	*£874,500*	*£1,065,960*	
19	**Contribution**	**£364,000**	**£500,500**	**£544,040**	
20	*Fixed costs:*				
21	Production overheads	£269,000	£269,000	£269,000	
22	Selling and distribution overheads	£112,000	£112,000	£147,000	
23	*Total fixed costs*	*£381,000*	*£381,000*	*£416,000*	
24	**Forecast profit/ (loss)**	**-£17,000**	**£119,500**	**£128,040**	
25					
26	**Price per bag**	£2.50	£2.50	£2.30	
27	**Contribution per bag**	£0.91	£0.91	£0.78	
28	**Forecast profit / (loss) per bag**	-£0.04	£0.22	£0.18	
29					
30					

Point 12 requires you to copy and paste the information into a new worksheet, so you can use **GOALSEEK**. This function is very useful if you want to change one input number and see how everything else is affected. It is important you copy and paste everything, including formats and formulas, otherwise **GOALSEEK** cannot be used. To use **GOALSEEK**, you must be careful how you build the budget spreadsheet. If everything is not properly linked to, say, the activity level, the **GOALSEEK** will not work properly.

The screenshot that follows shows the **GOALSEEK** required. The forecast profit cell to be set to £150,000 is D24, and the bags sold, in D6, is the number that will change. If you have not used **GOALSEEK** before, refer to the Osborne Books Spreadsheet Skills for Management Accounting Tutorial.

Once points 1 to 13 are complete, the 'Target Profit £150,000' worksheet should look like the worksheet shown on the following page – the forecast profit is £150,000 and 728,255 bags must be sold to achieve it.

	A	B	C	D	E
1	**Miss Molly Pet Treats Ltd**	Date produced		04/06/2021	
2	**Product : Woofily Good Treats**				
3	**Budget for year ending 30 June 20-3**				
4					
5					
6	Bags sold	400,000	550,000	728,255	
7					
8		£	£	£	
9	Revenue	£1,000,000	£1,375,000	£1,674,987	
10	*Direct materials (all variable):*				
11	Rice	£32,000	£44,000	£55,347	
12	Vitamins	£160,000	£220,000	£276,737	
13	Cheese	£160,000	£220,000	£276,737	
14	Sausage	£120,000	£165,000	£207,553	
15	*Direct labour (all variable):*				
16	Baking	£78,000	£107,250	£139,170	
17	Packaging	£86,000	£118,250	£153,443	
18	*Total variable costs*	*£636,000*	*£874,500*	*£1,108,987*	
19	Contribution	£364,000	£500,500	£566,000	
20	*Fixed costs:*				
21	Production overheads	£269,000	£269,000	£269,000	
22	Selling and distribution overheads	£112,000	£112,000	£147,000	
23	*Total fixed costs*	*£381,000*	*£381,000*	*£416,000*	
24	Forecast profit/ (loss)	-£17,000	£119,500	£150,000	
25					
26	Price per bag	£2.50	£2.50	£2.30	
27	Contribution per bag	£0.91	£0.91	£0.78	
28	Forecast profit / (loss) per bag	-£0.04	£0.22	£0.21	
29					
30					
31					

You can download the answer file, 'MATST Ch 7 Miss Molly Pets Treats Ltd answer', from the Osborne Books website.

Chapter Summary

- Budgets are based on pre-determined costs and revenues set in advance.

- Budgeted/standard costs and revenues are set for:

  - sales revenue

  - direct materials

  - direct labour

  - overheads

  - operating profit (sales revenue minus direct materials, direct labour and production overheads)

- Budgets are part of the decision-making, planning and control processes of a business or organisation.

- Fixed budgets are set at the beginning of the time period and then adhered to and monitored whatever the circumstances.

- Flexible budgets are altered to vary in line with the level of activity.

- A knowledge of the behaviour of costs enables:

  - identification of the amounts of fixed and variable costs within a semi-variable cost

  - preparation of flexible budgets for revenue and costs

  - identification of the break-even point (see Chapter 8)

- Variances are used as a method of cost and revenue control. Variances can be either favourable (F) or adverse (A), and are acted upon if they are significant.

- There are a number of reasons why variances occur and, often, there is an inter-relationship (sub-variance) within variances – eg an adverse direct material variance may be resolved by reducing wastage or by buying at a cheaper price.

- Rolling budgets are kept up-to-date by adding a new budget period once the most recent budget period is complete.

budget

a financial plan for a business that is prepared in advance

operating profit

sales revenue minus direct materials, direct labour and overheads

fixed budget

budget which remains the same whatever the level of activity

flexible budget

budget which changes with the level of activity and takes into account different cost behaviour patterns

high/low method

method used to identify the amounts of fixed and variable costs within total costs

variance

the difference between the budgeted cost or revenue and the actual cost or revenue

favourable variance

where actual costs are lower than budgeted costs, or where actual revenues are higher than budgeted revenues

adverse variance

where actual costs are higher than budgeted costs, or where actual revenues are lower than budgeted revenues

controllable costs

costs which can be influenced by the manager/supervisor

non-controllable costs

costs which cannot be influenced by the manager/supervisor in the short term

rolling budget

budget which is kept up-to-date by adding a new budget period once the most recent budget period is completed to give the moving annual total (MAT)

Activities

7.1 The Accounts Supervisor of Nerca Manufacturing Limited has provided you with the following information:

- at 10,000 units of output, total costs are £50,000

- at 15,000 units of output, total costs are £65,000

You are to use the high/low method to identify the amount of fixed costs. The supervisor tells you that there is a constant unit variable cost up to this volume, and that there are no stepped fixed costs.

7.2 Boxster Limited makes boxes for customers in the food and drink industry. Using costing software, the company has prepared a budget for the next quarter for one of its boxes, BB4. This box is produced in batches and the budget is based on selling and producing 1,000 batches.

One of the customers of Boxster Limited has indicated that it may be significantly increasing its order level for box BB4 for the next quarter and it appears that activity levels of 1,200 batches and 2,000 batches are feasible.

The semi-variable costs should be calculated using the high/low method. If 3,000 batches are sold the total semi-variable cost will be £7,500 and there is a constant unit variable cost up to this volume.

Complete the table below and calculate the budgeted profit per batch of BB4 at the different activity levels.

Batches produced and sold	1,000	1,200	2,000
	£	£	£
Sales revenue	35,000		
Variable costs:			
• Direct materials	7,500		
• Direct labour	10,500		
• Overheads	6,000		
Semi-variable costs:	4,500		
• Variable element			
• Fixed element			
Total cost	28,500		
Total profit	6,500		
Profit per batch (to two decimal places)	6.50		

7.3 Today's date is 1 April 20-9.

You work as a Finance Assistant for First Class Flooring, a business producing and selling wooden flooring. It is owned by George and Janek. George and Janek have asked you to prepare some volume analysis for them, as they are looking at how much profit they could make in the next quarter at different levels of output.

Download the spreadsheet file 'MATST Chapter 7 Activities data' from the Osborne Books website.

Save the spreadsheet file in an appropriate location and rename it to 'MATST Chapter 7 Activities answer', so you can refer back to it.

Open the renamed file.

You are to calculate the profitability of First Class Flooring for different levels of output for the next quarter to 30 June 20-9.

In the worksheet called '7.3 Output Analysis':

1   **Amend all text** in this sheet to Calibri font.

2   Use 'copy' and 'paste values' to insert the figures from the worksheet '7.3 Budget' column C into the correct positions in column G of the '7.3 Output Analysis' worksheet.

3   **Insert** a row underneath row 3.

4   Enter 'Percentage of Current Budget' in A4.

5   In F4, G4, H4 and I4 **calculate** the % of each output vs 'Current Budget'. **Format** the cells % to two decimal places.

6   **Calculate** the budget for each output for the revenue and each cost, using **absolute referencing** where necessary.

7   **Format** the costs and revenues to currency £0,000.

8   **Format** all column headings in rows 2-4 as bold.

9   **Calculate** the operating profit for each level of output in row 16. Use **conditional formatting** to show profit in green font and losses in red font.

10 Perform a **spell check** and ensure all contents can be seen.

Save the file as 'MATST Chapter 7 Activities answers' and compare this to the answer file on the Osborne Books website.

7.4   The budget for direct labour is £10,800; the actual cost is £12,200. The budget for direct materials is £4,600; the actual cost is £4,350.

Which **one** of the following statements is correct?

(a)	direct labour variance £1,400 adverse; direct materials variance £250 adverse
(b)	direct labour variance £1,400 favourable; direct materials variance £250 favourable
(c)	direct labour variance £1,400 adverse; direct materials variance £250 favourable
(d)	direct labour variance £1,400 favourable; direct materials variance £250 adverse

7.5   The budget for sales revenue is £34,800; the actual sales revenue is £35,900. The budget for direct materials is £8,200; the actual cost is £8,650.

Which **one** of the following statements is correct?

(a)	sales revenue variance £1,100 adverse; direct materials variance £450 adverse
(b)	sales revenue variance £1,100 favourable; direct materials variance £450 favourable
(c)	sales revenue variance £1,100 adverse; direct materials variance £450 favourable
(d)	sales revenue variance £1,100 favourable; direct materials variance £450 adverse

7.6   A budget for 8,000 units of output shows a direct materials cost of £17,400 and a direct labour cost of £12,600. Actual output is 9,000 units.

Which **one** of the following gives the correct figures for the flexed budget?

(a)	direct materials £19,575; direct labour £14,175
(b)	direct materials £19,575; direct labour £12,600
(c)	direct materials £17,400; direct labour £14,175
(d)	direct materials £17,400; direct labour £12,600

7.7   The budget for 10,000 units of output shows a fixed overheads cost of £20,200. Actual output is 12,000 and the actual cost of fixed overheads is £21,000.

For the flexed budget identify whether the following statements are true or false by putting a tick in the relevant column of the table below.

Flexed budget	True	False
Fixed overheads are shown in the flexed budget at a cost of £24,240		
Fixed overheads are shown in the flexed budget at a cost of £21,000		
Fixed overheads are shown in the flexed budget at a cost of £20,200		
There is a fixed overheads variance of £800 adverse		
There is a fixed overheads variance of £2,040 adverse		
There is no fixed overheads variance		

7.8   Identify whether the following causes of variances would show as Adverse or Favourable by ticking the relevant column.

Cause of variance	Adverse	Favourable
Increase in material prices		
Fewer materials are wasted		
Cheaper materials are used		
Theft of materials		
An increase in direct labour pay		
More efficient use of direct labour		
Overtime is paid to direct labour		
A cheaper electricity supplier is used for the fixed overhead		
Selling prices are increased		
An increase in the number of units sold		

7.9   You work as an Accounts Assistant for Onslow Limited, a manufacturing business.

The company's budgeting software gives you the original budget costs and the actual performance for last month for product O14. Actual output was 90 per cent of budgeted output.

(a)   Complete the table below to show a flexed budget and the resulting variances against the budget. Show the actual variance amount, for each cost, in the column headed 'variance'.

Note:

- Adverse variances must be denoted with a minus sign or brackets.

- Enter 0 where any figure is zero.

	Original budget	Flexed budget	Actual	Variance
Output level	100%	90%	90%	
	£	£	£	£
Direct materials	4,700		5,200	
Direct labour	10,800		8,900	
Fixed overheads	4,100		4,500	
Total	19,600		18,600	

(b)   Which **one** of the following might have caused the variance for direct materials?

(a)	An increase in material prices	
(b)	More efficient use of materials	
(c)	A decrease in material prices	
(d)	Fewer material wasted	

7.10 You are the bookkeeper for Catering for Occasions, a business which provides catering services. It is owned by Amy Cox.

Amy has asked you to produce some management accounts information for her, analysing the year's performance against budget.

Download the spreadsheet file 'MATST Chapter 7 Activities data' from the Osborne Books website.

Save the spreadsheet file in an appropriate location and rename it to 'MATST Chapter 7 Activities data', so you can refer back to it.

Open the renamed file.

In the worksheet '7.10 Variance analysis':

1   Insert 'Catering for Occasions' in cell A1 in **bold, font size 11**. Insert 'Year ended 31 December 20-4' in cell A2, in the same **format**.

2   Ensure all data can be viewed, adjusting the **column width** as needed.

3   **Spell check** the information on the worksheet.

4   In cell C3 enter '£' and **copy** across to E3.

5   Use '**copy**' and '**paste link**' to insert figures from the worksheet '7.10 Budget and actual data' columns C and D into the correct positions in columns C and D of the '7.10 Variance analysis' worksheet.

6   **Format** all text and data to be Times New Roman.

7   **Insert a row** underneath row 2. Insert another row under row 4.

8   **Enter** '% of Budget' in F4. **Merge** and **centre** cells E2 and F2.

9   **Calculate** the £ variance for each item of revenue and each cost, for cells E6 - E16, using different **formulas** for revenue and cost variances. Use **custom formatting** to show favourable variances in black and adverse variances in red, as a '-' (minus) figure.

10 **Calculate** the variance % of budget in cells F6 - F16.

11 **Format** cells F6 to F16 to percentage to two decimal places.

12 **Format** the budget and actual figures to 0,000.

13 **Calculate** the operating profit for the budget (cell C17), actual results (cell D17) and, using cells C17 and D17, the variance value (cell E17).

14 Put an **IF statement** in E18 to show 'Balanced' if the variance £ column total equals E17 and 'check' if it does not.

15 **Insert a header** 'Catering for Occasions Year ended 31 December 20-4'.

16 **Insert a footer** to show 'Variance analysis' current time, and date.

17 Set the **print orientation** to landscape.

Save the file as 'MATST Chapter 7 Activities answers' and compare this to the answer file on the Osborne Books website.

7.11   Wyvern Ltd budgeted to manufacture and sell 30,000 units of product WV10 for the year ending 31 December. However, due to a shortage of raw materials it was only able to manufacture and sell 27,000 units.

(a)   Complete the following table to show a flexed budget and the resulting variances against this budget for the year. Show the actual variance amount, for sales revenue and each cost, in the column headed 'Variance'.

Note:

- Adverse variances must be denoted with a minus sign or brackets.
- Enter 0 where any figure is zero.

	Original budget	Flexed budget	Actual	Variance
Units sold	30,000	27,000	27,000	
	£000	£000	£000	£000
Sales revenue	1,800		1,650	
Less costs:				
Direct materials	550		500	
Direct labour	340		297	
Fixed overheads	650		645	
Operating profit	260		208	

(b)   Referring to your answer for part (a), which **one** of the variances has had the greatest impact in increasing the operating profit?

(a)	Sales revenue	
(b)	Direct materials	
(c)	Direct labour	
(d)	Fixed overheads	

7.12 Perran Ltd budgeted to manufacture and sell 22,000 units of product P14 for the year ending 31 December. However, due to an increase in demand it was able to manufacture and sell 27,500 units.

(a) Complete the following table to show a flexed budget and the resulting variances against this budget for the year. Show the actual variance amount, for sales revenue and each cost, in the column headed 'Variance'.

Note:

- Adverse variances must be denoted with a minus sign or brackets.

- Enter 0 where any figure is zero.

	Original budget	Flexed budget	Actual	Variance
Units sold	22,000	27,500	27,500	
	£000	£000	£000	£000
Sales revenue	1,400		1,875	
Less costs:				
Direct materials and direct labour	300		360	
Variable overheads	500		645	
Fixed overheads	420		480	
Operating profit	180		390	

(b) Which **one** of the following might have caused the variance for direct materials and direct labour?

(a)	An increase in material prices	
(b)	More efficient use of direct labour	
(c)	A increase in employees' pay	
(d)	More material wasted	

7.13 Excalibur Limited, a manufacturing business, has prepared budgeted information for three of its products, EX27, EX45 and EX67, for the next financial year.

Product	EX27	EX45	EX67
Sales revenue (£)	57,600	93,600	81,000
Direct materials (£)	20,250	41,400	42,750
Direct labour (£)	17,550	19,800	18,750

The company expects to produce and sell 9,000 units of EX27 and 12,000 units of EX45. The budgeted sales demand for EX67 is 25% greater than that of EX45. Budgeted fixed overheads are £33,845.

Complete the table below (to two decimal places) to show the budgeted contribution per unit of EX27, EX45 and EX67 sold, and the company's budgeted profit or loss for the year from these products.

	EX27 (£)	EX45 (£)	EX67 (£)	Total (£)
Sales volume (units)				
Selling price per unit				
Less: variable costs per unit				
Direct materials				
Direct labour				
Contribution per unit				
Total contribution				
Less: fixed overheads				
Budgeted *profit/(loss)				

* delete as appropriate

7.14 Excalibur Limited, a manufacturing business, has budgeted to manufacture 10,000 units of product EX94 last month. However, due to an increase in demand, it was able to manufacture 11,200 units.

(a) Complete the table below to show a flexed budget and the resulting variances against this budget for the month. Show the actual variance amount for each cost in the column headed 'Variance'.

Note:

- Adverse variances must be denoted with a minus sign or brackets.

- Enter 0 where any figure is zero.

	Original budget	Flexed budget	Actual	Variance
Units sold	10,000	11,200	11,200	
	£	£	£	£
Raw material A1	3,200		3,925	
Raw material A4	1,250		1,325	
Skilled labour	4,850		5,060	
Unskilled labour	1,225		1,440	
Variable overheads	4,025		4,310	
Fixed overheads	5,740		6,140	
Total costs	20,290		22,200	

(b) Which **one** of the following might have caused the variance for skilled labour?

(a)	An increase in employees' pay	
(b)	A reduction in employees' pay	
(c)	A higher paid grade of labour used	
(d)	Less efficient use of skilled labour	

7.15   Complete the following sentences which describe types of budgets:

(a)   A ……………..……….. budget changes with the level of activity and takes into account different cost behaviour patterns.

(b)   A ……………..……….. budget remains the same whatever the level of activity.

(c)   A ……………..……….. budget is kept up-to-date by adding a new budget period once the most recent budget period is completed.

7.16   Cuisinera Ltd manufactures cast-iron cooking pans and trays.

The Management Accountant has prepared budgeted data for the manufacture of product P39. At a production level of 1,500 units the budget shows a forecast loss of £2,500.

If production is increased to 2,000 units the Management Accountant has calculated that:

- the revenue per unit will decrease by 5% for all units

- variable materials costs will decrease by £2 per unit for all units

- variable labour costs will decrease by 10% for all units

- fixed costs will increase by £2,000

(a)   You are to complete the table below to show the forecast profit/(loss) for the manufacture and sale of 1,800 units and 2,000 units.

Enter your answers to the nearest whole pound (£); enter any loss figure with a minus sign or brackets.

	1,500 units	1,800 units	2,000 units
	£	£	£
Revenue	30,000		
Variable materials costs	12,000		
Variable labour costs	10,500		
Contribution to fixed costs	7,500		
Fixed costs	10,000		
Forecast profit/(loss)	(2,500)		

(b)   Which **one** of the following might be the reason for the change in labour costs at the level of 2,000 units?

(a) More efficient use of labour	
(b) An increase in employees' pay	
(c) Overtime paid for the increase in production	
(d) A higher grade of labour used	

8 Short-term decisions

this chapter covers...

In this chapter we see how cost accounting information is used to help a business to make short-term decisions. The techniques we will look at include:

- *break-even analysis*

- *margin of safety*

- *target profit*

- *profit-volume (contribution-sales) ratio*

- *'special order' pricing*

These techniques make use of the principles of marginal costing, which have been covered in Chapter 6.

SHORT-TERM DECISIONS

what is meant by short-term decisions?

By short-term decisions we mean those actions which will affect the costs and revenues of a business over the next few weeks and months, up to a maximum of one year ahead. For example, an ice cream manufacturer will make the decision to increase production over the summer months in order to meet higher sales.

types of short-term decisions

The decisions that we will be looking at include:

■ Break-even analysis, where the break-even point is the output level (units manufactured or services provided) at which the sales revenue is just enough to cover all the costs. Break-even analysis answers questions such as:

– what output do we need in order to break-even?

– at current levels of output we are above break-even, but how safe are we?

– we have to make a profit of £1,000 per week; what level of output do we need to achieve this?

– what is the effect on profit if we sell more than we think?

■ Marginal costing is used in short-term decision-making to identify the fixed and variable costs that are required to make a product or to provide a service. Once these are known, questions about pricing can be answered:

– if we increase prices, sales revenues are expected to fall but how will our profit be affected?

– if we decrease prices, sales revenues are expected to increase but how will our profit be affected?

– a potential customer wants to buy our product but at a lower price than we usually charge; how will our profit be affected?

what information is needed?

Decision-making is concerned with the future and always involves making a choice between alternatives. To help with decision-making it is important to identify **relevant (avoidable) costs and irrelevant (unavoidable) costs.**

Relevant costs are those costs that are changed by a decision.

Irrelevant costs are those costs that are not affected by a decision.

In order to make a decision, information is needed about costs and revenues:

- **future costs and revenues**
  - it is the expected future costs and revenues that are relevant
  - past costs and revenues are only useful in so far as they provide a guide to the future
  - costs already spent (called **sunk costs**) are irrelevant to decision-making

- **differential costs and revenues**
  - only those costs which alter as a result of decision-making are relevant and are avoidable costs
  - where costs are the same for each alternative, they are irrelevant and are unavoidable costs
  - thus any cost that changes when a decision is made is a relevant cost

In the short term, a business or organisation always attempts to make the best use of existing resources. This involves focusing on the relevant costs and revenues that will change as a result of a decision being made, such as:

- selling prices

- variable costs and the variable element of semi-variable costs

- contribution per unit of output, which is selling price minus variable cost

- marginal cost, which is the cost of producing one extra unit of output

Fixed period costs and the fixed element of semi-variable costs are irrelevant in decision-making as they do not alter in short-term decision-making, eg the rent of a car factory is most likely to be the same when 11,000 cars are produced each year instead of 10,000 previously. Although, remember that, in the long term, all costs are variable. Also, note that, in the long term, all costs are relevant and avoidable – for example, if a business decided to stop production and cease to trade.

reporting decisions

With decision-making it is essential that the costing information of estimated costs and revenues is reported to managers, or other appropriate people, with **professional competence**, in a clear and concise way. **Professional competence** is an **ethical principle** which requires accounting staff to maintain their professional knowledge and skill in order to provide a competent, professional service to employers and clients.

The information reported should include recommendations which are supported by well-presented reasoning. The decisions will not be taken by the person who has prepared the information, but the decision-makers will be influenced by the recommendations of the report. Remember that managers, and other appropriate people, do not always have an accounting background, so any form of presentation must be set out with professional competence and should use as little technical accounting terminology as possible.

Methods of presentation include:
- verbal presentations, including Zoom presentations
- written reports/emails

Both of these require a similar amount of preparation; the steps are:
- plan the report
- check that the plan deals with the tasks set
- be aware of the context in which the report is written
- express the report, verbal or written, in clear and concise English

written reports

The written report should include:
- an introduction, which sets out the task or the problem
- the content of the report, which explains the steps towards a solution and may include accounting calculations
- a conclusion, which includes a recommendation of the decision to be taken
- an appendix, which can be used to explain fully the accounting calculations, and to detail any sources of reference consulted

In this chapter we will see a written report on short-term decisions which makes recommendations – see page 285.

verbal presentations

A verbal presentation, including Zoom, requires the same professional competence in preparation and content as a written report and is probably the more difficult to present. Accordingly, verbal presentations often include support material in the form of handouts or computer presentations. Such material can be used to explain accounting data and to make key points and recommendations.

COSTS, CONTRIBUTION AND PROFIT

To help with short-term decision-making, costs are classified by their behaviour as either variable costs or fixed costs (with semi-variable costs being split between their fixed and variable elements). For example, a car manufacturer will need to identify:

- the variable product costs of each car

- the total fixed period costs of running the business over the period

When the manufacturer sells a car it receives the selling price, which covers the variable costs of the car. As the selling price is greater than the variable costs there will also be an amount of money – the contribution – available to pay off the fixed period costs incurred. The contribution formula (which we have seen in Chapter 6) is:

selling price per unit *less* variable cost per unit = contribution per unit

It follows that the difference between the sales income and the variable costs of the units sold in a period is the **total contribution** that the sales of all the units in the period make towards the fixed costs of the business.

A business can work out its profit for any given period from the total contribution and fixed costs figures:

total contribution *less* total fixed costs = profit

A statement of profit or loss (income statement) can be prepared in the following format:

		£
	Sales revenue	X
less	Variable costs	X
equals	Contribution	X
less	Fixed costs	X
equals	PROFIT	X

BREAK-EVEN

Break-even is often referred to as CVP (cost, volume, profit) analysis because we look at the costs of output, the volume of output, and the profit made.

Break-even is the point at which neither a profit nor a loss is made.

The break-even point is the output level (units manufactured or services provided) at which the sales revenue is just enough to cover all the costs. Break-even is the point at which the profit (or loss) is zero. The output level can be measured in a way that is appropriate for the particular business or organisation – either units of output or sales revenue. The break-even formula is:

$$\frac{fixed\ costs\ (£)}{contribution\ per\ unit\ (£)} = number\ of\ units\ to\ break\text{-}even$$

The formula for break-even in sales revenue is:

break-even point (units of output) x selling price per unit

This can also be calculated using the profit-volume (PV) ratio – see page 278.

In order to use break-even analysis, we need to know:

- selling price (per unit)
- costs of the product
  - variable costs (such as materials, labour) per unit
  - overhead costs, and whether these are fixed or variable
- limitations, such as maximum production capacity, maximum sales

The Case Study of Fluffy Toys Limited which follows shows how the break-even point can be worked out.

Case Study

FLUFFY TOYS LIMITED: BREAK-EVEN

situation

Fluffy Toys Limited manufactures soft toys and is able to sell all that can be produced. The variable product costs (materials and direct labour) of each toy are £10 and the selling price is £20 each. The fixed period costs of running the business are £5,000 per month. How many toys need to be produced and sold each month for the business to cover its costs, ie to break-even?

solution

This problem can be solved by calculation, by constructing a table, or by means of a graph. Which method is used depends on the purpose for which the information is required:

- the **calculation method** is quick to use and is convenient for seeing the effect of different cost structures on break-even point
- the **table method** shows the amounts of fixed and variable costs, sales revenue, and profit at different levels of production
- the **graph method** is used for making presentations – for example, to the directors of a company – because it shows in a visual form the relationship between costs and sales revenue, and the amount of profit or loss at different levels of production

Often the calculation or table methods are used before drawing a graph. By doing this, the break-even point is known and suitable scales can be selected for the axes of the graph in order to give a good visual presentation.

calculation method

The contribution per unit is:

	Selling price per unit	£20
less	Variable costs per unit	£10
equals	Contribution per unit	£10

Each toy sold gives a contribution (selling price less variable costs) of £10. This contributes towards the fixed costs and, in order to break-even, the business must have sufficient £10 'lots' to meet the fixed costs. Thus, with fixed costs of £5,000 per month, the break-even calculation is:

$$\frac{fixed\ costs\ (£)}{contribution\ per\ unit\ (£)} = \frac{£5,000}{£10} = 500\ toys\ each\ month$$

The break-even point is:

- in units of output, 500 toys each month
- in sales revenue, £10,000 each month (500 toys x £20)

table method

Units of output	Fixed costs A	Variable costs B	Total cost C	Sales revenue D	Profit/(loss)
			A + B		D − C
	£	£	£	£	£
100	5,000	1,000	6,000	2,000	(4,000)
200	5,000	2,000	7,000	4,000	(3,000)
300	5,000	3,000	8,000	6,000	(2,000)
400	5,000	4,000	9,000	8,000	(1,000)
500	5,000	5,000	10,000	10,000	nil
600	5,000	6,000	11,000	12,000	1,000
700	5,000	7,000	12,000	14,000	2,000

graph method

A graphical presentation uses money amounts as the common denominator between fixed costs, variable costs, and sales revenue.

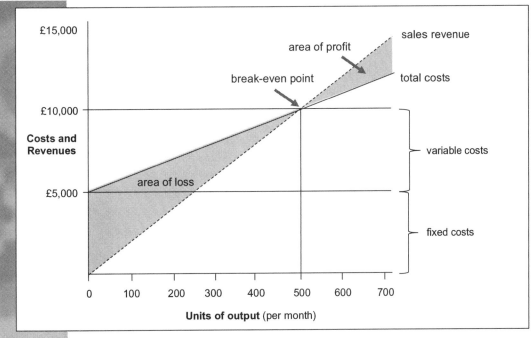

notes to the graph

- With a break-even graph, it is usual for the vertical (Y) axis to show money amounts; the horizontal (X) axis shows units of output/sales.
- The sales revenue and total costs lines are straight and diagonal.
- The fixed costs are unchanged at all levels of output, in this case they are £5,000 (but there might be stepped fixed costs).
- The variable costs commence, on the vertical axis, *from the fixed costs amount*, not from 'zero'. This is because the cost of producing zero units is the fixed costs.
- The fixed costs *plus* the variable costs form the *total costs* line.
- The point at which the total costs and sales revenue lines cross is the break-even point.
- From the graph we can read off the break-even point both in terms of units of output, 500 units on the horizontal axis, and in sales revenue, £10,000 on the vertical axis.
- The 'proof' of the break-even chart is:

		£
	Sales revenue (500 units at £20 each)	10,000
less	Variable costs (500 units at £10 each)	5,000
equals	Contribution	5,000
less	Fixed costs	5,000
equals	PROFIT/LOSS	nil

INTERPRETATION OF BREAK-EVEN

When interpreting break-even, it is all too easy to concentrate solely on the break-even point. The graph, for example, tells us much more than this: it also shows the profit or loss at any level of output/sales revenue contained within the graph. To find this, simply measure the gap between sales revenue and total costs at a chosen number of units, and read the money amounts off on the vertical axis (above break-even point it is a profit; below, it is a loss). For example, the graph in the Case Study above shows a profit or loss at:

- 700 units = £2,000 profit
- 200 units = £3,000 loss

Break-even analysis, whether by calculation, by table, or by graph, can be used by all types of businesses and organisations. For example, a shop will wish to know the sales it has to make each week to meet costs; a sports centre will wish to know the ticket sales that have to be made to meet costs; a club or society might wish to know how many raffle tickets it needs to sell to meet the costs of prizes and of printing tickets.

Once the break-even point has been reached, the **additional** contribution forms the profit. For example, if the business considered in the Case Study above was selling 650 toys each month, it would have a total contribution of 650 x £10 = £6,500; of this the first £5,000 will be used to meet fixed costs, and the remaining £1,500 represents the profit (which can be read off the break-even graph). This can be shown by means of a statement of profit or loss as follows:

		£
	Sales revenue (650 units at £20 each)	13,000
less	Variable costs (650 units at £10 each)	6,500
equals	Contribution (to fixed costs and profit)	6,500
less	Monthly fixed costs	5,000
equals	PROFIT FOR MONTH	1,500

BREAK-EVEN: MARGIN OF SAFETY

The margin of safety is the amount by which sales exceed the break-even point. Margin of safety can be expressed as:

- a number of units
- a sales revenue amount
- a percentage, using the following formula

$$\frac{current\ output - break\text{-}even\ output}{current\ output} \times 100 = percentage\ margin\ of\ safety$$

worked example: margin of safety

In the Case Study earlier in this chapter, Fluffy Toys Limited (pages 273-275), if current output is 700 units, while the break-even point is 500 units, the margin of safety is:

- 200 units (ie 700 – 500)

- £4,000 of sales revenue (ie 200 units at £20 each)

- 29 per cent, ie

$$\frac{700 - 500}{700} \times \frac{100}{1}$$

By interpreting this margin of safety we can say that production/sales could fall by these values before the business reaches break-even point and ceases to make a profit.

Margin of safety is especially important in times of recession as it expresses to management the amount of the 'cushion' which current production/revenue gives beyond the break-even point. Where there is a comparison to be made between two or more products, each with different margins of safety, the product with the highest margin of safety is looked on favourably; however, margin of safety is only one factor in decision-making.

BREAK-EVEN: TARGET PROFIT

A further analysis of break-even is to calculate the production costs and sales revenue in order to give a certain amount of profit – the **target profit.** This is calculated as:

$$\frac{fixed\ costs\ (\pounds) + target\ profit\ (\pounds)}{contribution\ per\ unit\ (\pounds)} = number\ of\ units\ of\ output$$

The sales revenue to achieve the target profit is calculated as:

number of units of output x sales revenue per unit (£) = target sales revenue (£)

Thus, if Fluffy Toys Limited (see the Case Study on pages 273-275) required a profit of £2,000 per month, the calculation is:

$$\frac{\pounds5,000 + \pounds2,000}{\pounds10} = 700\ units\ of\ output,\ with\ a\ sales\ revenue\ of\ \pounds14,000$$

* 700 units x £20 each = £14,000

This target profit can then be shown by means of a statement of profit or loss as follows:

		£
	Sales revenue (700 units at £20 each)	14,000
less	Variable costs (700 units at £10 each)	7,000
equals	Contribution (to fixed costs and profit)	7,000
less	Monthly fixed costs	5,000
equals	TARGET PROFIT FOR MONTH	2,000

Target profit can also be calculated by making use of the profit-volume (contribution-sales) ratio (see below).

BREAK-EVEN: PROFIT-VOLUME RATIO

The profit-volume (PV) ratio analyses the relationship between the amount of contribution and the amount of the value of sales. It is often referred to as the contribution-sales (CS) ratio. PV ratio is calculated as:

$$\frac{contribution\ (£)}{selling\ price\ (£)} = profit\text{-}volume\ ratio$$

The ratio, or percentage, can be calculated on the basis of a single unit of production or for the whole business. Note that the higher the PV ratio, the better for the business.

In break-even analysis, if fixed costs are known, we can use the PV ratio to find the sales revenue at which the business breaks-even, or the sales revenue to give a target profit.

worked example: profit-volume ratio

Referring back to the Case Study (Fluffy Toys Limited), the PV ratio (on a per unit basis):

$$\frac{contribution\ (£)}{selling\ price\ (£)} = \frac{£10^*}{£20} = 0.5\ or\ 50\%$$

* selling price (£20) – variable costs (£10) = contribution £10

Fixed costs are £5,000 per month, so the sales revenue needed to break-even is:

$$\frac{fixed\ costs\ (£)}{PV\ ratio} = \frac{£5,000}{0.5\ (see\ above)} = £10,000$$

As the selling price is £20 per toy, we can get back to the break-even in units of output as follows:
£10,000 ÷ £20 = 500 units

If the directors of Fluffy Toys Limited wish to know the sales revenue that must be made to achieve a target profit of £2,000 per month, the PV ratio is used as follows:

$$\frac{\text{fixed costs + target profit}}{\text{PV ratio}} = \text{required level of sales}$$

$$\frac{£5,000 + £2,000}{0.5} = £14,000$$

As the selling price is £20 per toy, we can get to the units of output as follows:

£14,000 ÷ £20 = 700 units to achieve a target profit of £2,000.

WHEN TO USE BREAK-EVEN ANALYSIS

Break-even analysis is often used:

before starting a new business

The calculation of break-even point is important in order to see the sales revenue needed by the new business in order to cover costs, or to make a particular level of profit. The feasibility of achieving the level can then be considered by the owner of the business, and other parties such as the bank manager.

when making changes

The costs of a major change will need to be considered by the owners and/or managers. For example, a large increase in production will, most likely, affect the balance between fixed and variable costs. Break-even analysis will be used as part of the planning process to ensure that the business remains profitable.

to measure profits and losses

Within the limitations of break-even analysis, profits and losses can be estimated at different levels of output from current production. Remember that this can be done only where the new output is close to current levels and where there is no major change to the structure of costs.

to answer 'what if?' questions

Questions such as 'what if sales revenue falls by 10 per cent?' and 'what if fixed costs increase by £1,000?' can be answered – in part at least – by break-even analysis. The effect on the profitability of the business can be seen, subject to the limitations noted earlier. A question such as 'what if sales revenue increases by 300 per cent?' is such a fundamental change that it can only be answered by examining the effect on the nature of the fixed and variable costs and then recalculating the break-even point.

to evaluate alternative view points

Businesses often have a choice of production methods – this is particularly true of a manufacturing business. For example, a product could be made:

- either, by using a labour-intensive process, with a large number of employees supported by basic machinery

- or, by using an automated process (such as robotics or artificial intelligence) with very few employees

In the first case, the cost structure will be high variable costs (labour) and low fixed costs (depreciation of machinery). In the second case, there will be low variable costs and high fixed costs. Break-even analysis can be used to examine the relationship between the costs which are likely to show a low break-even point in the first case, and a high break-even point in the second. In this way, the management of the business is guided by break-even analysis; management will also need to know the likely sales revenues, and the availability of money with which to buy the machinery.

'SPECIAL ORDER' PRICING

'Special order' pricing is where a business uses spare capacity to make extra sales of its product at a lower price than its normal selling price.

'Special order' pricing, which makes use of marginal costing techniques, is normally used once the business is profitable at its current level of output, ie it has reached break-even. Additional sales – at 'special order' prices – can be made at a selling price above marginal cost, but below absorption cost. In this way, profits can be increased, provided that the additional sales are spare capacity. The key to increasing profit from additional sales is to ensure that a contribution to profit is made from the special order: the Case Study which follows illustrates this principle.

WYVERN BIKE COMPANY: SPECIAL ORDERS

situation

The Wyvern Bike Company produces 100 bikes a week, and sells them for £200 each. Its costs are as follows:

Weekly costs for producing 100 bikes

	£
Direct materials (£40 per bike)	4,000
Direct labour (£50 per bike)	5,000
Production overheads (fixed)	5,000
Total cost	14,000

The owner of the company has been approached by an internet sales company which wishes to buy:

- either 50 bikes each week at a price of £120 per bike
- or 100 bikes each week at a price of £80 per bike

The bikes can be produced in addition to existing production, with no increase in overheads. The special order is not expected to affect the company's existing sales. How would you advise the owner?

solution

The *absorption cost* of producing one bike is £140 (£14,000 ÷ 100 bikes). The internet sales company is offering either £120 or £80 per bike. On the face of it, with an absorption cost of £140, both orders should be rejected. However, as there will be no increase in production overheads, we can use *marginal costing* to help with decision-making.

The *marginal cost* per bike is £90 (direct materials £40 + direct labour £50), and so any contribution, ie selling price less marginal cost, will be profit:

- **50 bikes at £120 each**

  Although below absorption cost, the offer price of £120 is above the marginal cost of £90 and increases profit by the amount of the £30 extra contribution, ie (£120 – £90) x 50 bikes = £1,500 extra profit.

- **100 bikes at £80 each**

  This offer price is below absorption cost of £140 and marginal cost of £90; therefore there will be a fall in profit if this order is undertaken of (£80 – £90) x 100 bikes = £1,000 reduced profit.

Weekly statements of profit or loss

	Existing production of 100 units	Existing production + 50 units @ £120 each	Existing production + 100 units @ £80 each
	£	£	£
Sales revenue (per week):			
100 bikes at £200 each	20,000	20,000	20,000
50 bikes at £120 each	–	6,000	–
100 bikes at £80 each	–	–	8,000
	20,000	26,000	28,000
Less production costs:			
Direct materials (£40 per unit)	4,000	6,000	8,000
Direct labour (£50 per unit)	5,000	7,500	10,000
Production overheads (fixed)	5,000	5,000	5,000
PROFIT	6,000	7,500	5,000

The conclusion is that the first special order from the internet sales company should be accepted, and the second declined. The general rule is that, once the fixed overheads have been recovered (ie break-even has been reached), provided additional units can be sold at a price above marginal cost, then profits will increase.

COST AND REVENUE PLANNING

The principles of marginal costing can also be used to establish the effect of changes in costs and revenues on the profit of the business. Such changes include

- a reduction in selling prices in order to sell a greater number of units of output and to increase profits

- an increase in selling prices (which may cause a reduction in the number of units sold) in order to increase profits

Any change in selling prices and output will have an effect on sales revenues and on variable costs; there may also be an effect on fixed costs. The best way to show such changes is to use a columnar layout which shows costs and revenues as they are at present and then – in further columns – how they will be affected by any proposed changes. This method is used in the Case Study which follows.

Case Study

BROOKES AND COMPANY: COST AND REVENUE PLANNING

situation

Brookes and Company produces tool kits for bikes. The company produces 100,000 tool kits each year and the costs per unit of output are:

	£
Direct materials	2.20
Direct labour	2.00
Variable production overheads	0.80
Fixed production overheads	0.40
Fixed non-production overheads	0.60
	6.00

The selling price per tool kit is £10.00

The Managing Director of the business has been thinking about how to increase profits for next year. He has asked you, as an Accounts Assistant, to look at the following two proposals from a management accounting viewpoint.

Proposal 1

To reduce the selling price of each tool kit to £9.00. This is expected to increase sales by 20,000 kits each year to a total of 120,000 kits. Apart from changes in variable costs, there would be no change in fixed costs.

Proposal 2

To increase the selling price of each tool kit to £12.00. This is expected to reduce sales by 20,000 kits each year to a total of 80,000 kits. Apart from changes in variable costs, there would be a reduction of £5,000 in fixed production overheads.

You are to prepare a report for the Managing Director stating your advice, giving reasons and workings. Each of the two proposals is to be considered on its own merits without reference to the other proposal.

solution

The following calculations, presented in columnar format, will form an appendix to the report to the Managing Director. Note that the three money columns deal with the existing production level, and then the two proposals.

For additional information, the break-even point and margin of safety are calculated at each of the output levels.

	existing output (100,000 units)	proposal 1 (120,000 units)	proposal 2 (80,000 units)
BROOKES AND COMPANY			
Cost and revenue planning for next year			
	£	£	£
Sales revenue			
100,000 units at £10.00 per unit	1,000,000		
120,000 units at £9.00 per unit		1,080,000	
80,000 units at £12.00 per unit			960,000
TOTAL REVENUE	1,000,000	1,080,000	960,000
Direct materials at £2.20 per unit	220,000	264,000	176,000
Direct labour at £2.00 per unit	200,000	240,000	160,000
Variable production overhead at £0.80 per unit	80,000	96,000	64,000
Fixed production overhead	40,000	40,000	35,000
Fixed non-production overhead	60,000	60,000	60,000
TOTAL COSTS	600,000	700,000	495,000
PROFIT	400,000	380,000	465,000

Tutorial notes:

* fixed production overheads: 100,000 units at £0.40 per unit (note £5,000 reduction under proposal 2)

* fixed non-production overheads: 100,000 units at £0.60 per unit

Break-even

$$\frac{\text{fixed costs (£)}}{\text{contribution per unit (£)}} \quad = \quad 20{,}000 \text{ units} \quad 25{,}000 \text{ units} \quad 13{,}572 \text{ units}$$

Margin of safety

$$\frac{\text{current output} - \text{break-even output}}{\text{current output}} \times 100 \quad = \quad 80\% \quad 79\% \quad 83\%$$

REPORT

To: Managing Director

From: Accounts Assistant

Date: Today

Cost and revenue planning for next year

Introduction

- You asked for my comments on the proposals for next year's production.

- I have looked at the expected profits if

  - we continue to sell 100,000 units each year at a selling price of £10.00 each

  - selling price is reduced to £9.00 per unit, with sales volume expected to increase to 120,000 units each year

  - selling price is increased to £12.00 per unit, with sales volume expected to decrease to 80,000 units each year

Report

- Please refer to the calculations sheet.

- At existing levels of production, the contribution (selling price – variable costs) per unit is:

  £10.00 – (£2.20 + £2.00 + £0.80) = £5.00 per unit x 100,000 units = £500,000

  Fixed costs total £100,000.

  Therefore profit is £400,000.

- For proposal 1, the contribution per unit is:

  £9.00 – (£2.20 + £2.00 + £0.80) = £4.00 per unit x 120,000 units = £480,000

  Fixed costs total £100,000.

  Therefore profit is £380,000.

- For proposal 2, the contribution per unit is:

  £12.00 – (£2.20 + £2.00 + £0.80) = £7.00 per unit x 80,000 units = £560,000

  Fixed costs total £95,000.

  Therefore profit is £465,000.

Conclusion

- Proposal 2 maximises the contribution from each unit of output, has the lowest break-even point and the highest margin of safety.

- Although we expect to sell fewer units, the total contribution is greater.

- There is a small reduction in fixed costs under this proposal.

- Before proposal 2 is adopted, we would need to be sure of the accuracy of the expected fall in sales volume.

MARGINAL COSTING IN DECISION-MAKING

We have seen how marginal costing principles can be useful in short-term decision-making. Nevertheless, there are a number of points that must be borne in mind:

■ **fixed period costs must be covered**

A balance needs to be struck between the output that is sold at above marginal cost and the output that is sold at absorption cost. The overall contribution from output must cover the fixed period costs of the business and provide a profit. Overall output should be sold at a high enough price to provide a contribution equal to or greater than fixed costs.

■ **separate markets for marginal cost**

It is sensible business practice to separate out the markets where marginal cost is used. For example, a business would not quote a price based on absorption cost to retailer A and a price based on marginal cost to retailer B, when A and B are both in the same town! It would be better to seek new markets – perhaps abroad – with prices based on marginal cost.

■ **effect on customers**

One of the problems of using marginal cost pricing to attract new business is that it is difficult to persuade the customer to pay closer to, or above, absorption cost later on. Thus one of the dangers of using marginal cost is that profits can be squeezed quite dramatically if the technique is used too widely.

■ **problems of product launch on marginal cost basis**

There is great temptation to launch a new product at the keenest possible price – below absorption cost (but above marginal cost). If the product is highly successful, it could well alter the cost structure of the business. However, it could also lead to the collapse of sales of older products so that most sales are derived from output priced on the marginal cost basis – it may then be difficult to increase prices to above absorption cost levels.

■ **special edition products**

Many businesses use marginal costing techniques to sell off older products at a keen price. For example, car manufacturers with a new model due in a few months' time will package the old model with 'special edition' features and sell it at a low price (but above marginal cost).

- **'last minute' sales**

  'Last minute' businesses sell products such as empty hotel rooms and unsold flight seats which have no value once the opportunity to sell has passed – for example, the flight has taken off. As the deadline approaches the business (or its computer algorithm) uses marginal costing to work out the lowest price that will cover the marginal costs of the product and make a small contribution to fixed costs.

SPREADSHEET SKILLS FOR MANAGEMENT ACCOUNTING

using spreadsheets to support short-term decision-making

In this chapter, you have studied how to use cost-volume profit-volume analysis and estimates of future costs and revenues to determine contribution and break-even points. In real life, spreadsheets will usually be used for this. Different scenarios can easily be analysed when a spreadsheet is built to be flexible, if costs, volumes and revenues can be changed.

Product managers may want this type of information to consider different scenarios. Using protection on a worksheet can ensure the integrity of the formulas, allowing product managers to consider several different options for price and volume, before finalising decisions with the finance department.

The break-even point can be established by using a spreadsheet, either using formulas or linking data to a break-even graph. Putting the information into a graph often helps managers understand the concept of break-even and shows how profits change as outputs increase.

Let's perform some cost-volume-profit analysis using spreadsheets in the following Case Study.

Case Study

SPREADSHEET SKILLS TO PROVIDE MANAGEMENT ACCOUNTING INFORMATION

situation

Blue Sky Kites makes kites and sells them via the internet. A new design, the 'Easy Breath' kite, is a light-weight kite which uses built-in channels that are blown up to keep its shape. This makes it quite simple to carry around, so the design is expected to be popular.

The owners of Blue Sky Kites, Ed and Tom, would like you to do some cost-volume-profit analysis on the new product.

The following costs have been determined:

Materials per kite: £16.50

Labour cost per kite: £7.00

Selling price per kite: £50.00

Fixed overheads per month: £24,000

Download the spreadsheet file 'MATST Ch 8 Spreadsheet Case Study Blue Sky Kites data' from the Osborne Books website.

Save the spreadsheet file in an appropriate location and rename it 'MATST Ch 8 Spreadsheet Case Study Blue Sky Kites answer'.

Open the renamed file.

On the worksheet 'Easy Breath Kite', you are required to:

1 **Insert** the information for the Easy Breath Kite for sales price per kite, variable cost per kite and fixed costs per month (cells D5:D7).

2 Complete the table for the different levels of output (cells B9:F16). **Calculate** the fixed costs, variable costs, total costs, sales revenue and profit/(loss), using the information in cells D5:D7, and **absolute referencing**, in an appropriate formula.

3 **Calculate** the break-even units in cell D19, using an appropriate formula, using **ROUNDUP** to the nearest whole number.

4 **Calculate** the break-even revenue in cell D20, using an appropriate **formula**.

5 Using an appropriate formula, **calculate** the margin of safety % if 1,200 kites are sold, in cell D21.

6 **Hide** columns B and C.

7 **Insert a line graph** on the existing worksheet showing the total costs and sales revenue for the number of kites sold using the data from the table.

8 **Title the graph** 'Easy Breath Kite Projection', **font size 14, format bold**.

9 **Change the colour** of the 'Total Costs' line to small blue dashes and the 'Sales Revenue' line to long red dashes.

10 **Amend the vertical axis** to show units in steps of £5,000.

11 **Move the legend** to the right-hand side.

12 **Add the title** 'Amount' to the vertical axis, font size 12.

13 **Add the title** 'Number of Kites Sold' to the horizontal axis, font size 12.

solution

The 'Easy Breath Kite' worksheet currently looks like this:

	A	B	C	D	E	F	G
1	**Blue Sky Kites**						
2	*Easy Breath Kite*						
3	*Cost Information*						
4				£			
5	Sales price per kite						
6	Variable cost per kite						
7	Fixed costs per month						
8	Units	Costs (Materials & Labour)	Fixed Costs	Total Costs	Sales Revenue	Profit/ (Loss)	
9	0						
10	200						
11	400						
12	600						
13	800						
14	1000						
15	1200						
16	1400						
17							
18							
19	Break-even, units						
20	Break-even revenue, £						
21	Margin of safety %						
22							

Points 1 to 5 use spreadsheet skills you have already used in the activities in this book. Once you have completed points 1 to 2, the 'Easy Breath Kite' worksheet will look like that shown on the next page:

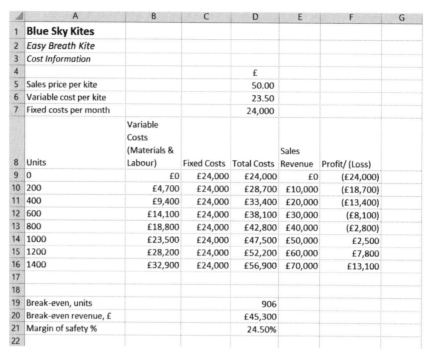

	A	B	C	D	E	F	G
1	**Blue Sky Kites**						
2	*Easy Breath Kite*						
3	*Cost Information*						
4				£			
5	Sales price per kite			50.00			
6	Variable cost per kite			23.50			
7	Fixed costs per month			24,000			
8	Units	Variable Costs (Materials & Labour)	Fixed Costs	Total Costs	Sales Revenue	Profit/(Loss)	
9	0	£0	£24,000	£24,000	£0	(£24,000)	
10	200	£4,700	£24,000	£28,700	£10,000	(£18,700)	
11	400	£9,400	£24,000	£33,400	£20,000	(£13,400)	
12	600	£14,100	£24,000	£38,100	£30,000	(£8,100)	
13	800	£18,800	£24,000	£42,800	£40,000	(£2,800)	
14	1000	£23,500	£24,000	£47,500	£50,000	£2,500	
15	1200	£28,200	£24,000	£52,200	£60,000	£7,800	
16	1400	£32,900	£24,000	£56,900	£70,000	£13,100	
17							
18							
19	Break-even, units			906			
20	Break-even revenue, £			£45,300			
21	Margin of safety %			24.50%			
22							

This table is like that in the Fluffy Toys Limited Case Study you looked at earlier in the chapter. If you found any elements of this difficult, go back and review this again.

The formulas used in the spreadsheet are shown below:

	A	B	C	D	E	F	G
1	**Blue Sky Kites**						
2	*Easy Breath Kite*						
3	*Cost Information*						
4				£			
5	Sales price per kite			50			
6	Variable cost per kite			=16.5+7			
7	Fixed costs per month			=24000			
8	Units	Variable Costs (Materials & Labour)	Fixed Costs	Total Costs	Sales Revenue	Profit/(Loss)	
9	0	=$D$6*A9	=$D$7	=B9+C9	=$D$5*A9	=E9-D9	
10	200	=$D$6*A10	=$D$7	=B10+C10	=$D$5*A10	=E10-D10	
11	400	=$D$6*A11	=$D$7	=B11+C11	=$D$5*A11	=E11-D11	
12	600	=$D$6*A12	=$D$7	=B12+C12	=$D$5*A12	=E12-D12	
13	800	=$D$6*A13	=$D$7	=B13+C13	=$D$5*A13	=E13-D13	
14	1000	=$D$6*A14	=$D$7	=B14+C14	=$D$5*A14	=E14-D14	
15	1200	=$D$6*A15	=$D$7	=B15+C15	=$D$5*A15	=E15-D15	
16	1400	=$D$6*A16	=$D$7	=B16+C16	=$D$5*A16	=E16-D16	
17							
18							
19	Break-even, units			=ROUNDUP(D7/(D5-D6),0)			
20	Break-even revenue, £			=+D19*D5			
21	Margin of safety %			=(1200-D19)/1200			
22							

Using formulas in the table which refer to the cost information in D5 to D7 makes it simple to update, should the sales price, variable costs or fixed costs change. It also means the spreadsheet can easily be used for other products.

The rest of the question is focused on creating a break-even graph. It is often easier to use visual tools, such as graphs to show the break-even point, as it is clear how total costs and sales revenue changes as more kites are sold.

If you have not used graphs very often, refer to the Osborne Books Spreadsheets for Management Accounting Tutorial to help you with any elements you are unsure of.

Once the remaining points 6 to 13 are complete, the 'Easy Breath Kite' chart should look like this. Note: To highlight the break-even point an arrow and text box have been added to the picture below.

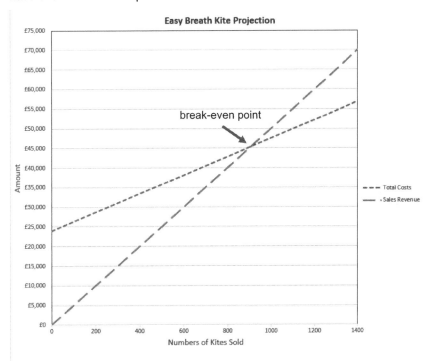

As you can see, the chart agrees with and illustrates the calculations. The calculated break-even revenue of £45,300 is the point where sales revenue and total costs meet, as is the calculated break-even number of kites sold, 906. The graph can be used by the management at Blue Sky Kites to plan for certain levels of output and predict the resulting profit or loss.

As the spreadsheet is built using formulas and only the costs and revenues are input, it could be used for sensitivity analysis to consider different pricing and/or cost scenarios. This spreadsheet then provides a useful tool when assessing new products.

You can download the answer file, 'MATST Ch 8 Spreadsheet Case Study Blue Sky Kites answer', from the Osborne Books website.

Chapter Summary

- Short-term decisions are those actions which will affect the costs and revenues over the next few weeks and months.

- Break-even analysis distinguishes between fixed period costs and variable product costs.

- The relationship between sales revenue, fixed costs and variable costs is used to ascertain the break-even point, by means of a calculation, a table, or a graph.

- Break-even analysis can show:

  - break-even point in units of production

  - break-even point in sales revenue

  - profit or loss at given levels of production and sales revenue

- 'Special order' pricing is where a business uses spare capacity to make extra sales of its product at a lower price than normal. In order to increase profits the special order selling price must be above marginal cost.

- Marginal costing principles are used in short-term decision-making for break-even and 'special order' pricing.

Key Terms

relevant costs	those costs that are changed by a decision
irrelevant costs	those costs that are not affected by a decision
sunk costs	past costs which are irrelevant to decision-making
professional competence	ethical principle requiring accounting staff to maintain their professional knowledge and skill
cost behaviour	the way in which costs behave in different ways as the volume of output or activity changes
contribution	selling price less variable cost
cost, volume, profit (CVP)	analysis of the costs of output, the volume of output, and the profit made

break even

the point at which neither a profit nor a loss is made, calculated in units of output as follows:

$$\frac{fixed\ costs\ (£)}{contribution\ per\ unit\ (£)}$$

margin of safety (%)

the amount by which sales exceed the break-even point; calculated as a percentage as follows:

$$\frac{current\ output - break\text{-}even\ output}{current\ output} \times\ 100$$

target profit (units)

the output that needs to be sold to give a certain amount of profit, calculated in number of units of output as follows:

$$\frac{fixed\ costs\ (£) + target\ profit\ (£)}{contribution\ per\ unit}$$

profit-volume (PV) ratio

ratio which expresses the amount of contribution in relation to the amount of the value of sales:

$$\frac{contribution\ (£)}{selling\ price\ (£)}$$

PV ratio is used to calculate the sales revenue needed to break-even as follows:

$$\frac{fixed\ costs\ (£)}{PV\ ratio}$$

marginal cost

the cost of producing one extra unit of output

Activities

8.1 Mike Etherton, a manufacturer of cricket bats, has the following monthly costs:

Material cost	£8 per bat
Labour cost	£12 per bat
Selling price	£35 per bat
Fixed overheads	£12,000

You are to:

(a) Read from the graph (below) the profit or loss if 200 bats, and 1,200 bats are sold each month.

(b) Prepare a table showing costs, sales revenue, and profit or loss for production of bats in multiples of 100 up to 1,200. Does the table confirm your answer to (a)?

(c) If production is currently 1,000 bats per month, what is the margin of safety, in units and as a percentage?

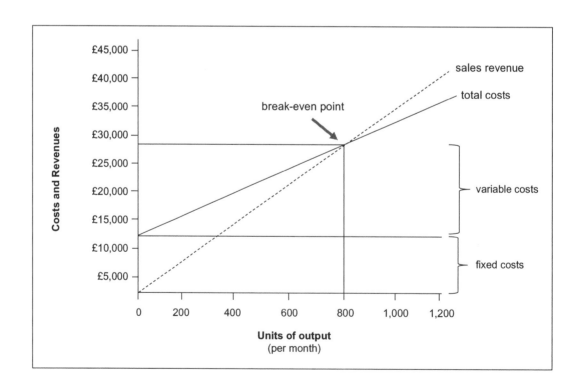

8.2 Wyvern Limited makes a product which is numbered WV5. The selling price of product WV5 is £28 per unit and the total variable cost is £16 per unit. Wyvern Limited estimates that the fixed costs per quarter associated with this product are £24,000.

(a) Calculate the budgeted break-even, in units per quarter, for product WV5.

units

(b) Calculate the budgeted break-even revenue, in £ per quarter, for product WV5.

£

(c) Complete the table below to show the budgeted margin of safety in units, and the margin of safety percentage if Wyvern Limited sells 2,500 units or 4,000 units of product WV5 per quarter.

Units of WV5 sold per quarter	2,500	4,000
Margin of safety (units)		
Margin of safety percentage		

(d) If Wyvern Limited wishes to make a profit of £18,000 per quarter, how many units of WV5 must it sell?

units

(e) If Wyvern Limited reduces the selling price of WV5 by £1, what will be the impact on the break-even point and the margin of safety per quarter, assuming no change in the number of units sold?

(a)	The break-even point will decrease and the margin of safety will increase	
(b)	The break-even point will stay the same but the margin of safety will decrease	
(c)	The break-even point will decrease and the margin of safety will stay the same	
(d)	The break-even point will increase and the margin of safety will decrease	

8.3 Riley Limited has made the following estimates for next month:

Selling price	£25 per unit
Variable cost	£10 per unit
Fixed costs for the month	£300,000
Forecast output	30,000 units
Maximum output	40,000 units

As an Accounts Assistant, you are to carry out the following tasks:

Task 1

Calculate:

- the profit-volume ratio
- the break-even point in units next month
- the break-even point in sales revenue next month
- the margin of safety in units and sales revenue at the forecast output for next month
- the number of units to generate a profit of £100,000 next month

Task 2

Calculate the profit for next month at:

- the forecast output
- the maximum output

Task 3

One of the managers has suggested that, if the selling price were reduced to £20 per unit, then sales would be increased to the maximum output.

- For this new strategy, you are to calculate:
    - the profit-volume ratio
    - the break-even point in units
    - the break-even point in sales revenue
    - the margin of safety in units and sales revenue
    - the forecast profit
- Prepare a report for the General Manager advising whether you believe that the new strategy should be implemented. (Use a copy of the report form in the Appendix.)

8.4 You are the bookkeeper for Catering for Occasions, owned by Amy Cox. The business caters for weddings and parties.

You have been given the sales information for January to June by Amy. She would like you to do some analysis of her jobs over the last six months. You are to calculate the actual break-even point, along with some other key information, to help Amy improve her quotation process.

Open the file 'MATST Chapter 8 Activities data'.

Save the file as 'MATST Chapter 8 Activities answers'.

In the worksheet '8.1 Jan-June jobs':

1 **Unhide the rows** for March to May.

2 **Edit the header** to show 'Catering for Occasions Jan - June sales'.

3 Find the average sales and contribution for each month, using **SUBTOTAL**.

4 In J2, use **COUNTA** to find the total number of events so far in the year, referring to column A.

5 Use **cell fill** to colour the average sales (C39), average contribution (F39) and number of jobs (J2) in light green.

6 **Calculate** the average contribution/sales ratio to **two decimal places** in cell C41, based on the food/drink costs and wages costs being the only variable costs.

7 Using the total overheads in the worksheet '8.4 Overheads' and the average contribution/sales ratio, use an appropriate formula to **calculate** the break-even revenue for the six months of January to June in cell C43 to the nearest £, using the **currency format**.

8 Using an appropriate formula, **calculate** the break-even number of events in the year in cell C45, rounding the number of events as appropriate. **Format the cell** to no decimal places.

9 Using an appropriate formula, **calculate** the margin of safety, in terms of events, rounding the number of events as appropriate. **Format** cell C47 to no decimal places.

10 Put a single line **border** around cells A41:C47 and **highlight the cell area** in light yellow.

Save your answer and compare it to 'MATST Chapter 8 Activities answers', which is available to download on the Osborne Books website.

8.5 You are an Accounts Assistant at Durning Foods Limited. The company produces ready meals which are sold in supermarkets and convenience stores. You have just received the following email from the General Manager:

EMAIL
From: General Manager
To: Accounts Assistant
Subject: Production line of Indian meals
Date: 8 October 20-8
Please prepare a cost and revenue plan for the Indian meals production line for November.
We plan to sell 36,000 meals in November and will base our projection on the cost and revenue behaviour patterns experienced during July to September.

The management accounting records show the following for July, August and September:

DURNING FOODS LIMITED: Production line for Indian meals
Actual results for July to September 20-8

	July	August	September
Number of meals sold	33,500	31,000	34,700
	£	£	£
Direct materials	25,125	23,250	26,025
Direct labour	15,075	13,950	15,615
Direct expenses	6,700	6,200	6,940
Overheads for the production line	12,525	12,150	12,705
Other production overheads	4,000	4,000	4,000
Total cost	63,425	59,550	65,285
Sales revenue	67,000	62,000	69,400
Profit	3,575	2,450	4,115

Tutorial note:

* direct costs are variable

* overheads for the production line are semi-variable

Task 1

Use the above information to identify the projected cost and revenue figures for November based on their behaviour during July to September.

Task 2

After you have completed Task 1, the General Manager sends you the following email:

EMAIL
From: General Manager
To: Accounts Assistant
Subject: Production line of Indian meals
Date: 14 October 20-8

Thank you for your work on the cost and revenue projections for November.

Our Buying Department has found an alternative supplier of materials – meat, rice and sauces. The buyers say that the quality is better than we use at the moment and the price is 20 per cent cheaper. However, we will need to buy in larger quantities to get such good prices. To allow for this, I would like to increase production and sales to 40,000 meals in November.

Could you please recalculate the cost and revenue projections for November 20-8 based on the increased activity and taking advantage of the cheaper prices?

Also, please calculate the break-even point in terms of the number of meals to be sold in November if we make this change. Please include a note of the margin of safety we will have.

- Use your identified cost and revenue behaviour patterns to adjust for the change in material costs and to prepare a revised projection for November 20-8 based on sales of 40,000 meals.
- Calculate the break-even point in terms of meals to be sold in November if the lower priced materials are used.
- Calculate the margin of safety, expressed as a percentage of the increased planned activity for November.

8.6   You are the bookkeeper for Luke Graham, a sole trader, who runs Trendy Togs, a clothing business.

Today's date is 10 July 20X6.

Luke Graham is considering opening a shop and he has asked you to do some analysis for him. He would like you to determine what level of revenue he will need to break-even and make a profit. Luke has been given some cost information by a friend who owns a coffee shop, Coffee and Cake, in the same area he is looking to set up the shop, to help him.

(a)   You have been given a spreadsheet containing the Coffee and Cake cost data. You will need to adjust the data, in line with Luke's instructions, to create the break-even information for Trendy Togs' shop.

Download the spreadsheet file 'MATST Chapter 8 Activities data' from the Osborne Books website, if you have not already done so.

Open the renamed file.

In the worksheet called '8.6 Break-even analysis', if you have not already done so:

1   **Insert** 'Trendy Togs' in cell A1 in **bold**, font size 12.

2   **Insert** 'Break-even analysis new shop' in cell A2 in bold, font size 12.

3   **Spell check** the text information on the '8.6 Coffee and Cake data' worksheet then copy the information in A4-A12 over into the '8.6 Break-even analysis' worksheet, starting at A5.

4   **Link** the costs across from the '8.6 Coffee and Cake data' worksheet into the '8.6 Break-even analysis' worksheet and '**copy'** and '**paste link**' to the correct place in column B.

5   Increase staff costs from 1.5 people to 2 by amending the **formula** in cell B5. Amend the text to reflect this change.

6   Increase 'Electricity' and 'Rates' costs by 5%.

7   **Insert** depreciation of '£5000', based on Luke's estimate.

8   Increase 'Rent' and 'Insurance' costs by 10%.

9   In cell B3 enter '£'.

10   **Calculate** the total in cell B15.

11   **Format** all text to be in Arial.

12   **Adjust width of column** A so all text can be seen.

(b) Luke has asked you to calculate the break-even revenue and how much he would have to sell to achieve a profit of £50,000. The contribution/sales ratio is 0.5.

You are required to complete the table underneath the cost information to show the Break-even revenue and the revenue needed for a profit of £50,000.

In the worksheet 8.6 'Break-even analysis':

1. Underneath the text 'Target profit' **insert** the amount £50,000 in cell C19.

2. **Link cells** B21 and C21 to the total fixed costs from the working above.

3. On the line for 'Revenue Required', use a **formula** to calculate the revenue required assuming the margin of 50%.

4. **Insert** a title 'Break-even analysis new shop' at the top of the table in cells A17-C17, using the **text formatting** in cell A2, **merged** and **centred** over the table.

5. Ensure figures are **formatted** £0,000.

(c) Luke Graham has now asked you what the revenue would need to be if he wished to earn £75,000 of profit.

In the worksheet 8.6 'Break-even analysis':

1. **Insert a column** between the Break-even and Target Profit columns.

2. Complete the new column, **calculating** the Target profit at £75,000.

(d) Luke has decided he would like to set up a bonus scheme for the staff. He will pay a bonus of 1.5% of sales for every £ of sales above the break-even revenue. He would like you to calculate how much the bonus will be at revenue levels of £160,000, £300,000 and £400,000.

In the worksheet '8.6 Break-even analysis':

1. **Insert** 'Bonus' in cell C27.

2. The bonus payment should qual 1.5% of sales above the break-even revenue amount, which has been calculated in cell B23. **Use absolute referencing** for the break-even revenue amount. Where no bonus is payable, the **IF statement** should show 'No bonus'.

3. **Copy** and **paste** the **IF statement** in cell C29 into cells C30 and C31 to calculate the bonus payable at revenues of £300,000 and £400,000 respectively.

Save your answer and compare it to 'MATST Chapter 8 Activities answers', which is available to download on the Osborne Books website.

8.7 Westfield Limited makes 2,000 units of product Exe each month. Information from the computer system shows that the company's costs are:

Monthly costs for making 2,000 units of Exe

	£
direct materials	6,000
direct labour	4,000
production overheads (fixed)	8,000
total cost	18,000

Each unit of Exe is sold for £12.

The management of the company has been approached by a buyer who wishes to purchase:

- *either* 200 units of Exe each month at a price of £6 per unit

- *or* 500 units of Exe each month at a price of £4 per unit

The extra units can be produced in addition to existing production, with no increase in overheads. The special order is not expected to affect the company's existing sales. How would you advise the management?

8.8 Popcan Limited manufactures and sells a soft drink which the company sells at 25p per can. Currently output is 150,000 cans per month, which represents 75 per cent of production capacity. The company has an opportunity to use the spare capacity by producing the product for a supermarket chain which will sell it under their own label. The supermarket chain is willing to pay 18p per can.

Use the following information from the computer system to advise the management of Popcan Limited if the offer from the supermarket should be accepted:

POPCAN LIMITED	
Costs per can	
	pence
Direct materials	5
Direct labour	5
Production overheads (variable)	4
Production overheads (*fixed)	6
* fixed production overheads are apportioned on the basis of current output	

8.9 What is meant by the principle of professional competence? Choose **one** answer.

(a)	An accounting qualification is always proof of professional competence	
(b)	The Accounts Supervisor is the person who ensures compliance with ethical principles	
(c)	Anyone with an accounting qualification can report to clients on all aspects of decision-making	
(d)	Accounting staff are required to maintain their knowledge and skills to provide a competent service	

8.10 Scandi Toys Ltd manufactures a range of wooden toys for babies and toddlers.

(a) The following cost data is available for product C18, a wooden play cooker.

Units	Total Cost £
300	15,000
500	20,000

Calculate the variable cost for each unit of C18.

£ [ ]

Calculate the total cost of producing 600 units of C18.

£ [ ]

(b) The following information is available for product T12, a pull-along wooden train:

Selling price per unit	£25
Variable cost per unit	£12
Total fixed costs	£2,600
Budgeted production	500 units

Calculate the break-even point in units for T12.

[ ] units

Calculate the margin of safety in units for T12 at budgeted production of 500 units.

	units

Calculate the number of units of T12 that must be sold in order to produce a profit of £5,200.

	units

8.11 This Activity is about short-term decision-making.

Complete the following statements by selecting the correct options to complete the gaps.

Select your options, which can be used more than once, from the following list: break-even, fixed, profit, profit-volume, selling, target, variable.

Selling price minus .... costs equals contribution.

Total contribution minus .... costs equals profit.

.... point is where neither a profit nor a loss is made.

Current output minus .... output equals margin of safety.

Contribution divided by selling price equals .... ratio.

Production costs and sales revenues can be used to calculate a given level of profit, known as the .... profit.

9 Cash budgeting and resources ratios

this chapter covers...

- the purpose of a cash budget

- the differences between cash and profit

- the principles of forecasting cash receipts and payments:

    - sales, purchases and production

    - trade receivables and payables

    - acquisition and disposal of non-current assets

    - capital and loans, loan repayments and drawings

- the funding methods for the acquisition of non-current assets:

    - cash purchase

    - part exchange

    - borrowing in the form of loans and hire purchase

- the importance of liquidity and the use of resources ratios:

    - inventory holding period

    - trade receivables collection period

    - trade payables payment period

- the working capital cycle

- ways of improving cash flow

PURPOSE OF A CASH BUDGET

A cash budget details the forecast bank receipts and payments, usually on a month-by-month basis for the next three, six or twelve months, in order to show the forecast bank balance at the end of each month throughout the budget period.

Note that, although we call it a cash budget, it details receipts and payments through the bank account – it focuses on the liquid funds of a business held at the bank.

The cash budget focuses on the *liquidity* of a business, ie the ability to have sufficient money in the bank to pay its way on a day-to-day basis. Without liquidity even a profitable business will eventually run out of money to pay its suppliers, wages and expenses. It is often a lack of cash (lack of liquidity) that causes businesses to fail.

From the cash budget, the managers of a business can decide what action to take when a surplus of cash is shown to be available or, as is more likely, when a bank overdraft needs to be arranged.

DIFFERENCES BETWEEN CASH AND PROFIT

Sometimes people in business get confused between 'cash' and 'profit' and may say: "I am making a profit, but why is my bank overdraft increasing?"

The difference between cash and profit is:

■ cash is money in the bank or held as physical cash (eg in the cash till)

■ profit is a calculated figure which shows the surplus of income over expenditure for a period: it takes note of adjustments for accruals and prepayments and non-cash items such as depreciation and provision for doubtful receivables. It does not include capital expenditure (ie the purchase of non-current assets), or owner's drawings/dividends, or loans raised and repaid

The reasons why a business can be making a profit but its bank balance is reducing (or its bank overdraft is increasing) include:

■ capital expenditure – the purchase of non-current assets reduces cash but profit is affected only by the amount of depreciation on the asset

■ increase in trade receivables – if more goods are being sold, this should lead to an increase in profit but, until trade receivables pay, there is no benefit to the bank balance

■ decrease in trade payables – if trade payables are paid earlier than usual there will be no effect on profit but the bank balance will reduce (or a bank overdraft will increase)

- increase in inventory – if more inventory is purchased there will be an increase in profit as it is sold, but paying for inventory will reduce the money at bank (or increase an overdraft) until the money from extra sales is received

- prepayment of expenses at the year end – as a prepayment is an expense for next year, early payment will have no effect on the current year's profit, but the bank balance will be affected by the payment

- loan repaid – this has no effect on profits (although loan interest may be reduced), but the bank balance will be affected by the repayment

- drawings/dividends paid to owners – will have no effect on profit, but the bank balance will be affected by the payment

Clearly the above will work in reverse for a business that is making reduced profits. To some extent, it may see money flowing into the bank account – collecting receipts from trade receivables, reduced payments to trade payables, sale of non-current assets, etc.

LAYOUT OF A CASH BUDGET

A format for a cash budget, with example figures for a new business, follows. Note how the format is ideally suited for the use of a spreadsheet – which enables changes to be made easily and the effect of 'what if' questions (eg 'what if sales increase by 20 per cent?') to be seen.

MIKE ANDERSON, TRADING AS 'ART SUPPLIES' CASH BUDGET FOR THE SIX MONTHS ENDING 30 JUNE 20-8						
	Jan	Feb	Mar	Apr	May	Jun
	£	£	£	£	£	£
Receipts						
Capital introduced	20,000					
Trade receivables	-	-	3,000	6,000	6,000	10,500
Total receipts for the month	20,000	-	3,000	6,000	6,000	10,500
Payments						
Non-current assets	8,000					
Inventory	5,000					
Trade payables	-	2,000	4,000	4,000	7,000	7,000
Operating expenses	1,600	1,600	1,600	1,600	1,600	1,600
Drawings	1,000	1,000	1,000	1,000	1,000	1,000
Total payments for the month	15,600	4,600	6,600	6,600	9,600	9,600
Net cash flow	4,400	(4,600)	(3,600)	(600)	(3,600)	900
Opening bank balance/(overdraft)	-	4,400	(200)	(3,800)	(4,400)	(8,000)
Closing bank balance/(overdraft)	4,400	(200)	(3,800)	(4,400)	(8,000)	(7,100)

Note that the cash budget consists of three main sections:

- Receipts for the month

- Payments for the month

- Summary of bank account

Within receipts and payments, a business can choose as many row items and descriptions as it requires – there is no set format for a cash budget.

The summary of the bank account – at the bottom of the cash budget – shows net cash flow (total receipts minus total payments) added to the bank balance at the beginning of the month. This gives the estimated closing bank balance or overdraft at the end of the month. An overdraft is shown either with brackets or with a minus sign.

benefits of a cash budget

The use of a cash budget enables a business to:

- monitor its cash resources

- plan future expenditure, eg financing new non-current assets

- control costs and revenues to ensure that either:

    - a bank overdraft is avoided (so saving interest and charges payable), or

    - a bank overdraft or loan can be arranged in advance

- reschedule payments where necessary to avoid bank borrowing, eg delay the purchase of non-current assets

- coordinate the activities of the various sections of the business, eg the production department buys in materials not only to meet the expected sales of the sales department but also at a time when there is cash available

- communicate the overall aims of the business to the various sections and to check that the cash will be available to meet their needs

- identify any possible cash surpluses in advance and take steps to invest the surplus on a short-term basis (so earning interest)

FORECASTING CASH RECEIPTS AND PAYMENTS

Receipts

Receipts are analysed to show the amount of money expected to be received from:

- cash sales

– trade receivables, ie credit sales

– disposal of non-current assets

– capital introduced

– loans received

Payments

Payments show how much money is expected to be paid in respect of:

– cash purchases

– trade payables, ie credit purchases

– production costs, such as expenses

– acquisition of non-current assets*

– repayment of capital

– drawings

– loans repaid

* important note: depreciation of non-current assets does not feature in cash budgets because it is a non-cash expense, ie no cash flow.

The timing of receipts and payments is important when preparing a cash budget. Businesses prepare budgets for purchases, sales, expenses, the acquisition/disposal of non-current assets. From these budgets the timing of cash receipts and payments can be estimated and the requirement for capital, or loans, or a bank overdraft, can be anticipated.

Note that the timing of receipts from trade receivables and payments to trade payables is important. This is because many businesses buy and sell their materials and products on credit terms – the payments and receipts may well not be in the same months as indicated by the purchases and sales budgets. This aspect of cash budgets is explained below.

CASH FLOWS FROM TRADE RECEIVABLES AND TO TRADE PAYABLES

Within a cash budget it is necessary to take note of the timing of receipts from trade receivables and payments to trade payables. This is because many businesses buy their materials and sell their products on credit terms – the payments and receipts may well not be in the same months as indicated by the purchases and sales budgets. The Worked Examples on the next pages show how payments and receipts can be calculated.

Trade receivables

The period of credit allowed to customers – the time between making a sale and receiving payment – affects the cash flow of the business in that this period is being financed by the seller. It is important that, as well as having good products and being able to sell them, cash flows in from customers are received without delay and by the due date. Customers who don't pay on time will need to be chased and some businesses will employ a Credit Controller to do this in a systematic way.

For example, a business has agreed trade terms of 30 days with its customers. This means that sales made in January should be paid for in February, the sales made in February should be paid for in March, etc. The cash budget needs to record these receipts from credit sales for the month when they are expected to be received.

Note that, for trade receivables, it may be necessary to allow for prompt payment discount and irrecoverable debts – these will affect the expected cash receipts shown in the cash budget.

worked example – receipts from trade receivables

situation

You are to calculate receipts from trade receivables for January to June using the following information (ignore VAT):

- the amount of trade receivables at 1 January is £14,000

- credit sales are budgeted to be £30,000 per month from January to March, and £40,000 per month from April to June

- half of the trade receivables pay in the month of sale and take advantage of 2% prompt payment discount (PPD)

- the remainder of trade receivables pay in the month after sale, without prompt payment discount – however, 3% of these will not pay and should be regarded as irrecoverable debts

solution

RECEIPTS FROM TRADE RECEIVABLES						
	January	**February**	**March**	**April**	**May**	**June**
	£	£	£	£	£	£
Month of sale	15,000	15,000	15,000	20,000	20,000	20,000
PPD	(300)	(300)	(300)	(400)	(400)	(400)
Following month	14,000	15,000	15,000	15,000	20,000	20,000
Irrecoverable debts	(420)	(450)	(450)	(450)	(600)	(600)
Receipts for month	28,280	29,250	29,250	34,150	39,000	39,000

Trade payables

An important aspect of running a business is to ensure that trade payables are paid on time. Delaying payment beyond the due date may well mean that suppliers refuse to deliver any further goods, which will lead to production problems and have an effect on the whole business. Suppliers usually offer a period of credit, and so the period between taking delivery of the goods and making payment for them gives the buyer a period when its purchases are being financed by the seller. Nevertheless, the buyer needs to ensure that cash is available in the bank account to meet payments to trade payables as they fall due.

Payments to suppliers link to the cash budget, which records payments to trade payables – and the master budget – where the amount of trade payables is shown as a liability on the forecast statement of financial position.

For example, a business has agreed trade terms of 60 days with its suppliers. This means that purchases made in January should be paid for in March, the purchases made in February should be paid for in April, etc. The cash budget needs to record these payments for credit purchases for the month when they are expected to be made.

Note that for trade payables, it may be necessary to allow for prompt payment discount, which will affect the expected cash payments shown in the cash budget.

worked example – payments to trade payables

situation

You are to calculate payments to trade payables for July to December using the following information (ignore VAT):

- the amount of trade payables at 1 July is £12,000
- credit purchases are budgeted to be £25,000 per month in July and August, £30,000 per month in September and October, and £34,000 per month in November and December
- half of the trade payables allow prompt payment discount (PPD) of 3% and are paid in the month of purchase
- the remainder of trade payables are paid in the month after purchase, without prompt payment discount

solution

PAYMENTS TO TRADE PAYABLES						
	July	August	September	October	November	December
	£	£	£	£	£	£
Month of purchase	12,500	12,500	15,000	15,000	17,000	17,000
PPD	(375)	(375)	(450)	(450)	(510)	(510)
Following month	12,000	12,500	12,500	15,000	15,000	17,000
Payments for month	24,125	24,625	27,050	29,550	31,490	33,490

Case Study	

CASH BUDGET FOR A NEW BUSINESS

situation

Your friend, Evie Myles, is setting up a business which sells art supplies to schools and colleges. She is to start trading on 1 January 20-4 with an initial capital of £15,000 which she will pay in to her business bank account. On this date she will buy office equipment at a cost of £5,000.

For the next six months Evie has budgeted her purchases, sales and expenses as follows (ignore VAT):

	Purchases £	Sales £	Expenses £
January	8,000	4,000	1,000
February	6,000	5,500	1,250
March	5,000	7,000	1,500
April	5,500	7,500	1,500
May	5,500	8,000	1,750
June	4,000	6,500	*2,000

* including depreciation of office equipment £500

She will pay for purchases in the month after purchase; likewise she expects her customers to pay for sales in the month after sale. Expenses will be paid in the month they are incurred. She will take £600 each month from the business as drawings.

Evie asks you to prepare a cash budget for the first six months of her new business.

solution

EVIE MYLES CASH BUDGET FOR THE SIX MONTHS ENDING 30 JUNE 20-4						
	Jan £	**Feb** £	**Mar** £	**Apr** £	**May** £	**Jun** £
Receipts						
Capital introduced	15,000					
Trade receivables	-	4,000	5,500	7,000	7,500	8,000
Total receipts for the month	15,000	4,000	5,500	7,000	7,500	8,000
Payments						
Non-current assets	5,000					
Trade payables	-	8,000	6,000	5,000	5,500	5,500
Expenses	1,000	1,250	1,500	1,500	1,750	*1,500
Drawings	600	600	600	600	600	600
Total payments for the month	6,600	9,850	8,100	7,100	7,850	7,600
Net cash flow	8,400	(5,850)	(2,600)	(100)	(350)	400
Opening bank balance/(overdraft)	-	8,400	2,550	(50)	(150)	(500)
Closing bank balance/(overdraft)	8,400	2,550	(50)	(150)	(500)	(100)

* excluding depreciation £500 (a non-cash expense)

Evie's cash budget shows:

∞ a reduction in the bank balance during the early months of the new business

∞ the need for a small overdraft facility – to be negotiated with the bank

∞ an improving cash flow at the end of the period

Note that, in order to avoid a bank overdraft, Evie could consider funding the non-current assets by other means than cash purchase – see below.

FUNDING NON-CURRENT ASSETS

Funding methods available for the acquisition of non-current assets include cash purchase, part-exchange, loans and hire purchase.

Note: in AAT Assessments you could be asked to identify the suitability of each funding method in the context of a business situation.

cash purchase

This is where the business has sufficient cash in its bank account – or in an interest-bearing deposit account – to pay in full for the new asset. Alternatively, a business might buy an asset on standard commercial credit terms, eg 30 days, and then make payment for the asset from the bank account before the end of the term – legal title to the asset is usually acquired at the date of purchase, ie before the date of payment.

part-exchange

This is where an old asset is 'traded in' as part of the purchase price of a new asset, the balance remaining due being paid either in cash or by borrowing; part exchange is especially common when a new vehicle – car or van – is being purchased.

borrowing – loans

A loan agreement with a bank or a finance company is a method of funding the purchase of non-current assets, such as vehicles, machinery, computers and office equipment. The bank or finance company lends an agreed sum of money to the business, which uses the funds to purchase the asset. Ownership of the asset belongs to the business from the start – unlike hire purchase – although the bank or finance company will often require security to back their loan. The borrower makes agreed repayments which cover the cost and the interest (which may be fixed for the term of the loan). Loans are available for periods of up to seven years (sometimes longer).

Note that a bank overdraft is not the same as a loan – instead it is a short-term facility which allows a business to overdraw its bank account and, usually, is reviewed each year. A bank overdraft is not a suitable funding method for non-current assets.

borrowing – hire purchase

A hire purchase agreement from a finance company enables a business (the hirer) to have the use of a non-current asset on payment of a deposit. The finance company owns the asset and the hirer makes regular instalment payments – monthly, quarterly or half-yearly – which pay the cost plus interest over a set period. At the end of the hire purchase period, ownership of the asset usually passes from the finance company to the business. Hire purchase is a medium-term agreement which is often used to finance non-current assets such as vehicles, machinery, computers and office equipment.

USE OF RESOURCES RATIOS

Use of resources ratios measures how efficiently the owners and/or managers control the current aspects of the business – inventories, trade receivables and trade payables. Like all accounting ratios, comparison needs to be made either with figures for the previous year, or with a similar business.

inventory holding period (days)

$$\frac{Inventories}{Cost\ of\ sales} \times 365$$

Inventory holding period is the number of days' inventories held on average. This figure will depend on the type of goods sold by the company. For example, a market trader selling fresh flowers, who finishes each day when sold out, will have an inventory holding period of one day. By contrast, a jewellery shop – because it may hold large quantities of jewellery – will have a much longer inventory holding period, perhaps sixty or ninety days, or longer. Nevertheless, it is important for a business to keep its inventory holding period as short as possible, subject to being able to meet the needs of most of its customers. A company which is improving in efficiency will generally have a shorter inventory holding period comparing one year with the previous one, or with the inventory holding period of similar companies.

Note that inventory holding period can only be calculated where a business buys and sells goods; it cannot be used for a business that provides a service.

trade receivables collection period (days)

$$\frac{Trade\ receivables}{Revenue} \times 365$$

This calculation shows how many days, on average, trade receivables take to pay for goods sold to them by the business. The collection time can be compared with that for the previous year, or with that of a similar business. In the UK, most trade receivables should make payment within about 30 days; however, with international trade, it may take longer for the proceeds to be received. A comparison from year-to-year of the collection period is a measure of the efficiency at collecting the money that is due to it and we are looking for some reduction in trade receivables' days over time. Ideally trade receivables' days should be shorter than trade payables' days, thus indicating that money is being received from trade receivables before it is paid out to trade payables.

trade payables payment period (days)

$$\frac{\textit{Trade payables}}{\textit{Cost of sales}} \quad x \ 365$$

This calculation is the opposite aspect to that of trade receivables: here we are measuring the speed it takes to make payment to trade payables. While trade payables can be a useful temporary source of finance, delaying payment too long may cause problems. This ratio is most appropriate for businesses that buy and sell goods; it is not so important for a business that provides a service. Generally we would expect to see the trade payables' days period to be longer than the trade receivables' days, ie money is being received from trade receivables before it is paid out to trade payables. We would also be looking for a similar figure for trade payables' days from one year to the next: this would indicate a stable company.

working capital cycle (days)

Working capital cycle = Inventory days + Receivable days – Payable days

This is a further use of the ratios covering the working capital items of inventory, trade receivables and trade payables. The working capital cycle measures the period of time between payment for goods received into inventory and the collection of cash from customers in respect of their sale. The shorter the time between the initial outlay and the ultimate collection of cash, the lower the amount of working capital needed by the business.

The working capital cycle is illustrated in the diagram on the next page:

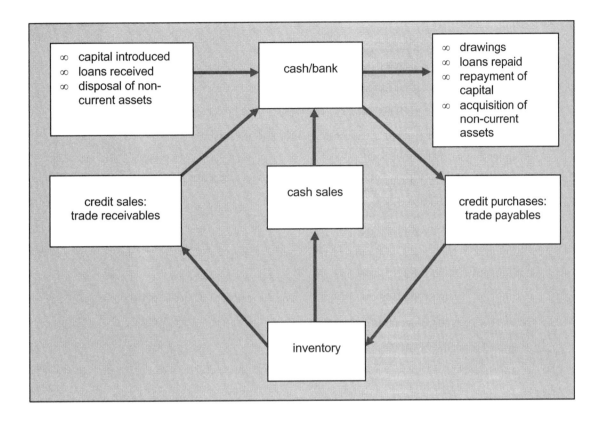

IMPROVING CASH FLOW

When the working capital cycle has been calculated, it needs to be compared either with the working capital cycle for the previous year, or with a similar business. It will show either a better position, ie the time has been reduced, or a worse position, ie the time has been increased.

As we have seen earlier in this chapter, liquidity is important for the survival of a business. Preparing a cash budget and using resources ratios are tools that are used by a business to ensure that there is sufficient liquidity, without which the business is heading for failure.

Of course, the liquidity needs will vary from business to business. For example, a market trader selling fruit and vegetables will need a much smaller cushion of liquidity than, say, a furniture manufacturer. Here the market trader will buy stock for the stall the day before and sell the goods for cash, which then gives the liquidity to buy stock for the next market day. By contrast, the furniture manufacturer will buy in materials on credit terms, pay expenses of running the factory, and give credit terms to furniture shops that stock its products.

Where a business has insufficient liquidity – and many new businesses are set up with too little liquidity – there are two options to improve the situation:

■ raise additional finance from the owners in the form of capital

■ raise additional debt finance in the forms of loans, overdrafts, hire purchase

For smaller businesses, family and friends may be prepared to help out with finance.

To improve the cash flow of the working capital cycle, businesses have the following options:

■ speed up the rate of debt collection (and lower the number of receivable days)

■ slow down the rate of payment to suppliers (and increase the number of payable days)

■ reduce inventory (and lower the number of inventory days)

■ offer prompt payment discount (PPD) to customers

■ dispose of non-current assets

However, it may not be possible to put these into practice as there could be unintended consequences – reducing inventory might mean that a poorer service is offered to customers, speeding up debt collection might mean that customers seek other suppliers who offer better terms, and slowing payment to suppliers might mean that they refuse to supply unless payment is made immediately. Offering PPD reduces the profitability of the business and, once offered to customers, will prove difficult to withdraw at a later stage. The sale of non-current assets – unless surplus to requirements – could affect the ability of the business to continue to trade.

Case Study

MANAGING WORKING CAPITAL

situation

You are the Accounts Assistant at Builders Supplies Limited.

The following figures have been extracted from the accounting software:

	last year	this year
	£	£
Revenue	685,400	722,300
Cost of sales	372,700	405,500
Trade receivables	45,500	70,350
Trade payables	37,250	55,050
Inventory	62,750	75,400

All purchases and sales are made on credit.

Today, you have been asked to:

∞ Calculate the resources ratios for last year and this year

 – inventory holding period (days)

 – trade receivables collection period (days)

 – trade payables payment period (days)

Show your calculations (using a 365 day year) and take each to the nearest whole day.

∞ calculate the working capital cycle in days for last year and this year

∞ make brief notes on your findings for the accountant, to include suggestions for improvement where necessary

solution

RESOURCES RATIOS	last year (days)	this year (days)
inventory holding period *inventories/cost of sales x 365*	$\frac{62,750}{372,700}$ x 365 = 61	$\frac{75,400}{405,500}$ x 365 = 68
trade receivables collection period *trade receivables/revenue x 365*	$\frac{45,500}{685,400}$ x 365 = 24	$\frac{70,350}{722,300}$ x 365 = 36
trade payables payment period *trade payables/cost of sales x 365*	$\frac{37,250}{372,700}$ x 365 = 36	$\frac{55,050}{405,500}$ x 365 = 50
inventory days *plus* receivable days *minus* payable days	61 +24 –36	68 +36 –50
WORKING CAPITAL CYCLE	= 49	= 54

Notes:

∞ Whilst the revenue of the business has increased during the year, the working capital cycle has deteriorated by five days.

∞ Inventory days have increased, which is not good for liquidity. Which inventory lines are affected? Is any of the inventory out-of-date/unsaleable?

∞ Receivable days have increased, again not good. What are the stated terms of payment? Are there any irrecoverable debts?

∞ Payable days have increased, which means extra credit is being taken from trade payables. This could lead to supply and liquidity problems in the future if trade payables insist on cash payment terms. Have extra credit terms been negotiated with suppliers?

∞ In summary, the working capital cycle has increased, which indicates that there is less liquidity in the business. All of the resources ratios have deteriorated – the business does need to address its worsening liquidity position.

SPREADSHEET SKILLS FOR MANAGEMENT ACCOUNTING

using spreadsheets to support cash management, including calculating resources ratios

In this chapter, you have studied how to forecast cash receipts and payments, using a suggested format. At work, the finance department will set up spreadsheets to do this, using current information to calculate future cash receipts and payments and forecast bank balances.

It is useful if the assumptions in the cash budget then link to the cash flow, via appropriate formulas. Different scenarios can be considered quickly if, for example, the business wants to change the terms of credit, as the new cash balances will then be calculated automatically. It is a good idea to protect the cash flow formulas in the worksheet, so no-one can make amendments that may 'corrupt' the cash flow. This is particularly important if the spreadsheet is complex.

A spreadsheet may also be used for reporting the resources ratios, part of monitoring working capital. It could highlight adverse and positive changes in these ratios, either graphically or using formatting, to help managers understand them more easily.

Let's complete a forecast cash flow for a small business in the following Case Study.

Case Study

SPREADSHEET SKILLS TO PRODUCE A CASH FLOW

situation

Charlie and Monty are setting up new business, which produces a range of products aimed at customers with limited outdoor space. The 'Pantry in a Pot' range includes plants chosen for planting in window boxes and pots.

You must create a cash flow budget for the next six months for the new product range. The budgeted information is included on the spreadsheet 'MATST Ch 9 Spreadsheet Case Study Pantry in a Pot data' on the Osborne Books website.

You also have the following information:

- Credit customers are to be given 30 days terms. Charlie and Monty expect 90% of customers to pay on time, with the remaining 10% paying in the following month.

- Purchases are paid for in the month after purchase. December's purchases are expected to be £8,716.

- Labour costs and production overheads are paid in the month they are incurred. Included in production overheads is depreciation on equipment of £1,400 per month.

- Administration, marketing and distribution overheads will be paid for during the month they are incurred in.

- A new packing area for the 'Pantry in a Pot' range is being set up in the gardening sheds at the start of January, costing £30,000.

- Charlie and Monty are investing capital of £60,000 at the start of January. The business has also applied for a loan of £35,000, expected in February. The first monthly loan repayment of £650 is due on 1 March.

- The expected opening bank balance is £0 at the start of January.

Download the spreadsheet file 'MATST Ch 9 Spreadsheet Case Study Pantry in a Pot data' from the Osborne Books website.

Save the spreadsheet file in an appropriate location and rename it 'MATST Ch 9 Spreadsheet Case Study Pantry in a Pot answer'.

Open the renamed file.

On the worksheet 'Pantry in a Pot information':

1   **Insert** the customer payment information into cells B3 and B4.

2   **Cell fill** all information on sales (cells A2:H9) with orange, on purchases (cells A10:H12) with green, on labour costs (cells A13:H15) with blue and on overheads (cells A16: H19) with pink.

3   **Format** all cells in A6:H20 with a **single line border**.

4   **Format** all rows with months in (rows 6, 10, 13 and 16) to **bold, italic, font size 12.**

5   **Insert two rows** above row 19.

6   In row 19, **insert** 'Depreciation' in A19 and the depreciation amount for each month in cells B19:G19, **calculating** the total in cell H19.

7   In row 20, **insert** 'Production overheads (exc dep'n)' in A20 and **calculate** this for each month. **Calculate** the total in cell H20.

On the worksheet 'Pantry in a Pot cash flow':

8   Using appropriate **formulas to link** to the information in the worksheet 'Pantry in a Pot information', **calculate** the receipts from cash sales and credit sales for January to June.

9   **Insert** the remaining receipts in row 7 (loan and capital) where appropriate.

10 **Calculate,** using an appropriate formula, total receipts for each month January to June.

11 **Insert** the payment of January purchases in B10. Using appropriate **formulas, link** the payment descriptions from the worksheet 'Pantry in a Pot information' and also **calculate** the payments for January to June for:
    - 'Purchases (on credit)'
    - 'Wages and salaries',
    - 'Production overheads (exc dep'n)'
    - 'Administration, marketing and distribution'.

    Show each type of cash payment on a separate row.

12 **Insert** 'Non-current assets' into A14 and any payments for non-current assets in row 14.

13 **Insert** the 'Loan repayment' into cell A15 and the appropriate payments into row 15.

14 Using appropriate formulas, **calculate** the total payments for each month (cells B16:G16) and the net cash flow (cells B17:G17).

15 **Insert** the opening cash balance into cell B18 and, using appropriate formulas, **calculate** the closing balance for January and the opening and closing balances for February to June (cells C19:G19).

16 Use **conditional formatting** to show positive closing balances in the month as green fill with green text and negative closing balances as red fill with red text.

17 Format cells with numbers to **format** 0,000.

18 **Protect** cells A4:G19 using the password '123'.

solution

The 'Pantry in a Pot information' worksheet currently looks like this:

	A	B	C	D	E	F	G	H	I
1	Pantry in a Pot cash flow forecast								
2	Credit sales:								
3	% of customer who pay on 30 days:								
4	% of customers who pay on 60 days:								
5									
6	Month of sale	Jan	Feb	Mar	Apr	May	Jun	Total	
7		£	£	£	£	£	£	£	
8	Cash sales	£0	£7,340	£25,080	£27,010	£28,560	£32,400	120,390	
9	Credit sales	£5,600	£14,450	£57,840	£61,600	£82,500	£87,100	309,090	
10	Month of purchase	Jan	Feb	Mar	Apr	May	Jun	Total	
11		£	£	£	£	£	£	£	
12	Purchases (on credit)	24,614	25,827	34,579	36,954	40,528	44,576	207,078	
13	Labour costs	Jan	Feb	Mar	Apr	May	Jun	Total	
14		£	£	£	£	£	£	£	
15	Wages and salaries	16,584	17,722	22,212	23,900	25,487	26,589	132,494	
16	Overhead costs	Jan	Feb	Mar	Apr	May	Jun	Total	
17		£	£	£	£	£	£	£	
18	Production overheads (inc dep'n)	6,600	6,600	6,600	6,600	6,600	6,600	39,600	
19	Adminstration, marketing and distribution	3,500	3,700	4,500	4,600	4,600	4,700	25,600	
20									

Points 1 to 4 use spreadsheet skills you have already used in the activities in this book. Once you have completed points 1 to 4, the 'Pantry in a Pot information' worksheet will look like the one shown on the next page:

	A	B	C	D	E	F	G	H	I
1	Pantry in a Pot cash flow forecast								
2	Credit sales:								
3	% of customer who pay on 30 days:	90%							
4	% of customers who pay on 60 days:	10%							
5									
6	Month of sale	Jan	Feb	Mar	Apr	May	Jun	Total	
7		£	£	£	£	£	£	£	
8	Cash sales	£0	£7,340	£25,080	£27,010	£28,560	£32,400	120,390	
9	Credit sales	£5,600	£14,450	£57,840	£61,600	£82,500	£87,100	309,090	
10	Month of purchase	Jan	Feb	Mar	Apr	May	Jun	Total	
11		£	£	£	£	£	£	£	
12	Purchases (on credit)	24,614	25,827	34,579	36,954	40,528	44,576	207,078	
13	Labour costs	Jan	Feb	Mar	Apr	May	Jun	Total	
14		£	£	£	£	£	£	£	
15	Wages and salaries	16,584	17,722	22,212	23,900	25,487	26,589	132,494	
16	Overhead costs	Jan	Feb	Mar	Apr	May	Jun	Total	
17		£	£	£	£	£	£	£	
18	Production overheads (inc dep'n)	6,600	6,600	6,600	6,600	6,600	6,600	39,600	
19	Adminstration, marketing and distribution	3,500	3,700	4,500	4,600	4,600	4,700	25,600	
20									

The different colours highlight the different receipts and payments going into the cash flow.

The next three points are to deduct depreciation, which is not a cash flow, from production overheads. By inserting two new lines, this amendment can easily be seen on this worksheet. By having all the 'data' on the 'Pantry in a Pot information' worksheet, it is clear to managers the level of predicted sales, purchases, wages and salaries, etc.

By the end of point 7, the 'Pantry in a Pot information' worksheet looks like this:

	A	B	C	D	E	F	G	H	I
1	Pantry in a Pot cash flow forecast								
2	Credit sales:								
3	% of customer who pay on 30 days:	90%							
4	% of customers who pay on 60 days:	10%							
5									
6	Month of sale	Jan	Feb	Mar	Apr	May	Jun	Total	
7		£	£	£	£	£	£	£	
8	Cash sales	£0	£7,340	£25,080	£27,010	£28,560	£32,400	120,390	
9	Credit sales	£5,600	£14,450	£57,840	£61,600	£82,500	£87,100	309,090	
10	Month of purchase	Jan	Feb	Mar	Apr	May	Jun	Total	
11		£	£	£	£	£	£	£	
12	Purchases (on credit)	24,614	25,827	34,579	36,954	40,528	44,576	207,078	
13	Labour costs	Jan	Feb	Mar	Apr	May	Jun	Total	
14		£	£	£	£	£	£	£	
15	Wages and salaries	16,584	17,722	22,212	23,900	25,487	26,589	132,494	
16	Overhead costs	Jan	Feb	Mar	Apr	May	Jun	Total	
17		£	£	£	£	£	£	£	
18	Production overheads (inc dep'n)	6,600	6,600	6,600	6,600	6,600	6,600	39,600	
19	Depreciation	1,400	1,400	1,400	1,400	1,400	1,400	39,600	
20	Production overheads (exc dep'n)	5,200	5,200	5,200	5,200	5,200	5,200	39,600	
21	Adminstration, marketing and distribution	3,500	3,700	4,500	4,600	4,600	4,700	25,600	
22									

Let's move onto creating the cash flow, using this information, on the 'Pantry in a Pot cash flow' worksheet.

The cash flow format used is similar to that in the Case Study earlier on in this chapter. The receipts section already has headings in. In point 8, your formulas must allow for some sales receipts to be received after 30 days (month of credit sale plus one) or after 60 days (month of credit sale plus two). You must use

absolute referencing to refer to the percentages of customers who pay on 30 days or 60 days, so you can copy and paste the formula across.

For example, the formula for March credit sales would be:

=('Pantry in a Pot information'!C9*'Pantry in a Pot information'!$B$3)+('Pantry in a Pot information'!B9*'Pantry in a Pot information'!$B$4)

Once points 8 to 10 are complete, the 'Pantry in a Pot cash flow' worksheet, will look like that shown on the next page.

	A	B	C	D	E	F	G	H
1	**Pantry in a Pot cash flow forecast**							
2		Jan	Feb	Mar	Apr	May	Jun	
3		£	£	£	£	£	£	
4	*Receipts*							
5	Cash sales	0	7340	25080	27010	28560	32400	
6	Credit sales	0	5040	13565	53501	61224	80410	
7	Other	50000	35000					
8	Total receipts	50000	47380	38645	80511	89784	112810	
9	*Payments*							
10								
11								
12								
13								
14								
15								
16	Total payments							
17	Net cash flow							
18	Opening balance							
19	Closing balance							
20								

If your figures do not agree, use **show formulas** to look at your formulas and compare them to those shown in the 'Pantry in a Pot cash flow' worksheet in the file 'MATST Ch 9 Spreadsheet Case Study Pantry in a Pot answer' on the Osborne Books website. If you are unsure if the formulas are correct, you could confirm one or two figures using your calculator. Remember, the spreadsheet is simply a tool you use to apply management accounting knowledge!

The formulas for payment headings and payments are more straightforward. Some costs are paid for in the month of purchase. The cost for purchases for January is input from the information at the start of the question, as is the non-current assets payment and the loan repayments. Part of the difficulty in producing a cash flow forecast is bringing together data from various sources, so be prepared for this.

Once points 1 to 14 are completed, your 'Pantry in a Pot cash flow' worksheet should look like that shown on the next page.

	A	B	C	D	E	F	G	H
1	**Pantry in a Pot cash flow forecast**							
2		Jan	Feb	Mar	Apr	May	Jun	
3		£	£	£	£	£	£	
4	*Receipts*							
5	Cash sales	0	7340	25080	27010	28560	32400	
6	Credit sales	0	5040	13565	53501	61224	80410	
7	Other	50000	35000					
8	Total receipts	50000	47380	38645	80511	89784	112810	
9	*Payments*							
10	Purchases (on credit)	8716	24614	25827	34579	36954	40528	
11	Wages & salaries	16584	17722	22212	23900	25487	26589	
12	Production overheads (exc dep'n)	5200	5200	5200	5200	5200	5200	
13	Adminstration, marketing and distribution	3500	3700	4500	4600	4600	4700	
14	Non-current assets	30000						
15	Loan repayment			650	650	650	650	
16	Total payments	64000	51236	58389	68929	72891	77667	
17	Net cash flow	-14000	-3856	-19744	11582	16893	35143	
18	Opening balance							
19	Closing balance							
20								
21								
22								

The final formulas to calculate the opening balance and closing balance are straightforward. For January, the opening balance is £0. The closing bank balance is the opening bank balance plus the net cash flow in the month. For January, the formula for the closing bank balance in cell B19 is:

=B18+B17.

The opening bank balance for February in cell C18 is:

=B19

Point 16 uses conditional formatting to highlight when the closing bank balance is positive or negative ie in an overdraft. As the cash flow clearly shows, Charlie and Monty will need to find a way to manage the cash for the first four months, as the business is only cash generative in month 5.

Finally, formatting the cells makes the numbers easier to read and protecting the worksheet ensures the cash flow formulas cannot be amended incorrectly.

Once all points are complete, the 'Pantry in a Pot cash flow' worksheet will look like that shown on the next page.

	A	B	C	D	E	F	G	H
1	**Pantry in a Pot cash flow forecast**							
2		Jan	Feb	Mar	Apr	May	Jun	
3		£	£	£	£	£	£	
4	*Receipts*							
5	Cash sales	-	7,340	25,080	27,010	28,560	32,400	
6	Credit sales	-	5,040	13,565	53,501	61,224	80,410	
7	Other	60,000	35,000					
8	Total receipts	60,000	47,380	38,645	80,511	89,784	112,810	
9	*Payments*							
10	Purchases (on credit)	8,716	24,614	25,827	34,579	36,954	40,528	
11	Wages & salaries	16,584	17,722	22,212	23,900	25,487	26,589	
12	Production overheads (exc dep'n)	5,200	5,200	5,200	5,200	5,200	5,200	
13	Adminstration, marketing and distribution	3,500	3,700	4,500	4,600	4,600	4,700	
14	Non-current assets	30,000						
15	Loan repayment			650	650	650	650	
16	Total payments	64,000	51,236	58,389	68,929	72,891	77,667	
17	Net cash flow	- 4,000	- 3,856	- 19,744	11,582	16,893	35,143	
18	Opening bank balance	-	- 4,000	- 7,856	- 27,600	- 16,018	875	
19	Closing bank balance	- 4,000	- 7,856	- 27,600	- 16,018	875	36,018	
20								

You can download the answer file, 'MATST Ch 9 Spreadsheet Pantry in a Pot answer', from the Osborne Books website to compare to your answer in detail.

Chapter Summary

- A cash budget is prepared in order to show the forecast bank balance throughout the budget period.

- The cash budget focuses on the liquidity of the business.

- The format of a cash budget is ideally suited to the use of a spreadsheet.

- The use of a cash budget enables a business to monitor its cash resources and to plan future expenditure.

- The timing of receipts from trade receivables and payments to trade payables is important in the preparation of a cash budget.

- Funding methods available for the acquisition of non-current assets include cash purchase, part-exchange, loans, and hire purchase.

- Use of resource ratios measure how efficiently the current aspects of the business are controlled – principally inventories, trade receivables and trade payables.

- The working capital cycle measures the period of time between payment for goods received into inventory and the collection of cash from customers.

- A business with insufficient liquidity should consider raising additional finance from the owners or from debt finance.

- To improve the cash flow of the working capital cycle, a business should consider:

  - speeding up debt collection from trade receivables

  - slowing down the rate of payment to trade payables

  - reducing inventory

Key Terms		
	cash budget	a forecast of bank receipts and payments in order to show the forecast bank balance throughout the budget period
	liquidity	the ability of a business to have sufficient money in the bank to pay its way on a day-to-day basis
	cash	money in the bank or held as physical cash
	profit	a calculated figure which shows the surplus of income over expenditure for a period
	net cash flow	total cash receipts minus total cash payments
	cash purchase	method of funding the acquisition of non-current assets when the business has sufficient cash to pay in full for the new asset
	part-exchange	where an old asset is 'traded in' as part of the purchase price of a new non-current asset
	loans	a loan agreement with a bank or finance company to borrow money to purchase a non-current asset
	hire purchase	agreement between a finance company and a hirer which enables the hirer to have the use of a non-current asset against a deposit and regular instalment payments
	inventory holding period (days)	inventories/cost of sales x 365
	trade receivables collection period (days)	trade receivables/revenue x 365
	trade payables payment period (days)	trade payables/cost of sales x 365
	working capital cycle (days)	inventory days + receivable days − payable days

Activities

9.1 You are to calculate receipts from trade receivables for April to September using the following information (ignore VAT):

- the amount of trade receivables at 1 April is £10,000

- credit sales are budgeted to be £25,000 per month from April to July, and £30,000 per month in August and September

- half of the trade receivables pay in the month of sale and take advantage of 3% prompt payment discount

- the remainder of trade receivables pay in the month after sale, without prompt payment discount – however, 2% of these will not pay and should be regarded as irrecoverable debts

RECEIPTS FROM TRADE RECEIVABLES						
	April	**May**	**June**	**July**	**August**	**September**
	£	£	£	£	£	£
Month of sale						
PPD						
Following month						
Irrecoverable debts						
Receipts for month						

9.2 You work at Pershore Furniture Ltd and have been asked by your manager to calculate receipts from trade receivables for July to December using the following information (ignore VAT).

The amount of trade receivables at 1 July is £250,000.

Credit sales are budgeted to be £300,000 for July to September, £200,000 in October and £250,000 in November and December.

40% of trade receivables pay in the month of sales, utilising a 2% prompt payment discount.

The remainder of trade receivables pay in the month after sale. 1% of these will not pay and should be considered irrecoverable debts.

Download the file 'MATST Chapter 9 Activities data' from the Osborne Books website and rename it 'MATST Chapter 9 Activities answers'.

Open the renamed file.

In the worksheet called '9.2 Pershore Furniture':

1   **Insert** the credit sales for the months July to December in cells B12:G12.

2   **Format** cells B6:B9 as **percentages** to 0 decimal places. **Insert** the percentages for trade receivables who pay in the month of sale, prompt payment discount, percentage of customers who pay in the month after sale and irrecoverable debts (cells B6:B9).

3   **Merge and centre** cells B14 to H14.

4   Using appropriate **formulas**, **calculate** the cash receipts by month for July to December (cells B16:G22), adjusting for discounts and irrecoverable debts. Use a separate row for each month of sale. On each row, include a **formula** for total receipts for the month of sale (column H).

5   Using an appropriate formula, **calculate** the total receipts for July to December (cells B23:H23).

6   **Format** row 15 in **bold** and row 23 in **bold and italic**.

7   **Create a stacked 2D column chart**, showing the cash receipts for July to December.

8   **Title the chart** 'Pershore Furniture Ltd Cash receipts July to December, showing breakdown by month of sale' **format** bold italic, font size 14.

9   **Insert a comment** in cell B16 'Trade receivables 1 July £250,000 still due from June's sales, adjusted for irrecoverable debts'.

10   **Label** the vertical **axis** Amount, font size 11. **Label** the horizontal **axis** 'Month of cash receipt'.

11   **Copy the chart** onto a new worksheet named '9.2 PF Ltd Cash receipts chart'. Ensure it is clear to read.

12   **Set the margins** so the chart is centred horizontally and vertically on the page, ready to print for your manager.

Save the file as 'MATST Chapter 9 Activities answers' and compare your answer to this spreadsheet on the Osborne Books website.

9.3 You are to calculate payments to trade payables for October to March using the following information (ignore VAT):

- the amount of trade payables at 1 October is £12,500

- credit purchases are budgeted to be £30,000 per month in October and November, £40,000 per month in December and January, and £35,000 per month in February and March

- half of the trade payables allow prompt payment discount of 2% and are paid in the month of purchase

- the remainder of trade payables are paid in the month after purchase, without prompt payment discount

PAYMENTS TO TRADE PAYABLES						
	October	November	December	January	February	March
	£	£	£	£	£	£
Month of purchase						
PPD						
Following month						
Payments for month						

9.4 You are preparing the cash budget of Wilkinson for the first six months of 20-8. The following budgeted figures are available (ignore VAT):

	Sales £	Purchases £	Wages and salaries £	Other expenses £
January	65,000	26,500	17,500	15,500
February	70,000	45,000	18,000	20,500
March	72,500	50,000	18,250	19,000
April	85,000	34,500	18,500	18,500
May	65,000	35,500	16,500	20,500
June	107,500	40,500	20,000	22,000

The following additional information is available:

- Sales income is received in the month after sale, and sales for December 20-7 amounted to £57,500

- 'Other expenses' each month includes an allocation of £1,000 for depreciation; all other expenses are paid for in the month in which they are incurred

- Purchases, and wages and salaries are paid for in the month in which they are incurred

- The bank balance at 1 January 20-8 is £2,250

Task 1

Prepare a month-by-month cash budget for Wilkinson for the first six months of 20-8, using the layout which follows.

Task 2

Advise Wilkinson the amount of bank overdraft facility that will be required, and for what time period.

WILKINSON CASH BUDGET FOR THE SIX MONTHS ENDING 30 JUNE 20-8						
	Jan £	Feb £	Mar £	Apr £	May £	Jun £
Receipts						
Trade receivables						
Total receipts for the month						
Payments						
Trade payables						
Wages and salaries						
Other expenses						
Total payments for the month						
Net cash flow						
Opening bank balance/(overdraft)						
Closing bank balance/(overdraft)						

9.5 Jayne Smith has recently been made redundant; she has received a redundancy payment and this, together with her accumulated savings, amounts to £10,000. She has decided to set up her own business selling stationery and this will commence trading with an initial capital of £10,000 on 1 January 20-2. On this date she will buy a van for business use at a cost of £6,000. She has budgeted her purchases, sales and expenses for the next six months as follows (ignore VAT):

	Purchases	Sales	Expenses
	£	£	£
January	4,500	1,250	750
February	4,500	3,000	600
March	3,500	4,000	600
April	3,500	4,000	650
May	3,500	4,500	650
June	4,000	6,000	700

She will pay for purchases in the month after purchase; likewise, she expects her customers to pay for sales in the month after sale. All expenses will be paid for in the month they are incurred.

Task 1

Jayne realises that she may need a bank overdraft before her business becomes established. Prepare a month-by-month cash budget for the first six months of Jayne Smith's business, using the layout which follows.

Task 2

What is the maximum bank overdraft shown by the cash budget? Suggest two ways in which Jayne Smith could amend her business plan in order to avoid the need for a bank overdraft.

| JAYNE SMITH | | | | | | |
| CASH BUDGET FOR THE SIX MONTHS ENDING 30 JUNE 20-2 | | | | | | |
	Jan £	Feb £	Mar £	Apr £	May £	Jun £
Receipts						
Capital introduced						
Trade receivables						
Total receipts for the month						
Payments						
Van						
Trade payables						
Expenses						
Total payments for the month						
Net cash flow						
Opening bank balance/(overdraft)						
Closing bank balance/(overdraft)						

9.6 A-Z Taxis needs a new taxi to meet an increase in business. The business is profitable but the owner, Ken Molina, doesn't want to use current monies to fund the purchase. Which **one** of the following funding methods would you suggest he considers?

(a) Cash purchase	
(b) Purchase on 30 days' credit terms	
(c) Bank overdraft	
(d) Hire purchase	

9.7 A hire purchase agreement is a:

(a) medium-term agreement where a finance company funds an asset and the business makes instalment payments to pay the cost plus interest	
(b) short-term agreement to fund an asset on 30 days' commercial credit terms	
(c) medium-term agreement under which a bank or finance company lends the funds to a business to enable it to buy the asset	
(d) type of bank overdraft	

9.8 **(a)** Complete the following sentence:

The financing method whereby a business trades in an old asset to meet part of the payment for a new asset is known as [   ]

Select from the following: cash purchase, hire purchase, loan, part-exchange.

(b) A school needs a new photocopier for the school office. Who is the appropriate person to give authority for this capital expenditure? Choose **one**.

(a) the school secretary	
(b) the head teacher	
(c) the school caretaker	
(d) year 11 students	

9.9 Which **one** of the following is the working capital cycle?

(a) inventory days + receivable days – payable days	
(b) inventory days + payable days – receivable days	
(c) payable days + receivable days – inventory days	
(d) payable days + receivable days + inventory days	

9.10   You are the Accounts Assistant at Exbury Limited.
The following figures have been extracted from the accounting software:

	last year £	this year £
Revenue	564,300	532,900
Cost of sales	289,500	276,200
Trade receivables	58,250	50,150
Trade payables	29,850	27,050
Inventory	35,650	34,450

All purchases and sales are made on credit.

Task 1

Calculate the resources ratios for last year and this year using the layout which follows:
–   inventory holding period (days)
–   trade receivables collection period (days)
–   trade payables payment period (days)

Show your calculations (using a 365 day year) and take each to the nearest whole day.

Task 2

Calculate the working capital cycle in days for each year, using the layout below:

Task 3

Make brief notes on your findings for the Accountant, to include suggestions for improvement where necessary.

Task 1

RESOURCES RATIOS	last year (days)	this year (days)
inventory holding period		
trade receivables collection period		
trade payables payment period		

Task 2

WORKING CAPITAL CYCLE	last year (days)	this year (days)
inventory days receivable days payable days		
WORKING CAPITAL CYCLE		

Task 3

Notes:

9.11 Goodwin Ltd is a manufacturer of garden furniture. The directors of Goodwin Ltd are reviewing the working capital cycle of the business for the year-ended 31 October 20-2.

Extracts from the financial statements give the following information:

Year end	31 October 20-2 £
Revenue	1,240,354
Cost of sales	620,847
Inventory	45,186
Trade receivables	125,176
Trade payables	77,045

(a) You are to complete the table below for Goodwin Ltd to show the working capital cycle in days for the year ended 31 October 20-2. Enter answers to the nearest whole day, using a 365 day year.

Year end	31 October 20-2 Days
Trade receivables collection period	
Trade payables payment period	
Inventory holding period	
Working capital cycle	

(b) Which **one** of the following actions will shorten the working capital cycle of Goodwin Ltd?

(a) Increasing the trade receivables collection period	
(b) Reducing the trade payables payment period	
(c) Increasing the inventory holding period	
(d) Reducing the trade receivables collection period	

9.12 You work for SF Engineering Ltd, a specialist engineering company. You are preparing some information for the board meeting and have been asked to produce some ratio analysis.

The financial accountant has already input the numbers from the financial statements into a worksheet '9.12 SF Engineering Ltd', and wants you to complete the calculations and amend some of the formatting.

In the worksheet '9.12 SF Engineering Ltd':

1   Place a **thick black border** around cells A11 to D19.

2   **Format** rows 11 and 12 to bold.

3   Using an appropriate formula, **calculate** the inventory holding period (days) in cells B14 and C14. Use **ROUNDUP** to calculate this to the nearest whole day.

4   Using an appropriate formula, **calculate** the trade receivables collection period (days) in cells B16 and C16. Use **ROUNDUP** to **calculate** this to the nearest whole day.

5   Using an appropriate formula, **calculate** the trade payables payment period (days) in cells B18 and C18. Use **ROUNDUP** to **calculate** this to the nearest whole day.

6   Use **conditional formatting**, including an appropriate formula, in cells B14, B16 and B18 to cell fill green with black font if the ratio is better in 20-9 than in 20-8.

7   Use **conditional formatting**, including an appropriate formula, in cells B14, B16 and B18 to cell fill red with black font if the ratio is worse in 20-9 than in 20-8.

8   Use an **IF statement** in cells D14, D16 and D18 to show 'Better' if the 20-9 ratio is better than 20-8 and 'Worse' if it is worse than 20-8.

9.13 Identify whether each of the following actions will improve or worsen the cash flow of a business in the short term.

Action	Improve	Worsen
Reducing the credit terms offered to customers from 30 days to 20 days		
Increasing inventory holding period from 25 days to 40 days		
Doubling the credit limits of all existing customers		
Negotiating with suppliers to increase credit terms from 35 days to 45 days		
Changing customer credit terms from 30 days net to 2.5% prompt payment discount within 14 days or 30 days net		

Answers to chapter activities

CHAPTER 1: AN INTRODUCTION TO MANAGEMENT ACCOUNTING

1.1   (d)   Preparation of management accounting information in a straightforward and honest way

1.2

Responsibility centre	Criteria	Department Cee	Department Dee
Cost centre	Low cost	£10,000 ✔	£12,000 X
Profit centre	High profit	£5,000 ✔	£4,000 X
Revenue centre	High sales	£55,000 ✔	£35,000 X
Investment centre	High %	20% ✔	15% X

Advice to the owner: Department Cee is performing better than Department Dee for all four of the criteria. However, both sections are earning profits which contribute to the overheads of the business, so both should continue to trade.

1.3

	A	B	C	D	E
1	Outdoors and Active!				
2	Year ended 31 March 20-3				
3		Tents	Outdoor Clothing	Sleeping Bags	
4		£'000	£'000	£'000	
5	Revenue	4,920	5,630	3,680	
6					
7	Costs				
8	Materials	1,600	2,060	1,900	
9	Labour	1,970	1,430	650	
10	Overheads	540	320	420	
11	Total cost	4,110	3,810	2,970	
12					
13	Profit earned	810	1,820	710	
14	Profit %	16.5%	32.3%	19.3%	
15					
16	Investment made	3,750	3,690	1,290	
17	Return on investment %	21.6%	49.3%	55.0%	
18					
19					
	Divisional Performance ⊕				

Note: Your design may look slightly different however the key spreadsheet elements, for example borders and cell fill, must be included. The spreadsheet file for this answer is entitled 'MATST Chapter 1 Outdoors and Active! Divisional Performance 31 March 20-3' and is available to download from the Osborne Books website.

1.4

REPORT
To: Finance Director **From:**   Accounts Assistant **Date:**   today

Costs and revenue for last year

I report on the details of the costs and revenue for last year of each segment of the business. Details are as follows:

	Newspapers and magazines	Books	Stationery
Cost Centre	£000	£000	£000
• materials	155	246	122
• labour	65	93	58
• expenses	27	35	25
• total	247	374	205
Profit Centre			
Revenue	352	544	230
less Costs (see above)	247	374	205
Profit	105	170	25
Revenue Centre	352	544	230
Investment Centre			
Profit (see above)	105	179	25
Investment	420	850	250
Expressed as a percentage	25%	20%	10%

1.5
- raw materials: variable

- factory rent: fixed

- electricity: semi-variable

- direct labour: variable

- indirect labour: fixed

- commission paid to sales staff: variable

Classifying costs by behaviour identifies them as being fixed, or semi-variable, or variable. This helps with decision-making – the business might be able to alter the balance between fixed and variable costs in order to increase profits. For example, a furniture manufacturing business will have to make decisions on whether to use direct labour (variable cost) or machinery (fixed cost) for many of the production processes. The decision will be based very much on the expected level of sales, ie for lower sales it is likely to make greater use of direct labour, while for higher sales a more machine-intensive method of production might be used.

1.6

		Fixed	Semi-variable	Variable
(a)	Rates of business premises	✔		
(b)	Royalty paid to designer for each unit of output			✔
(c)	Car hire with fixed rental and charge per mile		✔	
(d)	Employees paid on piecework basis			✔
(e)	Straight-line depreciation	✔		
(f)	Direct materials			✔
(g)	Telephone bill with fixed rental and a charge for each call made		✔	
(h)	Office salaries	✔		

1.7   Points 1 to 11 completed

	A	B	C	D	E	F
1		Tom's Nurseries			Cost categories:	
2		Quarter ended 30 June 20-5			Variable cost	
3					Semi-variable cost	
4	Cost description	Actual cost	Cost category		Fixed cost	
5	Compost	£ 16,421	Variable cost			
6	Compostable pots	£ 15,400	Variable cost			
7	Plastic pots	£ 5,600	Variable cost			
8	Seed costs	£ 20,432	Variable cost			
9	Wages of seed planters and cultivators	£ 35,498	Variable cost			
10		£ 93,351	**Variable cost Total**			
11	Fixed hire cost for delivery lorries, plus charge per mile	£ 6,900	Semi-variable cost			
12	Power to heat greenhouses (standing charge plus rate per	£ 12,300	Semi-variable cost			
13		£ 19,200	**Semi-variable cost Total**			
14	Depreciation of greenhouses	£ 4,700	Fixed cost			
15	Depreciation of office equipment	£ 600	Fixed cost			
16	Hire of additional temporary greenhouses	£ 3,000	Fixed cost			
17	Rates of nursery	£ 11,450	Fixed cost			
18	Salary of administrative staff	£ 12,000	Fixed cost			
19		£ 31,750	**Fixed cost Total**			
20		£ 144,301	**Grand Total**			
21						
22						
23						

Points 12 and 13 completed

1 2 3		B	C	D	E	F
	1	Tom's Nurseries			Cost categories:	
	2	Quarter ended 30 June 20-5			Variable cost	
	3				Semi-variable cost	
	4	Actual cost	Cost category		Fixed cost	
+	10	£ 93,351	Variable cost Total			
+	13	£ 19,200	Semi-variable cost Total			
+	19	£ 31,750	Fixed cost Total			
−	20	£ 144,301	Grand Total			
	21					
	22					
	23					

Formulas when points 1 to 13 completed

	B	C	D	E
1	Tom's Nurseries			Cost categories:
2	Quarter ended 30 June			Variable cost
3				Semi-variable cost
4	Actual cost	Cost category		Fixed cost
10	=SUBTOTAL(9,B5:B9)	Variable cost Total		
13	=SUBTOTAL(9,B11:B12)	Semi-variable cost Total		
19	=SUBTOTAL(9,B14:B18)	Fixed cost Total		
20	=SUBTOTAL(9,B5:B18)	Grand Total		
21				
22				

The answer file for this question, 'MATST Chapter 1 Activities answer' can be downloaded from the Osborne Books website.

1.8

Tubular steel	direct materials
Factory supervisor's salary	indirect labour
Wages of employee operating moulding machine	direct labour
Works canteen assistant's wages	indirect labour
Business rates of factory	indirect expenses
Electricity to operate machines	indirect expenses*
Factory heating and lighting	indirect expenses
Plastic for making chair seats	direct materials
Hire of special machinery for one particular order	direct expenses
Grease for the moulding machine	indirect materials
Depreciation of factory machinery	indirect expenses
Depreciation of office equipment	indirect expenses

* Note: the cost of electricity to operate machines has been classified above as an indirect expense. This is often the case because it is not worthwhile analysing the cost of power for each unit of production. An industry that uses a lot of power will often have meters fitted to each machine so that costs may be identified and allocated to production as a direct expense. Other, lesser users of electricity, are unlikely to calculate the separate cost and will consider power to be an indirect expense. Whichever treatment is used – indirect expenses or direct expenses – it is important that it is applied consistently.

1.9

Cost Item	Classification
Dressings	direct materials
Disposable scalpels	direct materials
Surgeon's salary	direct labour
Floor cleaning materials	indirect materials
Laundry	indirect expenses*
Depreciation of staff drinks machine	indirect expenses*
Theatre heat and light	indirect expenses*
Porter's wages	indirect labour
Anaesthetic gas	direct materials
Depreciation of theatre equipment	indirect expenses
Maintenance of theatre equipment	indirect expenses
CDs for music in theatre	indirect expenses
Anaesthetist's salary	direct labour

* These items have been classified as indirect expenses – this is the most likely classification. If the money amount of any item was large, it would be worthwhile looking at the costing system to see if the item could be identified as a direct expense.

1.10

Cost item	Total cost £	Prime cost £	Production overheads £	Admin costs £	Selling and distribution costs £
Wages of employees working on the bottling line	6,025	6,025			
Wages of employees in the stores department	2,750		2,750		
Bottles	4,050	4,050			
Safety goggles for bottling line employees	240		240		
Advertisement for new employees	125			125	
Depreciation of bottling machinery	500		500		
Depreciation of sales staff's cars	1,000				1,000
Royalty paid to local farmer	750	750			
Trade exhibition fees	1,500				1,500
Computer stationery	210			210	
Sales staff salaries	4,095				4,095
TOTALS	21,245	10,825	3,490	335	6,595

1.11 (b) Salaries of maintenance staff

1.12 (d) Cost of paper

1.13 (a) Production overheads

1.14 (c) Administration costs

1.15 (c) A product cost is included in inventory valuation

1.16

Statement	Management accounting	Financial accounting
Providing financial statements for shareholders		✔
Producing financial reports on future activities	✔	
Providing financial information to assist with decision-making	✔	
Controlling the expenditure of the business	✔	
Liaising with HMRC for VAT and tax purposes		✔
Producing financial reports as and when they are needed	✔	

CHAPTER 2: MATERIALS COSTS

2.1   Stock item D

- reorder level = (3 units per day x 7 days) + 30 units = 51 units
- maximum reorder quantity = 350 units – 30 units = 320 units

Stock item E

- reorder level = (4 units per day x 7 days) + 40 units = 68 units
- maximum reorder quantity = 350 units – 40 units = 310 units

2.2 Points 1 to 11 complete

	A	B	C	D	E	F
1	Date		Bamboo	Glue	Wax	
2			Kilograms	Litres	Litres	
3	07-Apr			70	30	
4	08-Apr		2,300		20	
5	10-Apr			30	30	
6	14-Apr				30	
7	21-Apr		1,700	40	28	
8	26-Apr				20	
9	30-Apr		1,330	70		
10	02-May				20	
11	08-May		2,100		30	
12	10-May			120	30	
13	16-May		2,300		30	
14	21-May			76	25	
15	26-May		1,000		25	
16	04-Jun				30	
17						
18	58	Days	10,730	406	348	Total
19						
20	Maximum inventory		5,000	150	80	
21	Average daily usage		185	7	6	
22	Average lead time, days		6	4	4	
23	Inventory buffer		1,000	50	40	
24	Re-order level		2,110	78	64	
25	Maximum order quantity		4,000	100	40	
26	Minimum order quantity		1,110	28	24	
27						

Formulas for points 1 to 11 complete

	A	B	C	D	E	F
1	Date		Bamboo	Glue	Wax	
2			Kilograms	Litres	Litres	
3	44293			70	30	
4	44294		2300		20	
5	44296			30	30	
6	44300				30	
7	44307		1700	40	28	
8	44312				20	
9	44316		1330	70		
10	44318				20	
11	44324		2100		30	
12	44326			120	30	
13	44332		2300		30	
14	44337			76	25	
15	44342		1000		25	
16	44351				30	
17						
18	=DAYS(A16,A3)	Days	=SUM(C3:C16)	=SUM(D3:D16)	=SUM(E3:E16)	Total
19						
20	Maximum inventory		5000	150	80	
21	Average daily usage		=ROUND(C18/$A18,0)	=ROUND(D18/$A18,0)	=ROUND(E18/$A18,0)	
22	Average lead time, days		6	4	4	
23	Inventory buffer		1000	50	40	
24	Re-order level		=(C21*C22)+C23	=(D21*D22)+D23	=(E21*E22)+E23	
25	Maximum order quantity		=C20-C23	=D20-D23	=E20-E23	
26	Minimum order quantity		=C21*C22	=D21*D22	=E21*E22	
27						
28						

The answer file for this question, 'MATST Chapter 2 Activities answers' can be downloaded from the Osborne Books website.

2.3   **Economic Order Quantity (EOQ)** $= \sqrt{\dfrac{2 \times 72{,}000 \times 20}{£2}}$

$$= \sqrt{\dfrac{2{,}880{,}000}{£2}}$$

$$= \sqrt{1{,}440{,}000}$$

$$= 1{,}200 \text{ kg}$$

2.4 **(a)** **FIFO**

INVENTORY RECORD

Date	Receipts			Issues			Balance		
	Quantity (units)	Cost per unit	Total Cost	Quantity (units)	Cost per unit	Total Cost	Quantity (units)	Cost per unit	Total Cost
20-4		£	£		£	£		£	£
January	20	3.00	60.00				20	3.00	60.00
February	10	3.60	36.00				20	3.00	60.00
							10	3.60	36.00
							30		96.00
March				8	3.00	24.00	12	3.00	36.00
							10	3.60	36.00
							22		72.00
April	10	4.00	40.00				12	3.00	36.00
							10	3.60	36.00
							10	4.00	40.00
							32		112.00
May				12	3.00	36.00			
				4	3.60	14.40	6	3.60	21.60
				16		50.40	10	4.00	40.00
							16		61.60

(b) **AVCO**

INVENTORY RECORD

Date	Receipts			Issues			Balance		
	Quantity (units)	Cost per unit	Total Cost	Quantity (units)	Cost per unit	Total Cost	Quantity (units)	Cost per unit	Total Cost
20-4		£	£		£	£		£	£
January	20	3.00	60.00				20	3.00	60.00
February	10	3.60	36.00				20	3.00	60.00
							10	3.60	36.00
							30	3.20	96.00
March				8	3.20	25.60	22	3.20	70.40
April	10	4.00	40.00				22	3.20	70.40
							10	4.00	40.00
							32	3.45	110.40
May				16	3.45	55.20	16	3.45	55.20

2.5 **(a)** **FIFO**

INVENTORY RECORD: TYPE X

Date	Receipts			Issues			Balance		
	Quantity (units)	Cost per unit	Total Cost	Quantity (units)	Cost per unit	Total Cost	Quantity (units)	Cost per unit	Total Cost
20-4		£	£		£	£		£	£
January	100	4.00	400.00				100	4.00	400.00
February				80	4.00	320.00	20	4.00	80.00
March	140	4.20	588.00				20	4.00	80.00
							140	4.20	588.00
							160		668.00
April	100	3.80	380.00				20	4.00	80.00
							140	4.20	588.00
							100	3.80	380.00
							260		1,048.00
May				20	4.00	80.00			
				120	4.20	504.00	20	4.20	84.00
				140		584.00	100	3.80	380.00
							120		464.00
June	80	4.50	360.00				20	4.20	84.00
							100	3.80	380.00
							80	4.50	360.00
							200		824.00

(b)   AVCO

INVENTORY RECORD: TYPE X

Date	Receipts			Issues			Balance		
	Quantity (units)	Cost per unit	Total Cost	Quantity (units)	Cost per unit	Total Cost	Quantity (units)	Cost per unit	Total Cost
20-4		£	£		£	£		£	£
January	100	4.00	400.00				100	4.00	400.00
February				80	4.00	320.00	20	4.00	80.00
March	140	4.20	588.00				20	4.00	80.00
							140	4.20	588.00
							160	4.18	668.00
April	100	3.80	380.00				160	4.18	668.00
							100	3.80	380.00
							260	4.03	1,048.00
May				140	4.03	564.20	120	4.03	483.80
June	80	4.50	360.00				120	4.03	483.80
							80	4.50	360.00
							200	4.22	843.80

Note: The cost per unit is calculated to two decimal places and is used to work out the issue costs.
The total cost balance is the difference between the previous total cost balance and the issues. Take care to note how you should round when using AVCO.

(a)   FIFO

INVENTORY RECORD: TYPE Y

Date	Receipts			Issues			Balance		
	Quantity (units)	Cost per unit	Total Cost	Quantity (units)	Cost per unit	Total Cost	Quantity (units)	Cost per unit	Total Cost
20-4 January	200	£ 10.00	£ 2,000.00		£	£	200	£ 10.00	£ 2,000.00
February	100	9.50	950.00				200 100 300	10.00 9.50	2,000.00 950.00 2,950.00
March				200 40 240	10.00 9.50	2,000.00 380.00 2,380.00	60	9.50	570.00
April	100	10.50	1,050.00				60 100 160	9.50 10.50	570.00 1,050.00 1,620.00
May	140	10.00	1,400.00				60 100 140 300	9.50 10.50 10.00	570.00 1,050.00 1,400.00 3,020.00
June				60 40 100	9.50 10.50	570.00 420.00 990.00	60 140 200	10.50 10.00	630.00 1,400.00 2,030.00

(b)   AVCO

INVENTORY RECORD: TYPE Y

Date	Receipts			Issues			Balance		
	Quantity (units)	Cost per unit	Total Cost	Quantity (units)	Cost per unit	Total Cost	Quantity (units)	Cost per unit	Total Cost
20-4		£	£		£	£		£	£
January	200	10.00	2,000.00				200	10.00	2,000.00
February	100	9.50	950.00				200	10.00	2,000.00
							100	9.50	950.00
							300	9.83	2,950.00
March				240	9.83	2,360.00	60	9.83	590.00
April	100	10.50	1,050.00				60	9.83	590.00
							100	10.50	1,050.00
							160	10.25	1,640.00
May	140	10.00	1,400.00				160	10.25	1,640.00
							140	10.00	1,400.00
							300	10.13	3,040.00
June				100	10.13	1,013.00	200	10.13	2,027.00

Note: The cost per unit is calculated to two decimal places and is used to work out the issue costs. For AVCO there is invariably going to be an element of rounding when working to two decimal places. For example the issue total in March at £9.83 per unit is £2,359.20, but is rounded to £2,360 so that this and the total cost of £590 (rounded from £589.80) equal February's total cost of £2,950.

The total cost balance is the difference between the previous total cost balance and the issues. Take care to note how you should round when using AVCO.

2.6   Task 1

INVENTORY RECORD								
Product: Wholewheat flour								
Date	Receipts			Issues			Balance	
	Quantity (kg)	Cost per kg	Total Cost	Quantity (kg)	Cost per kg	Total Cost	Quantity (kg)	Total Cost
20-4 Balance at 1 May		£	£		£	£	10,000	£ 2,500
6 May	20,000	0.30	6,000				30,000	8,500
10 May				10,000	0.25	2,500		
				10,000	0.30	3,000		
				20,000		5,500	10,000	3,000
17 May	10,000	0.35	3,500				10,000	3,000
							10,000	3,500
							20,000	6,500
20 May				10,000	0.30	3,000		
				5,000	0.35	1,750		
				15,000		4,750	5,000	1,750

Task 2

20-4	Code number	Debit £	Credit £
6 May	3000	6,000	
6 May	5000		6,000
10 May	3300	5,500	
10 May	3000		5,500
17 May	3000	3,500	
17 May	5000		3,500
20 May	3300	4,750	
20 May	3000		4,750

2.7   **(a)**

$$\text{Economic Order Quantity (EOQ)} = \sqrt{\frac{2 \times 57,600\text{kg} \times £25}{£2}}$$

$$= \sqrt{\frac{2,880,000}{£2}}$$

$$= \sqrt{1,440,000}$$

$$= \underline{1,200 \text{ kg}}$$

(b) and **(c)**

Inventory record for plastic grade P5

Date	Receipts			Issues			Balance	
	Quantity (kg)	Cost per kg	Total Cost	Quantity (kg)	Cost per kg	Total Cost	Quantity (kg)	Total Cost
		£	£		£	£		£
Balance at 22 June							4,400	10,560
23 June	1,200	2.634	3,161				5,600	13,721
25 June				1,000	2.450	2,450	4,600	*11,271
26 June	1,200	2.745	3,294				5,800	14,565
29 June				1,500	2.511	3,767	4,300	**10,798

* £13,721 – £2,450   ** £14,565 – £3,767

2.8

	Transaction	Account debited	Account credited
1	Receipt of materials into inventory, paying on credit	Inventory	Trade payables control
2	Issue of materials from inventory to production	Production	Inventory
3	Receipt of materials into inventory, paying immediately by bank transfer	Inventory	Bank
4	Return of materials from production to inventory	Inventory	Production

2.9 (d) Valuing inventory in order to maximise profit

2.10 Points 1 to 5 complete – rows 3 to 54

	Range	Colour and cushions	Size	Total number	Valuation method	IAS 2 value of item	Total inventory value
4	Cosy	Oatmeal	Single	13	Cost	£266.50	£3,464.50
5	Cosy	Oatmeal	Double	25	Cost	£475.50	£11,887.50
6	Cosy	Oatmeal	King size	12	Cost	£595.60	£7,147.20
7	Cosy	Oatmeal	Queen size	12	Cost	£485.50	£5,826.00
8	Cosy	Oatmeal	Super king size	25	Cost	£695.50	£17,387.50
9	Dreamy City	Grey	Single	55	Cost	£226.50	£12,457.50
10	Dreamy City	Grey	Double	59	Cost	£405.50	£23,924.50
11	Dreamy City	Grey	King size	36	Cost	£545.60	£19,641.60
12	Dreamy City	Grey	Queen size	29	Cost	£445.50	£12,919.50
13	Dreamy City	Grey	Super king size	21	Cost	£665.50	£13,975.50
14	Cosy City	Grey	Single	23	Cost	£266.50	£6,129.50
15	Cosy City	Grey	Double	6	Cost	£475.50	£2,853.00
16	Cosy City	Grey	King size	17	Cost	£595.60	£10,125.20
17	Cosy City	Grey	Queen size	6	Cost	£485.50	£2,913.00
18	Cosy City	Grey	Super king size	14	Cost	£695.50	£9,737.00
19	Sleepy City	Grey	Single	2	Cost	£209.00	£418.00
20	Sleepy City	Grey	Double	5	Cost	£405.50	£2,027.50
21	Sleepy City	Grey	King size	4	Cost	£525.60	£2,102.40
22	Sleepy City	Grey	Queen size	9	Cost	£425.50	£3,829.50
23	Sleepy City	Grey	Super king size	6	Cost	£605.50	£3,633.00
24	Cosset	Oatmeal	Single	26	Cost	£275.00	£7,150.00
25	Cosset	Oatmeal	Double	15	Cost	£465.00	£6,975.00
26	Cosset	Oatmeal	King size	21	Cost	£630.00	£13,230.00
27	Cosset	Oatmeal	Queen size	10	Cost	£575.00	£5,750.00
28	Cosset	Oatmeal	Super king size	9	Cost	£695.00	£6,255.00
29	Nest City	Grey	Single	16	Cost	£219.00	£3,504.00
30	Nest City	Grey	Double	30	Cost	£415.50	£12,465.00
31	Nest City	Grey	King size	12	Cost	£535.60	£6,427.20
32	Nest City	Grey	Queen size	12	Cost	£435.50	£5,226.00
33	Nest City	Grey	Super king size	14	Cost	£615.50	£8,617.00
34					Cost Min		£418.00
35					Cost Max		£23,924.50
36	Dreamy	Midnight	Single	32	NRV	£199.00	£6,368.00
37	Dreamy	Midnight	Double	29	NRV	£399.00	£11,571.00
38	Dreamy	Midnight	King size	10	NRV	£549.00	£5,490.00
39	Dreamy	Midnight	Queen size	17	NRV	£429.00	£7,293.00
40	Dreamy	Midnight	Super king size	10	NRV	£599.00	£5,990.00
41	Sleepy	Midnight	Single	13	NRV	£199.00	£2,587.00
42	Sleepy	Midnight	Double	20	NRV	£289.00	£5,780.00
43	Sleepy	Midnight	King size	19	NRV	£489.00	£9,291.00
44	Sleepy	Midnight	Queen size	15	NRV	£399.00	£5,985.00
45	Sleepy	Midnight	Super king size	31	NRV	£589.00	£18,259.00
46	Nest	Midnight	Single	13	NRV	£199.00	£2,587.00
47	Nest	Midnight	Double	38	NRV	£389.00	£14,782.00
48	Nest	Midnight	King size	24	NRV	£529.00	£12,696.00
49	Nest	Midnight	Queen size	6	NRV	£420.00	£2,520.00
50	Nest	Midnight	Super king size	13	NRV	£579.00	£7,527.00
51					NRV Min		£2,520.00
52					NRV Max		£18,259.00
53					Grand Min		£418.00
54					Grand Max		£23,924.50

2.2 Usage | Inventory by size chart | 2.10 Inventory Analysis | **NRV Cost Analysis**

Points 6 to 13 complete

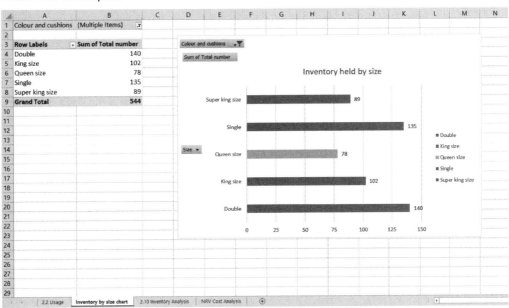

The answer file for this question, 'MATST Chapter 2 Activities answers' can be downloaded from the Osborne Books website.

CHAPTER 3: LABOUR COSTS

3.1   N Ball: 35 hours x £11.00 per hour = £385.00 (no bonus)

T Smith: 37 hours x £10.00 per hour = £370.00 + bonus £10.00 = £380.00

L Lewis: 38 hours x £10.00 per hour = £380.00 + bonus £15.00 = £395.00

M Wilson: 36 hours x £12.00 per hour = £432.00 + bonus £12.00 = £444.00

3.2   • L Fry: £400.00 (time rate)
   • R Williams: £450.00 (piecework rate)
   • P Grant: £435.00 (piecework rate)

3.3 Points 1 to 4 completed

	A	B	C	D	E	F	G	H	I	J	K	L	M	N	O	P	Q	R
1	Deerpark Ltd								W/c 30/03/20-9									
2	Ali Ghalid	Charlotte Holmes	Jamal Khalid	Jane Finley	Kris Chumak	Sara Jones	Tonya Bradley		Gross pay	Ali Ghalid	Charlotte Holmes	Jamal Khalid	Jane Finley	Kris Chumak	Sara Jones	Tonya Bradley	Total	
3	T-shirt	Shirt	Shirt	Sweatshirt	Sweatshirt	Sweatshirt	Shirt		Items produced									
4	T-shirt	T-shirt	Sweatshirt	T-shirt	Sweatshirt	Shirt	Shirt		Sweatshirt	11	10	15	14	16	13	16	95	
5	Sweatshirt	T-shirt	Shirt	T-shirt	Shirt	Sweatshirt	Shirt		T-shirt	16	9	7	19	7	6	1	65	
6	Shirt		Sweatshirt	Sweatshirt	Sweatshirt	Shirt	Sweatshirt		Shirt	13	16	13	0	14	17	22	95	OK
7	T-shirt	Sweatshirt	Shirt	T-shirt	Sweatshirt	Shirt	Shirt											
8	T-shirt	Shirt	Sweatshirt	Sweatshirt	Sweatshirt	Shirt	Shirt		Gross pay	327	310	305	226	324	327	376	2195	
9	T-shirt	Shirt	Shirt	T-shirt	Shirt	Shirt	Shirt											
10	T-shirt	Shirt	Sweatshirt	T-shirt	Sweatshirt	Sweatshirt	Sweatshirt											
11	Sweatshirt	T-shirt	Sweatshirt	Sweatshirt	T-shirt	Shirt	Shirt											
12	T-shirt	Shirt	Shirt	Shirt	Shirt	Shirt	Shirt											
13	T-shirt	Sweatshirt	T-shirt	Sweatshirt	Shirt	Sweatshirt	Shirt		Rate per item									
14	Sweatshirt	Shirt	Shirt	T-shirt	Sweatshirt	Shirt	Shirt		Sweatshirt	8								
15	Shirt	Sweatshirt	Sweatshirt	Sweatshirt	Shirt	T-shirt	Sweatshirt		T-shirt	6								
16	T-shirt	T-shirt	Sweatshirt	Sweatshirt	Sweatshirt	Shirt	Shirt		Shirt	11								
17	T-shirt	Shirt	Sweatshirt	Sweatshirt	T-shirt	Sweatshirt	Shirt											
18	T-shirt	T-shirt	T-shirt	Shirt	Sweatshirt	Shirt	Shirt											
19	Sweatshirt	Shirt	Shirt	T-shirt	Sweatshirt	Shirt	Shirt											
20	Sweatshirt	T-shirt	Shirt	Sweatshirt	Shirt	Shirt	Shirt											
21	Shirt	Shirt	T-shirt	Sweatshirt	Shirt	Shirt	Shirt											
22	Shirt	Sweatshirt	Sweatshirt	Sweatshirt	Shirt	Sweatshirt	Shirt											
23	Sweatshirt	Shirt	Sweatshirt	T-shirt	Shirt		Shirt											
24	Shirt	Sweatshirt	Shirt	T-shirt	Shirt	T-shirt	Sweatshirt											
25	Shirt	Sweatshirt	T-shirt	T-shirt	Shirt	Shirt	Sweatshirt											
26	Shirt	Sweatshirt	T-shirt	T-shirt	Shirt	Shirt	Shirt											
27	Sweatshirt	Sweatshirt	Shirt	T-shirt	Shirt	Sweatshirt	T-shirt											
28	Shirt	T-shirt	T-shirt	Sweatshirt	Sweatshirt	T-shirt	Shirt											
29	T-shirt	Shirt	Shirt	Sweatshirt	T-shirt	Shirt	Shirt											
30	Sweatshirt	T-shirt	T-shirt	T-shirt	Sweatshirt	Sweatshirt	Shirt											
31	Sweatshirt	Shirt	Shirt	Sweatshirt	Shirt	Shirt	Shirt											
32	Sweatshirt	Sweatshirt	Sweatshirt	T-shirt	T-shirt	Sweatshirt	Sweatshirt											
33	Shirt	Shirt	Shirt	T-shirt	T-shirt	Shirt	Shirt											
34	Shirt	Shirt	Sweatshirt	T-shirt	Sweatshirt	Shirt	Sweatshirt											
35	T-shirt	Sweatshirt	Sweatshirt	T-shirt	Shirt	T-shirt	Shirt											
36	T-shirt	Shirt	Sweatshirt		Sweatshirt	Shirt	Sweatshirt											
37	Shirt	Shirt	Sweatshirt		Shirt	T-shirt	Sweatshirt											
38	T-shirt				T-shirt	Shirt	Shirt											
39	Shirt				Sweatshirt		Sweatshirt											
40	T-shirt						Sweatshirt											
41	Shirt						Shirt											
42	Sweatshirt																	
43																		
44																		

Points 1 to 4 – formulas Columns I to M

	I	J	K	L	M
1	W/c 30/03/20-9				
2	Gross pay	Ali Ghalid	Charlotte Holmes	Jamal Khalid	Jane Finley
3	Items produced				
4	Sweatshirt	=COUNTIF(A$3:A$42,$I4)	=COUNTIF(B$3:B$42,$I4)	=COUNTIF(C$3:C$42,$I4)	=COUNTIF(D$3:D$42,$I4)
5	T-shirt	=COUNTIF(A$3:A$42,$I5)	=COUNTIF(B$3:B$42,$I5)	=COUNTIF(C$3:C$42,$I5)	=COUNTIF(D$3:D$42,$I5)
6	Shirt	=COUNTIF(A$3:A$42,$I6)	=COUNTIF(B$3:B$42,$I6)	=COUNTIF(C$3:C$42,$I6)	=COUNTIF(D$3:D$42,$I6)
7					
8	Gross pay	=(J4*$J$14)+(J5*$J$15)+(J6*$J$16)	=(K4*$J$14)+(K5*$J$15)+(K6*$J$16)	=(L4*$J$14)+(L5*$J$15)+(L6*$J$16)	=(M4*$J$14)+(M5*$J$15)+(M6*$J$16)

Points 1 to 4 – formulas Columns I, N to R

	I	N	O	P	Q	R
1	W/c 30/03/20-9					
2	Gross pay	Kris Chumak	Sara Jones	Tonya Bradley	Total	
3	Items produced					
4	Sweatshirt	=COUNTIF(E$3:E$42,$I4)	=COUNTIF(F$3:F$42,$I4)	=COUNTIF(G$3:G$42,$I4)	=SUM(J4:P4)	
5	T-shirt	=COUNTIF(E$3:E$42,$I5)	=COUNTIF(F$3:F$42,$I5)	=COUNTIF(G$3:G$42,$I5)	=SUM(J5:P5)	
6	Shirt	=COUNTIF(E$3:E$42,$I6)	=COUNTIF(F$3:F$42,$I6)	=COUNTIF(G$3:G$42,$I6)	=SUM(J6:P6)	=IF(COUNTA(A3:G42)-Q4-Q5-Q6=0,"OK","Check")
7						
8	Gross pay	=(N4*$J$14)+(N5*$J$15)+(N6*$J$16)	=(O4*$J$14)+(O5*$J$15)+(O6*$J$16)	=(P4*$J$14)+(P5*$J$15)+(P6*$J$16)	=SUM(J8:P8)	

Points 5 and 6 completed – columns H to R

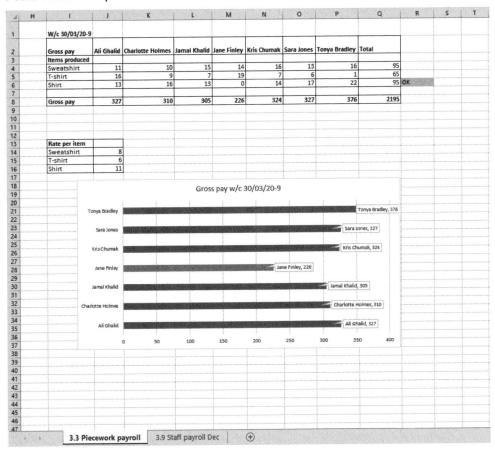

	Ali Ghalid	Charlotte Holmes	Jamal Khalid	Jane Finley	Kris Chumak	Sara Jones	Tonya Bradley	Total	
W/c 30/03/20-9									
Gross pay									
Items produced									
Sweatshirt	11	10	15	14	16	13	16	95	
T-shirt	16	9	7	19	7	6	1	65	
Shirt	13	16	13	0	14	17	22	95	OK
Gross pay	327	310	305	226	324	327	376	2195	
Rate per item									
Sweatshirt	8								
T-shirt	6								
Shirt	11								

3.3 Piecework payroll   3.9 Staff payroll Dec

3.4 Gross wages

			£
•	Anna Kurtin:	35 hours at £10.50 per hour =	367.50
		4 hours overtime at £14.00 per hour =	56.00
		production bonus 45 x 50p =	22.50
			446.00
•	Pete Singh:	35 hours at £12.00 per hour =	420.00
		3 hours overtime at £16.00 per hour =	48.00
		4 hours overtime at £18.00 per hour =	72.00
		production bonus 57 x 50p =	28.50
			568.50

Piecework rate for Anna Kurtin
£446.00 ÷ 45 = £9.91 per 1,000 copies printed

3.5

		MOULDING	FINISHING
•	Time saved	–	500
•	Bonus (£)	–	2,525*
•	Total labour cost (£)	41,160	47,975

* £45,450 ÷ 4,500 hours = £10.10 x 500 hours = £5,050 x 50% = £2,525

3.6 **(a)** Week 1: 450 hours at £10.20 per hour = £4,590

50 hours at £5.10 (overtime premium) = £255

Total gross earnings for Week 1 = £4,590 + £255 = £4,845

Week 2: 400 hours at £10.20 per hour = £4,080 = Total gross earnings

(b) Week 1: Normally treated as indirect labour cost would be overtime premium on 50 hours,

ie 50 x £5.10 = £255 (as above)

Week 2: Normally treated as indirect labour cost would be 20 hours of non-production work at basic pay, ie 20 x £10.20 = £204

3.7 **Employee's weekly time sheet for week ending 15 April 20-6**

Employee: T Mantle			Production Centre: Finishing			
Employee number: 170			Basic pay per hour: £14.00			
	Hours spent on production	Hours worked on indirect work	Notes	Basic pay £	Overtime premium £	Total pay £
Monday	6	0		84	0	84
Tuesday	5	2	2 hours maintenance	98	7	105
Wednesday	7	0		98	7	105
Thursday	6	3	3 hours training	126	21	147
Friday	8	0		112	14	126
Saturday	5	0		70	28	98
Sunday	0	0		0	0	0
Total	37	5		588	77	665

3.8   **Task 1**

Dr		Wages Control Account		Cr
	£			£
Cash/bank (net wages)	7,500	Production (direct labour)		6,500
HM Revenue & Customs		Production overheads		
(income tax & NIC)	1,450	(indirect labour)		2,700
Pension contributions	750	Non-production overheads		
		(administration)		500
	9,700			9,700

Task 2

20-4	Code number	Debit £	Credit £
26 March	3300	6,500	
26 March	5200		6,500
26 March	3500	2,700	
26 March	5200		2,700
26 March	3700	500	
26 March	5200		500

3.9   Points 1 to 13 completed

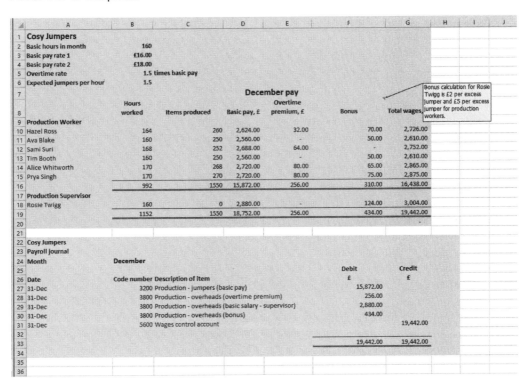

Points 1 to 10 completed – formulas used

	A	B	C	D	E	F	G	H
1	**Cosy Jumpers**							
2	Basic hours in month	160						
3	Basic pay rate 1	16						
4	Basic pay rate 2	18						
5	Overtime rate	1.5						
6	Expected jumpers per hour	1.5	times basic pay					
7								
8					December pay			
9	Production Worker	Hours worked	Items produced	Basic pay, £	Overtime premium, £	Bonus	Total wages, £	Bonus calculation for Rosie Twigg is £2 per excess jumper and £5 per excess jumper for production workers.
10	Hazel Ross	164	260	=B10*$B$3	=IF(B10>$B$2,(B10-$B$2)*($B$3)*($B$5),0)	=IF(((C10-(B10*$B$6))*5)>0,((C10-(B10*$B$6))*5),0)	=D10+E10+F10	
11	Ava Blake	160	250	=B11*$B$3	=IF(B11>$B$2,(B11-$B$2)*($B$3)*($B$5),0)	=IF(((C11-(B11*$B$6))*5)>0,((C11-(B11*$B$6))*5),0)	=D11+E11+F11	
12	Sumi Suri	168	252	=B12*$B$3	=IF(B12>$B$2,(B12-$B$2)*($B$3)*($B$5),0)	=IF(((C12-(B12*$B$6))*5)>0,((C12-(B12*$B$6))*5),0)	=D12+E12+F12	
13	Tim Booth	160	250	=B13*$B$3	=IF(B13>$B$2,(B13-$B$2)*($B$3)*($B$5),0)	=IF(((C13-(B13*$B$6))*5)>0,((C13-(B13*$B$6))*5),0)	=D13+E13+F13	
14	Alice Whitworth	170	268	=B14*$B$3	=IF(B14>$B$2,(B14-$B$2)*($B$3)*($B$5),0)	=IF(((C14-(B14*$B$6))*5)>0,((C14-(B14*$B$6))*5),0)	=D14+E14+F14	
15	Prya Singh	170	270	=B15*$B$3	=IF(B15>$B$2,(B15-$B$2)*($B$3)*($B$5),0)	=IF(((C15-(B15*$B$6))*5)>0,((C15-(B15*$B$6))*5),0)	=D15+E15+F15	
16		=SUM(B10:B15)	=SUM(C10:C15)	=SUM(D10:D15)	=SUM(E10:E15)	=SUM(F10:F15)	=SUM(G10:G15)	
17	Production Supervisor							
18	Rosie Twigg	160	0	=B18*$B$4	=IF(B18>$B$2,(B18-$B$2)*($B$4)*($B$5),0)	=IF(((C16-(B16*$B$6))*2)>0,((C16-(B16*$B$6))*2),0)	=D18+E18+F18	
19		=B18+B16	=C18+C16	=D18+D16	=E18+E16	=F18+F16	=G18+G16	
20							=SUM(D19:F19)-G19	
21								
22	**Cosy Jumpers**							
23	**Payroll journal**							
24	**Month**	December						
25								
26	**Date**	**Code number**	**Description of item**			**Debit £**	**Credit £**	
27	44561	3200	Production - jumpers (basic pay)			=D16		
28	44561	3800	Production - overheads (overtime premium)			=E19		
29	44561	3800	Production - overheads (basic salary - supervisor)			=D18		
30	44561	3800	Production - overheads (bonus)			=F19		
31	44561	5600	Wages control account				=G19	
32								
33						=SUM(F27:F31)	=SUM(G27:G31)	
34								

3.10 Total cost of direct labour for October:

		£
16,000 hours x £10 per hour	=	160,000
1,600 hours x £5 per hour (overtime premium)	=	8,000

Total cost of direct labour = £160,000 + £8,000 = £168,000

Cost bookkeeping entries:

	Debit	Credit
	£	£
• production – 'Mulligan' clubs (1500)	168,000	
• wages control (5000)		168,000

3.11 **(a)** £645, ie 43 standard hours at £15

(b) £675, ie Monday £120, Tuesday £120, Wednesday £150, Thursday £165, Friday £120

(c) £650, ie above the standard hours produced

(d) £735, ie 44 actual hours at £15, plus flat-rate bonus of £75 for the week

3.12 **(a)**

Labour cost	Hours	£
Basic pay	416	4,160
Overtime rate 1	30	375
Overtime rate 2	15	225
Total cost before team bonus		4,760
Bonus payment		1,000
Total cost including team bonus		5,760

(b) The direct cost per equivalent unit for March is £5,760/12,000 equivalent units = **£0.48**

(c) The equivalent units of production with regard to labour for April will be 9,800 units + (1,500 units x 80% complete) = **11,000 units.**

The bonus payable will be 1,000 units x £10.60 per hour x 5% = **£530**

CHAPTER 4: OVERHEADS AND EXPENSES

4.1 **(a)**

OVERHEAD ANALYSIS SHEET		
	MOULDING	FINISHING
Budgeted total overheads (£)	9,338	3,298
Budgeted machine hours	1,450	680
Budgeted overhead absorption rate (£)	6.44*	4.85**

* £9,338 ÷ 1,450 hours

** £3,298 ÷ 680 hours

(b)

JOB OVERHEAD ANALYSIS SHEET		
	MOULDING	FINISHING
Job machine hours	412	154
Budgeted overhead absorption rate (£)	6.44	4.85
Overhead absorbed by job (£)	2,653.28*	746.90**

* 412 hours x £6.44 per hour

** 154 hours x £4.85 per hour

(c) **Direct labour hour**

- With this method, production overhead is absorbed on the basis of the number of direct labour hours worked.

- While this is a commonly-used method, it is inappropriate where some output is worked on by hand while other output passes quickly through a machinery process and requires little direct labour time.

- This method may be appropriate for Wyvern Fabrication Company; however, much depends on the balance between direct labour hours and machine hours in the two production departments.

4.2 **(a)**

Budgeted overheads	Basis of apportionment	Total £	Dept A £	Dept B £	Dept C £
Rent and rates	Floor space	7,210	3,090	1,545	2,575
Depn. of machinery	Carrying amount	10,800	5,400	3,240	2,160
Supervisor's salary	Production-line employees	33,000	17,600	8,800	6,600
Machinery insurance	Carrying amount of machinery	750	375	225	150
Totals		51,760	26,465	13,810	11,485

(b)   37 hours x 48 weeks =   1,776 direct labour hours per employee

Dept A: 8 employees =   £26,465/14,208 hours =   £1.86 per direct labour hour

Dept B: 4 employees =   £13,810/7,104 hours =   £1.94 per direct labour hour

Dept C: 3 employees =   £11,485/5,328 hours =   £2.16 per direct labour hour

4.3   **(a)**

Budgeted overheads	Basis of apportionment	Total £	Machining £	Finishing £	Maintenance £
Rent and rates	Floor space	5,520	2,760	1,840	920
Buildings insurance	Floor space	1,320	660	440	220
Machinery insurance	Carrying amount	1,650	1,200	450	–
Lighting and heating	Floor space	3,720	1,860	1,240	620
Dep'n of machinery	Carrying amount	11,000	8,000	3,000	–
Supervisor's salary	No. of employees	30,000	18,000	9,000	3,000
Maintenance dept salary	Allocation	23,590	–	–	23,590
Factory cleaning	Floor space	4,800	2,400	1,600	800
		81,600	34,880	17,570	29,150
Re-apportionment of maintenance dept	Value of machinery	–	21,200	7,950	(29,150)
		81,600	56,080	25,520	–

(b)   35 hours x 47 weeks = 1,645 direct labour hours per employee

Machining Dept: 6 employees = 9,870 hours = £5.12 per direct labour hour

Finishing Dept: 3 employees = 4,935 hours = £5.17 per direct labour hour

4.4

Budgeted overheads	Total	Business studies	General studies	Administration	Technical support
		£	£	£	£
Overheads	81,600	40,000	20,000	9,600	12,000
Technical support	–	6,000	3,000	3,000	(12,000)
				12,600	–
Administration	–	8,400	4,200	(12,600)	–
	81,600	54,400	27,200	–	–

4.5 **(a)** $\dfrac{\text{total overheads}}{\text{total hours}} = \dfrac{£74,900 \text{ (total of all overhead costs)}}{3,290 \text{ (35 hours x 47 weeks x 2 partners)}}$ = £22.77 per partner hour

(b) $\dfrac{£74,900 + £100,000}{3,290}$ = £53.16 per partner hour

(c) 2 hours x 47 weeks x £22.77 = £2,140.38 per partner (ie £4,280.76 in total)

4.6 **(a)** Direct labour hour: (3 hours x 80 seats) + (3.5 hours x 40 seats)
= 380 direct labour hours per month = £2.63 per hour.
Machine hour: (1 hour x 80 seats) + (2.5 hours x 40 seats)
= 180 machine hours per month = £5.56 per hour.
Alternative methods could be based on a percentage of certain costs, eg direct labour.

(b) **Direct labour hour**
'Standard' £42.50 + £7.89 (3 x £2.63) = £50.39
'De Luxe' £62.00 + £9.21 (3.5 x £2.63) = £71.21

Machine hour
'Standard' £42.50 + £5.56 = £48.06
'De Luxe' £62.00 + £13.90 (2.5 x £5.56) = £75.90
Note: some figures have been rounded to the nearest penny

(c) See text page 131. The machine hour rate charges most to 'de luxe' model. On balance, direct labour hours may be the best method to use because the products are more labour-intensive than machine-intensive. Whichever method is used, the total amount of overheads absorbed will be the same in the end.

4.7 **Task 1**

Budgeted fixed overheads for November 20-1	Basis	Total £	Warehouse £	Manufact-uring £	Maintenance £	Admin £
Depreciation	**Carrying amount**	9,150	1,830	6,100	305	915
Rent	**Floor space**	11,000	1,650	6,600	1,100	1,650
Other property overheads	**Floor space**	6,200	930	3,720	620	930
Administration overheads	**Allocated**	5,450				5,450
Staff costs	**Allocated**	27,370	3,600	9,180	8,650	5,940
		59,170	8,010	25,600	10,675	14,885

Task 2

Budgeted fixed overhead absorption rate for the manufacturing department:
£25,600 ÷ 10,000 hours = £2.56 per machine hour

4.8   Task 1

Budgeted fixed overheads for August 20-3	Basis	Total £	Accommo-dation £	Restaurant £	Bar £	Kitchen £	Administration £
Bedroom repairs	Allocated	3,200	3,200				
Electricity	Metered	1,700	550	250	150	700	50
Rent of premises	Floor space	9,000	5,850	1,350	900	450	450
Kitchen repairs	Allocated	1,025				1,025	
Staff costs	Allocated	23,595	4,550	6,740	3,045	2,310	6,950
Other property overheads	Floor space	4,000	2,600	600	400	200	200
		42,520	16,750	8,940	4,495	4,685	7,650
Administration			4,590	1,530	765	765	(7,650)
		42,520	21,340	10,470	5,260	5,450	–

Task 2

Budgeted fixed overhead absorption rate for the kitchen:

£5,450 ÷ 1,000 hours = £5.45 per labour hour

4.9

Points 1 to 9 completed

	A	B	C	D	F	G	H	I	J	K	L	M
1	Bill's Bicycles											
2	Budgeted overhead rates 20-6											
3												
4	Apportionment basis											
5	Overhead	Basis			Frame making	Assembly	Warehouse	Adminstration	Total		Basis of apportionment	
6	Buildings insurance	% of floor space			40%	30%	20%	10%	100%		Allocation	
7	Depreciation of non-current	Carrying amount of non-current assets			£400,000	£240,000	£120,000	£40,000	£800,000		% of floor space	
8	Lighting and heating	% of floor space			40%	30%	20%	10%	100%		Carrying amount of non-current assets	
9	Rent and rates	% of floor space			40%	30%	20%	10%	100%		No of employees	
10	Managers' salaries	No of employees			45	35	10	10	100			
11												
12												
13	Bugdeted fixed overheads for year to 30 November 20-6											
14	Overhead	Basis			Frame making	Assembly	Warehouse	Administration	Total			
15	Buildings insurance	% of floor space			2,400	1,800	1,200	600	6,000	OK		
16	Depreciation of non-current	Carrying amount of non-current assets			70,000	42,000	21,000	7,000	140,000	OK		
17	Lighting and heating	% of floor space			6,400	4,800	3,200	1,600	16,000	OK		
18	Rent and rates	% of floor space			7,280	5,460	3,640	1,820	18,200	OK		
19	Managers' salaries	No of employees			45,900	35,700	10,200	10,200	102,000	OK		
20	Indirect staff costs	Allocation			96,000	75,600	216,000	170,000	557,600	OK		
21					227,980	165,360	255,240	191,220	839,800			
22	Warehouse				102,096	153,144	-255,240					
23	Administration				95,610	95,610		-191,220				
24	Total				425,686	414,114	0	0	839,800			
25												
26												
27	Overhead Recovery Rate:	Machine/Labour hrs	Rate, £									
28												
29	Frame making		250,000	1.71								
30	Assembly		59,400	6.98								
31												
32												
33												
34												
35												

4.9 Apportionment | 4.9 Basis of apport't

Points 1 to 9 – formulas used

Columns A to G

Bill's Bicycles

Budgeted overhead rates 20-6

	A	B	F	G
Apportionment basis			**Frame making**	**Assembly**
Overhead	**Basis**			
Buildings insurance	% of floor space		=HLOOKUP($B6,'Activity I Basis of apport'!$A$3:$D$8,2,FALSE)	=HLOOKUP($B6,'Activity I Basis of apport'!$A$3:$D$8,3,FALSE)
Depreciation of non-current assets	Carrying amount of non-current assets		=HLOOKUP($B7,'Activity I Basis of apport'!$A$3:$D$8,2,FALSE)	=HLOOKUP($B7,'Activity I Basis of apport'!$A$3:$D$8,3,FALSE)
Lighting and heating	% of floor space		=HLOOKUP($B8,'Activity I Basis of apport'!$A$3:$D$8,2,FALSE)	=HLOOKUP($B8,'Activity I Basis of apport'!$A$3:$D$8,3,FALSE)
Rent and rates	% of floor space		=HLOOKUP($B9,'Activity I Basis of apport'!$A$3:$D$8,2,FALSE)	=HLOOKUP($B9,'Activity I Basis of apport'!$A$3:$D$8,3,FALSE)
Managers' salaries	No of employees		=HLOOKUP($B10,'Activity I Basis of apport'!$A$3:$D$8,2,FALSE)	=HLOOKUP($B10,'Activity I Basis of apport'!$A$3:$D$8,3,FALSE)
Bugdeted fixed overheads for year to 30			**Frame making**	**Assembly**
Overhead	**Basis**			
Buildings insurance	% of floor space		=F6/$J6*$E15	=G6/$J6*$E15
Depreciation of non-current assets	Carrying amount of non-current assets		=F7/$J7*$E16	=G7/$J7*$E16
Lighting and heating	% of floor space		=F8/$J8*$E17	=G8/$J8*$E17
Rent and rates	% of floor space		=F9/$J9*$E18	=G9/$J9*$E18
Managers' salaries	No of employees		=F10/$J10*$E19	=G10/$J10*$E19
Indirect staff costs	Allocation		='Activity I Basis of apport'!E4	='Activity I Basis of apport'!E5
Warehouse			=SUM(F15:F20)	=SUM(G15:G20)
Administration			=0.4*H21	=0.6*H21
Administration			=0.5*I21	=0.5*I21
Total			=SUM(F21:F23)	=SUM(G21:G23)

	A	B	C
Overhead Recovery Rate:		**Machine/Labour hrs**	**Rate, £**
Frame making		250000	=ROUNDUP(F24/B29,2)
Assembly		59400	=ROUNDUP(G24/B30,2)

Points 1 to 9 – formulas used

Columns H to K

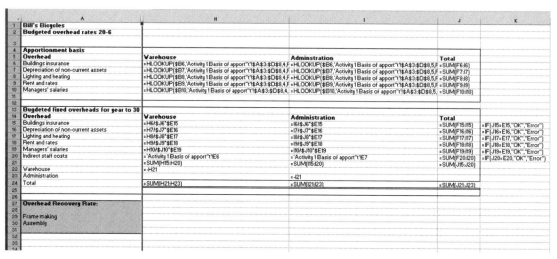

	A	H	I	J	K
1	Bill's Bicycles				
2	Budgeted overhead rates 20-6				
3					
4	Apportionment basis				
5	Overhead	Warehouse	Administration	Total	
6	Buildings insurance	=HLOOKUP($B6,'Activity 1 Basis of apport'!$A$3:$D$8,4,F	=HLOOKUP($B6,'Activity 1 Basis of apport'!$A$3:$D$8,5,F	=SUM(F6:I6)	
7	Depreciation of non-current assets	=HLOOKUP($B7,'Activity 1 Basis of apport'!$A$3:$D$8,4,F	=HLOOKUP($B7,'Activity 1 Basis of apport'!$A$3:$D$8,5,F	=SUM(F7:I7)	
8	Lighting and heating	=HLOOKUP($B8,'Activity 1 Basis of apport'!$A$3:$D$8,4,F	=HLOOKUP($B8,'Activity 1 Basis of apport'!$A$3:$D$8,5,F	=SUM(F8:I8)	
9	Rent and rates	=HLOOKUP($B9,'Activity 1 Basis of apport'!$A$3:$D$8,4,F	=HLOOKUP($B9,'Activity 1 Basis of apport'!$A$3:$D$8,5,F	=SUM(F9:I9)	
10	Managers' salaries	=HLOOKUP($B10,'Activity 1 Basis of apport'!$A$3:$D$8,4,	=HLOOKUP($B10,'Activity 1 Basis of apport'!$A$3:$D$8,5,	=SUM(F10:I10)	
11					
12					
13	Bugdeted fixed overheads for year to 30				
14	Overhead	Warehouse	Administration	Total	
15	Buildings insurance	=H6/$J6*$E15	=I6/$J6*$E15	=SUM(F15:I15)	=IF(J15=E15,"OK","Error")
16	Depreciation of non-current assets	=H7/$J7*$E16	=I7/$J7*$E16	=SUM(F16:I16)	=IF(J16=E16,"OK","Error")
17	Lighting and heating	=H8/$J8*$E17	=I8/$J8*$E17	=SUM(F17:I17)	=IF(J17=E17,"OK","Error")
18	Rent and rates	=H9/$J9*$E18	=I9/$J9*$E18	=SUM(F18:I18)	=IF(J18=E18,"OK","Error")
19	Managers' salaries	=H10/$J10*$E19	=I10/$J10*$E19	=SUM(F19:I19)	=IF(J19=E19,"OK","Error")
20	Indirect staff costs	='Activity 1 Basis of apport'!E6	='Activity 1 Basis of apport'!E7	=SUM(F20:I20)	=IF(J20=E20,"OK","Error")
21		=SUM(H15:H20)	=SUM(I15:I20)	=SUM(J15:J20)	
22	Warehouse	=-H21			
23	Administration		=-I21		
24	Total	=SUM(H21:H23)	=SUM(I21:I23)	=SUM(J21:J23)	
25					
26					
27	Overhead Recovery Rate:				
28					
29	Frame making				
30	Assembly				
31					
32					
33					

Data validation – point 1

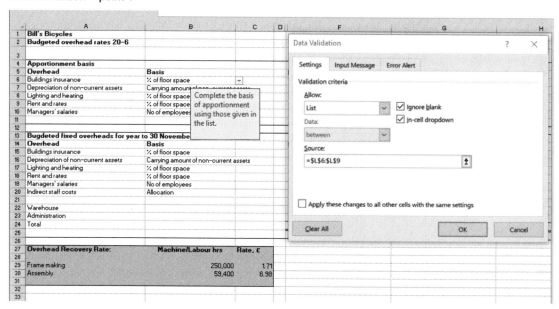

4.10

Budgeted overheads	Basis of apportionment	Moulding £	Finishing £	Maintenance £	Stores £	Admin £	Totals £
Depreciation charge for machinery	Carrying amount of machinery	1,200	750				1,950
Power for production machinery	Power usage	1,736	868				2,604
Rent and rates of premises	Floor space	1,425	760	570	665	855	4,275
Light and heat for premises	Floor space	975	520	390	455	585	2,925
Indirect labour	Allocated			32,200	27,150	28,450	87,800
Totals		5,336	2,898	33,160	28,270	29,890	99,554
Re-apportion Maintenance		24,870	8,290	(33,160)			
Re-apportion Stores		16,962	11,308		(28,270)		
Re-apportion Administration		14,945	14,945			(29,890)	
Total overheads to production centres		62,113	37,441				99,554

4.11 **(a)**   (d) cutting £20 per hour; assembly £75 per hour

 (b)   (a) cutting £9 per hour; assembly £25 per hour

 (c)   (b) cutting over-absorbed £7,400; assembly under-absorbed £3,500

4.12

Dr	Production Overheads Account: Moulding Department (3400)		Cr
	£		£
Bank (overheads incurred)	5,000	Production	4,800
		Statement of profit or loss	
		(under-absorption)	200
	5,000		5,000

Dr	Production Overheads Account: Finishing Department (3500)		Cr
	£		£
Bank (overheads incurred)	7,000	Production	7,500
Statement of profit or loss			
(over-absorption)	500		
	7,500		7,500

20-6	Code number	Debit £	Credit £
26 May	3000	4,800	
26 May	3400		4,800
26 May	3000	7,500	
26 May	3500		7,500
26 May	6000	200	
26 May	3400		200
26 May	3500	500	
26 May	6000		500

4.13 **(a)** Example of Overhead Recovery Journal worksheet

Points 1 to 4 completed

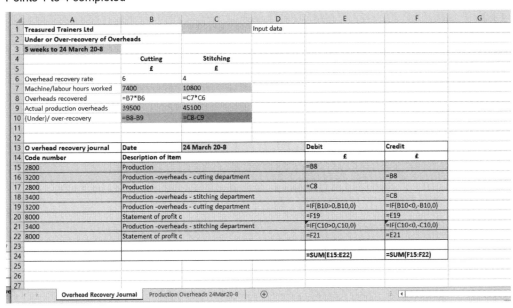

Formulas used in example of Overhead Recovery Journal worksheet

Points 1 to 4 completed

(b) 3D column chart of production overheads, including data table

Points 1 to 2 completed

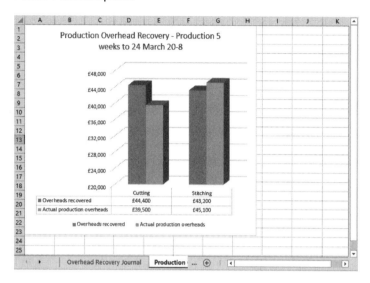

Note: Your journal and graph may look slightly different to this answer. However, the key spreadsheet elements, for example the **IF statement**, **colour fill** for each section of the journal, all cells except cells being **protected** must be included.

The answer file, 'MATST Chapter 4 Treasured Trainers Overhead Recovery Calculation and Journal' is available to download on the Osborne Books website.

4.14

Dr	**Production Overheads Account: Baking Department (2600)**			Cr
	£			£
Bank (overheads incurred)	11,500	Production		12,000
Statement of profit or loss				
(over-absorption)	500			
	12,000			12,000

Dr	**Production Overheads Account: Finishing Department (2800)**			Cr
	£			£
Bank (overheads incurred)	5,000	Production		4,800
		Statement of profit or loss		
		(under-absorption)		200
	5,000			5,000

20-6	Code number	Debit £	Credit £
11 March	2000	12,000	
11 March	2600		12,000
11 March	2000	4,800	
11 March	2800		4,800
11 March	2600	500	
11 March	5000		500
11 March	5000	200	
11 March	2800		200

4.15 **(a)**

Department	£
Paint	13,992
Wallpaper	10,416

(b)

Department	£	over-absorbed	under-absorbed
Paint	368		✔
Wallpaper	726	✔	

(c)

Over-absorbed overheads are **debited** to production overheads and **credited** to the statement of **profit or loss.**

Under-absorbed overheads are **added** to the total cost of production and **reduce** profits.

CHAPTER 5: METHODS OF COSTING

5.1 The method of costing for each business should be justified; however, the following are the most likely methods:

- *accountant* – job costing, because each job will take a different length of time and is likely to involve a number of staff, each with different skill levels

- *bus company* – service costing, where the object is to find the cost per unit of service, eg passenger mile; job costing used for 'one-offs', eg quoting for the transport for a trip to the seaside for an old people's home

- *baker* – batch costing, where identical units are produced in batches, eg loaves; job costing could be used for 'one-off' items, eg a wedding cake

- *sports centre* – service costing, or job costing for 'one-off', eg hire of the main sports hall for an exhibition

- *hotel* – different methods of costing are likely to be used, eg service costing for the rooms, batch costing in the restaurant, and job costing for special events

- *wedding* – job costing, because each wedding is separately identifiable to which costs can be charged

5.2

			£	£
(a)	Direct materials:	100m x £7.50	750.00	
		75m x £4.00	300.00	
				1,050.00
	Direct labour:	28 hours x £12.50		350.00
	Variable overheads:	28 hours x £10.00		280.00
	TOTAL COST			1,680.00
(b)	Profit (20% of total cost)			336.00
	SELLING PRICE			2,016.00

5.3

JOB COST RECORD		
Replacement Cylinder Head		
		£
Direct materials		1,000.00
100 kg of high-strength steel at £10 per kg		
Direct Labour		
Foundry:	10 hours at £15.00 per hour	150.00
Finishing:	15 hours at £12.00 per hour	180.00
Overheads		
Foundry:	80% of direct labour cost	120.00
Finishing:	12 machine hours x £20 per hour	240.00
TOTAL COST		1,690.00
Profit (25% of total cost)		422.50
SELLING PRICE		2,112.50

5.4   Point 1 completed

	A	B	C	D
1	**Material PM821**			
2				
3		Period	Price per tonne	
4		1	65	
5		2	67	
6		3	66	
7		4	69	
8		5	71	
9		6	74	
10		7	73	
11		8	70	
12		9	77	
13		10	79	
14		11	81	
15		12	78	
16		13	82	
17		14	84	
18		15	80	
19		16	81	
20		17	79	
21		18	83	
22		19	85	
23		20	83	
24		21	85	
25		22	82	
26		23	86	
27		24	84	
28	**Quote period**	27	90.09884	
29				

The formula in C28 is =FORECAST(B28,C4:C27,B4:B27).

Points 2 to 7 completed

	A	B	C	D	E	F	G	H	I
1	**Quotation for Job MC980**								
2	To be completed in period 27								
3									
4		Unit	Quantity	Price	Cost				
5	**Direct materials**			£	£				
6	PM821 tarmac	Tonnes	20	90.10	1,802.00				
7	Hardcore	Tonnes	30	35.40	1,062.00				
8	**Direct labour**								
9	Site preparation team	Hours	375	15.00	5,625.00	Sheriden Amos · E9 ···			
10	Tarmac laying team	Hours	120	18.10	2,172.00	Confirmed with Site Prep Manager			
11	**Overheads**					11/05/2021 17:47			
12	Site preparation O/H	60% of direct labour cost			3,375.00				
13	Tarmac laying O/H	£30 per labour hour			3,600.00	Reply			
14									
15	Total cost				17,636.00				
16	Margin 20%				4,409.00				
17	Selling price				22,045.00				
18					OK				
19									
20									
21									
22									

Points 2 to 7 – formulas used

Columns A to E

	A	B	C	D	E	F
1	Quotation for Job MC980					
2	To be completed in period 27					
3						
4		Unit	Quantity	Price	Cost	
5	Direct materials			£	£	
6	PM821 tarmac	Tonnes	20	=ROUND('5.3 Forecast PM821'!C28,2)	=D6*C6	
7	Hardcore	Tonnes	30	35.4	=D7*C7	
8	Direct labour					
9	Site preparation team	Hours	375	15	=D9*C9	
10	Tarmac laying team	Hours	=4*30	18.1	=D10*C10	
11	Overheads					
12	Site preparation O/H	60% of direct labour cost			=0.6*E9	
13	Tarmac laying O/H	£30 per labour hour			=30*C10	
14						
15	Total cost				=SUM(E6:E14)	
16	Margin 20%				=E15/0.8*0.2	
17	Selling price				=E16+E15	
18					=IF(E16/E17=0.2,"OK","Check")	
19						
20						

Points 8 to 15 completed

The screenshot shown below is set to 'Page Layout' view, to show the amended header.

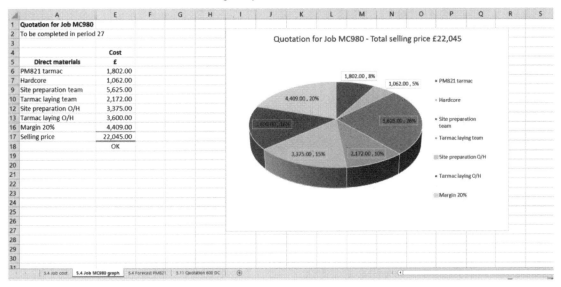

The spreadsheet 'MATST Chapter 5 Activities Answer' is available on the Osborne Books website, to enable you to view the chart in colour.

5.5

	£
Total costs:	
Depreciation of electric trains £60,000* x 6 trains	360,000
Leasing charges for track	1,000,000
Maintenance charges for trains	910,000
Power for trains	210,000
Wages of drivers and conductors	480,000
Administration	520,000
	3,480,000

* (£1,300,000 – £100,000) ÷ 20 years = £60,000 per train per year

Total cost per passenger mile:

$$\frac{£3,480,000}{\text{1m journeys x 4 miles}} = £0.87 \text{ total cost per passenger mile}$$

5.6

Cost element	Costs	Completed units	Work-in-progress			Total equivalent units	Cost per unit	WIP valuation
			Units	% complete	Equivalent units			
	A	B	C	D	E	F	G	H
					C x D	B + E	A ÷ F	E x G
	£						£	£
Direct materials	11,500	20,000	5,000	100	5,000	25,000	0.46	2,300
Direct labour	9,000	20,000	5,000	50	2,500	22,500	0.40	1,000
Production overheads	18,000	20,000	5,000	50	2,500	22,500	0.80	2,000
Total	38,500						1.66	5,300

- Cost per toy is £1.66 each
- Work-in-progress valuation is £5,300

5.7 **(a)** **(Note:** normal wastage, with scrap sales)

Dr				Production Account				Cr
	Quantity (litres)	Unit cost	Total cost		Quantity (litres)	Unit cost	Total cost	
		£	£			£	£	
Materials	22,000	0.25	5,500	Normal wastage	2,000	0.20	400	
Labour		0.15	3,300	Finished goods	20,000	0.53	10,600	
Overheads		0.10	2,200					
	22,000		11,000		22,000		11,000	

Tutorial note:

The cost per unit of the expected output is:

$$\frac{£11,000 - £400}{20,000 \text{ litres}} = £0.53 \text{ per litre}$$

(b)

	Debit £	Credit £
Normal wastage account	400	

5.8   (**Note:** abnormal loss, with scrap sales)

Dr				Production Account				Cr
	Quantity (kg)	Unit cost	Total cost		Quantity (kg)	Unit cost	Total cost	
		£	£			£	£	
Materials	42,000	0.25	10,500	Normal wastage	2,000	0.20	400	
Labour		0.10	4,200	Finished goods	39,500	0.41	16,195	
Overheads		0.05	2,100	Abnormal wastage	500	0.41	205	
	42,000		16,800		42,000		16,800	

Tutorial note:

The cost per unit of the expected output is:

$$\frac{£16,800 - £400^*}{40,000 \text{ kilos}} = £0.41 \text{ per kg}$$

*(2,000 kg x 20p)

Dr	Normal Wastage Account		Cr
	£		£
Production account	400	Bank	400

Dr	Abnormal Wastage Account		Cr
	£		£
Production account	205	Bank (500 kg x 20p)	100

5.9   **(a)**   £0.61   (£8,400 + £6,240) ÷ 24,000 units

        (b)   £0.95   (£25,680 – £2,880) ÷ 24,000 units

        (c)   £0.80   (£8,400 + £6,240 + £4,560) ÷ 24,000 units

        (d)   £19,200   £8,400 + £6,240 + £4,560

        (e)   £22,800   £25,680 – £2,880

5.10 **(a)**

Cost card for 1,500 'Bude' jackets	£
Direct material:	
Cloth	13,750
Lining	5,000
Total direct material	18,750
Direct labour:	
Cutting	16,800
Sewing	24,000
Finishing	11,250
Total direct labour	52,050
Variable production overhead	23,700
Fixed production overhead	15,000
Total estimated absorption cost	109,500

(b)

Debit	Production	£11,250
Credit	Wages control	£11,250

(c) Estimated prime cost per batch

£ | 70,800 |

Estimated marginal cost per batch

£ | 94,500 |

(d) The total revenue PeachTree will receive for the batch

£ | 165,000 |

The estimated profit for each jacket

£ |37 |

5.11 Points 1 to 10 completed

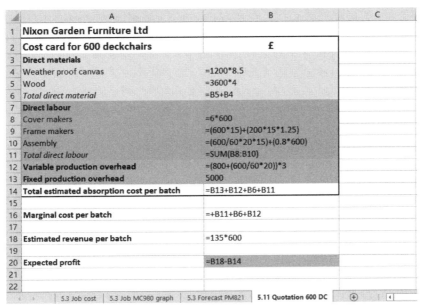

	A	B	C	D	E
1	Nixon Garden Furniture Ltd				
2	Cost card for 600 deckchairs	£			
3	Direct materials				
4	Weather proof canvas	10,200			
5	Wood	14,400			
6	Total direct material	24,600			
7	Direct labour				
8	Cover makers	3,600			
9	Frame makers	12,750			
10	Assembly	3,480			
11	Total direct labour	19,830			
12	Variable production overhead	3,000			
13	Fixed production overhead	5,000			
14	Total estimated absorption cost per batch	52,430			
15					
16	Marginal cost per batch	£47,430			
17					
18	Estimated revenue per batch	£81,000			
19					
20	Expected profit	£28,570			
21					
22					

5.3 Job cost | 5.3 Job MC980 graph | 5.3 Forecast PM821 | **5.11 Quotation 600 DC**

Points 1 to 10 – formulas used

	A	B	C
1	Nixon Garden Furniture Ltd		
2	Cost card for 600 deckchairs	£	
3	Direct materials		
4	Weather proof canvas	=1200*8.5	
5	Wood	=3600*4	
6	Total direct material	=B5+B4	
7	Direct labour		
8	Cover makers	=6*600	
9	Frame makers	=(600*15)+(200*15*1.25)	
10	Assembly	=(600/60*20*15)+(0.8*600)	
11	Total direct labour	=SUM(B8:B10)	
12	Variable production overhead	=(800+(600/60*20))*3	
13	Fixed production overhead	5000	
14	Total estimated absorption cost per batch	=B13+B12+B6+B11	
15			
16	Marginal cost per batch	=+B11+B6+B12	
17			
18	Estimated revenue per batch	=135*600	
19			
20	Expected profit	=B18-B14	
21			
22			

5.3 Job cost | 5.3 Job MC980 graph | 5.3 Forecast PM821 | **5.11 Quotation 600 DC**

Conditional formatting (point 10)

	A	B	C	D	E	F
1	Nixon Garden Furniture Ltd					
2	Cost card for 600 deckchairs	£				
3	Direct materials					
4	Weather proof canvas	=1200*8.5				
5	Wood	=3600*4				
6	Total direct material	=B5+B4				
7	Direct labour					
8	Cover makers	=6*600				
9	Frame makers	=(600*15)+(200*15*1.25)				
10	Assembly	=(600/60*20*15)+(0.8*600)				
11	Total direct labour	=SUM(B8:B10)				
12	Variable production overhead	=(800+(600/60*20))*3				
13	Fixed production overhead	5000				
14	Total estimated absorption cost per batch	=B13+B12+B6+B11				
15						
16	Marginal cost per batch	=+B11+B6+B12				
17						
18	Estimated revenue per batch	=135*600				
19						
20	Expected profit	=B18-B14				

Conditional Formatting Rules Manager   ?   ×

Show formatting rules for: Current Selection ▾

⊞ New Rule...   ▱ Edit Rule...   ✕ Delete Rule   ⊞ Duplicate Rule   ∧ ∨

Rule (applied in order shown)	Format	Applies to	Stop If True
Cell Value > 25000	AaBbCcYyZz	=$B$20	☐

OK   Close   Apply

The spreadsheet 'MATST Chapter 5 Activities Answer' is available on the Osborne Books website for you to compare your answer to.

CHAPTER 6: MARGINAL, ABSORPTION AND ACTIVITY BASED COSTING

6.1   **(a)**

Marginal cost per coffee machine	£
Direct materials	25.00
Direct labour	20.00
MARGINAL COST	45.00

(b)

Absorption cost per coffee machine	£
Direct materials	25.00
Direct labour	20.00
Fixed production overheads £270,000 ÷ 15,000 machines	18.00
ABSORPTION COST	63.00

(c)

COFFEEWORKS LIMITED

Statement of profit or loss: 15,000 coffee machines

	£	£
Sales revenue (15,000 x £80)		1,200,000
Direct materials (15,000 x £25)	375,000	
Direct labour (15,000 x £20)	300,000	
Fixed production overheads	270,000	
TOTAL COST		945,000
GROSS PROFIT		255,000
Less non-production overheads		200,000
NET PROFIT		55,000

6.2 **(a)**

Marginal cost per barbecue	£
Direct materials	30.00
Direct labour	25.00
MARGINAL COST	55.00

(b)

Absorption cost per barbecue	£
Direct materials	30.00
Direct labour	25.00
Fixed production overheads 150,000 ÷ 10,000 barbecues	15.00
ABSORPTION COST	70.00

(c)

COOK-IT LIMITED

Statement of profit or loss: 10,000 barbecues

	£	£
Sales revenue (10,000 x £90)		900,000
Direct materials (10,000 x £30)	300,000	
Direct labour (10,000 x £25)	250,000	
Fixed production overheads	150,000	
TOTAL COST		700,000
GROSS PROFIT		200,000
Less non-production overheads		125,000
NET PROFIT		75,000

6.3

MAXXA LIMITED

Statement of profit or loss for the month ended 31 January 20-7

	MARGINAL COSTING		ABSORPTION COSTING	
	£	£	£	£
Sales revenue 3,000 units at £8 each		24,000		24,000
Variable costs				
Direct materials at £1.25 each	5,000		5,000	
Direct labour at £2.25 each	9,000		9,000	
	14,000			
Less Closing inventory (marginal cost*)				
1,000 units at £3.50 each	3,500			
	10,500			
Fixed production overheads	6,000		6,000	
			20,000	
Less Closing inventory (absorption cost*)				
1,000 units at £5 each			5,000	
Less Cost of sales		16,500		15,000
Gross profit		7,500		9,000
Less non-production overheads		4,000		4,000
Net profit		3,500		5,000

* Closing inventory of 1,000 units (4,000 manufactured – 3,000 sold) is calculated on the basis of this month's costs:

marginal costing, variable costs only, ie £1.25 + £2.25 = £3.50 per unit

absorption costing, variable and fixed costs, ie £20,000 ÷ 4,000 units = £5 per unit

The difference in the profit is caused only by the closing inventory figures: £3,500 under marginal costing, and £5,000 under absorption costing. With marginal costing, the full amount of the fixed production overheads has been charged in this year's statement of profit or loss; by contrast, with absorption costing, part of the fixed production overheads (here £6,000 x 1,000/4,000 units = £1,500) has been carried forward in the inventory valuation.

6.4

Points 1 to 10 completed

	A	B	C	D	E	F	G
1	Bill's Bicycles						
2	Year ended 30 November 20-6						
3	Bicycles produced, units	22,000					
4	Bicycles sold, units	20,000					
5	Sales price per unit	£450					
6	Materials cost per unit	£75					
7	Frame making labour, hrs	3					
8	Frame making rate	£16.50					
9	Assembly, hrs	5					
10	Assembly rate	£18.00					
11	Fixed production overheads	£862,400					
12			Freewheeler Electric Bicycle				
13		Marginal cost statement		Absorption cost statement			
14		£	£	£	£		
15	Sales revenue		9,000,000		9,000,000		
16	*Variable costs*						
17	Materials	1,650,000		1,650,000			
18	Labour- frame making	1,089,000		1,089,000			
19	Labour - assembly	1,980,000		1,980,000			
20		4,719,000					
21	Less: Closing inventory	429,000					
22		4,290,000					
23	Fixed production overheads	862,400		862,400			
24				5,581,400			
25	Less: Closing inventory			507,400			
26	Less: Cost of sales		5,152,400		5,074,000		
27	Gross profit		3,847,600		3,926,000		
28	Less: Non-production overheads						
29	Administration	239,200		239,200			
30	Distribution	1,468,700		1,468,700			
31	Marketing	362,400		362,400			
32			2,070,300		2,070,300		
33	Net profit		1,777,300		1,855,700		
34	Additional profit under Absorption costing				£78,400		
35							
36	Production overhead absorbed per unit of production				£39.20		
37							
38							

Points 1 to 10 – formulas used

⊿	A	B	C	D	E	F
1	Bill's Bicycles					
2	Year ended 30 November 20-6					
3	Bicycles produced, units	22000				
4	Bicycles sold, units	20000				
5	Sales price per unit	450				
6	Materials cost per unit	75				
7	Frame making labour, hrs	3				
8	Frame making rate	16.5				
9	Assembly, hrs	5				
10	Assembly rate	18				
11	Fixed production overheads	862400				
12			**Freewheeler Electric Bicycle**			
13			Marginal cost statement		Absorption cost statement	
14		£	£	£	£	
15	Sales revenue		=B5*B4		=C15	
16	*Variable costs*					
17	Materials	=B6*B3		=B17		
18	Labour- frame making	=B7*B8*B3		=B18		
19	Labour - assembly	=B9*B10*B3		=B19		
20		=B19+B18+B17				
21	Less: Closing inventory	=B20/B3*(B3-B4)				
22		=B20-B21				
23	Fixed production overheads	=B11		=B11		
24				=D23+D19+D18+D17		
25	Less: Closing inventory			=D24/B3*(B3-B4)		
26	Less: Cost of sales		=B23+B22		=D24-D25	
27	Gross profit		=C15-C26		=E15-E26	
28	Less: Non-production overheads					
29	Administration	239200		239200		
30	Distribution	1468700		1468700		
31	Marketing	362400		362400		
32			=SUM(B29:B31)		=SUM(D29:D31)	
33	Net profit		=C27-B29-B30-B31		=E27-D29-D30-D31	
34	Additional profit under Absorption c				=E33-C33	
35						
36	Production overhead absorbed per unit of production				=ROUND((D23/B3),2)	
37						

The spreadsheet 'MATST Chapter 6 Activities Answer' is available to download on the Osborne Books website.

6.5   **(a)**

ACTIVTOYS LIMITED

Statement of profit or loss for the year ended 31 December 20-1

	MARGINAL COSTING		ABSORPTION COSTING	
	£	£	£	£
Sales revenue 1,300 frames at £125 each		162,500		162,500
Variable costs				
Direct materials at £25 each	37,500		37,500	
Direct labour at £30 each	45,000		45,000	
	82,500			
Less Closing inventory (marginal cost*)				
200 frames at £55 each	11,000			
	71,500			
Fixed production overheads	82,500		82,500	
			165,000	
Less Closing inventory (absorption cost*)				
200 frames at £110 each			22,000	
Less Cost of sales		154,000		143,000
Gross profit		8,500		19,500
Less non-production overheads		8,000		8,000
Net profit		500		11,500

* Closing inventory of 200 frames (1,500 manufactured – 1,300 sold) is calculated on the basis of this year's costs:

marginal costing, variable costs only, ie £25 + £30 = £55 per frame x 200 frames = £11,000
absorption costing, variable and fixed costs, ie £165,000 ÷ 1,500 frames = £110 per frame x 200 frames = £22,000

(b)   Reasons for different profit figures:

- The difference in the profit figures is caused by the closing inventory figures: £11,000 under marginal costing and £22,000 under absorption costing – the same costs have been used, but fixed production overheads have been treated differently.

- Only fixed production overheads are dealt with differently using the techniques of marginal and absorption costing – both methods charge non-production overheads in full to the statement of profit or loss in the year to which they relate.

- With marginal costing, the full amount of the fixed production overheads has been charged in this year's statement of profit or loss; by contrast, with absorption costing, part of the fixed production overheads (here, £11,000) has been carried forward to next year in the inventory valuation.

Comment on the directors' statement:

- A higher profit does not mean more money in the bank.

- The two costing methods simply treat fixed production overheads differently and, in a year when there is no closing inventory, total profits to date are exactly the same – but they occur differently over the years.

- For financial statements, Activtoys Limited must use the absorption cost inventory valuation of £22,000 in order to comply with IAS 2, *Inventories*.

- For accounting staff, ethical considerations must apply – profit statements must be prepared without manipulation or bias.

6.6 **(a)** Activity based costing is a costing method which charges overheads to production on the basis of activities. The cost per unit of a product can be calculated based on its use of activities.

(b) A cost driver is an activity which causes costs to be incurred.

(c) Cost pools are groups of overhead costs that are incurred by the same activities.

6.7 Benefits of activity based costing (ABC) over absorption costing:

- more accurate – it identifies what causes overheads to be incurred for a particular activity

- more objective – overheads are charged to production on the basis of activities

- selling prices – more accurate because overheads are analysed to the products which use the activities

- appropriate for capital-intensive industries where overheads are high and complex in nature

6.8 Points 1 to 3 completed

	A	B	C	D	E	F	G	H	I
22									
23	*Absorption overhead calculations*		Piccolo	Medio	Grande	Giganto	Total		
24	Machine hours per product		3.00	3.50	4.00	4.50			
25	Machine hours for production		2,700	6,720	1,600	2,250	13,270		
26									
27	Overhead rate		£12.18						
28									
29	Overhead per product		£36.54	£42.63	£48.72	£54.81			
30									
31									
32	*Activity Based Costing calculations*		Piccolo	Medio	Grande	Giganto	Total		
33			£	£	£	£	£		
34	Set ups		30,600.00	20,400.00	13,600.00	17,000.00	81,600.00		
35	Raw material stores costs		14,527.26	25,826.23	1,345.12	16,141.40	57,840.00		
36	Quality inspections		15,600.00	3,900.00	1,300.00	1,300.00	22,100.00		
37			60,727.26	50,126.23	16,245.12	34,441.40	161,540.00		
38									
39	Overhead per product		£67.47	£26.11	£40.61	£68.88			
40									
41									
42									

Points 1 to 3 – formulas used

	A	B	C	D	E	F	G	H
1	**Pizzaiola Ltd**							
2	**Quarter ended 31 March 20-2**							
3								
4	**Budgeted production overhead costs**		£					
5	Set up costs		81600					
6	Raw material store costs		57840					
7	Quality Inspection costs		22100					
8			=SUM(C5:C7)					
9								
10								
11	*Production information*		Piccolo	Medio	Grande	Giganto	Total	
12	Machine hours per product		3	3.5	4	4.5		
13	Machine hours (total)		=3*C20	=3.5*D20	=4*E20	=4.5*F20	=SUM(C13:F13)	
14								
15	Batches		18	24	8	10		
16	Batch size		50	80	50	50		
17	Set ups		18	12	8	10	=SUM(C17:F17)	
18	Issues of materials from raw materials s		=15*C15	=20*D15	=25*E15	=30*F15	=SUM(C18:F18)	
19	Quality Inspections		24	6	2	2	=SUM(C19:F19)	
20	No of items produced		=+C16*C15	=+D16*D15	=+E16*E15	=+F16*F15	=SUM(C20:F20)	
21								
22								
23	*Absorption overhead calculations*		Piccolo	Medio	Grande	Giganto	Total	
24	Machine hours per product		3	3.5	4	4.5		
25	Machine hours for production		=C24*C20	=D24*D20	=E24*E20	=F24*F20	=SUM(C25:F25)	
26								
27	Overhead rate		=ROUNDUP(C8/G25,2)					
28								
29	Overhead per product		=$C$27*C24	=$C$27*D24	=$C$27*E24	=$C$27*F24		
30								
31								
32	*Activity Based Costing calculations*		Piccolo	Medio	Grande	Giganto	Total	
33			£	£	£	£	£	
34	Set ups		=$C$5*C17/$G$17	=$C$5*D17/$G$17	=$C$5*E17/$G$17	=$C$5*F17/$G$17	=SUM(C34:F34)	
35	Raw material stores costs		=$C$6*C18/$G$18	=$C$6*D18/$G$18	=$C$6*E18/$G$18	=$C$6*F18/$G$18	=SUM(C35:F35)	
36	Quality inspections		=$C$7*C19/$G$19	=$C$7*D19/$G$19	=$C$7*E19/$G$19	=$C$7*F19/$G$19	=SUM(C36:F36)	
37			=SUM(C34:C36)	=SUM(D34:D36)	=SUM(E34:E36)	=SUM(F34:F36)	=SUM(G34:G36)	
38								
39	Overhead per product		=C37/C20	=D37/D20	=E37/E20	=F37/F20		
40								
41								
42								

Points 4 to 8 completed

	A	B	C	D	E	F	G	H	I	J	K	L	M
1	Pizzaiola Ltd												
2	Quarter ended 31 March 20-2												
3					Absorption costing				Activity Based Costing				
4													
5			Piccolo	Medio	Grande	Giganto		Piccolo	Medio	Grande	Giganto		
6	No of items produced		900	1920	400	500		900	1920	400	500		
7													
8	Product costs		£	£	£	£		£	£	£	£		
9	Aluminium		50.00	60.00	90.00	110.00		50.00	60.00	90.00	110.00		
10	Insulation		25.00	30.00	40.00	50.00		25.00	30.00	40.00	50.00		
11	Consumables (screws, etc)		14.00	15.00	18.00	20.00		14.00	15.00	18.00	20.00		
12	Pizza stone		35.00	40.00	60.00	75.00		35.00	40.00	60.00	75.00		
13	Chimney		25.00	25.00	30.00	40.00		25.00	25.00	30.00	40.00		
14	Thermometer		8.00	10.00	12.00	20.00		8.00	10.00	12.00	20.00		
15	Door handle		5.00	5.00	15.00	20.00		5.00	5.00	15.00	20.00		
16	Burner door		10.00	10.00	15.00	15.00		10.00	10.00	15.00	15.00		
17	Burner handle		5.00	5.00	10.00	10.00		5.00	5.00	10.00	10.00		
18	Total variable cost		177.00	200.00	290.00	360.00		177.00	200.00	290.00	360.00		
19	Production overhead (absorption)		36.54	42.63	48.72	54.81		67.47	26.11	40.61	68.88		
20	Production cost		213.54	242.63	338.72	414.81		244.47	226.11	330.61	428.88		
21	Markup - 40%		85.42	97.05	135.49	165.92		97.79	90.44	132.25	171.55		
22	Suggested price		298.96	339.68	474.21	580.73		342.26	316.55	462.86	600.44		
23													
24													
25	Current price							£300.00	£340.00	£480.00	£590.00		
26													
27	(Under)/ over price							-£42.26	£23.45	£17.14	-£10.44		
28													
29													

Points 4 to 8 completed – formulas used

Columns A to F

	A	B	C	D	E	F
1	Pizzaiola Ltd					
2	Quarter ended 31 March 20-2					
3						
4				Absorption costing		
5			*Piccolo*	*Medio*	*Grande*	*Gigante*
6	No of items produced		='6.8 Overhead information'!C15*'6.8 Overhead information'!C16	='6.8 Overhead information'!D15*'6.8 Overhead information'!D16	='6.8 Overhead information'!E15*'6.8 Overhead information'!E16	='6.8 Overhead information'!F15*'6.8 Overhead information'!F16
7						
8	Product costs		£	£	£	£
9	Aluminium		50	60	90	110
10	Insulation		25	30	40	50
11	Consumables (screws, etc)		14	15	18	20
12	Pizza stone		35	40	60	75
13	Chimney		25	25	30	40
14	Thermometer		8	10	12	20
15	Door handle		5	5	15	20
16	Burner door		10	10	15	15
17	Burner handle		5	5	10	10
18	Total variable cost		=SUM(C9:C17)	=SUM(D9:D17)	=SUM(E9:E17)	=SUM(F9:F17)
19	Production overhead (absorption)		='6.8 Overhead information'!C29	='6.8 Overhead information'!D29	='6.8 Overhead information'!E29	='6.8 Overhead information'!F29
20	Production cost		=C19+C18	=D19+D18	=E19+E18	=F19+F18
21	Markup - 40%		=C20*0.4	=D20*0.4	=E20*0.4	=F20*0.4
22	Suggested price		=C21+C20	=D21+D20	=E21+E20	=F21+F20
23						
24						
25	Current price					
26						
27	(Under) / over price					
28						

Columns G to K

	A	G	H	I	J	K	L
1	Pizzaiola Ltd						
2	Quarter ended 31 March 20-2						
3							
4			Activity Based Costing				
5			Piccolo	Medio	Grande	Giganto	
6	No of items produced		=C6	=D6	=E6	=F6	
7							
8	Product costs		£	£	£	£	
9	Aluminium		50	60	90	110	
10	Insulation		25	30	40	50	
11	Consumables (screws, etc)		14	15	18	20	
12	Pizza stone		35	40	60	75	
13	Chimney		25	25	30	40	
14	Thermometer		8	10	12	20	
15	Door handle		5	5	15	20	
16	Burner door		10	10	15	15	
17	Burner handle		5	5	10	10	
18	Total variable cost		=SUM(H9:H17)	=SUM(I9:I17)	=SUM(J9:J17)	=SUM(K9:K17)	
19	Production overhead (absorption)		=+'6.8 Overhead information'!C39	=+'6.8 Overhead information'!D39	=+'6.8 Overhead information'!E39	=+'6.8 Overhead information'!F39	
20	Production cost		=+H19+H18	=+I19+I18	=+J19+J18	=+K19+K18	
21	Markup - 40%		=+H20*0.4	=+I20*0.4	=+J20*0.4	=+K20*0.4	
22	Suggested price		=+H21+H20	=+I21+I20	=+J21+J20	=+K21+K20	
23							
24							
25	Current price		300	340	480	590	
26							
27	(Under-)/ over price		=H22+H25	=I22+I25	=J22+J25	=K22+K25	
28							

Conditional formatting

Points 4 to 9 completed

	A	B	H	I	J	K	L
1	**Pizzaiola Ltd**						
2	**Quarter ended 31 March 20-2**						
3				**Activity Based Costing**			
4							
5			*Piccolo*	*Medio*	*Grande*	*Giganto*	
6	No of items produced		900	1920	400	500	
7							
8	*Product costs*		£	£	£	£	
9	Aluminium		50.00	60.00	90.00	110.00	
10	Insulation		25.00	30.00	40.00	50.00	
11	Consumables (screws, etc)		14.00	15.00	18.00	20.00	
12	Pizza stone		35.00	40.00	60.00	75.00	
13	Chimney		25.00	25.00	30.00	40.00	
14	Thermometer		8.00	10.00	12.00	20.00	
15	Door handle		5.00	5.00	15.00	20.00	
16	Burner door		10.00	10.00	15.00	15.00	
17	Burner handle		5.00	5.00	10.00	10.00	
18	*Total variable cost*		*177.00*	*200.00*	*290.00*	*360.00*	
19	Production overhead (absorption)		67.47	26.11	40.61	68.88	
20	**Production cost**		**244.47**	**226.11**	**330.61**	**428.88**	
21	Markup - 40%		97.79	90.44	132.25	171.55	
22	Suggested price		342.26	316.55	462.86	600.44	
23							
24							
25	Current price		£300.00	£340.00	£480.00	£590.00	
26							
27	(Under)/ over price		-£42.26	£23.45	£17.14	-£10.44	
28							
29							

The spreadsheet 'MATST Chapter 6 Activities Answer' is available to download on the Osborne Books website.

6.9 (c) Agreeing with the finance director to use absorption costing for the closing inventory.

Note: a limited company must comply with accounting standards – under IAS 2, *Inventories*, absorption costing is acceptable, but marginal costing is not.

CHAPTER 7: ASPECTS OF BUDGETING

7.1

	high output	15,000 units	£65,000
less	low output	10,000 units	£50,000
equals	difference	5,000 units	£15,000

- amount of variable cost per unit:

$$\frac{£15,000}{5,000} = £3 \text{ variable cost per unit}$$

- at 10,000 units of output the cost structure is:

	total cost	£50,000
less	variable costs (10,000 units x £3 per unit)	£30,000
equals	fixed costs	£20,000

- check at 15,000 units of output when the cost structure is:

	variable costs (15,000 units x £3 per unit)	£45,000
add	fixed costs (as above)	£20,000
equals	total costs	£65,000

- therefore fixed costs, at these levels of output, are £20,000

7.2

Batches produced and sold	1,000	1,200	2,000
	£	£	£
Sales revenue	35,000	42,000	70,000
Variable costs:			
• Direct materials	7,500	9,000	15,000
• Direct labour	10,500	12,600	21,000
• Overheads	6,000	7,200	12,000
Semi-variable costs:	4,500		
• Variable element		1,800	3,000
• Fixed element		3,000	3,000
Total cost	28,500	33,600	54,000
Total profit	6,500	8,400	16,000
Profit per batch (to two decimal places)	6.50	7.00	8.00

7.3 Points 1 to 10 completed

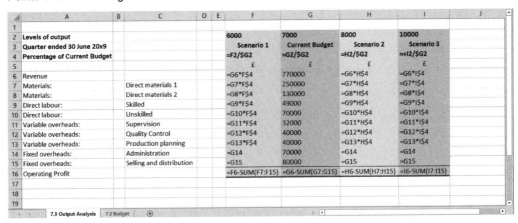

	A	B	C	D	E	F	G	H	I	J
1										
2	**Levels of output**					**6000**	**7000**	**8000**	**10000**	
3	**Quarter ended 30 June 20x9**					**Scenario 1**	**Current Budget**	**Scenario 2**	**Scenario 3**	
4	**Percentage of Current Budget**					**85.71%**	**100.00%**	**114.29%**	**142.86%**	
5						**£**	**£**	**£**	**£**	
6	Revenue					£660,000	£770,000	£880,000	£1,100,000	
7	Materials:		Direct materials 1			£214,286	£250,000	£285,714	£357,143	
8	Materials:		Direct materials 2			£111,429	£130,000	£148,571	£185,714	
9	Direct labour:		Skilled			£42,000	£49,000	£56,000	£70,000	
10	Direct labour:		Unskilled			£60,000	£70,000	£80,000	£100,000	
11	Variable overheads:		Supervision			£27,429	£32,000	£36,571	£45,714	
12	Variable overheads:		Quality Control			£34,286	£40,000	£45,714	£57,143	
13	Variable overheads:		Production planning			£34,286	£40,000	£45,714	£57,143	
14	Fixed overheads:		Administration			£70,000	£70,000	£70,000	£70,000	
15	Fixed overheads:		Selling and distribution			£80,000	£80,000	£80,000	£80,000	
16	Operating Profit					-£13,714	£9,000	£31,714	£77,143	
17										
18										
19										

7.3 Output Analysis   7.3 Budget

Points 1 to 10 showing formulas

	A	B	C	D	E	F	G	H	I	J
1										
2	Levels of output					6000	7000	8000	10000	
3	Quarter ended 30 June 20x9					Scenario 1	Current Budget	Scenario 2	Scenario 3	
4	Percentage of Current Budget					=F2/$G2	=G2/$G2	=H2/$G2	=I2/$G2	
5						£	£	£	£	
6	Revenue					=G6*F$4	770000	=G6*H$4	=G6*I$4	
7	Materials:		Direct materials 1			=G7*F$4	250000	=G7*H$4	=G7*I$4	
8	Materials:		Direct materials 2			=G8*F$4	130000	=G8*H$4	=G8*I$4	
9	Direct labour:		Skilled			=G9*F$4	49000	=G9*H$4	=G9*I$4	
10	Direct labour:		Unskilled			=G10*F$4	70000	=G10*H$4	=G10*I$4	
11	Variable overheads:		Supervision			=G11*F$4	32000	=G11*H$4	=G11*I$4	
12	Variable overheads:		Quality Control			=G12*F$4	40000	=G12*H$4	=G12*I$4	
13	Variable overheads:		Production planning			=G13*F$4	40000	=G13*H$4	=G13*I$4	
14	Fixed overheads:		Administration			=G14	70000	=G14	=G14	
15	Fixed overheads:		Selling and distribution			=G15	80000	=G15	=G15	
16	Operating Profit					=F6-SUM(F7:F15)	=G6-SUM(G7:G15)	=H6-SUM(H7:H15)	=I6-SUM(I7:I15)	
17										
18										
19										

7.3 Output Analysis   7.3 Budget

The spreadsheet 'MATST Chapter 7 Activities answers' is available to download on the Osborne Books website.

7.4 (c) direct labour variance £1,400 adverse; direct materials variance £250 favourable

7.5 (d) sales revenue variance £1,100 favourable; direct materials variance £450 adverse

7.6 (a) direct materials £19,575; direct labour £14,175

7.7

Flexed budget	True	False
Fixed overheads are shown in the flexed budget at a cost of £24,240		✔
Fixed overheads are shown in the flexed budget at a cost of £21,000		✔
Fixed overheads are shown in the flexed budget at a cost of £20,200	✔	
There is a fixed overheads variance of £800 adverse	✔	
There is a fixed overheads variance of £2,040 adverse		✔
There is no fixed overheads variance		✔

7.8

Cause of variance	Adverse	Favourable
Increase in material prices	✔	
Fewer materials are wasted		✔
Cheaper materials are used		✔
Theft of materials	✔	
An increase in direct labour pay	✔	
More efficient use of direct labour		✔
Overtime is paid to direct labour	✔	
A cheaper electricity supplier is used for the fixed overhead		✔
Selling prices are increased		✔
An increase in the number of units sold		✔

7.9 **(a)**

	Original budget	Flexed budget	Actual	Variance
Output level	100%	90%	90%	
	£	£	£	£
Direct materials	4,700	4,230	5,200	−970
Direct labour	10,800	9,720	8,900	820
Fixed overheads	4,100	4,100	4,500	−400
Total	19,600	18,050	18,600	−550

(b) (a) An increase in material prices

7.10 Points 1 to 14 completed

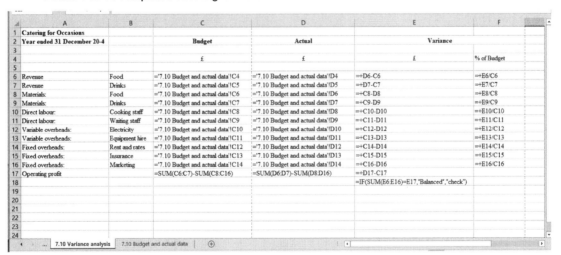

	A	B	C	D	E	F	G
1	**Catering for Occasions**						
2	**Year ended 31 December 20-4**		**Budget**	**Actual**	**Variance**		
3							
4			£	£	£	% of Budget	
5							
6	Revenue	Food	95,400	104,950	9,550	10.01%	
7	Revenue	Drinks	5,200	6,300	1,100	21.15%	
8	Materials:	Food	33,390	39,500	-6,110	-18.30%	
9	Materials:	Drinks	2,340	2,802	-462	-19.74%	
10	Direct labour:	Cooking staff	15,200	17,200	-2,000	-13.16%	
11	Direct labour:	Waiting staff	15,500	17,050	-1,550	-10.00%	
12	Variable overheads:	Electricity	4,000	4,200	-200	-5.00%	
13	Variable overheads:	Equipment hire	2,000	2,500	-500	-25.00%	
14	Fixed overheads:	Rent and rates	5,000	5,000	0	0.00%	
15	Fixed overheads:	Insurance	1,000	900	100	10.00%	
16	Fixed overheads:	Marketing	1,000	1,500	-500	-50.00%	
17	Operating profit		21,170	20,598	-572		
18					Balanced		
19							
20							

7.10 Variance analysis | 7.10 Budget and actual data

Points 1 to 14 completed showing formulas

	A	B	C	D	E	F
1	Catering for Occasions					
2	Year ended 31 December 20-4		Budget	Actual	Variance	
3						
4			£	£	£	% of Budget
5						
6	Revenue	Food	='7.10 Budget and actual data'!C4	='7.10 Budget and actual data'!D4	=+D6-C6	=+E6/C6
7	Revenue	Drinks	='7.10 Budget and actual data'!C5	='7.10 Budget and actual data'!D5	=+D7-C7	=+E7/C7
8	Materials:	Food	='7.10 Budget and actual data'!C6	='7.10 Budget and actual data'!D6	=+C8-D8	=+E8/C8
9	Materials:	Drinks	='7.10 Budget and actual data'!C7	='7.10 Budget and actual data'!D7	=+C9-D9	=+E9/C9
10	Direct labour:	Cooking staff	='7.10 Budget and actual data'!C8	='7.10 Budget and actual data'!D8	=+C10-D10	=+E10/C10
11	Direct labour:	Waiting staff	='7.10 Budget and actual data'!C9	='7.10 Budget and actual data'!D9	=+C11-D11	=+E11/C11
12	Variable overheads:	Electricity	='7.10 Budget and actual data'!C10	='7.10 Budget and actual data'!D10	=+C12-D12	=+E12/C12
13	Variable overheads:	Equipment hire	='7.10 Budget and actual data'!C11	='7.10 Budget and actual data'!D11	=+C13-D13	=+E13/C13
14	Fixed overheads:	Rent and rates	='7.10 Budget and actual data'!C12	='7.10 Budget and actual data'!D12	=+C14-D14	=+E14/C14
15	Fixed overheads:	Insurance	='7.10 Budget and actual data'!C13	='7.10 Budget and actual data'!D13	=+C15-D15	=+E15/C15
16	Fixed overheads:	Marketing	='7.10 Budget and actual data'!C14	='7.10 Budget and actual data'!D14	=+C16-D16	=+E16/C16
17	Operating profit		=SUM(C6:C7)-SUM(C8:C16)	=SUM(D6:D7)-SUM(D8:D16)	=+D17-C17	
18					=IF(SUM(E6:E16)=E17,"Balanced","check")	
19						
20						
21						
22						
23						
24						

7.10 Variance analysis | 7.10 Budget and actual data

Points 1 to 17 completed (shown as '7.10 Variance analysis' would appear when printed)

Catering for Occasions Year ended 31 December 20-4

Catering for Occasions
Year ended 31 December 20-4

		Budget	Actual	Variance	
		£	£	£	% of Budget
Revenue	Food	95,400	104,950	9,550	10.01%
Revenue	Drinks	5,200	6,300	1,100	21.15%
Materials:	Food	33,390	39,500	-6,110	-18.30%
Materials:	Drinks	2,340	2,802	-462	-19.74%
Direct labour:	Cooking staff	15,200	17,200	-2,000	-13.16%
Direct labour:	Waiting staff	15,500	17,050	-1,550	-10.00%
Variable overheads:	Electricity	4,000	4,200	-200	-5.00%
Variable overheads:	Equipment hire	2,000	2,500	-500	-25.00%
Fixed overheads:	Rent and rates	5,000	5,000	0	0.00%
Fixed overheads:	Insurance	1,000	900	100	10.00%
Fixed overheads:	Marketing	1,000	1,500	-500	-50.00%
Operating profit		21,170	20,598	-572	
			Balanced		

7.10 Variance analysis 20:32 04/06/2021

The spreadsheet 'MATST Chapter 7 Activities Answer' is available to download on the Osborne Books website.

7.11 **(a)**

	Original budget	Flexed budget	Actual	Variance
Units sold	30,000	27,000	27,000	
	£000	£000	£000	£000
Sales revenue	1,800	1,620	1,650	30
Less costs:				
Direct materials	550	495	500	–5
Direct labour	340	306	297	9
Fixed overheads	650	650	645	5
Operating profit	260	169	208	39

(b) (a) Sales revenue

7.12 **(a)**

	Original budget	Flexed budget	Actual	Variance
Units sold	22,000	27,500	27,500	
	£000	£000	£000	£000
Sales revenue	1,400	1,750	1,875	125
Less costs:				
Direct materials and direct labour	300	375	360	15
Variable overheads	500	625	645	−20
Fixed overheads	420	420	480	−60
Operating profit	180	330	390	60

(b) (b) More efficient use of direct labour

7.13

	EX27 (£)	EX45 (£)	EX67 (£)	Total (£)
Sales volume (units)	9,000	12,000	15,000	
Selling price per unit	6.40	7.80	5.40	
Less: variable costs per unit				
Direct materials	2.25	3.45	2.85	
Direct labour	1.95	1.65	1.25	
Contribution per unit	2.20	2.70	1.30	
Total contribution	19,800	32,400	19,500	71,700
Less: fixed overheads				(33,845)
Budgeted profit/(loss)				37,855

7.14 **(a)**

	Original budget	Flexed budget	Actual	Variance
Units sold	10,000	11,200	11,200	
	£	£	£	£
Raw material A1	3,200	3,584	3,925	−341
Raw material A4	1,250	1,400	1,325	75
Skilled labour	4,850	5,432	5,060	372
Unskilled labour	1,225	1,372	1,440	−68
Variable overheads	4,025	4,508	4,310	198
Fixed overheads	5,740	5,740	6,140	−400
Total costs	20,290	22,036	22,200	−164

(b) (b) A reduction in employees' pay

7.15 **(a)** flexible
(b) fixed
(c) rolling

7.16 **(a)**

	1,500 units	1,800 units	2,000 units
	£	£	£
Revenue	30,000	36,000	38,000
Variable materials costs	12,000	14,400	12,000
Variable labour costs	10,500	12,600	12,600
Contribution to fixed costs	7,500	9,000	13,400
Fixed costs	10,000	10,000	12,000
Forecast profit/(loss)	(2,500)	(1,000)	1,400

(b) (a) More efficient use of labour

CHAPTER 8: SHORT-TERM DECISIONS

8.1　**(a)**　200 bats = £9,000 loss; 1,200 bats = £6,000 profit

(b)

Units of output	Fixed costs	Variable costs	Total cost	Sales revenue	Profit/(loss)*
	£	£	£	£	£
100	12,000	2,000	14,000	3,500	(10,500)
200	12,000	4,000	16,000	7,000	(9,000)
300	12,000	6,000	18,000	10,500	(7,500)
400	12,000	8,000	20,000	14,000	(6,000)
500	12,000	10,000	22,000	17,500	(4,500)
600	12,000	12,000	24,000	21,000	(3,000)
700	12,000	14,000	26,000	24,500	(1,500)
800	12,000	16,000	28,000	28,000	nil
900	12,000	18,000	30,000	31,500	1,500
1,000	12,000	20,000	32,000	35,000	3,000
1,100	12,000	22,000	34,000	38,500	4,500
1,200	12,000	24,000	36,000	42,000	6,000

* brackets indicate a loss

(c)　**margin of safety**

margin of safety units = 1,000 – 800 = <u>200 units</u>

$$\frac{\text{current output} - \text{break-even output}}{\text{current output}} = \frac{1,000 - 800}{1,000} \times 100 = \underline{20\%}$$

8.2 **(a)** **2,000 units** per quarter

Contribution: £28 – £16 = £12 per unit

Fixed costs: £24,000

Break-even: £24,000 ÷ £12

(b) **£56,000** per quarter

2,000 units x £28

(c)

Units of WV5 sold per quarter	2,500	4,000
Margin of safety (units)	500*	2,000**
Margin of safety percentage	20%*	50%**

* 2,500 units – 2,000 units to break-even

500 units ÷ 2,500 units of output x 100

** 4,000 units – 2,000 units to break-even

2,000 units ÷ 4,000 units of output x 100

(d) **3,500 units** per quarter

Fixed costs £24,000 + target profit £18,000 = £42,000

£42,000 ÷ £12

(e) (d) The break-even point will increase and the margin of safety will decrease

8.3 **Task 1**

- profit-volume (PV) ratio

$$\frac{\text{contribution (£)}}{\text{selling price (£)}} = \frac{£15^*}{£25} = 0.6 \text{ or } 60\%$$

* selling price £25 – variable cost £10

- break-even point in units next month

$$\frac{\text{fixed costs (£)}}{\text{contribution per unit (£)}} = \frac{£300,000}{£15} = 20,000 \text{ units}$$

- break-even point in sales revenue next month

$$\frac{\text{fixed costs (£)}}{\text{PV ratio}} = \frac{£300,000}{0.6} = £500,000$$

check: 20,000 units x selling price £25 per unit = £500,000

- margin of safety at output of 30,000 units next month

$$\frac{\text{current output} - \text{break-even output}}{\text{current output}} = \frac{30,000 - 20,000}{30,000} \times 100$$

= 33.3%, or 10,000 units, or £250,000 of sales revenue

- number of units to generate a target profit of £100,000 next month

$$\frac{\text{fixed costs (£)} + \text{target profit (£)}}{\text{contribution per unit (£)}} = \frac{£300,000 + £100,000}{£15} = 26,667 \text{ units}$$

Task 2

		Forecast output (30,000 units)	Maximum output (40,000 units)
		£	£
	sales revenue (at £25 each)	750,000	1,000,000
less	variable costs (at £10 each)	300,000	400,000
equals	contribution (to fixed costs and profit)	450,000	600,000
less	monthly fixed costs	300,000	300,000
equals	forecast profit for month	150,000	300,000

Task 3

- profit-volume (PV) ratio

$$\frac{£10^*}{£20} = 0.5 \text{ or } 50\%$$

* selling price £20 – variable cost £10

- break-even point in units

$$\frac{£300,000}{£10} = 30,000 \text{ units}$$

- break-even point in sales revenue

$$\frac{£300,000}{0.5} = £600,000$$

check: 30,000 units x selling price £20 per unit = £600,000

- margin of safety at maximum output of 40,000 units

$$\frac{40,000 - 30,000}{40,000} \times 100 = 25\%, \text{ or } 10,000 \text{ units, or } £200,000 \text{ of sales revenue}$$

- forecast profit at sales of 40,000 units

		£
	sales revenue (at £20 each)	800,000
less	variable costs (at £10 each)	400,000
equals	contribution (to fixed costs and profit)	400,000
less	monthly fixed costs	300,000
equals	forecast profit for month	100,000

REPORT

To: General Manager
From: Accounts Assistant
Date: Today

Proposal to reduce selling price

Introduction

- You asked me to report on the suggestion from one of the managers that the selling price for our product should be reduced from £25 per unit to £20.
- The manager has suggested that the effect of this reduction would be to increase output from the forecast of 30,000 units per month to our maximum output of 40,000 units per month.

Report

- As can be seen from the workings at current levels of output of 30,000 units per month:
  - contribution sales ratio is 60%
  - break-even point is 20,000 units
  - margin of safety is 33.3%
  - forecast profit is £150,000 per month

- If the manager's suggestion is adopted sales will increase to our maximum output of 40,000 units per month; this will give us:
  - contribution sales ratio of 50%
  - break-even point of 30,000 units
  - margin of safety of 25%
  - forecast profit of £100,000 per month

Conclusion

- From the data summarised above it can be seen that the manager's suggestion would reduce our contribution sales ratio, increase the break-even point, and reduce the margin of safety. All of these are movements in the wrong direction.

- The main point to note is that forecast profit will fall by £50,000 per month to £100,000 per month, and the volume of output will need to be higher.

- Although we would be working at maximum output if the suggestion is adopted, this does mean that there is no scope to increase output and sales in the future without major changes to our cost structure. We would not be able to meet requests for additional sales from our existing customers, and this could cause them to seek all of their supplies from our competitors.

- For these reasons, I would recommend that the manager's suggestion is not undertaken.

8.4   Points 1 to 10 completed

	A	B	C	D	E	F	G	H	I	J	K
1	Catering jobs										
2	Job	Month	Sales, £	Food/drink, £	Wages costs, £	Contribution, £		Number of events		30	
3	Smith wedding	January	1,500.00	450.05	349.60	700.35					
4	Jamal party	January	1,450.00	450.00	381.70	618.30					
5	Grosvenor wedding	January	1,200.00	360.00	318.40	521.60					
6	Zuckerman party	January	1,650.00	545.00	368.80	736.20					
7	Moore 50th wedding anniversi	January	1,500.00	515.00	361.40	623.60					
8	Wilber birthday	January	1,150.00	350.00	212.00	588.00					
9	Hanson birthday party	January	1,200.00	400.00	340.30	459.70					
10		January Avera	1,378.57			606.82					
11	Sykes wedding	February	1,875.00	562.56	437.00	875.44					
12	Muhammed party	February	1,812.50	562.50	477.13	772.87					
13	Sita wedding	February	1,500.00	450.00	398.00	652.00					
14	Harris party	February	1,950.00	481.00	350.00	1,119.00					
15		February Aver	1,784.38			854.83					
16	Gee party	March	1,875.00	643.75	451.75	779.50					
17	Ali wedding anniversary	March	1,437.50	437.50	265.00	735.00					
18	Bailey party	March	1,650.00	560.00	390.00	700.00					
19		March Average	1,654.17			738.17					
20	Murphy party	April	1,500.00	500.00	425.38	574.62					
21	Begum party	April	2,062.50	618.80	480.70	963.00					
22	Cheng wedding	April	1,993.75	618.75	525.00	850.00					
23		April Average	1,852.08			795.87					
24	Clark christening	May	1,650.00	495.00	437.80	717.20					
25	Rodriguez party	May	2,145.00	749.38	385.00	1,010.62					
26	O'Neill wedding	May	2,062.50	708.10	497.00	857.40					
27	Ahmed party	May	1,581.25	481.25	291.50	808.50					
28	Houghton party	May	1,815.00	616.00	429.00	770.00					
29	Akhtar wedding	May	1,650.00	550.00	410.00	690.00					
30		May Average	1,817.29			808.95					
31	Bondar wedding	June	2,681.25	885.00	621.25	1,175.00					
32	Carpenter party	June	2,055.63	602.00	364.35	1,089.28					
33	Ali wedding	June	2,359.50	770.00	536.25	1,053.25					
34	Welsh party	June	2,145.00	687.50	512.50	945.00					
35	Barr wedding	June	3,485.63	1,106.25	777.00	1,602.38					
36	Than party	June	2,672.31	752.50	45.47	1,874.34					
37	Dias wedding	June	3,067.35	962.50	670.30	1,434.55					
38		June Average	2,638.10			1,310.54					
39		Grand Average	1,889.22			876.56					
40											
41	Average contribution /sales ratio		0.46								
42											
43	Break-even revenue, £		£20,917								
44											
45	Break-even number of events		12								
46											
47	Margin of safety, events		18								
48											
49											

8.4 Jan-June jobs   8.4 Overheads   8.6 Coffee and cake data   8.6 Break-even analysis   ⊕

Points 1 to 10 showing formulas

	A	B	C	D	E	F	G	H	I	J
1	Catering jobs									
2	Job	Month	Sales, £	Food/drink, £	Wages costs, £	Contribution, £		Number of events		=COUNTA(A3:A37)
3	Smith wedding	January	1500	450.05	349.6	=C3-SUM(D3:E3)				
4	Jamal party	January	1450	450	381.7	=C4-SUM(D4:E4)				
5	Grosvenor wedding	January	1200	360	318.4	=C5-SUM(D5:E5)				
6	Zuckerman wedding	January	1650	545	368.8	=C6-SUM(D6:E6)				
7	Moore 50th wedding anniversary	January	1500	515	361.4	=C7-SUM(D7:E7)				
8	Wilber birthday	January	1150	350	212	=C8-SUM(D8:E8)				
9	Hanson birthday party	January	1200	400	340.3	=C9-SUM(D9:E9)				
10		January Average	=SUBTOTAL(1,C3:C9)			=SUBTOTAL(1,F3:F9)				
11	Sykes wedding	February	1875	562.56	437	=C11-SUM(D11:E11)				
12	Muhammed party	February	1812.5	562.5	477.13	=C12-SUM(D12:E12)				
13	Sita wedding	February	1500	450	398	=C13-SUM(D13:E13)				
14	Harris party	February	1950	481	350	=C14-SUM(D14:E14)				
15		February Average	=SUBTOTAL(1,C11:C14)			=SUBTOTAL(1,F11:F14)				
16	Gee party	March	1875	643.75	451.75	=C16-SUM(D16:E16)				
17	Ali wedding anniversary	March	1437.5	437.5	265	=C17-SUM(D17:E17)				
18	Bailey party	March	1650	560	390	=C18-SUM(D18:E18)				
19		March Average	=SUBTOTAL(1,C16:C18)			=SUBTOTAL(1,F16:F18)				
20	Murphy party	April	1500	500	425.38	=C20-SUM(D20:E20)				
21	Begum party	April	2062.5	618.8	480.7	=C21-SUM(D21:E21)				
22	Cheng wedding	April	1993.75	618.75	525	=C22-SUM(D22:E22)				
23		April Average	=SUBTOTAL(1,C20:C22)			=SUBTOTAL(1,F20:F22)				
24	Clark christening	May	1650	495	437.8	=C24-SUM(D24:E24)				
25	Rodriguez party	May	2145	749.38	385	=C25-SUM(D25:E25)				
26	O'Neill wedding	May	2062.5	708.1	497	=C26-SUM(D26:E26)				
27	Ahmed party	May	1581.25	481.25	291.5	=C27-SUM(D27:E27)				
28	Houghton party	May	1815	616	429	=C28-SUM(D28:E28)				
29	Akhtar wedding	May	1650	550	410	=C29-SUM(D29:E29)				
30		May Average	=SUBTOTAL(1,C24:C29)			=SUBTOTAL(1,F24:F29)				
31	Bondar wedding	June	2681.25	885	621.25	=C31-SUM(D31:E31)				
32	Carpenter party	June	2055.63	602	364.35	=C32-SUM(D32:E32)				
33	Ali wedding	June	2359.5	770	536.25	=C33-SUM(D33:E33)				
34	Welsh party	June	2145	687.5	512.5	=C34-SUM(D34:E34)				
35	Barr wedding	June	3485.63	1106.25	777	=C35-SUM(D35:E35)				
36	Than party	June	2672.31	752.5	45.47	=C36-SUM(D36:E36)				
37	Dias wedding	June	3067.95	962.5	670.3	=C37-SUM(D37:E37)				
38		June Average	=SUBTOTAL(1,C31:C37)			=SUBTOTAL(1,F31:F37)				
39		Grand Average	=SUBTOTAL(1,C3:C37)			=SUBTOTAL(1,F3:F37)				
40										
41	Average contribution /sales ratio		=+F39/C39							
42										
43	Break-even revenue, £		='8.4 Overheads'!B7/'8.4 Jan-June jobs '!C41							
44										
45	Break-even number of events		=ROUNDUP(C43/C39,0)							
46										
47	Margin of safety, events		=+J2-C45							
48										
49										

| 8.4 Jan-June jobs | 8.4 Overheads | 8.6 Coffee and cake data | 8.6 Break-even analysis | ⊕ |

The spreadsheet 'MATST Chapter 8 Activities answers' is available to download on the Osborne Books website.

8.5   Task 1

DURNING FOODS LIMITED: Production line for Indian meals

Planned results for November 20-8

Number of meals to be sold	36,000
	£
Direct materials at 75p per meal	27,000
Direct labour at 45p per meal	16,200
Direct expenses at 20p per meal	7,200
Overheads for the production line at £7,500 + 15p per meal	12,900
Other production overheads	<u>4,000</u>
Total cost	67,300
Sales revenue at £2.00 per meal	<u>72,000</u>
Profit	<u>4,700</u>

Workings (using figures for July):

- direct materials per meal   = £25,125 ÷ 33,500 meals   = £0.75
- direct labour per meal   = £15,075 ÷ 33,500 meals   = £0.45
- direct expenses per meal   = £6,700 ÷ 33,500 meals   = £0.20
- overheads for Indian meals production line

	Meals	£
high	34,700	12,705
low	31,000	12,150
difference	3,700	555

variable cost per meal	= £555 ÷ 3,700 meals	= £0.15
fixed cost	= £12,525 – (£0.15 x 33,500 meals)	= £7,500

- other production overheads: fixed cost = £4,000 per month
- sales revenue per meal = £67,000 ÷ 33,500 meals = £2.00

Task 2

DURNING FOODS LIMITED: Production line for Indian meals

Planned results for November 20-8: increased activity

Number of meals to be sold	40,000
	£
Direct materials at 75p – 20% = 60p per meal	24,000
Direct labour at 45p per meal	18,000
Direct expenses at 20p per meal	8,000
Overheads for the production line at £7,500 + 15p per meal	13,500
Other production overheads	4,000
Total cost	67,500
Sales revenue at £2.00 per meal	80,000
	12,500
Profit	

Break-even point

		£	£
Contribution per meal:			
	selling price		2.00
less	variable costs:		
	direct materials	0.60	
	direct labour	0.45	
	direct expenses	0.20	
	production line overheads	0.15	
			1.40
equals	contribution per meal		0.60

Fixed costs:		
	production line overheads	7,500
	other production overheads	4,000
		11,500

Break-even point:

$$\frac{£11,500}{£0.60} = 19,167 \text{ meals}$$

Margin of safety:

$$\frac{40,000 - 19,167}{40,000} \times 100 = 52\%$$

8.6 **(a)** to **(d)** all points completed

	A	B	C	D	E	F
1	**Trendy Togs**					
2	**Break-even analysis new shop**					
3		£				
4						
5	Staff (2 people)	36,000				
6	Electricity	6,300				
7	Depreciation on shop f	5,000				
8	Rent	22,000				
9	Rates	3,150				
10	Phone (fixed contract)	500				
11	Administration	5,000				
12	Insurance	1,100				
13	Marketing	2,000				
14						
15		81,050				
16						
17		Break-even analysis new shop				
18		Break-even	Target profit	Target profit		
19			£75,000	£50,000		
20						
21	Fixed Costs	£81,050	£81,050	£81,050		
22						
23	Revenue Required	£162,100	£312,100	£262,100		
24						
25						
26						
27	**Bonus calculation**	Revenue	Bonus			
28						
29	Bonus payable	£ 160,000	No bonus			
30	Bonus payable	£ 300,000	£ 2,069			
31	Bonus payable	£ 400,000	£ 3,569			
32						
33						
34						

8.6 Coffee and cake data | **8.6 Break-even analysis**

(a) to **(d)** all points completed showing formulas

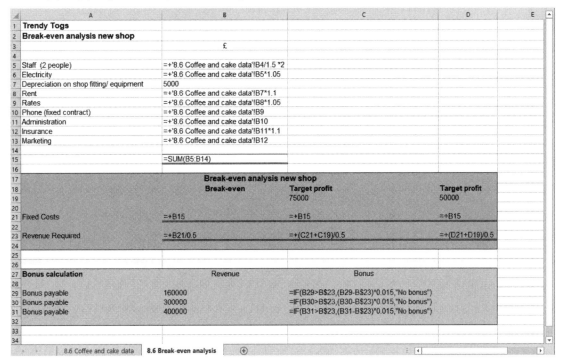

	A	B	C	D	E
1	**Trendy Togs**				
2	**Break-even analysis new shop**				
3		£			
4					
5	Staff (2 people)	=+'8.6 Coffee and cake data'!B4/1.5 *2			
6	Electricity	=+'8.6 Coffee and cake data'!B5*1.05			
7	Depreciation on shop fitting/ equipment	5000			
8	Rent	=+'8.6 Coffee and cake data'!B7*1.1			
9	Rates	=+'8.6 Coffee and cake data'!B8*1.05			
10	Phone (fixed contract)	=+'8.6 Coffee and cake data'!B9			
11	Administration	=+'8.6 Coffee and cake data'!B10			
12	Insurance	=+'8.6 Coffee and cake data'!B11*1.1			
13	Marketing	=+'8.6 Coffee and cake data'!B12			
14					
15		=SUM(B5:B14)			
16					
17			Break-even analysis new shop		
18		Break-even	Target profit	Target profit	
19			75000	50000	
20					
21	Fixed Costs	=+B15	=+B15	=+B15	
22					
23	Revenue Required	=+B21/0.5	=+(C21+C19)/0.5	=+(D21+D19)/0.5	
24					
25					
26					
27	**Bonus calculation**	Revenue	Bonus		
28					
29	Bonus payable	160000	=IF(B29>B$23,(B29-B$23)*0.015,"No bonus")		
30	Bonus payable	300000	=IF(B30>B$23,(B30-B$23)*0.015,"No bonus")		
31	Bonus payable	400000	=IF(B31>B$23,(B31-B$23)*0.015,"No bonus")		
32					
33					
34					

8.6 Coffee and cake data   **8.6 Break-even analysis**   ⊕

The spreadsheet 'MATST Chapter 8 Activities answer' is available to download on the Osborne Books website.

8.7 The marginal cost per unit of Exe is £5 (direct materials £3 + direct labour £2), and so any contribution, ie selling price less marginal cost, will be profit:

*   *200 units at £6 each*

The offer price of £6 is above the marginal cost of £5 and increases profit by the amount of the £1 extra contribution, ie (£6 – £5) x 200 units = £200 extra profit.

*   *500 units at £4 each*

This offer price is below the marginal cost of £5; therefore there will be a fall in profit if this order is undertaken of (£4 – £5) x 500 units = £500 reduced profit.

WESTFIELD LIMITED monthly statements of profit or loss	Existing production of 2,000 units	Existing production + 200 units @ £6 each	Existing production + 500 units @ £4 each
	£	£	£
Sales revenue (per month):			
2,000 units at £12 each	24,000	24,000	24,000
200 units at £6 each	–	1,200	–
500 units at £4 each	–	–	2,000
	24,000	25,200	26,000
Less production costs:			
Direct materials (£3 per unit)	6,000	6,600	7,500
Direct labour (£2 per unit)	4,000	4,400	5,000
Production overheads (fixed)	8,000	8,000	8,000
PROFIT	6,000	6,200	5,500

The conclusion is that the first special order should be accepted, and the second declined.

8.8

POPCAN LIMITED		
monthly statements of profit or loss		
	Existing production of 150,000 cans	Existing production + 50,000 cans at 18p each
	£	£
Sales revenue (per month):		
150,000 cans at 25p each	37,500	37,500
50,000 cans at 18p each	–	9,000
	37,500	46,500
Less production costs:		
Direct materials (5p per can)	7,500	10,000
Direct labour (5p per can)	7,500	10,000
Production overheads – variable (4p per can)	6,000	8,000
– fixed*	9,000	9,000
PROFIT	7,500	9,500
* 6p x 150,000 cans = £9,000		

The offer from the supermarket chain should be accepted because:

- the marginal cost of producing each can is 14p (direct materials 5p, direct labour 5p, variable production overheads 4p)

- the offer price is 18p per can, which is above marginal cost, and gives a contribution of 4p

- profits increase by the amount of the extra contribution, ie (18p – 14p) x 50,000 cans = £2,000 extra profit

8.9 (d) Accounting staff are required to maintain their knowledge and skills to provide a competent service

8.10 (a) Note that this is a semi-variable cost – use the high/low method to calculate the fixed and variable elements

The variable cost for each unit of C18: **£25**

The total cost of producing 600 units of C18: **£22,500**

(b) The break-even point in units for T12: **200** units

The margin of safety in units for T12 at budgeted production of 500 units: **300** units.

The number of units of T12 that must be sold in order to produce a profit of £5,200: **600** units.

8.11

Selling price minus **variable** costs equals contribution.

Total contribution minus **fixed** costs equals profit.

Break-even point is where neither a profit nor a loss is made.

Current output minus **break-even** output equals margin of safety.

Contribution divided by selling price equals **profit-volume** ratio.

Production costs and sales revenues can be used to calculate a given level of profit, known as the **target** profit.

CHAPTER 9: CASH BUDGETING AND RESOURCES RATIOS

9.1

RECEIPTS FROM TRADE RECEIVABLES						
	April	**May**	**June**	**July**	**August**	**September**
	£	£	£	£	£	£
Month of sale	12,500	12,500	12,500	12,500	15,000	15,000
PPD	(375)	(375)	(375)	(375)	(450)	(450)
Following month	10,000	12,500	12,500	12,500	12,500	15,000
Irrecoverable debts	(200)	(250)	(250)	(250)	(250)	(300)
Receipts for month	21,925	24,375	24,375	24,375	26,800	29,250

9.2   Points 1 to 6 completed

	A	B	C	D	E	F	G	H	I
1	**Pershore Furniture Limited**								
2	**Receipts from credit sales**								
3									
4									
5	**Customer information**								
6	Pay in month of sale, %	40%							
7	Prompt payment discount,%	2%							
8	Pay in month after sale, %	60%							
9	Irrecoverable debt, %	1%							
10									
11		July	August	September	October	November	December		
12	Credit sales	£300,000	£300,000	£300,000	£200,000	£250,000	£250,000		
13									
14					Cash receipts				
15	**Month of sale**	July	August	September	October	November	December	Total	
16	June	£247,500						£247,500	
17	July	£117,600	£178,200					£295,800	
18	August		£117,600	£178,200				£295,800	
19	September			£117,600	£178,200			£295,800	
20	October				£78,400	£118,800		£197,200	
21	November					£98,000	£148,500	£246,500	
22	December						£98,000	£98,000	
23	**Total**	**£365,100**	**£295,800**	**£295,800**	**£256,600**	**£216,800**	**£246,500**	**£1,676,600**	
24									
25									
26									

Points 1 to 6 completed showing formulas and comment for cell B16 is shown on the next page.

Points 7 to 12 completed

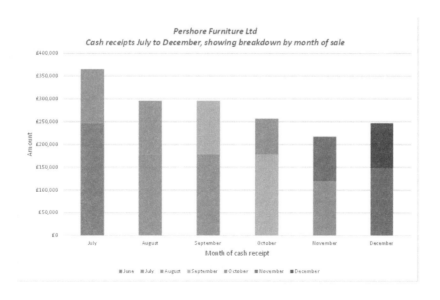

Pershore Furniture Ltd
Cash receipts July to December, showing breakdown by month of sale

The spreadsheet 'MATST Chapter 9 Activities answers' is available to download on the Osborne Books website.

9.3

PAYMENTS TO TRADE PAYABLES						
	October	November	December	January	February	March
	£	£	£	£	£	£
Month of purchase	15,000	15,000	20,000	20,000	17,500	17,500
PPD	(300)	(300)	(400)	(400)	(350)	(350)
Following month	12,500	15,000	15,000	20,000	20,000	17,500
Payments for month	27,200	29,700	34,600	39,600	37,150	34,650

9.4 Task 1

WILKINSON						
CASH BUDGET FOR THE SIX MONTHS ENDING 30 JUNE 20-8						
	Jan	Feb	Mar	Apr	May	Jun
	£	£	£	£	£	£
Receipts						
Trade receivables	57,500	65,000	70,000	72,500	85,000	65,000
Total receipts for the month	57,500	65,000	70,000	72,500	85,000	65,000
Payments						
Trade payables	26,500	45,000	50,000	34,500	35,500	40,500
Wages and salaries	17,500	18,000	18,250	18,500	16,500	20,000
Other expenses	14,500	19,500	18,000	17,500	19,500	21,000
Total payments for the month	58,500	82,500	86,250	70,500	71,500	81,500
Net cash flow	(1,000)	(17,500)	(16,250)	2,000	13,500	(16,500)
Opening bank balance/(overdraft)	2,250	1,250	(16,250)	(32,500)	(30,500)	(17,000)
Closing bank balance/(overdraft)	1,250	(16,250)	(32,500)	(30,500)	(17,000)	(33,500)

Task 2

A bank overdraft facility of £35,000 should be arranged for a period of six months. Sales for June are high at £107,500 with the income to be received in July. Wilkinson should review the overdraft requirement again in June.

9.5

Task 1

JAYNE SMITH						
CASH BUDGET FOR THE SIX MONTHS ENDING 30 JUNE 20-2						
	Jan	Feb	Mar	Apr	May	Jun
	£	£	£	£	£	£
Receipts						
Capital introduced	10,000					
Trade receivables	-	1,250	3,000	4,000	4,000	4,500
Total receipts for the month	10,000	1,250	3,000	4,000	4,000	4,500
Payments						
Van	6,000					
Trade payables	-	4,500	4,500	3,500	3,500	3,500
Expenses	750	600	600	650	650	700
Total payments for the month	6,750	5,100	5,100	4,150	4,150	4,200
Net cash flow	3,250	(3,850)	(2,100)	(150)	(150)	300
Opening bank balance/(overdraft)	-	3,250	(600)	(2,700)	(2,850)	(3,000)
Closing bank balance/(overdraft)	3,250	(600)	(2,700)	(2,850)	(3,000)	(2,700)

Notes:
- customers pay one month after sale, ie trade receivables from January settle in February
- suppliers are paid one month after purchase, ie trade payables from January are paid in February

Task 2

The cash budget shows the maximum bank overdraft to be £3,000 in May.

Jayne Smith could avoid the need for a bank overdraft in one or more of the following ways (the question asks for two ways):
- by commencing her business with a higher initial capital, eg £13,000
- by buying the van on hire purchase instead of by cash purchase
- by reducing her purchases to £3,000 for each of January and February
- by asking her suppliers for two months' credit for the initial purchases of £4,500 made in January
- by asking her customers to pay more quickly

9.6 (d) Hire purchase

9.7 (a) medium-term agreement where a finance company funds an asset and the business makes instalments to pay the cost plus interest

9.8 (a) part exchange

(b) (b) the head teacher

9.9 (a) inventory days + receivable days – payable days

9.10

Task 1

RESOURCES RATIOS	last year (days)	this year (days)
inventory holding period	$\frac{35,650}{289,500}$ x 365 = 45	$\frac{34,450}{276,200}$ x 365 = 46
trade receivables collection period	$\frac{58,250}{564,300}$ x 365 = 38	$\frac{50,150}{532,900}$ x 365 = 34
trade payables payment period	$\frac{29,850}{289,500}$ x 365 = 38	$\frac{27,050}{276,200}$ x 365 = 36

Task 2

WORKING CAPITAL CYCLE	last year (days)	this year (days)
inventory days	45	46
receivable days	+ 38	+ 34
payable days	– 38	– 36
WORKING CAPITAL CYCLE	= 45	= 44

Task 3

> **Notes:**
> - Whilst the turnover of the business has decreased during the year, the working capital cycle has improved by one day.
> - Inventory days have slightly increased but this is not significant provided that all of the inventory is saleable.
> - Receivable days have decreased, which indicates that the business has good credit control.
> - Payable days have decreased, which indicates that the business is in control of its payments.
> - The working capital cycle has improved slightly, which indicates good control over liquidity.

9.11 **(a)**

Year end	31 October 20-2 Days
Trade receivables collection period	37
Trade payables payment period	45
Inventory holding period	27
Working capital cycle	19

(b) (d) Reducing the trade receivables collection period

9.12 Points 1 to 8 completed

	A	B	C	D
1	**SF Engineering Ltd**			
2				
3	**Extracted from financial statements**	**30 Sept 20-9**	**30 Sept 20-8**	
4		**£**	**£**	
5	Revenue	1,458,900	1,313,100	
6	Cost of sales	875,340	725,600	
7	Trade receivables	245,300	278,900	
8	Trade payables	125,050	146,300	
9	Inventory	218,800	232,600	
10				
11	**Resources ratios**	**30 Sept 20-9**	**30 Sept 20-8**	**Change**
12		**Days**	**Days**	
13				
14	Inventory holding period	92	118	Better
15				
16	Trade receivables collection period	62	78	Better
17				
18	Trade payables payment period	53	74	Worse
19				
20				
21				

Points 1 to 8 completed – formulas used

	A	B	C	D
1	**SF Engineering Ltd**			
2				
3	**Extracted from financial statements**	**30 Sept 20-9**	**30 Sept 20-8**	
4		£	£	
5	Revenue	1458900	1313100	
6	Cost of sales	875340	725600	
7	Trade receivables	245300	278900	
8	Trade payables	125050	146300	
9	Inventory	218800	232600	
10				
11	**Resources ratios**	**30 Sept 20-9**	**30 Sept 20-8**	Change
12		**Days**	**Days**	
13				
14	Inventory holding period	=ROUNDUP(((B9/B6)*365),0)	=ROUNDUP(((C9/C6)*365),0)	=IF(B14<C14,"Better","Worse")
15				
16	Trade receivables collection period	=ROUNDUP(((B7/B5)*365),0)	=ROUNDUP(((C7/C5)*365),0)	=IF(B16<C16,"Better","Worse")
17				
18	Trade payables payment period	=ROUNDUP(((B8/B6)*365),0)	=ROUNDUP(((C8/C6)*365),0)	=IF(B18>C18,"Better","Worse")
19				
20				

The spreadsheet 'MATST Chapter 9 Activities answers' is available to download on the Osborne Books website.

9.13

Action	Improve	Worsen
Reducing the credit terms offered to customers from 30 days to 20 days	✔	
Increasing inventory holding period from 25 days to 40 days		✔
Doubling the credit limits of all existing customers		✔
Negotiating with suppliers to increase credit terms from 35 days to 45 days	✔	
Changing customer credit terms from 30 days net to 2.5% prompt payment discount within 14 days or 30 days net	✔	

Appendix: photocopiable resources

INVENTORY RECORD

Date	Receipts			Issues			Balance		
	Quantity (units)	Cost per unit	Total Cost	Quantity (units)	Cost per unit	Total Cost	Quantity (units)	Cost per unit	Total Cost
		£	£		£	£		£	£

EMPLOYEE'S WEEKLY TIME SHEET

	Hours spent on production	Hours worked on indirect work	Notes	Basic pay £	Overtime premium £	Total pay £
Employee:			Production/Investment Centre:			
Employee number:			Basic pay per hour:			
Monday						
Tuesday						
Wednesday						
Thursday						
Friday						
Saturday						
Sunday						
Total						

ALLOCATION AND APPORTIONMENT TABLE

Budgeted overheads	Basis of apportion-ment	Production centre £	Production centre £	Support centre £	Support centre £	Support centre £	Totals £
Totals							
Re-apportion support centre							
Re-apportion support centre							
Re-apportion support centre							
Total overheads to production centres							

WORK-IN-PROGRESS CALCULATION

Cost element	Costs A	Completed units B	Work-in-progress			Total equivalent units F	Cost per unit G	WIP value H
			Units C	% complete D	Equivalent units E			
	£				C x D	B + E	A ÷ F £	E x G £

PRODUCTION AND WASTAGE ACCOUNTS

Dr				Production Account			Cr
	Quantity £	Unit cost £	Total cost £		Quantity £	Unit cost £	Total cost £

Dr	Abnormal Wastage Account	Cr
£		£

Dr	Normal Wastage Account	Cr
£		£

BUDGET REPORT

	Flexed budget	Actual	Variance	Favourable (F) or Adverse (A)
Volume sold				
	£000	£000	£000	
Sales revenue				
Less costs:				
Direct materials				
Direct labour				
Variable overheads				
Operating profit				

REPORT
To:
From:
Date:

Index

432

for your notes

for your notes

for your notes

for your notes

for your notes

for your notes

for your notes

for your notes

for your notes

for your notes

for your notes

for your notes

for your notes

for your notes

for your notes